THE
LUCKIEST
GUERRILLA

A True Tale of Love, War and the Army

PATRICIA MURPHY MINCH

THE LUCKIEST GUERRILLA
A True Story of Love, War and the Army

by Patricia Murphy Minch

Published by
First Steps Publishing
PO Box 571
Gleneden Beach, OR 97388

Please note that the book contains some adult themes and references to wartime violence and racial epithets that may be considered profane, vulgar, or offensive by some readers.

This book is a memoir, a work of creative nonfiction. It reflects the author's present recollections of experiences over time. While all the events in this book are true, some identifying details and dialogue may have been changed or compressed to protect the privacy of the people involved.

Every effort has been made to be accurate. The author assumes no responsibility or liability for errors made in this book.

Cover Design by Suzanne Fyhrie Parrott

Unless otherwise noted, all photos are copyright of the author or in the public domain.

Socony Road Map of the Philippines 1940, Island of Luzon, Standars-Vacuum Oil Company, Philippines, Compiled and copyrighted 1940 by Percy Warner Tinan, sources of information: B.P.A. and U.S.C. & G.S. Maps, And Personal Road Tours.

ISBN: 978-1-937333-74-4 (hbk)
         978-1-937333-56-0 (pbk)
         978-1-937333-52-2 (ebk)

Library of Congress Control Number: 2018951720
Memoir, WWII, Luzon, Philippines

10 9 8 7 6 5 4 3 2 1

Printed in the
United States of America

DEDICATION

"The Filipino people were loyal, went without food so we could eat, and suffered torture and death at times to protect us. I wouldn't be alive today if it weren't for their support. Certainly our guerrilla action couldn't have succeeded without them." [1]

Arthur Philip Murphy
18 August 1964

This book is dedicated to each and every one of them, the unsung heroes who have been largely forgotten.

Patricia Murphy Minch

CONTENTS

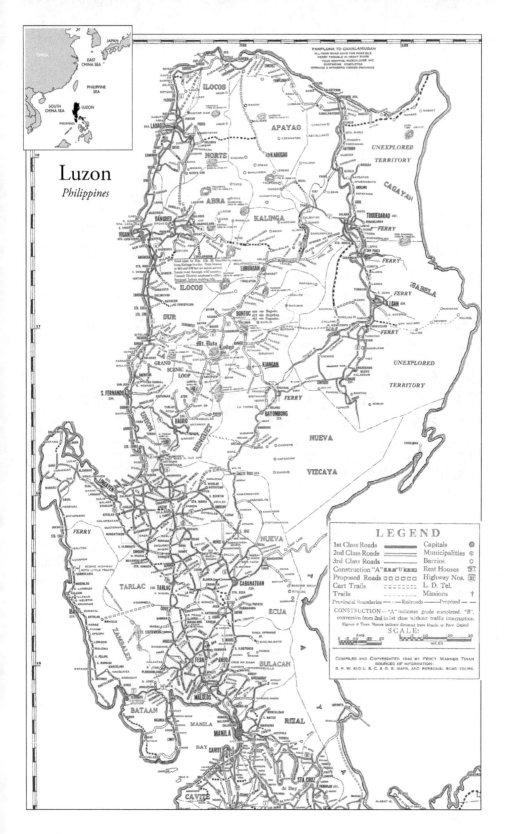

Luzon
Philippines

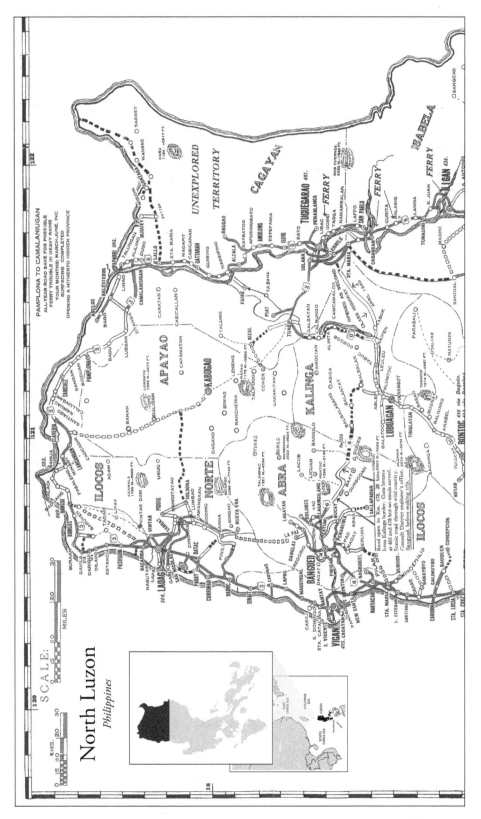

North Luzon
Philippines

SCALE:

MILES

KMS.

PAMPLONA TO CAMALANIUGAN
ALL-YEAR ROAD SAVE FOR POSSIBLE
FERRY TROUBLE IN HEAVY RAINS
(TOUR MONTHS: MARCH-JUNE). INC.
SURFACING COMPLETED
OPENING A HITHERTO HIDDEN PROVINCE

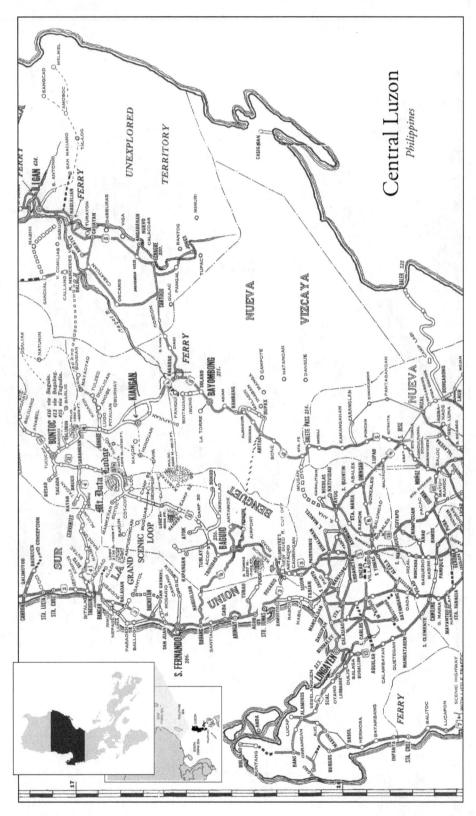

Central Luzon
Philippines

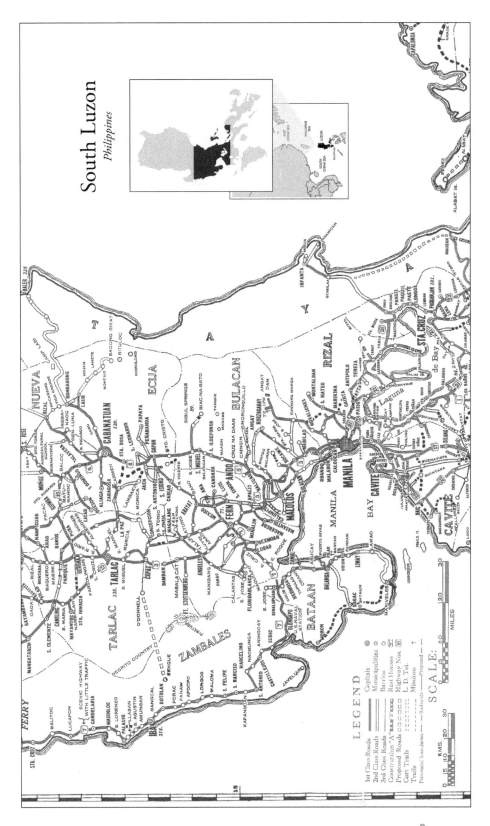

South Luzon

Philippines

Manila and Vicinity

Philippines

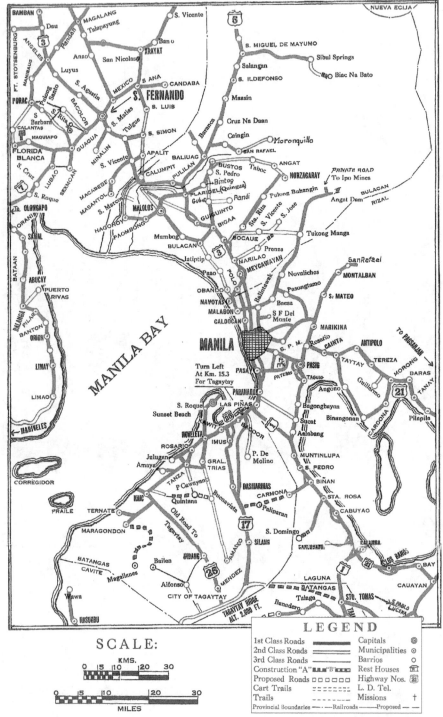

SCALE:

KMS.

0 5 10 20 30

0 5 10 20 30

MILES

PREFACE

ON A SUFFOCATING ARIZONA AFTERNOON in July 2005, I doggedly attacked the next item on a long list of required tasks to settle my mother's estate.

I had notified the Army and the Social Security Administration. I had met with the mortuary. I had submitted an obituary to the *East Valley Tribune*. Now came the hard part: going through the contents of her small house in Mesa, where she had lived for thirty-four years, deciding what to keep for myself, what to save for the grandchildren, what to put aside for an estate sale, and what to toss in the dumpster that now occupied the driveway, a hulking coffin waiting to swallow the last remnants of a life. Today's chore: the storeroom.

At first the going was easy. My mother had hoarded packing materials I could use to ship items to my home or to the grandchildren. The gardening supplies weren't a problem. I set shovels, rakes, pruners, hoses, and bottles of costly pesticides aside for the estate sale. Senior-citizen craft groups were active in the neighborhood, so I saved grocery bags filled with carefully collected driftwood and pinecones and Mason jars full of colored glass shards, worn smooth by the windblown desert sand. Salable, too, were the tools hanging on the pegboard above my father's workbench, though most hadn't been touched in decades. A box of Christmas ornaments slowed the work as I reminisced over each one. Those went into a "to be decided later" pile. When I came upon an early nineteenth century steamer trunk, more memories surfaced. My maternal grandmother had filled it with mementoes and photos from her immigrant parents and her own childhood and marriage. As little girls during World War II, my sister and I had listened, fascinated, as Grammy told and retold the stories connected with each keepsake, determined that we should know the histories of our ancestors. I tugged the steamer trunk over into a "save" pile. Two footlockers, stenciled on the sides with my father's name, rank, and an A.P.O. address, contained elaborate sterling silver serving pieces, unused and unpolished since my father's retirement from the Army, when formal entertaining was no longer required of an officer's wife. I added the footlockers and silver to the growing pile of things to be divvied up among the grandchildren.

By now I was hot, sweaty, and tired, but determined to cross the storeroom task off the list. Not as careful in my assessments as I'd been earlier in the day, with some boxes, I took a cursory look and relegated them to the dumpster. I might easily have thrown away the most valuable treasure of all.

At the back of the storeroom two unlabeled cardboard boxes were stacked, one on top of the other, their beige packing tape dry and cracked. Probably junk, I reasoned, but then opened the smaller one. Inside were hundreds of letters, carefully segregated into packets. When I picked one up, the rubber band disintegrated in my hands. I recognized my father's handwriting. Some of the letters were crinkly and brownish, the ink pale and smeared, as though they had gotten wet. Others, written on blue, tissue-thin airmail paper, were pristine. The postmarks ranged from the 1930s through the 1950s, though some had no postmark at all but were simply marked: "To be mailed after the war" or "Robin Hood: Please hide." Nearly all were addressed to my mother.

The second box, much larger, held a fascinating assortment of items: a pocket-sized red leather diary, its pages discolored, the writing barely legible; a fat manila envelope containing curled black-and-white photographs; a Samurai sword in a scabbard; a bolo knife, its hand-tooled leather sheath stained and brittle; an odd straw beanie with a feather and a button on top; a vicious-looking, double-bladed axe, the cutting edges dull and pitted; a woven rattan backpack filled with strange weavings; a handgun and holster with an attached paper tag bearing a number and a Japanese name; old Manila newspapers; decades-old issues of *World War II* magazine; faded copies of what looked like official communiqués to and from General Douglas MacArthur; and dozens of other documents I couldn't identify. I dragged the boxes into the house, uncorked a bottle of chilled sauvignon blanc, and began to read.

I had grown up an "Army brat" and had known from a very young age that my father had been a guerrilla in the Philippines during World War II. I knew the patch he wore on his uniform commemorated that service. I was familiar with my mother's beautiful jewelry that had once belonged to the first lady of the Philippines. I vividly remembered stories about eating snakes and lizards, even dogs fed to the bursting point with rice, then killed and roasted over an open fire, stories about living in grass huts and wearing G-strings—the types of things youngsters find fascinating—but I had rarely listened in on the more serious discussions of the war that sometimes took place when other officers and their wives came to call. As a young adult, I had stayed busy with my own family in California while my parents traveled the world. They'd visit a few times each year, but those visits were dominated by activities involving the grandchildren. If the subject of war came up at all, it involved Vietnam or the Middle East.

As I read through the letters, I became mesmerized. Here was a story I'd never heard before, a detailed, very personal look into my parents' lives during a tumultuous period in history, when the fate of the world hung in the balance. I shipped home to California the two cardboard boxes and my parents' extensive collection of books about World War II in the Pacific. Already I had decided to transcribe the letters into a more readable, permanent record for my family.

But it didn't stop there. The letters left many questions unanswered. The older books only raised additional questions, for the few brief mentions of my father and his wartime companions were vague and incomplete.

I acquired several newer titles about the guerrilla war in the Philippines. Not only did they fail to provide all the answers I sought, but in some cases gave false or misleading information.[1] These seemingly innocuous bits of misinformation—each of which I initially took at face value—pop up in even the most respected tomes about events involving my father. Only after many months of reading and becoming familiar with the various accounts did such discrepancies became apparent to me.

It's taken a decade of research to fill in the blanks. Along the way I unearthed several obscure accounts by others who were in North Luzon during the war, accounts filled with specific detail not found in the earlier, more widely cited sources. When I couldn't locate maps that showed the various guerrilla camps, I drew my own. Obtaining my parents' government personnel files, I read for the first time their actual job descriptions, the names of their bosses and coworkers, the dates involved, and their efficiency reports. Personal contact with descendants of some of those people yielded further information, documents, and photographs. I exchanged information with Rosie Osmeña Valencia, daughter of Esperanza Osmeña, the first lady of the Philippines, who was snatched, along with her family, from the clutches of the Japanese in October 1944, following a detailed plan put together by my father. I also discovered, to my astonishment, that my mother developed a close friendship with another Army officer, and that she was baptized a Catholic in anticipation of marrying him after the war, after my father's demise became official. I learned my parents' reunion was not the exquisite, happy ending of fairy tales; that even those men who survived years of unimaginable hardship often suffered what was then euphemistically termed "battle fatigue." I researched what became of the men who figured prominently in my father's ordeal, peripheral stories that have never been told and which I feel compelled to tell because I'm the only one left who can.

With this mountain of accumulated information, transcribing the letters was not enough. If I wanted to provide my descendants a complete record, I'd have to do more. I'd have to write a book, one both entertaining and easy to follow while remaining true to the facts, one containing actual photographs and documents and enough historical background to place the events into context, one with maps of a part of the world they may never see.

In the process, I came to realize my parents' story was not unique. It is also the story of millions of young couples caught up in many different wars, separated for years, in many cases forever. It is a story of loneliness, of uncertainty, of fear, of loss. It is a story of rebellion, of courage, of the brutality of war, of the resilience of a people—it is a story of survival.

Today, under a new president whose agenda differs markedly from that of his predecessors, the lessons learned from World War II have once again become relevant. What should be the level of our military preparedness? How should the United States deal with allies and enemies? How does today's definition of *torture* compare to that during WWII, when the *water cure* and much worse were commonly used by our enemies, when decapitation was the expected end for captured American guerrillas in North Luzon? How much *collateral damage* is acceptable in the conduct of war? What is the mission of American forces deployed to the Middle East, or should they be deployed at all? How much are the American people willing to pay? How many lives are we willing to sacrifice to try and persuade another culture of the innate *rightness* of our own, our government, and our way of life? Do our efforts actually bear fruit? And what about the stalwart spouses and families left behind in time of war? What are they owed, other than a cursory nod of gratitude? What is the *right* of the American people to know every detail of the inner workings of their government? Every detail of each action taken by their military? What is the proper balance between security and freedom?

These are all difficult issues, ferociously debated across our land. I hope this real account of what our fathers and grandfathers, our mothers and grandmothers—members of the "greatest generation"—endured to preserve the freedoms set forth in our Constitution and Bill of Rights might contribute, to some small degree, to the conversation.

~ Patricia Murphy Minch

INTRODUCTION

"I SHALL RETURN," promised General Douglas MacArthur in March 1942 when he was plucked from the besieged island fortress of Corregidor, whisked by PT boat through the enemy-infested waters of the South China Sea to Mindanao, and subsequently flown to the safety of Australia. He left behind a few generals and an underfed, undertrained, and poorly equipped army of American junior officers and Filipino soldiers to defend the Philippine Islands against a vastly superior Japanese invader.

The history books have labeled it the worst military disaster in our nation's history. Never had the United States been so thoroughly beaten, so completely humiliated as on Bataan and Corregidor in April and May of 1942, when our exhausted fighting men were ordered to lay down their arms, hoist white flags, and surrender. Their ammunition was gone. Their food was gone. They had no medicine. More than half were sick with malaria, dysentery, and dengue fever. They had no other option.

Following the surrender on Bataan, their brutal Japanese captors marched these poor unfortunates sixty-eight miles in the blazing sun, without food or water, north toward a filthy prison at Camp O'Donnell. Without weapons and without hope, the prisoners could only put one foot in front of the other and try to keep up. Thousands never made it.

Surrounded, with no escape route, the last defenders of Corregidor also laid down their weapons and raised their hands in the air. They were no match for the Japanese. All was lost.

Here and there in northern Luzon, the largest of the Philippine Islands, tiny remnants of the fallen army found themselves abandoned and alone, cut off from the main body ordered to retreat south to Bataan. They, too, were included in the surrender order. They had to obey.

In the gold mining regions high in the mountains of North Luzon, dozens of ex-pat American mining engineers and shift bosses were also stranded. Many had families. The Japanese ordered them to report to civilian internment camps. They had to do as they were told.

All over the Philippines, native civilians stoically awaited whatever conditions the powerful Japanese victors chose to impose on a defeated population. There was nothing they could do.

The vast majority, both military and civilian, bowed to the inevitable. But not all. Some stubborn, hardy individuals chose a different path, driven by a visceral hatred of the Japanese—they knew already the unspeakable atrocities of which the Japanese were capable—an innate instinct to survive, and eventually by an unquenchable desire to win.

As the grim enemy occupation took shape in mid-1942, approximately one hundred Americans remained loose in North Luzon.

Some had fled into the jungle at the time of the surrender on Bataan. Others had managed to escape from the Death March. A few had gotten away from the hell that was Camp O'Donnell. Those who never reached Bataan had disappeared into the mountains. Gradually a few leaders emerged among them, and the guerrilla movement was born. Over the next three years, right under the noses of the Japanese occupation forces, the movement grew as disparate pockets of American and Filipino guerrillas were organized into a fighting force totaling more than 22,000 men, poised to attack the hated enemy from the rear when General MacArthur finally made good on his promise.

"I have returned," the general said in October 1944 as he waded ashore on the beach at Leyte Gulf.

"We remained," they answered.

But it wasn't easy. Fewer than fifteen of the one hundred Americans survived the war.

Art Murphy was one of those. He was my father.

This is his story.

CHAPTER 1

HUMBLE BEGINNINGS
October 1913 to November 1940

ART MURPHY—or, more properly, Arthur Philip Murphy—was Grandma's Boy. No doubt about it. On the day Grandmother Sadie plucked him from the Maud Booth Home in Los Angeles, where he'd landed following his mother's premature death in 1918, Art became the center of her life, her *raison d'etre*.

At Maud Booth, five-year-old Art had fallen one night from an upper bunk—they were stacked three high—and injured his spine.

When the folks in charge couldn't locate the boy's father, they called Sadie, who took him into her home and nursed him back to health. The father married a second time, then a third time, and raised Art's two younger brothers, but since Sadie was unwilling to give him up, the father lost interest in his upbringing and rarely contributed to his support.

Twice divorced, Sadie was an unusual woman. Well-educated for her day, she also had plenty of horse sense,

Art in his woolen drawers and Buster Browns.

was tough, domineering, and usually got the better of anyone who crossed her. No sacrifice for Art was too great. Sadie considered him sickly, though, and insisted he wear long woolen underwear year-round to avoid catching cold, and Buster Brown girls' high-top shoes because she said he had weak ankles and flat feet. Team sports were forbidden. She regularly went after the neighborhood kids who taunted him with "Grandma's Boy."

To her great credit, Sadie encouraged Art to read. Whenever they moved—which they did frequently— she'd march him to the local library to get a card. Art spent most weekends in the library, and at closing always checked out the maximum number of books allowed. He read the children's classics and much more. By age nine he could expound on astronomy, giving facts and figures from memory. A seventh grade teacher dubbed him a juvenile expert in entomology and botany. He assembled a large natural science collection.

Sadie was frequently on welfare. Twice evicted for nonpayment of rent, several times they fled at midnight, before eviction proceedings began. But Sadie showed extraordinary resourcefulness in keeping them fed and a roof over their heads. She outwitted truant officers too. Art missed a lot of school, sometimes entire years.

Eventually their main source of income became an older man Art knew only as Uncle Mac. Perhaps Sadie was his mistress—Art never really knew. Sometimes Uncle Mac lived with them, but more often he worked elsewhere and sent money.

The best years were two during which the family lived in Yosemite National Park, where Uncle Mac found employment as a custodian at Camp Curry. Art was twelve. They occupied a rustic tent cabin, a fringe benefit of the job. Sadie wasn't as worried about Art's safety as she had been in the city, and after he completed his chores, he could do as he pleased. Unencumbered with school, he tramped the valley floor, hiked the mountain trails, knew every nook and cranny of the place, at ease with deer, raccoons, squirrels, chipmunks, the occasional bear or bobcat. Endless hours along the creeks, building rock dams and forts, whittling small boats, manning them with twig sailors, locked in make-believe naval battles. Pretending to be Tom Sawyer, Huck Finn—or perhaps Daniel Boone trekking north from Tennessee through the Cumberland Gap into the wilds of Kentucky.

When Uncle Mac rustled up a fishing pole, Art passed long days along the Merced River, teaching himself to cast, learning the deep holes where the biggest trout lurked—the main course for supper. Sadie dipped the fillets in beaten egg and seasoned flour and fried them in a sizzling skillet until they were brown and crisp on the outside but pink, sweet, and tender inside. Nothing tasted better.

Summer nights at Yosemite were special. Venturing onto the meadows, far from the tree line, lying on his back, gazing in awe at the heavens, feeling smug at how many constellations he could identify. *Where did it all come from?* Attending the ranger show at Camp Curry's outdoor amphitheater and watching the Fire Fall at nine. When park employees high atop Glacier Peak shoved the remnants of their huge bonfire over the mountain face, the incredible beauty of the red-hot coals floating gently earthward in the black velvet night—a recording of "Indian Love Call" echoing plaintively in the background—seemed to Art to embody all of nature, life, death, and eternity.

Sadie had a few books—he'd read them, most more than once. Not a problem in the summertime, but winter afternoons stretched long, gray, and cold. Yosemite Lodge's reading room had several inviting easy chairs, and Art pestered the desk clerk for permission to use it. For the first time the boy read poetry and essays. Ralph Waldo Emerson became his favorite. He tackled the Bible and a dusty old book about comparative religions, both of which piqued his curiosity. He tried to grasp the concept of God in the Bible, but found it vague and unsettling. He was skeptical. *How much closer could he possibly get to God than lying on his back on the valley floor and gazing at all the incredible majesty above?* To him, Nature *was* God, and it filled him with a sense of serenity and peace.

Art never learned why, but after the Yosemite years Uncle Mac disappeared. Sadie moved them back to Los Angeles, into a small upstairs flat across the street from Hollywood High School, where Art enrolled as a sophomore. Three years there became the longest uninterrupted period he'd ever attended school. He earned straight A's; worked on the yearbook, becoming editor his senior year; and became a finalist in the school's oratorical contest. He enrolled in ROTC and rose to cadet major. Grandma still considered him too fragile for team sports, so he joined the fencing club.

Sadie meddled continuously. At the drop of a hat, she'd march across the street into the principal's office—sometimes in her house-coat, petticoat flapping—and raise holy hell. Classmates whispered and snickered behind cupped hands. In his senior year Art demanded she stop micromanaging his life. She sulked for months. Their relationship never quite recovered.

Art had no trouble getting into UCLA. Given maximum credit for his high school ROTC service, he was admitted to the advanced course as a freshman and served as an instructor for two years. He rowed men's crew one year, but had to quit the following season when the long prac-

Art in his UCLA letter sweater

tices interfered with his job. He lettered in fencing every year. As a senior, he edited the *Southern Campus*, another "All American" yearbook. Voted Theta Chi's most valuable senior, he was also chosen one of sixteen UCLA seniors "best distinguished in scholarship, loyalty, and service to Alma Mater." He lived with Sadie but otherwise supported himself by working as a dishwasher, busboy, and fry cook at an all-night diner.

Graduating in 1937 with a bachelor's degree in political science and a minor in journalism, Art was accepted at Yale Law and offered a partial scholarship. But he hadn't managed to save a dime. He was also worn out. Hitching a ride on a cross-country freight to New Haven, then seeing if he could somehow make it all happen—he simply didn't have the energy. He didn't abandon the idea, but chose to take time out to rest. For employment that summer, he returned to Yosemite, his own personal paradise, and worked as a cook at Yosemite Lodge. There he met a young woman, quite unlike any he'd ever known, and his heart exploded, just like fireworks on the 4th of July.[1]

LILLIAN ISLEA BUFFUM WORKED AT THE LODGE as a waitress. Having lost her father in a refinery explosion in Long Beach when she was barely sixteen, she, too, had grown up in difficult circumstances, the eldest of four children of a widowed mother scrambling to survive the Great Depression of the 1930s. A petite, spunky, blue-eyed blonde, at age twenty Lillian had graduated from the University of California at Berkeley with a degree in English and a minor in education, and though she'd completed a fifth year and obtained a teaching credential, her practice teaching year had been a disappointment. She'd come to Yosemite to find some new direction—and perhaps have a little fun.

Their courtship was brief and intense. In their off-duty hours, they wandered the trails on horseback, playing verbal tennis, the subjects ranging from the meaning of life and the origin of the universe to how to make the best-tasting scrambled eggs. Art insisted a tiny pinch of saffron held the secret to the eggs. They shared every detail of their lives and found much in common. When Art proposed, Lillian accepted. There was no thought of an engagement ring; he gave her his Theta Chi pin, and she wore it proudly.

Art and Lillian on horseback - 1937

Lillian kept their engagement a secret from her family because her mother had a *grand plan* that didn't include marriage. She envisioned young Lillian living at home in Berkeley, getting a teaching job, and using her earnings to help put her brother Cecil through school. Cecil, once he finished school, was to help finance the education of the next younger sister, and so on. Young and in love, Lillian was tired of all the years of scrimping and doing without. Becoming Art's wife would open the door to an idyllic future, one filled with new ideas, new places, and new adventures, wrapped in a warm cocoon of security and true love. Or so she thought.

A T SUMMER'S END, LILLIAN RETURNED to Berkeley, and a few days later Art came to visit. He drove down from Yosemite in "Cynthia," his 1934 Dodge, and stayed two days. She introduced him as her friend. Her mother was cordial. Her siblings laughed at his jokes and seemed to like him. They went out with her college friends and had a fine time. Art returned to Yosemite to wind up his job commitment, and they promised to write daily. On October 18, Lillian got this letter:

"Dear Miss Buffum. Allow me to recall myself to you. The name is Murphy, Arthur Philip Murphy. We met during your recent stay here in Yosemite. I believe we went out together a few times and, if my memory is correct, I asked you to marry me and you accepted. I do not wish to be presumptuous, but I should think that would be sufficient acquaintance to merit correspondence with me. Don't you think so? It is now Monday evening and I haven't heard from you. I know you aren't ill, for Ramona Taylor received a letter written by you yesterday evening. I would think that I deserve at least equal consideration. There would have been time for two letters, had you been especially desirous of writing them. Or don't you know my address? It's Box 182, Yosemite National Park, California. I may also be reached at Yosemite Lodge, in care of the chef's office. Or don't you have money enough to buy stamps? To cover that contingency, I'm enclosing a three-cent stamp, which will cover the postage for one letter. Additional ones will be forthcoming, if necessary.

"Aw, gee, honey, why haven't you written? It's bad enough to be up here, away from you, but without hearing from you, it's awful! I thought you said you were going to write me Saturday nite. When they brought the mail in, I rushed over, only to find no letter. Then I thought you'd sent it to my box, but there was no letter there either. I know you're busy, but you should be able to find time to write me if you love me as much as I love you. Even if you haven't anything to say, at least let me know you're thinking of me.

"I know I'll see you soon, but it seems like ages, so please write.

Love, Art."[2]

Two weeks later Art returned to Berkeley driving Cynthia, freshly washed and waxed. They told her mother they were going to Southern California to attend the wedding of some college friends and would be staying with Art's grandmother. This wasn't a complete untruth; a fraternity brother and his fiancée *were* getting married in Los Angeles and had asked them to act as witnesses. And they *did* stay with Sadie in her upstairs flat on Sunset Avenue.

Art landed a job with the Los Angeles Newspaper Service Bureau, where within months he was promoted to attorney service manager, dealing primarily with the Bureau's lawyers. He learned a great deal about the legal profession and sometimes stood in for one of the lawyers in a closed-session legal proceeding. He started at $75 per month.

Lillian went to work as a social worker for the County of Los Angeles.

Art at desk at LANSB

ART AND LILLIAN WERE MARRIED on November 27, 1937, in a simple civil ceremony before a justice of the peace. They had no honeymoon, no formal wedding picture.

Their first daughter, Eleanor Ann, was named for Art's deceased mother. Eleanor was premature and weighed well under five pounds. Lillian had taken a bad fall down the grassy slope in front of their rented cottage one morning on her way to work, and she'd gone into labor a few hours later. The tiny girl was born without complication, but they couldn't take her home for several weeks. Even then they were scared of her and carried her around on a pillow.

That summer Art attended Civilian Military Training Camp at the Presidio of Monterey and the next summer spent two weeks with the 364th Infantry at Camp Ord, as it was known then. He was paid for attending these reserve summer camps, in addition to his salary at the Bureau, and the extra money finally finished paying off the hospital bill for Eleanor's birth.

Once they'd saved a few dollars, they took Eleanor to the Bay Area for the 1939 San Francisco World's Fair and to show her off to Lillian's family, who by then were speaking to her again.

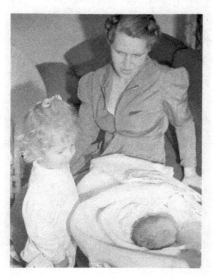

Their second child was supposed to have been the son Art wanted so badly, but instead they got Patricia Lee, a strapping nearly-nine-pounder. Eleanor wasn't pleased and often asked when they were going to take her back. They tried to explain that that wasn't exactly how things worked when you had a baby sister.

Lillian, Eleanor, newborn Patricia

CHAPTER 2

YOU'RE IN THE ARMY NOW

October to November 1940

IN SEPTEMBER OF 1939, HITLER was continuing to stir things up in Europe by annexing Austria, then invading Poland, Belgium, Holland, and France. His forces bombed England in preparation for landing an invasion force there. He made a pact of nonaggression with Russia and then abrogated it by attacking that country. According to some newspaper accounts, the consensus was growing in Washington that Hitler had to be stopped. The government began calling up reserve officers, a few at a time.

ART RECEIVED ORDERS to report to Fort Ord for extended active duty in mid-October 1940. They decided Lil and the children should move up north as soon as Art could find them a place. On November 22, Lillian got this letter:

> "Dearest. I didn't get a chance to write yesterday. I spent most of the day getting my tent straightened up, followed by a big Thanksgiving

Inspecting troops at Camp Ord

dinner. I ate a drumstick! Then I went to a show in Monterey with a couple of other fellows. Afterwards we had a sandwich in Carmel, came home, went to bed, and FROZE! It was 36 degrees when I got up this morning. My bed is like a rock— no springs, just a canvas cot and a so-called mattress, which I'm quite sure isn't a Sealy product.

"Today I did a bit of shopping. It'll give you a laugh. My first purchase was long woolen underwear! I've always despised it, as you know, but now I love it! I'm going to wear it day and nite. I also bought a sleeping bag and an air mattress 'cause we're leaving on a three-day hike tomorrow and I'll have to sleep on the ground.

"Honey, this place is monstrous. There are 13,000 men here at Camp Ord, and there will be 20,000 before long. Yesterday we drove by Camp Clayton, which is being built next to Ord and will hold another 20,000! They're building hundreds of two-story frame barracks and two movie theaters. Several nearby yards provide lumber, and a dozen truckloads of crushed rock are always poised, ready for delivery. The only way to appreciate what's taking place here is to think of the biggest camp you can comprehend, and then realize this one is even bigger!

"Regarding rentals, I understand there are some $40-per-month furnished houses in Monterey and Carmel if you're lucky enough to grab one. I'm going house-hunting soon, but I have to know about Fort Benning before I make a decision. Benning is only for three months, though, and then I'd return here. They give you $190 for transportation each way, and rail fare is only $40. I'd like to go to Benning. It's an officers' school and you get real training there. I've been told you can visit New York for a few days on the way back.

"I reported to my commanding officer this afternoon, and he was bewildered at how useless I am. (Everything in the Army has changed during the past year!) He hasn't decided what to do with me yet. The likely alternatives are heavy weapons officer, intelligence officer and adjutant, or supply officer. Whatever I do, I have lots to learn. That's why I like the Benning idea.

"The latest rumor is that this division is slated for eventual foreign duty—Alaska, the Philippines, or Panama.

"They're going to close up this nice, warm writing room now, so I'll end with my love for you and the babies. Love, Art.

"P.S. Do you think you'll still love me after seeing me in long woolen drawers?"[1]

Art began searching in earnest for a rental. A fraternity brother, Tom Sawyer, was also awaiting shipment overseas and wanted to bring his wife Helen and their six-month-old baby up from Los Angeles to wait until she could follow him. By combining their respective rental allowances, Art and Tom found a place. He wrote to tell Lil about it:

"Sit down, my dear, and get a good grip on yourself for I have lots of news! First, we are now one-half lessees of 'The Sand Box,' a cottage situated on the shores of lovely Carmel Bay! Through the large window in the front room, the bay lies spread out before you, framed by whispering pines. Across the road is a ribbon of sand where already I can see you and Eleanor strolling, Eleanor with her sand bucket and shovel, stopping to pick up shells every few steps. The front room has a high ceiling, walls of knotty pine, and a large fireplace. At the back of the house we have a sunny, bright bedroom with an alcove for Eleanor and Patricia. The kitchen has a breakfast nook, but no ice box. During this weather, one isn't really needed, and by the time one becomes necessary, we'll be able to afford it easily inasmuch as we're paying only $30 a month in rent. (The Sawyers' $25 makes a total of $55.) In back there's a fenced yard so a certain little girl can't wander too far afield. There's a laundry tub in the kitchen, I think.

The Sandbox in Carmel, CA.

"Last nite I went to a regimental party. The ladies wanted to know when you'd be up and said they were looking forward to meeting you. The caste system does not obtain here, evidently. The nicest lady I met was a major's wife! She said it's a great saving to buy food at the commissary. You save 8 cents per pound on butter.

"You probably want to know a lot of things about the house, so sit down and write me a list of questions. Also, go ahead and have the car fixed. I can pay about $35 and the balance on February 1st. Redouble your efforts to find a trailer. Think of some warm clothes for yourself. A pair of wool slacks would be very useful. Also shoes for walking in the sand. By the way, informality is the keynote of regimental parties, so don't buy any formals. Yes, you can borrow on your clothing budget, some!

"I could go on like this all nite, but you probably want to get started on those questions, so I'll stand by. Just think, honey, in a few days we'll be in each other's arms. I can almost feel your body close to mine right now. (Gilmore seems to feel it too. He wants his Annie!) Till then…love, Art."[2]

The Sand Box was everything Art had said it would be, but their little cadre didn't live there intact for very long. Tom shipped out a few weeks later, and Helen abruptly decided to return to her folks in Los Angeles until she could follow him. Not having the Sawyers to share the rent put a sizeable dent in their budget, but it was nice having the place all to themselves—and especially nice to move the children into a room of their own.

CHAPTER 3

CHANGE OF PLANS

January to February 1941

ART NEVER GOT TO FORT BENNING. Late in November there was a call for volunteers for a one-year overseas assignment to the Philippine Islands, which could be extended to two at the option of the volunteer. American officers were needed as instructors to train an expanding native army. The offer was mighty enticing to a lot of young reserve officers on active duty for the first time—a glamorous life in a far-away, fascinating part of the world. So many volunteered that at infantry bases all around the country names were thrown in a hat. Art's was the first one drawn at Camp Ord. He and Lillian were ecstatic! Scheduled to ship out from Fort Mason in San Francisco in mid-January, traveling via Hawaii and Guam, Art's family would follow as soon as his duty station was known and living arrangements completed, a few months at most.

Art and Lillian say good-bye

Art and Lillian met another young couple at Camp Ord, Brewster and Roberta Gallup, and became instant friends.

They called him Brew and her Bert. Brew had also drawn one of the slots in the Philippines. They didn't have children, only a little terrier named Scratty, but Bert loved Eleanor and Patricia, and she and Lil decided to join forces in The Sand Box until they could all sail off to the Philippines.

#NH 93756, USAT U.S. Grant, (U.S. Army Transport, 1919-1941) Underway in Manila Bay, 11 May 1938. Photographed by the U.S. Army Air Corps Second Observation Squadron. Note the U.S. flag painted on her side. U.S. Naval History and Heritage Command Photograph.

On January 20, 1941, a Monday, Art and Brew boarded the USAT *Grant* for the three-week voyage to Manila. This photo was taken on the deck, just before Art and Lil exchanged one last kiss and said good-bye. She blinked back her tears and kept smiling.

Lil and Bert spent their days making plans, revising lists, shopping for all the things they felt they'd need to take. They had no idea what would be available in the Philippines, so they played it safe and began stocking up.

On January 29 Art wrote to bring Lil up to date:

"My darling. It's been almost ten days since we said good-bye, ten days wonderful in every respect except that you're not with me to share the joys of this voyage. We're now in tropical waters, and the weather is quite warm, so we're all wearing summer clothes. We'll arrive in Honolulu tomorrow evening. But I'd better back up and start at the beginning.

"After leaving the pier, we sailed not out under the Golden Gate, but under the Oakland Bay Bridge, where we anchored for four hours while they made some adjustments to the radio compass. I went down to lunch and got my first surprise. Those dining rooms we saw were the crew and second-class dining rooms. The first-class salon is like a big hotel—a waiter for every four persons. And the food is like the Ritz! We even had fresh strawberries.

"Brew was assigned a cabin at the other end of the ship, and he has a different mess schedule too, so I'm not sure how much we're going to see of each other.

"We finally got underway, passed beneath the Golden Gate Bridge at 18 minutes to five, and hit the rolling sea. The population on deck dwindled in a hurry. You should have seen the empty chairs at dinner! It's taken two or three days for everyone to recover. I wasn't bothered and ate like a horse.

"(After lunch) Flash! We just blew the head off one of our boilers! It means we have to coast in to Hawaii, and then delay in Honolulu for repairs that might take as long as three weeks! Everyone is tickled pink!¹

And two days later:

"Hello, my darling. I can't tell you what a lucky break it was that we had this engine trouble and I'm 'stuck' here for a few days. When we do sail, I'm going to throw a ton of leis over the side so I'll be sure to come back. It is heaven and paradise all rolled into one. I can't believe fate could be so unkind as to let me come here without the one I love. I'll just tell you about a few things you'll encounter when you come through, unless you can finagle it so that your transport breaks down too.

1. The hibiscus blossoms grow in a bewildering array of colors. Their fragrance permeates the air.

2. Everything is lush and green, the parks, around the buildings, along the streets, in yards, even in the alleys.

3. It's warm, but it's a lazy sort of warmth.

4. It's cosmopolitan. There are no race problems here. Whites, natives, Chinese, and Japanese meet and mix in the same places. White men and native or Japanese girls go places together and no one raises an eyebrow. The Smiths and the Wongs and the Kauis live next door to one another and occupy the same tables at nite spots. And some of these native girls are real honeys! I don't think it would be a bit hard to go native.

5. Honolulu proper is disappointing, with Standard service stations, Kress 5 and 10's, Piggly Wiggly's, and even a Mode O'Day Shoppe. But from Waikiki on

out, you return to nature quickly, no billboards or anything like that. And the scenery! You'll just have to see it for yourself.

"Love, Art."[2]

On February 9, the *Grant* crossed the International Date Line. He described the festivities:

"Dearest. Well, I'm no longer an 'unwashed pollywog' but a hardened 'shellback,' having been duly brought before the court of Neptunus Rex and accused of having 'openly

proclaimed to all of Monterey and Fort Ord that I was going to bring my wife and children with me and then having cruelly deserted them,' also of having 'carried two cameras all over Honolulu, ostensibly to photograph military secrets.' I was—well, I'll let you find out for yourself when you come over.

"My darling, when you come over, I'm going to try so hard to make you happy. With servants to look after the youngsters and household, and entertainment and recreation so immediate and inexpensive, I want us to really live and to really know each other. We've been so rushed and tired ever since we got married. Do you know that you've never flirted with me, never realized how eminently desirable you are to me, and used that power to excite and thrill me with anticipation and compel me to court you again and again? I realize I've never given you the little attentions a wife of your desirability deserves. I'm going to make things different when you come. I love you so much!

"A bit of advice: Don't hang your clothes near an open porthole. One of my roommates had two suits ruined when a big wave splashed in.

"I almost forgot to tell you, we stopped for drinks at the Royal Hawaiian Hotel. It's about the swankiest place I've ever seen.

"I've just been down and done a big washing. How I wish you were here! I love you. Art"[3]

On February 13, he wrote again:

"All is bustle and confusion this morning, for our assignments have been posted. I'm to be stationed at Fort McKinley, which makes it almost certain that we'll have quarters when you come.

"To refresh your memory, Fort McKinley is seven or eight miles south of Manila and is the largest post in the Islands. There are two regiments of infantry stationed there, both Philippine Scout outfits.

"At noon today we were just 700 miles from Guam. We'll arrive there Saturday afternoon and pull out at midnight or early the next morning. In either case, we should arrive in Manila late Thursday, though we may not go ashore until the next morning. Just one week more! All my love, Art.

"P.S. By the way, Brewster Gallup was assigned to Corregidor, which means I probably won't be seeing much of him in P.I. either."[4]

On the 14th, he wrote again, but there were ominous overtones to his letter:

"My sweetheart. There's a horrible rumor going around that all Army families are being evacuated from Manila at once. Everyone on board is worried stiff. It's nothing official, though, and some of the married officers have received wires from their regiments welcoming them 'and their families' and saying quarters have been arranged. So it looks like it's just a rumor. If it should be true, they'll never get me to sign up for that extra year, unless there's a war, in which case I wouldn't have a say in it anyway.

"We received a wire yesterday from the Governor General of Guam inviting us to a dinner dance tomorrow nite. We'll anchor in Agana, the principal city of Guam. It's too shallow to dock the ship there, so we have to anchor in the bay and be taken ashore in small boats. They also say the bay is alive with sharks. Last trip they caught a six-footer right off the deck of the transport! I'd rather be swimming with you, not sharks!"[5]

And as part of a letter that same afternoon:

"According to the paper this morning, all hell is expected to break loose in the Far East at any moment, with Japan moving on Singapore or the Dutch East Indies. It hardly seems to me that Japan would be so dumb. She couldn't last over six months!

"It's exciting to think that in a few hours I'll get one, and maybe two, letters from those I love most in the whole world. It's a terrible feeling being so cut off by time and distance. I wanted to send you a Valentine greeting via radio, but only life or death messages are accepted for transmission over the ship's radio.

"Once again, my darling, I love you and miss you. I hope that when you read these lines, you'll already have your reservations to come and join me. Love, Art.

"P.S. Don't forget to bring sunglasses, and a new hat for Annie."[6]

Telegram regarding Art arriving in Manila, Feb 7, 1941

Late in the day on February 17, he said in part:

"Due to a strong tail wind, we've been zooming along at 14 miles per hour ever since we left Guam. We'll arrive in Manila on Thursday morning, as you probably know from the radiogram I sent this morning. They let up restrictions on them all at once, and I grabbed the opportunity for I knew you must be worried stiff by what you've been reading in the papers.

"They called in everyone with portable radios today and told them to quit spreading rumors based on news broadcasts. When we get to Manila, and not before, we'll really know what the score is."[7]

The tight knot in Lillian's stomach wouldn't go away. Preparations for their adventure took on a nervous grimness.

CHAPTER 4

FORT WILLIAM MCKINLEY

February to March 1941

ON FEBRUARY 20, 1941, THE *GRANT* SLID INTO PORT, greeted by a brass band and a big crowd. From the pier they were driven to a fancy *bienvenida* or welcoming get-together at the Army & Navy Club on the shore of beautiful Manila Bay. It was quite a party, their first introduction to the active social life that lay in store in the months ahead.

THE PHILIPPINES—A VAST ARCHIPELAGO of more than 7,000 islands stretching over 115,000 square miles in the western Pacific Ocean—had been a Spanish colony for more than three centuries, from the time Ferdinand Magellan first discovered it in 1521. When Spain lost the brief Spanish-American War in 1898, by the terms of the Treaty of Paris, the United States agreed to pay Spain $20 million for the Islands, worth half a billion of today's dollars.[1]

That turn of events didn't sit well with the Filipino people, most of whom wanted their independence, not another colonial master. Two days before the U.S. Congress was to ratify the treaty, fighting broke out between American forces and Filipino nationalists led by Emilio Aguinaldo. The ensuing Philippine-American War, also called the Philippine Insurrection, lasted until 1902, when Aguinaldo was captured and most organized Filipino resistance fell apart. President Theodore Roosevelt proclaimed a general amnesty for the defeated nationalists and officially declared the conflict over on July 4, 1902.[2]

The United States installed a colonial governor, introduced many social reforms, established schools, and implemented plans for economic development, all designed to win over the Filipino people. They were promised eventual full independence. In the meantime, the U.S. remained responsible for defending the colony, the task handled by two U.S. Army regiments consisting primarily of Filipino soldiers commanded by American officers. These two regiments were the 45th Infantry (Philippine Scouts) and the 57th Infantry (Philippine Scouts), both based at Fort McKinley.[3]

In 1934 the United States Congress passed the Tydings-McDuffie Act, by which the Philippines became a self-governing commonwealth, though still dependent upon America for its defense. Manuel L. Quezon was inaugurated commonwealth president in 1935, the first native Filipino to head a government of the Philippines.[4]

President Quezon then invited an American general, Douglas MacArthur—who'd spent much of his career in the Philippine Islands—to come out of retirement and return to Manila as head of the newly created Philippine Division, charged with preparing the Islands militarily for full independence in 1946. MacArthur devised a plan incorporating the already existing Philippine Scouts and the civilian police force known as the Philippine Constabulary, creating the new Philippine Commonwealth Army. That Army would grow to four hundred thousand men as additional Filipino recruits were inducted periodically into reserve units and trained over the ensuing ten-year period. In 1941, MacArthur's plan was still in its adolescence, and none of its components were operating at full strength.[5] Art's job with Company K of the 57th Infantry (PS) was to help train new Philippine Scout recruits.

ART GOT TWO LETTERS from Lil upon arriving at McKinley, and she was very confused. She'd done some checking on her own and had been told no dependents were sailing in

March or April. At the same time, Roberta Gallup had gotten an April 22nd sailing date! Nobody seemed to know exactly what was going on. Art made inquiries too, and it appeared there was a big scare on. All forces in the Islands were being brought up to war strength, and everyone was working a full day, not the usual situation.[6]

Temporary quarters at McKinley

Art's first day at Fort McKinley was a disappointment. Actually, he was disgusted with the place. The Philippine Islands weren't a luscious green like Hawaii; they looked sort of dried up. It was damned hot, and it was purportedly the coolest month of the year.[7]

Art's new roommates were Archie McMaster, Earl Hallgren, and Lars Jensen. He liked them right away, but their quarters were less than ideal—only one closet and one dresser for all four. Because the building had a single attic, fellows snoring at the other end kept everyone awake. Many of the newly arrived families were quartered in the same building, one family per room, so there wasn't much privacy and the kids made a real racket. Art and his roommates were told this was just temporary, though, and after the *Grant* sailed, they'd be better taken care of.[8]

At first Art spent money like a drunken sailor. Each of them was assigned a houseboy to do laundry, polish shoes, and take care of little errands. Not one for all the men in a room, but a *personal* houseboy. Art's was named Emilio, and he was cross-eyed. He explained that he had to have his own electric iron, wash pan, clothespins, and soap, because if he had to borrow anything, he'd lose face. Art had to pay him 25 pesos ($12.50) per month.[9] It seemed a pretty inefficient arrangement, but Art didn't make a fuss. He had more important things to think about.

McKinley was a maze. You had to call a taxi to go anywhere, and then hang on for dear life as the driver drove at breakneck speed on the left-hand side of the street.[10]

It took a week for a letter to go by air on the Pan American

Art in front of large building at McKinley

Clipper from the Philippines to Carmel. Art wrote to Lil almost daily but combined those dailies into a weekly letter to save postage. In his first letter, he tried to disillusion her a bit so she wouldn't be disappointed when she came over:

"Dearest sweetheart. I have a bit of time, so I'll tell you more about this place. The houses are big, old, rambling barns, with ancient plumbing, nothing the least bit exotic about them. The huge rooms will always look bare no matter how much furniture you cram in. Then there's the weather. As long as you sit still and in a breeze, you're okay, but as soon as you move about, you're wringing wet. So keep in mind, regarding clothes and undies, it's quantity you need. You need to change often, as a shower and fresh clothes make you feel fine, for a little while.

"Service here isn't the safest thing in the world. You have to look out for cobras and carabao (water buffalo), both wild and tame. They'll charge the smell of a white man, and it evidently takes a ton of bullets to kill one. In spite of everything bad, though, there's something fascinating about the place. You notice it the cool of the morning. You'll find out when you come.

"Yesterday morning I went swimming in the club pool and in the afternoon went horseback riding. Last nite cocktails and a buffet supper were served around the pool, followed by dancing afterwards. The orchestra was the best I've ever heard. I missed you so much that I got a little tipsy.

"I've already had to order a bunch of new clothes. There's constant social life here, and the dress is quite formal, especially in the evening. I've ordered a white suit, a white tropical dress uniform, and a white tux jacket.

"McMaster, Hallgren, and Jensen have all ordered new formal wear too, and as soon as it's delivered, we're going to have a joint picture-taking session so we'll have something to send home to show our wives where all our money went!

"I guess I should tell you a little about my roommates. Earl Hallgren is about my age, hails from Omaha, Nebraska, and has a wife, Florence, but no children. He was a lawyer in civilian life. Lars Jensen is a few years older and is from Minneapolis, Minnesota. His wife's name is Myrtle, and they have a little girl about Eleanor's age. He calls her Peachy. Archie McMaster is the old man of the group—I think he's thirty-four—and he's also from Nebraska. We call him Mac. He and his wife have, or had, three children. It's pretty sad. One of his little daughters died from some disease just two days after he shipped out. But his wife is expecting another baby, so that's good. Anyway, they're all swell, and we've been making plans to see the country together, as much as we can squeeze in, and afford.

"These natives are different from U.S. Filipinos. They're sort of like children. They always say 'Yes, sir' to everything you say, even if they don't understand a word. They love the Army, though, and the Philippine Scouts always have a long waiting list. A private makes 18 pesos ($9.50) a month, which I'm told is a princely salary here, so I might have to revisit the question of money with Emilio, my houseboy.

This U.S. Army photo is of Art conducting heavy weapons training at Fort McKindley with some of the boys of Company K. (1941)

"By the way, be careful what you repeat of what I tell you of the Army here—it's against orders. This place is full of foreign agents. We went to a bar in Manila the other day, and a German there bought us all we wanted to drink and then tried to pump us.

"Well, darling, I have to close now and get over to my company. Remember, I love you and want to hold you close so much. I want to make love to you in so many different ways. When I think of your wonderful body, the way it looked the last nite we were together, it drives me almost mad. Gilmore is straining as I write these words. He wants his Annie.

Kiss the babies for me.

Love, Art."[11]

Art had a bull session with the battalion adjutant one afternoon. He said there was an area fifty miles north of McKinley marked *unexplored* on the map and another area even farther north whose inhabitants sent the head of their last white visitor back to civilization on a raft! He also told Art about War Plan Orange, an elaborate system of secret plans for defense of the Islands in case of attack. He said any plane, Army or otherwise, that flew over Corregidor, the island guarding the entrance to Manila Bay, would be fired upon without warning.[12]

ON FEBRUARY 28 THE BIG BLOW FELL. First, orders went out that no more dependents would be brought over. Second, officers were forbidden to send for their families via commercial transportation. Third, all families already in the Philippines would be sent back to the States as fast as transportation became available. Fourth, no officers now on duty would be sent back "until they can be adequately replaced." Everyone was down in the dumps.[13]

McKinley threw a regimental *despedida* or farewell party for the wives sailing on the *Grant*, and though it was forced, everyone was brave and kept smiling. Art smiled too, but he knew just how they felt. His big hope became that the U.S. Congress wouldn't change the law so they could require him to stay after November.[14]

He did his best to adjust to the new reality:

"Hello, my darling. Well, I'm over my gloom now, so I'll turn to more cheerful subjects. I've been working hard trying to make soldiers out of my little brown recruits. They come from all over the Islands. Some have never worn shoes before. They have wonderful memories once you've gotten them to understand something, but you have to be careful what you say for they'll take everything literally. If you rebuke them, they'll be sad for a week. I feel more like a Boy Scout master than a soldier.

"Our older boys are really good and know their stuff. This is their career. I'm told the marksmanship average of the poorest company in the Scouts is better than the best average of any Regular Army company in the States. In some ways they seem simple, but in other ways they're way too deep for you. I'm told you can never know them completely.

"We went on a five-mile march today. Afterward, my clothes were sopping wet with sweat. Strangely enough, the natives don't have the endurance I do. I can't march in front of them for I'd march them right into the ground with my longer strides, though they'd never complain but would go right on until they dropped from exhaustion. I'm told that if one of their officers is threatened, they'll give their life to save his without batting an eye.

"Luzon is surrounded by Japs, it's true, but it's not as bad as it sounds. Most of the island is impassable jungle. There are only a few places where they could land and have a route of approach toward Manila, and we can defend those. Also, take some comfort from this thought: All our plans and training are for defense of the Islands. There'll be trouble only if we're attacked. Then we might have to hold out as long as six months before reinforcements arrive. My company's initial missions are quite safe, though I can't tell you what they are. We'll make it plenty tough for them if they try it. But everyone still thinks it's all a lot of hooey! All my love to you and the babies, Art."[15]

Two weeks later, after virtually all dependents had been evacuated, Art and his roommates were assigned one of the vacated houses, right next door to the post commander, General Jonathan Wainwright. The place had two small bedrooms and a bigger one, so they drew straws. McMaster and Hallgren got the singles, and Art and Lars Jensen shared the big one. Art and Jensen commandeered the tiny nursery to use as a darkroom.

The house was furnished with *bejuco* furniture, the bent bamboo kind with loose cushions like you'd find on a lanai back in the States. Art bought a lamp, also made of bamboo, because there wasn't enough light to read, and they each bought a bolo knife and hung them on the wall. Those bolos were really impressive—razor sharp and mean-looking—and each came with a gorgeous hand-tooled leather sheath. All four began collecting them, as their budgets would allow. An integral part of the decor were the many little lizards that lived on the ceilings and walls, most welcome guests because they existed on a steady diet of mosquitos.

Art in what they called "tropical undress," the standard attire at home.

Art and his roommates didn't stop missing their wives and groused regularly about the situation. At McKinley nothing seemed particularly ominous. In fact, many wives of British officers stationed in Hong Kong had been evacuated from there to McKinley "to wait out the unpleasantness." They couldn't figure out, if it was safe enough for the British women, why it wasn't safe enough for theirs. For weeks, despite the orders that had come down, they discussed alternate ways of getting their wives over to the Philippines, perhaps coming over by private transport, as some wives had done already, and living as tourists in Manila. The wife of one of the fellows (Van Houston) was doing just that. He told the higher-ups at McKinley that his wife had set sail in spite of his telling her to stay home. Headquarters just grunted and said that it guessed there was nothing that could be done about a "headstrong woman." Of course, she'd have to go home eventually, unless the order was revoked, but she'd sure as hell be the last woman in the Philippines to go. Art told Lil to start checking into the possibility of taking a trip to Manila, what it would involve in the way of passports and paperwork. They even cooked up a code by inventing an imaginary pregnant friend, Mary. If Lil found the prospects to be favorable, she was to send Art a telegram that Mary had had a boy; if the prospects seemed dim and unworkable, she would wire that Mary had had a girl. You never knew who might be reading your telegrams before they got delivered.

Around the middle of March he wrote to Lil:

"Sweetheart. I just got back from a three-day reconnaissance trip up in the provinces around Lingayen Gulf. Twenty-eight of us had a fine time riding around in command cars and learning about the country. We left the post at 6 a.m. on Friday, loaded to the gills with pistols, ammunition, canteens, field glasses, maps, and other gear, and drove in convoy up the central valley that runs between here and Lingayen.

In full uniform, with palm trees in background.

"At Lingayen we stayed in one of the Philippine Army barracks in a coconut grove near the beach, perfect for swimming after riding in the dust all day. The first evening we went downtown to shoot pool and had half the town for an audience. The second night we went to the local movie and saw *The Real Glory* with Gary Cooper, Andrea Leeds, and a cast of two thousand Filipinos. Inside the theater, on each side of the screen, a lighted sign read 'Use the Toilet'! Just an old Spanish custom, I guess.

"At nite we slept under mosquito netting, and before supper each nite had an appetizer of two quinine pills to prevent malaria.

"We went partway up to Baguio. There's quite a change when you hit the hills. Fewer people and villages. It's cooler, and you shed the lethargic feeling you have in the flat country.

"After being here a few weeks, I can see what they mean when they say this isn't a white man's country. On the post, it's all right; you live in sort of a vacuum. But outside, you can't drink the water; you can't use the ice; you can't eat or drink out of the utensils; you don't put your bare feet on the ground; you sleep under mosquito nets and take quinine; you can't eat native fruits or vegetables, and so on. It's interesting and picturesque, but you have to come here to appreciate how many conveniences and safeguards we take for granted at home.

"I heard a rumor to the effect that dependents might come on the April boat after all, but don't count on it.

"After our trip, I'm pretty sure the Japs would be crazy to attack us. The terrain is such that we would mess them up quite badly even before reinforcements arrived.

"The Clipper is due in today, and I'm going to wait and see what you have to say before I use up the rest of my peso's worth of postage. As always, I love you so much. Art."[16]

Next, Art's outfit took a reconnaissance trip to Bataan.

"I chewed some sugarcane, saw the kind of tree kapok grows on, and cut open a breadfruit, which turned out to be green. We camped in a grove of mango trees. The second day we marched ten miles, pouring sweat all the way. When we came out of the bush, a truck filled with iced Cokes and beer was waiting—ah, heaven! The last day we went down to the tip of the Bataan Peninsula. Here at last I saw a real jungle, tall hardwood trees covered with creeping vines and other assorted vegetation. But nary an orchid, monkey, or python did I see. I had along a .22 pistol, but all I could find to shoot at were crows. I killed one."[17]

When they got back, Van Houston's wife had arrived. She shared a tip about reservations on the de la Rama line, the outfit she'd sailed with. She said even if their passenger list was full, a woman traveling alone could usually get passage by signing up as a stewardess; that she wouldn't have to do any work but would get paid just the same. Art wondered if Lil's mother would be willing to take care of the babies for a few months, but then realized this would probably be a tough sell with Lil.[18]

And, in spite of all the uproar about dependents not coming over, damned if they didn't give the Van Houstons a little house right on the post.[19]

A day later:

> "I've been on special duty as assistant provost marshal, meaning I served as chief of police every other day. The most interesting part of the job was taking custody of a prisoner. This captain was a Philippine Scout officer and a graduate of West Point who'd made the mistake of trying to sell some of our secret defense plans to a Jap agent who turned out to be Secret Service. The captain was awaiting confirmation of a 15-year sentence at hard labor. He was being held in a single cell with two soldiers guarding him day and night, and when he took his daily exercise walk, three guards covered him with riot guns. I had to inspect every bite of food he ate and make sure there were no knives or anything on his tray that could be used as a weapon or to commit suicide. To top it all off, he was the mildest, most inoffensive-looking guy I ever saw. Two days later I had to take him to Manila to appear in a civil action, with orders to shoot him dead if he tried to get away."[20]

CHAPTER 5

SEEING THE SIGHTS
April through July 1941

ON APRIL 8, 1941, Art wrote to Lil to bring her up to date:

"My darling. I'm now back on duty with the company. We march every day, anywhere from five to twelve miles, and yesterday we stayed out all nite. I hear that around May 1st we're going up near Fort Stotsenburg for several weeks of combat firing. I also hear it's nice and hot up there.

"Last Sunday my housemates and I went down south of Manila into Batangas Province. The high point was when we went up on Tagaytay Ridge and looked over Lake Taal 2,000 feet below us. There's always a cool breeze there and they have a lovely lodge. The lake has the crater of an extinct volcano in the center. I sent you a postcard from there via regular mail.

"This picture shows, left to right, Lars Jensen, Earl Hallgren, Archie McMaster, and me. I've got to get some shorts made. I think my legs are better-looking than theirs, so if they're willing to wear 'em, I guess I can too.

"I haven't seen Brew Gallup since I arrived. Remember, he's on Corregidor, but he might as well be in China. It's eight miles from here to Manila and then thirty more by boat. I never seem to have time or taxi fare to even get to Manila.

Jensen, Hallgren, McMaster, and Art

"I'm glad to hear you and Bert are getting along so well and get an occasional invite to a party. You girls need a little fun too. It's good to be able to dance sometimes, and I guess I could put up with it if you got a little peck on the cheek from some amorous dance partner. But that's all! I did attend some dances when we first got here, but now that most of the women have gone, I'm not too hot on dancing with Hallgren, Mac, or Jensen.

"My poor little bunny! I can tell from your letters just how you feel! But buck up and just let day follow day, and all at once you'll come to and find us together. Try to develop some new interests. And don't worry, for I am quite safe. Please send me a letter on each Clipper—I look forward to them so much—and continue to mention our babies and the other intimate things of our love. They bring you so close to me. I can still feel the softness of your lips and neck, the fullness of your breasts, the sweetness of the insides of your legs and—but here I cannot put my ecstasy into words. I love you. Art."[1]

A week later he wrote again:

"My dearest. Your letter that came today was so perfect, so nice and long, I felt that we'd had a long talk in which you told me everything I wanted to know.

"We had an alert at four this morning, then a five-mile hike. I sneaked over to the post office and got your letter and read it over and over during the hike, pausing frequently to flick away the sweat dripping off the end of my nose. By the way, it's spring here now. The trees and flowers are blooming and the birds are building nests. There's a tree on post called a flame tree, and it's covered with the most beautiful brilliant red flowers you ever saw. I don't see how it's possible in this heat and drought. The golf course has cracks big enough to lose a ball in.

"I have to get up at four tomorrow for another hike, fifteen miles this time. We sure get enough hiking done here. I guess we have to because we're short of gasoline for training purposes. That several weeks in the field which had been scheduled has been called off because there isn't enough gas. I just hope they don't decide to have us march there!

"Last weekend I went over to Corregidor to see Brew, but I missed him. The biggest thrill was when the boat pulled away from the Manila dock and I half imagined I was headed home. My biggest disappointment came when I realized I wasn't, that and when they collected my camera as I stepped off the boat. They simply do not allow them, it seems. Too many military secrets to photograph. I only wish I could tell you all the things they have waiting to surprise our little yellow friends! It's just too bad for any boat, other than U.S. military, that comes too close to 'The Rock.' They shoot first and ask questions later. Every bit of beach is covered by entrenched machine guns, all loaded and ready to shoot. By the way, I got my camera back when I left.

"It's now 11 p.m. and I have to get up at four, so nighty night. All my love, Art."[2]

BY THE MIDDLE OF APRIL 'round-the-clock construction was going on to build a huge air-raid shelter on the post. In the event of hostilities, the plan was to evacuate all American citizens to McKinley and declare Manila an open city. The newspapers reported the Philippine high command, the Dutch foreign minister, and the British commander of Singapore were meeting for an "informal conversation" in Manila, and that 2,200 U.S. troops were expected to arrive on the next ship.

In early May Art wrote to share his thoughts.

"My loved one. I finally have a few moments to myself. We're on the go so much that even when we do quit working, my mind keeps churning. Also, the rainy season has started. On my way over to the club for supper the other evening, it started to sprinkle a few drops. After arriving at the club, it began raining like it does at home. Then it started to RAIN! You couldn't hear the person across the table talking. Then it stopped all at once. The next morning the cracks in the golf course had closed up and the green grass was sprouting.

Since then we've had some rain every day. When the sun's out, you feel miserable due to the steaminess, but now, at twilight, it's very, very nice.

"After nearly three months in the Philippines, I'm beginning to look at the natives as individual human beings. Up to this point, without realizing it, I've been looking at them just as natives, a class all having the same characteristics. But now I'm realizing there are big natives, little natives, good natives, bad natives, intelligent natives, dumb natives, and so forth. This change of attitude came as a bit of a surprise. It just sort of snuck up on me.

"I love you so much, my darling. I've settled down a little bit now. At first I was wild at being separated from you, like a wild animal would be when first caged. Now I recognize the futility of ranting and raving, but I miss you down inside just the same.

So much of life is apart from you,
Day still somehow would follow day,
Each crowded hour would claim from me its smile,
But I would not waltz as though to music heard,
But as one walks through a wood where every flower is dead,
Where every bird is mute.

"That's about the way I am now. I don't pine all day—I don't have time to—and at nite I'm so tired I sleep. But deep inside, the peace and joy are missing, that peace and joy that come with being with the ones I love, who are a part of me. I love you, my darling. Art."[3]

The balance of May dragged. They worked from seven until eleven-thirty in the morning and then had classes until one. The afternoons were free, but the problem then became one of boredom. Most of them ended up taking a long nap, then showering, dressing for dinner, shooting the bull or playing a little bridge after dinner, and then turning in early so they could do it all over again the next day. There wasn't much opportunity for field trips, although Art still hoped to get up to Baguio and into the headhunter country to take pictures.

Most conversations centered on the continuing political uncertainty. One day it seemed as though Japan was stepping up its saber-rattling, but then things would quiet down. With each change in sentiment, rumors flew regarding how much longer the government could keep reserve officers who'd only signed up for one year of active duty. If things really got hot, Art knew they could probably keep him regardless of the form he hadn't signed.

He continued to write to Lil every day, but there wasn't much to say until June 10, when he got two letters at once, and a *very* special photograph.[4] Lil and Roberta had evidently decided their hubbies needed some perking up, and somewhere they got the idea to stage a private photo session and take nude pictures of each other.

"My dearest. Your two letters came this morning. They were so nice and fat and said so many nice things that I felt ashamed of the skimpy letters I've been writing. And the picture—you can imagine what happened to Gilmore when I looked at it! No, I don't think there's anything wrong with our wanting pictures like that of each other when we can't have the real thing, though in my case at present it might be a little difficult to get any taken of myself 'en entère'— kind of hard to explain to the person snapping the shutter.

I don't see how Brew and I could get together on a deal like that, but Hallgren does have a camera with a self-timing device that I might borrow someday when everyone's gone. You were probably right in saying that Gilmore wouldn't be much to look at, unless I took a look at your picture before the shutter went off! Anyway, you two gals must be pretty chummy. I'd sure like to have been a fly on the wall!

"About the job, honey, it's your decision if you want to stay home with the babies and diapers or you'd be happier doing something more stimulating. It's all right with me either way. I don't feel that you'll fail in your 'duty as a mother' if you want to work. There are two things to be considered, though. First, I've always had a feeling you were happier when you had an interest and position in the outside world. Second, if anything should happen to me, my government insurance would only pay about $51 per month.

"We decided we didn't like the breakfasts at the mess, so we're going to start preparing our own. We'll each save 11 pesos on our mess bill. I went down today to buy the last of our equipment, mainly silverware and dishes. Shopping here is maddening. Some little items—as, today, a cooking fork— that you could get anywhere in the States, you can't find here. I've told my housemates I make the best scrambled eggs in the world, but I'll be damned if I can find any saffron.

"I'm going to try to get to Baguio next week. Jensen is going Monday, and I put in my detached service request today for the same period. I may not make it, though, because I've been put in charge of one of the rehabilitation details scheduled to make repairs around the post during the next week and a half. I'm hoping the DS request will slide through and I'll not only finally get to Baguio but get out of the detail besides. It'll probably be raining most of the time I'm up there, but I'll have to put up with that if I want to see the place for as soon as the rainy season ends, I want to go down to the southern islands, and after that it'll be time to go home.

"That picture certainly isn't very conducive to writing about such things as I've been talking about. I keep looking at the curve of your thigh where it disappears into the shadow. I keep remembering how heavy your breasts were when I held them in my hands. Physical love is such a wonderful thing, even as is the spiritual. It makes me so happy to read your letters telling how you miss me in a physical way and how you'd like to have a nude picture of me too. It gives me the feeling we're partners in love on an equal basis. People who consider the physical aspect of love degrading and something to be ashamed of speak from ignorance. And such persons are not in the minority, I'm afraid.

"Well, my darling, I'd better turn in so I'll have plenty of time to dream about you. Love, Art."[5]

ON JULY 26, 1941, President Roosevelt called General Douglas MacArthur back into the U.S. Army to head up a new organization, the United States Army Forces Far East. USAFFE included the U.S. Army's Philippine Division, the Far East Air Force, several National Guard units that had lately arrived from the States, and the nationalized Philippine Army, more than one hundred thousand troops in all. General Jonathan Wainwright took over MacArthur's former command of the Philippine Division, and MacArthur moved his headquarters from Manila over to Corregidor. Clark Field, sixty miles north of Manila, was slated to become the main Far East Air

Force location, with an authorized strength of three hundred B-17 bombers, the much-ballyhooed "Flying Fortress," and a whole slew of P-40 fighters, making Clark the largest bomber base in the world. Manila Bay was to have twenty-nine naval submarines. War Plan Orange 3 was in place, detailing defensive plans for every military unit in the Islands. According to news reports, Roosevelt was ordering massive shipments of materiel to the Bataan Peninsula, purportedly enough ammunition and supplies to last six months, ample time to assemble a naval convoy to bring in additional supplies and reinforcements from the States. In the event the Japanese were foolish enough to mount an attack, the Americans were going to be ready![6] While all of this activity was taking place, the first lieutenants at Fort McKinley generally weren't privy to the details.

A SURPRISE ALERT WAS CALLED ABOUT NOON on July 29, and for a while everybody thought the Japanese actually were on their way. Everyone usually knew when the alerts were coming, but that wasn't the case with this one. It really gave Art a funny feeling. He realized how unprepared he was for the real thing, so he put everything he'd have to take to war in one drawer in his dresser, and posted written instructions as to how he wanted Emilio to pack up what was left—that is, if *he* was left to do it.[7]

On July 30 Art wrote to Lil:

> "My sweet. I just missed being sent to Bataan on guard duty for a month today. Company L was going and was short one officer, whom they decided to make up from our company. They were going to send me first but then decided to draw lots. Lieutenant Parks was the unlucky man, so I'll miss out on malaria for a while longer. Nearly everyone who goes to Bataan gets it.
>
> "Darling, I loved so much the little things you told about

the babies—or should I say our daughter and the baby? Also the photos. It's the only way I have of keeping track of them and remembering that I have two daughters. They aren't able to write, so you have to be the scribe for all three of you. They're such sweet little darlings and I love them so much. I wish that, if nothing else, I could have one of them with me. There are *two*, you know, and you have them both! By the end of the first day, Eleanor would probably come in holding 'Oscar' by the tail. Have I told you about Oscar, the big lizard who lives in our attic? He's about three feet long and looks like a snake with legs—vilest-looking brute you ever saw! Anyway, give our girls each a big kiss and a bear hug from their daddy.

"I love you so much, my darling, and want to be with you so much these days. We could have such fun in spite of all the uncertainty here. Don't worry, my sweet, and keep your chin up and a smile on your lips. If we just keep on wanting to be together, somehow it'll come true. Till then, once again, I love you. Art."[8]

Then it appeared that the so-called crisis was over because the officers' equitation class started up again. It had been discontinued just before Art got to McKinley, but he was now required to attend riding school two hours a week. Unfortunately, he failed to show up for the first meeting of the class because it was pouring rain and he couldn't find a ride to the other end of the post where the thing was taking place. Twelve fellow officers didn't make it either, and all were restricted to base for a week. Art told the regimental executive officer who handed out the sentences just what he thought of the dirty deal.[9]

At this point he was pretty disgruntled, and wrote in part of a letter to Lil:

"Which brings up my 'love for the Army' and my 'desire to get a commission' of which you spoke in your letter. I have neither love nor respect for the Army as exhibited here in the Islands. It is the cheapest, pettiest, most hypocritical outfit you can imagine. Practically all the regular officers are still living in the old days before the emergency. Instead of getting ready to defend the Islands from attack, they waste time fussing with inconsequential details and putting on 'eyewash' for the benefit of their superiors. For example, in spite of the fact that the last women (except nurses) have left, all incoming officers are still required to buy those tropical full-dress uniforms, which cost more than all the rest of our uniforms put together. During the hottest weather, if you wear a sport shirt with your coat to supper, the brass hats are aghast. The general is 'very displeased' if an officer doesn't stop in the middle of his instruction and run over and report according to a prescribed formula when his nibs appears in the vicinity. The commanding officer of our regiment is one of the worst. He seems obsessed with a desire to be a brigadier general, and his ridiculous efforts to this end are obvious to all.

"First was his 'athletic program.' In spite of the fact the men were being worked to death at that time, he decided they needed exercise. The program required each of us to spend a week's pay to purchase a gym uniform with the regimental coat-of-arms on the chest. And some baseballs and boxing gloves wouldn't do. Each company was ordered to use its company fund—ordinarily set aside to provide little things for the comfort of the men—to construct elaborate outdoor gymnasiums, which had to be painted up in colored paint to look pretty and, incidentally, to impress the general. A prize for excellence was awarded to a company whose equipment, painted baby blue, included swings and a teeter-totter!

"I was so disgusted that I had our mechanic put up a slide made out of split bamboo, and also a May Pole! But instead of appreciating the subtle sarcasm, Headquarters commented on our 'improvements'! Now, with the rain, all that equipment stands useless and rusting away. But the colonel got a letter of compliment from the commanding general.

"Next there was a notice in the officers' bulletin that any officer who objected to having six pesos added onto his bill so the regiment could have 100 percent subscriptions to the *Infantry Journal*—and get its name on the honor roll in said magazine—would have to file an official protest. It is forbidden to force officers to make such contributions, but this was a way of getting around it as no one would have the nerve to protest. Well, I did! Headquarters was again aghast. I was the one scoundrel standing in the way of this glorious honor to the regiment and, incidentally, its commanding officer! I simply said that I read the *Infantry Journal* at the Officers' Club, where I paid five pesos a month for the privilege, and that I couldn't afford the expenditure. After a stormy session, we compromised that I *would* subscribe, with payment to be made at some undetermined future date.

"So I'm afraid I'll never get a regular commission from here. Where there's sensible work to be done, I do fine. But when it comes to eyewash, hocus-pocus, pish-tush and fuddly-duddly, I just don't get in step at all. My view is that we're over here to do a job so important that we have to make the sacrifice of being separated from our loved ones, and that fooling around with all this nonsense instead of concentrating every effort toward that end is nothing short of criminal. If the rest of the Army is fooling around like we are here, God help the United States if we get into a war!

"Also, reserve officers are not exactly loved around here. The day after I missed the riding class, I was on guard duty. The regular officer who was supposed to relieve me didn't show up. I called his quarters and was informed he was out riding, so I reported him just to see what would happen. Nothing did. Evidently horseback riding is more important than guard duty. Every regular officer lives in constant fear of his efficiency report, which will help make or break his Army career. This makes for apple-polishing and a fear of doing anything any differently than it's been done for decades. The reserve officer, who has no Army career and so doesn't give a damn about his efficiency report—and is often critical of the way things are done—is not appreciated in the least. But enough of this!

"I've used up my letter without telling you that I love you more than anything in the world. Yes, I too miss the 'thrill of being married,' only to me it's not only a thrill but also a feeling of peace and contentment, of being at ease in one's own little world. And we're going to be so happy in not so many months when we're together again. Once again, I love you, Art.

"P.S. Love to my little hellions, too, from their daddy."[10]

Over the next week the brass hats started to get the jitters again. First they issued every man a complete supply of ammunition, heretofore kept under lock and key, and required him to have it and his weapon within reach at all times in case he might be called upon to go fight parachute troops. Cavalry and scout cars began patrolling all likely parachute landing spots. They even started construction on a new entrance to the big U-shaped air-raid shelter they'd built earlier. No one knew what was coming next. Everyone was expecting the Philippine Army to be mobilized any day, and Art figured, if that happened, he'd be sent out to help train it and probably help command it. Everyone hoped it would mean temporary promotions, to avoid the complication of being outranked by Filipino officers.

On August 8 he wrote to Lillian:

"My darling. Your letter of July 28th arrived today. Yes, I was pretty low when I wrote about the Army, and you're quite right in your advice, but remember, you've done your share of damning the Army since I came over here.

"Nothing much has happened since my last letter. Ten regiments of the Philippine Army reserves will be called into active service at the end of August. U.S. Army officers will be sent out with them. But probably not me. It looks like at last I might get to Baguio, not just on detached service but on a permanent basis. The division adjutant called two nights ago and said there was a vacancy at Camp John Hay for a first lieutenant and would I be interested in transferring up there. I, of course, jumped at the chance.

"Today I found out my name was recommended to Division Headquarters by the 57th Infantry. I figured at first they just wanted to get rid of me and my big mouth, but I'm told I'm actually going to be getting a letter of commendation for my file, with five endorsements, so I guess all my past transgressions have been forgiven. I'll wire you if I get the job.

"The other highlight I have to report is our new uniform: tropical helmets and roll-collar, short-sleeve shirts. The helmets have already been issued while we're awaiting specifications on the shirts to have them made. The helmets are provoking such comments as 'Dr. Livingstone, I presume?' and 'Hello, Bug Hunter,' but they really are the berries! They look snazzy and they're cool. The Stetsons allowed no circulation. Perspiration just collected inside until you removed your hat, and then it gushed down in your face. The shirts will be a good idea too, because wristbands and neckbands are favorite places for prickly heat. I don't know if we'll get shorts like the Navy has, but I hope so. Also, all our men are being issued M-1 (Garand) rifles.

"I love you so much, my darling. To me you're the most perfect woman and wife in the whole world. I know that things don't look good for our being together for quite a while, but remember that I will be constantly thinking

of and loving you and the babies and doing everything in my power to bring us together again. Remember, if we just keep loving each other, everything is bound to come out all right.

"*Au revoir*, my love. Art."[11]

CHAPTER 6

MOVING, AND MOVING AGAIN

January to November 1941

THE RUMORS CONCERNING THE STATUS of the wives gradually became more than rumors. Lil and Bert each wrote several times to the War Department to request clarification, and, finally, on March 3, Lil received a reply back that seemed to put the matter to rest, at least as far as the Army was concerned. It was clear to the War Department that wives and families would not be going overseas.[1]

They decided to look for a less expensive place to live. The $55-a-month rent at The Sand Box was too high if they were going to be there for any length of time. They found a furnished stucco bungalow on Shell Avenue in Pacific Grove and made the move on

April 1. Their new home was only two blocks from the bay, so they could still enjoy the beach and the sand. Their only problem was the place was infested with fleas, and they had to set off bug bombs several times to get them under control.

Lillian, Eleanor, and Patricia in Pacific Grove

Roberta went to work in the credit department of Holman's Department Store in Pacific Grove. Holman's didn't pay big salaries, but they treated their employees like family. They sponsored the Holman Club, which acted as a social hub and afforded employees ample opportunity to get together outside of work. No one seemed to mind if Lil occasionally tagged along with Bert to the evening activities, when she could find a babysitter.[2]

THE HOSTESS HOUSE AT THE PRESIDIO of San Francisco became one of their regular haunts, particularly toward the latter part of May, when dependents began arriving from the Philippines. Most were confused and unsettled, but they needed to make financial and travel arrangements to proceed to their stateside homes, so several of the "left-behind" wives put together a volunteer help network to provide transportation and other assistance. It proved a mutually beneficial arrangement because a few had actually met Art or Brew. They told stories about life in the Philippines. It couldn't compare to being there, but it was better than nothing.

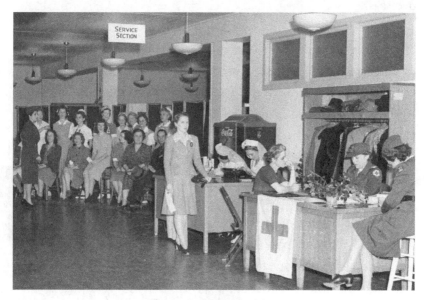

Lillian at Red Cross blood drive

The help group grew from three to a dozen women and began including luncheons and bridge parties. They referred to themselves as the "Philippine Wives' Club," although they were never officially sanctioned by anyone, paid no dues, and had no formal structure. They volunteered as a group at the Red Cross Auxiliary, helping with blood drives, rolling bandages, or whatever else was asked of them. Lil did attend a couple of the bridge parties and luncheons, although she much preferred the Red Cross work, where they were actually doing something useful. Babysitting was always a consideration.

This official photograph shows Lil (standing) and some of the other members of the Philippine Wives' Club.

ON JUNE 1, 1941, A MILITARY DRAFT was instituted, and Lillian's brother Cecil figured it wouldn't be long before he'd have to go overseas too. He and his fiancée Jane were desperate to get married and get a place of their own before that happened, but Cecil was paying the lion's share of the rent and other expenses for the house he still shared with his mother and youngest sister, Lucille. Lil felt a considerable weight on her shoulders and could think of only one solution: move in with her family in Oakland. She talked it over with Bert, who reluctantly agreed it was the right thing to do. Another member of the Philippine Wives' Club was looking for a place at the time and could team up with Roberta. Lil called her mother and proposed that she and the girls move in with the family and pick up Cecil's share of the expenses, freeing Cecil and Jane to get married. Lillian Sr. readily agreed.

It didn't go as smoothly as Lil had hoped. They had been living in a fairly modest bungalow in Oakland, but her mother promptly went out and rented a larger, more expensive house on Spruce Street in Berkeley, two stories with a good-sized backyard, three bedrooms, and a glassed-in porch on the second floor, perfect for Eleanor and Trisha. It meant Lil's share of the expenses increased, but it was too late to back out. On August 1 she and the children made the move.

The new arrangement took some adjustment. Lil and her mother had differing ideas about many things, including raising children. Lil had always attempted to make hers behave and observe boundaries—and wasn't above taking a coat hanger to them now and then—whereas her mother welcomed this opportunity to spoil them rotten. They did their best to get along.

Patricia's first birthday

Trisha's first birthday was hard for Lil because she knew how much Art would have wanted to be there to take pictures. She made a little cake and tried to take the spontaneous photos he liked. It's a good thing she clicked the shutter when she did, for ten seconds later the frosting was all over Trisha's face and down her front!

When school began again in the fall, Lil's mother got a job working in a girls' co-op residence house near the UC Berkeley campus, and their lives became easier. Lil handled the home chores during the day, and the girls were usually in bed when Lillian Sr. got home later in the evening.

Lil wrote to Art every day, sent snapshots, and tried to include stories about little things that happened so he wouldn't feel completely shut out.

She also tried to keep him abreast of news about his family and their friends. Many of his fraternity brothers were already in the service, but everyone was moving around so rapidly that it wasn't easy to keep track of them. Theta Chi was trying to track the members in uniform too, and they asked for a short biographical piece about Art. Lil did the best she could and sent it off.

WHILE LIL LOVED BEING AT HOME with the girls, she found that most things were routine and could be accomplished without much thought, leaving her too much time to ponder. The ponderings only led her in circles, and she always came back to the same unanswerable question: *What was going to happen?* She missed Roberta and the fun they'd had as housemates. Lil also envied Bert's job at Holman's, where she did stimulating work and interacted daily with interesting people. In a letter to Art she told him she was thinking about getting a job. He was very supportive.

Thanksgiving came and went uneventfully. Lillian Sr. cooked the turkey while Lil, Charlotte, and Lucille did the rest. Cecil and Jane were there too, and they had a nice, quiet family gathering. Well, as quiet as it ever was with Eleanor and Trisha around.

Lil made an appointment for a good studio portrait to send to Art for Christmas, in addition to the camera filters he'd been wanting. When the proofs came, she was quite happy with the results. She framed and wrapped Art's copy, along with his new filters and a Santa Claus drawing Eleanor had made for him, and rushed the package to the post office so it would get to the Philippines by Christmas.

The news was full of predictions of a war between Japan and the U.S. Japanese envoys and their families were leaving Mexico and the Panamanian countries and coming to Los Angeles to board Japanese steamers for home. If it was a war-of-nerves game they were playing, as far as Lil was concerned, they were winning. The constant uncertainty was getting her down. If war was declared, she knew Art wouldn't be coming home anytime soon, and even if war wasn't declared, it sounded as though they were going to keep him over there anyway. She didn't know what to think or what to hope for. She tried to busy herself with everyday chores and plans for the holidays and tried to ignore thoughts of what a war might mean. She was lonely and, yes, at times a bit depressed, but no one knew it. As Art had coached, she kept a stiff upper lip and a smile on her face.[3]

Then Lil got a bright idea. She asked Roberta to come for Christmas. With that prospect to look forward to, she updated the Christmas card list and planned presents for the children. She found a secondhand tricycle for Eleanor and took it to a nearby shop to be repainted.

Cecil and Jane chose to get married on Art's and Lil's fourth anniversary, November 27. They had a simple wedding at the University Presbyterian Church in Berkeley and then left for a one-week honeymoon in Las Vegas. When they returned, they spent Friday and Saturday, December 5 and 6, 1941, moving into their new apartment. They were very, very happy.

Christmas portrait of Lillian and girls

CHAPTER 7

CAMP JOHN HAY

August and September, 1941

WEDNESDAY, AUGUST 13, 1941:

"My sweetheart. Would you believe it! I'm sitting before a roaring fire in the fireplace! It's quite cold outside. You can smell the pine trees everywhere.

"Yes, I got the Baguio job! Lars Jensen and I both did. I got orders, effective yesterday, relieving me from McKinley and assigning me to the 1st Battalion, 43rd Infantry (Philippine Scouts), at Camp John Hay. Only four hours to get packed

Kennon (Zigzag) Road to Baguio

and cleared out! We arrived at seven last night, driving through rain most of the way. The road ended up making eight or ten zigzags up the side of a mountain onto the tableland where Baguio is situated at an elevation of 5,000 feet.

"Baguio is an English-speaking town. I saw signs saying Drug Store instead of *Botica* and Café instead of *Panciteria*. I'm told many of the local businesses are owned or operated by Chinese, Japanese, and just about every other nationality. Not far away, on nearby mountains, are huge gold and copper mines and vast lumbering operations. They employ primarily natives, but the managers, supervisors, and engineers are mostly Americans. Many of the upper-echelon people at the local mines even come from Northern California, up around the Mother Lode, if you can believe that! This is a resort town, where just about everybody who can afford it comes on vacation to get away from the sweltering heat and humidity of Manila. There are several fine hotels and oodles of ritzy resort homes scattered about.

"Camp John Hay is the most un-Army-like Army post you ever saw, more like a swanky country club or a big estate. There's even a botanical garden and an outdoor amphitheater where I'm told they have swell entertainment. The Officers' Club has a desk clerk and bellhops like a hotel, and scattered among the beautiful pine trees are cottages and apartments for visiting officers. They tell me that at any one time there'll be a hundred or more officers from other bases up here for R and R. The waiters at the main mess wear fancy uniforms and white gloves to serve you. And the food!!! For supper last nite we had consommé, fried chicken, mashed potatoes with chicken gravy, stewed tomatoes, fresh fruit salad, delicious apple pie, and coffee with real cream! I ate like a pig. Best of all, our food costs only a dollar a day.

"Jensen and I have been assigned the quarters of a major who's leaving. It's smaller than our quarters at McKinley, but it's a comfortable little cottage located within walking distance of the main mess and headquarters buildings. We have a couple of bedrooms, a living-dining room with a big fireplace, a bath, a kitchen with an electric water heater and a brand new electric stove, an office, and servants' quarters.

New quarters at Camp John Hay

"The post is like a big park with flowers, trees, rock gardens, and hedges everywhere, all perfectly manicured. Also an 18-hole golf course. There's a steak fry and dance every Saturday nite, the women at present being the two nurses on the post, some British Army officers' families (who've been extended guest privileges while their husbands are dealing with the Jap threat in Shanghai and Hong Kong), and the wives and daughters of the local mining barons.

"Just fifty feet from our front porch, the hill drops off into a deep gorge. They say the view is wonderful when the fog clears.

"I've been assigned to one of the two Philippine Scout companies here, Jensen to the other. Our men are highland Igorots. After 300 years of Spanish Catholic missionary work, you'd think the natives would all be Christians, but that isn't so. There are sixty-seven pagans in my company right now. My Company A is composed of men from the Bontoc tribe. Jensen's men are the Kalingas. Both are Igorot sub-tribes. Most of the older ones have their faces tattooed. I was told the marks on one man's face indicate he took fourteen heads in his younger days. This is headhunter country, but don't worry, my sweet, they aren't after ours! They love Americans.

"These mountain tribes are quite different from the lowlanders, who are short and skinny. These people are short, too, but quite muscular. The women carry heavy loads in baskets atop their heads. Back in the hills the men wear only gee strings and the women a wraparound skirt with nothing at all above the waist. How they do it in this cold weather is beyond me! The possibilities for photos, when the fog goes away, are unlimited, and in this temperature I'll have no trouble developing them. Also, wonderful native handcrafts can be bought locally, things like weavings and wood carvings.

"What are the disadvantages? There isn't much nite life. Jensen went downtown last nite and found the sidewalks had been rolled up for hours. There are only thirteen officers stationed here, which means no private life whatsoever, your business being everyone's business. And the rainy season lasts much longer up here. Of course, the worst thing is that the place is so nice it hurts that much more that my little family isn't here. We could have so much fun, if the youngsters didn't crawl out of the front yard and tumble down into the gorge. But I have company in my misery for, of the thirteen officers here, only one is a bachelor.

"We've been given a few days to get settled before they put us to work. Jensen and I plan to eat at the mess, at least for a while, and we'll hire a woman—the mountain men scorn such menial labor—to keep the house and do our washing and ironing. We're going to rent additional furniture from the club, get curtains made for the windows, and get some native curios to put on the walls and mantel.

"My sweet, I love you so much and miss you, tho it may not show in these lines of enthusiasm about my new station. It does make it a little easier when I have something to occupy my attention, but always remember that I love you more than anything in the world. Art."[1]

After a week, Art still hadn't done a lick of work. The post commander, Colonel John P. Horan, said he would assign the newcomers jobs "in due course." Jensen had already acquired himself a score of titles, but Art was so far only a company training officer of a company that did practically no training. However, the officers *with* jobs didn't do much either.

"Out of sheer boredom, we took up golf. You can rent clubs, so Jensen and I made a stab at nine holes, but got rained out in four. The next day we tried again and completed sixteen in spite of the rain. My score for sixteen holes was 93, so I was certainly no flash. Of course, this was the first time I'd ever played golf in my life. I got off a few fair drives but a great many of the other kind: topping the ball two or three feet, hooks, slices, and hitting trees. Jensen made 86, so we're good partners. I found the game intriguing. It gave me a thrill to smack one straight down the fairway. The course is a real whiz, up and down hills and across deep ravines. I'm going to buy a set of secondhand clubs. They'll pay for themselves in seventy games.

"Finally I saw the view from our front yard. On the other side of the gorge you can pick out the buildings of a gold mine. Baguio is in the middle of gold-mining country, with the Itogon Mine and Balatoc Mine being two of the largest in the world. They operate like individual villages, with homes provided for the families of the American managers, engineers, and supervisors, their own commissaries and transportation, just like a military post.

"Jensen and I went down to the weekly market day in Baguio. All the natives come in from the surrounding country, the men in gee strings and the women in their wrap-around skirt and a sort of shirtwaist blouse. Both smoke crudely rolled black cigars. They come to market not so much to buy and sell as to sit around on the sidewalk or along the curb and talk. I saw all kinds of things I knew you'd like, especially the hand-woven Baguio linens and the native carvings. I've decided to get enough of the stuff to turn a den into a 'Philippines Room' someday—furniture, rugs, pictures, wall decorations, the whole thing—but of course I'll have to save a little money first.

"The next day Colonel Horan ordered us to get fancied up in our tropical dress uniforms and attend President Manuel Quezon's birthday ball downtown. Baguio is the home of the president's summer residence, and whenever he has some occasion to celebrate, *everybody* is expected to show up. It was interesting meeting the biggest cheese in the whole country! He seemed a decent guy, smart, and good-looking too."[2]

On August 25th, Art had more idle time than usual, so he sat down and wrote Lillian a good long letter, probably two pesos' worth:

"My darling. This is our first clear day in a week. It rains ten inches a day. I even had to go down and draw hip boots. But today the sun came out and the clouds lifted and we could see the tops of the surrounding mountains.

"Camp John Hay has been designated as one of the officer training camps for the Philippine Army effective next Sunday, so I guess our idyllic existence here will end. We're busy getting a couple of empty barracks ready for them. My job is locating 350 beds by rounding up every spare bed on the post. As this includes beds being saved for possible guests and beds turned into living-room couches, I'm not so popular.

"The last few days have been the most perfect you can imagine. It rains regularly at three in the afternoon, but in the mornings we have the bluest sky and the snowiest white clouds so close overhead that it seems you could reach up and touch them. Huge, perfectly formed hibiscus flowers bloom everywhere. The other day I saw a butterfly as big as a bird, all black except for brilliant scarlet patches on each wing. Big iridescent blue ones too. This evening we had the most gorgeous sunset I've ever seen, the clouds pure golden and the sky the deepest of azure blues. A soft golden light enveloped everything, enhancing the colors, like a different world.

"You know, there's something that gets to you here— the life you live, the position you occupy, the experiences you have. The other day I realized that I don't want to come home, I just want to be with my wife and babies. There's nothing else back home that I miss. In retrospect, the Newspaper Service Bureau seems dull. I'm afraid I'll never again be happy at anything like that. I want us to go places, see things. I want us to live the life that's lived in places like this: the small society, the leisurely attitude toward life, the scotch-and-sodas with one's friends, being a member of an exclusive fraternity, the special privileges one has, the many things you can buy for a song!

"You may find my words a bit unusual, but I feel different now than I did a while ago. For one thing, I've learned I must accept the fact that we'll probably be separated for some time, so I cannot allow myself to miss you as acutely as I have or I'd go crazy. The cards are stacked against us, and we can't change that. Don't misunderstand. I do love you, just as I always have and always will. But I have to grow away from you in the sense that I've got to develop other interests to take the place of counting the days until I can sail home to you. With this new attitude I find I'm happier and can do my work better. I want you to develop the same attitude: love me just as much, but don't miss me so much. Don't brood about how unkind fate has been to us, and don't live only in memories of the past. They only make the present harder to bear. Pursue current interests, enough that you're never bored. You can be an individual now, so develop that individual. It'll enrich our lives when we're together again, when we start a new life in a new world. Learn some typing and shorthand, some Spanish, read about this country and ask me questions. I'll do my best to answer them.

"Be prepared to abandon that sense of insularity we developed living in our own little world. Here people do many things differently, have different customs and morals. For instance, gas stations don't occur with much frequency along the highways, so every so often these big red buses stop alongside the road and everyone piles out and goes, with no false modesty whatever. The women go standing up. They just hold their skirt out a little in front. I guess there's nothing on underneath. The simplicity of it all is quite refreshing.

"I learned today that we have four witch doctors in our company. I believe I told you that sixty-seven out of seventy-five of them are pagans. Yet they're head and shoulders above the lowland Filipino in native intelligence. The latter has the memory-book type of knowledge; he recites the book to you. These men 'savvy' what you're talking about. Also, they look you in the eye when they talk to you.

"Have I told you about my fellow officers here? We're quite a small group and I'll be mentioning them, so I'll give you a few details:

1. Lieutenant Colonel Horan, the post commander. A nice but eccentric old Joe. Very proper. Frowns on married officers showing any attention to any women whatsoever, yet tells about what 'big boobies' the woman had with whom he just danced.

2. Major Ketchum, Cavalry. Nickname 'Sandy.' Born to be a bachelor. A little shy and doesn't mix much, but a good egg.

3. Major Rumbold. A poor lost soul. Bored stiff and lonesome since his wife left. Wants to 'go down the mountain,' but the old man won't let him because he's a jack-of-all-trades.

4. Major Allen, post quartermaster. A Philippine Scout officer. He's been in the Islands twenty years. Nice, friendly old fellow who reminds me of an old-time grocer. His wife is allowed to stay here because she's a surgeon. Though middle-aged, they have the cutest little boy about two years old.

5. Major Giitter, adjutant to the C.O. Does everything exactly by the book. Can recite every Army rule and regulation from memory. Offends no one, but sort of tedious and boring. One of the C.O.'s fair-haired boys.

6. Captain Fellows, Coast Artillery. Doesn't mix much. Going home soon, he says.

7. Captain Simenson, a 'jawbone captain' and my company commander. Smart as a whip. Will be a general someday. Not afraid in the least of the old man. In case you didn't already know, 'jawbone' means he's a West Point graduate.

8. Captain Calvert, also 'jawbone,' an 'Army hat' and married to one. Quiet, serious, the slow-but-sure type.

9. Second Lieutenant Simpson. West Point. Pronounced Boston accent, but is from Virginia. Very friendly and affable.

10. Second Lieutenant Gasparini, an Italian Jew. An okay guy. Also West Point. His wife was the go-getter in the family.

11. Lieutenant Colonel Campbell, the post surgeon. Would make an ideal society doctor—mustache, glasses, and all. A man's man too.

12. First Lieutenant Lars Jensen, my sidekick. Is thirty-two, but you wouldn't know it. Our tastes complement each other perfectly. I really like him.

13. First Lieutenant Murphy. I guess you can write your own ticket on this one.

"I might add:

14. Ruby Bradley, a nurse, a little too old.

15. Bea Chambers, ditto, a little younger. Gets around.

"We make quite a heterogeneous bunch. I should add some British Army wives who are living at the mess while hubby 'fights for king and country.' I haven't gotten very well acquainted with any of them.

"Well, my darling, I've exhausted my supply of news and observations, and besides, my right hand is starting to cramp, so I'd better close for now, brush my toofies, and get to bed. Don't ever forget how much I love you and our babies. Please give them some hugs and kisses from their daddy, but save the best ones for yourself. Love, Art.

"P.S. Our house is lousy with cockroaches, though what they live on I haven't been able to figure out."[3]

They had some excitement the first week of September when a number-seven-signal typhoon hit Baguio. It blew like hell all night and most of the day. Water came in through the most tightly shuttered windows. Then it quit all at once and the sun came out and that was that.[4]

"Finally, we heard from Earl Hallgren. He's on his way down to Pangasinan Province for duty with the Philippine Army. McMaster is still at McKinley, but they both were promoted to captain after Jensen and I left.[5]

"The next Saturday we attended a party at the Philippine Military Academy. The Philippine Army officers had on their white mess uniforms, a replica of ours. Their wives were dressed fit to kill, some in Filipina formals, others in American dresses. They put on a formal dance, a *rigonondo*, with chairs arranged in a big square on the dance floor and the men seating and unseating the ladies and leading them across the room, accompanied by lots of bowing and hand flourishes, a court dance carried over from Spanish days. They served the strongest punch I've ever tasted, but I was able to safely navigate my way home, get up with a clear head, and play eighteen holes of golf the next morning. I forgot my score pretty quickly, though. It was lousy, well over 100.[6]

"There has been the usual spate of contradictory rumors regarding whether or not we'll really be kept for another year, and more of the Pollyanna-ish crowing about how the Japs wouldn't dare attack us. Mostly we ignore the gossip.

"Our big excitement is that Lars and I got new quarters. Major Rumbold finally went down the mountain, leaving his house vacant. First Colonel Horan said we could move in, then changed his mind and said no, and then changed it again and said yes. The place has a second bathroom we can convert into a darkroom, so we're happy as clams."[7]

Art took his company to inspect the positions they were expected to defend in the event of an attack. On September 26 he told Lil about it:

"My darling. Last week I went down the Kennon Road with my company to our beach positions. We camped in a coconut grove beside the bay. It's certainly a change going from here down to sea level—a distance of 25 miles, 5,000 feet in elevation, and about 20 degrees in temperature—from pines to coconut palms. Whenever I go down the Kennon Road, I'm reminded of the road into Yosemite between El Portal and El Capitan. There's the same rushing river, only this one's called the Bued and is a little muddy from mining debris. The same granite outcroppings and cascading waterfalls, the same narrow road hugging the edge of the river, blocked by rockslides every now and then. Kennon Road crosses and re-crosses the river more than a dozen times via narrow, one-way bridges over the deep gorge below. Of course, it's a bit different from Yosemite. Yosemite doesn't have brilliant red hibiscus flowers growing along the roads, nor does it have butterflies with six-inch wingspreads. And back home you wouldn't see the road workers clad only in gee strings, strange-looking grass headgear, and sporting a bolo, the all-purpose implement every man carries.

"You see native women along the road too, but never without something on their heads. Women carry everything on their heads. Even little girls carry their schoolbooks that way. This practice gives Filipino women a carriage that would put to shame the prize graduate of Mrs. Richbitch's Finishing School. Not so admirable are the cigars the women smoke. Down around Manila the women smoke long black cigarettes, but here they smoke big, fat, homemade stogies.

"Natives pan for gold along the rivers, and playing the gold stocks seems to be a favorite diversion. They say you can go in the stock exchange in Baguio at any time of day and see a bunch of Igorots, clad in gee strings, watching the price quotations!

"When we got back, we learned that Lieutenant Colonel Campbell, the post surgeon, and Captain Simenson, my company commander, had received radio orders to take the boat leaving on Monday for the States. As both were well-known, there've been a number of farewell parties for them. A prominent Chinese, who seems to have a finger in every business in town, gave them a farewell luncheon. There were more than twenty courses, four soup courses alone, one of them birds' nests. Another dish I found out later was roosters' testicles!

"After Simenson leaves, his place as my company C.O. is going to be taken by Captain Parker Calvert. He's already C.O. of Company B, but I guess they're running short of officers. He's a swell guy and should be easy to get along with. Not much sense of humor, though.

"Now we come to the big news! I played golf again yesterday. Remember what I've said about my score being 106 and the horrible slice I have? Well, recently I got some tips about curing the slice, and yesterday I tried them out and broke the century mark with a 92! Today I succeeded in cracking the 90 mark, to the tune of 85! One hole I got on the green in one stroke. I'm now dreaming of murdering the 80 mark.

"According to the sailing list, there are only 14 officers going home on this next transport. One of those is a captain who got caught in bed with a local 'lady' and was thrown in the brig, then told the officers in charge to go to hell, and finally got court-martialed and ordered back to the States, which I think is what he had in mind in the first place. Another is a captain down at Department Headquarters, where I guess he's gotten in good with the big shots.

"If you don't have anything else to do, you might go down to meet the *Coolidge* and say hello to the boys. They're mostly swell eggs. I imagine Rilla Calvert, Parker's wife, will be meeting them. By the way, her papa's not a colonel, he's a general! It might be wise to cultivate her friendship inasmuch as Parker will be my boss.

"Somebody said they have a Philippine Widows' Club at the Presidio of San Francisco. If so, you might meet other women with whom you share a common interest.

"Well, taps just blew, and I have to make a 5:30 inspection, so good night, my love. Art."[8]

Art and Lil continued to bat around the possibility there might be some way to get her over to the Philippines, particularly since there were by then several wives living incognito in Manila and even one or two in Baguio.

On October 1 the Army's Philippines Department put out a poop sheet entitled "Extension of Active Duty of Reserve Officers," with the main part reading:

1. Where the services of a Reserve Officer have been unsatisfactory and the commanders concerned do not recommend the extension, the active tour will not be extended. The officer will be returned to the United States at such time as will permit him to arrive at his home on the date of the expiration of his current tour of active duty.

2. Where the Reserve Officer does not desire extension and no cogent reasons are given why his tour should not be extended, extension will be made under the provisions of Public Law No. 2123, 77th Congress, approved August 18, 1941, for a period of six months provided his services are desired. Upon the expiration of this six-month period, if the need of his services no longer exists, consideration will then be given to his release.

3. Where the Reserve Officer desires extension and his request is approved by all commanders concerned, his tour of active duty will be extended for a period of one year.[9]

This turn of events resulted in several complications. On the outside chance the reasons Art had given for not wanting to be extended were considered "cogent," then he'd be sent home right away. The chances of that happening, though, were probably slim to none. If he were extended, it would be for only six months, not long enough to justify the hassle and expense of Lil and the babies coming over under cover. He told her to do some final checking on passports and other regulations governing foreign travel. When she got a definitive answer, if it was positive, she was to send him a radiogram about Mary having her baby, boy or girl, and then follow it up with a letter covering the details. If Mary had a boy, he'd immediately submit a request that his status be changed to a year's extension on the grounds that he now couldn't get his civilian job back and desired the extension as a means of saving money against hard times; and then, if that went through, he'd send for his family as soon as possible. If Mary had a girl, though, they'd let the six-month extension ride and hope it didn't turn into a second one.[10]

Jensen was a co-conspirator in all this. Lil and Myrtle Jensen traded letters back and forth. The plan was that Myrtle and Peachy would get themselves to San Francisco, and then Lil and Myrtle could coordinate things from there. Once or twice Jensen began getting cold feet, but he missed his family too, and didn't want to ignore any opportunity to get them over to the Philippines. A little firm talking on Art's part was usually enough to get him back on board. They kept their fingers crossed and waited for a wire.

CHAPTER 8

THE MOUNTAIN MAN
October and November 1941

ON OCTOBER 5 ART CELEBRATED his twenty-eighth birthday at the Army & Navy Club, where the orchestra played "Happy Birthday" for him, but otherwise it was no big deal.

A week later he and Lars were down at Fort McKinley again, this time attached to the Philippine Division for six days of maneuvers. There was no wire from Lillian. Art did, however, receive orders extending his tour of duty to May 19, 1942. Jensen did too. They were both anxious to get some word from their wives so they could put their plan into action. They were dead serious about the whole thing. At least Art was.[1]

On October 20 Art was out playing golf when he got word to call the post radio station right away to receive *a very urgent message*. The operator, his voice filled with sympathy and concern, tried hard to break the news gently: "Mary's baby is dead." It might have been funny, except that it meant Lil wasn't coming. Art forgot his golf game and went instead to the bar, settled in a dark corner, and pulled out the photo of his family. He had several stiff drinks—he didn't count how many—and what dripped down his cheeks wasn't perspiration.[2]

Regaining his composure, he wrote a short letter containing nothing but trivia:

"Sweetheart. There's nothing much happening to write about. My golf is lousy again, but, on the other hand, I'm even at poker. On Sunday we're all going down to Miramonte for a beach party. Then on Monday, Tuesday, and Wednesday they're giving seven of us a command car to take a trip up to Bontoc and the Banuae rice terraces, where I hope to get some good pictures. (Dee Dee Simenson used to call this the 'Tits and Terraces Trip.')

"The C.O. says that as soon as dry weather becomes a certainty, he's going to send our company on a five-day trip into the mountains. We'll have to carry our food and the rest of our gear on our backs. Sounds interesting.

"Last Sunday our Scout companies put on their tribal regalia and staged dances. I got some pretty fair photos, which I hope to finish up in time to enclose. And speaking of photos, in the enclosed one of me in the swim trunks, the chair leg in the rear makes me look pretty virile, don'tcha think?

"Well, I'd better go to bed now and hope I get a letter tomorrow. Good nite and love, Art."[3]

T HE FOLLOWING MONDAY THEY LEFT AT EIGHT and got to Bontoc, 150 kilometers from Baguio, about 2 p.m. There were seven of them: Captains Giitter and Calvert, Lieutenants Jensen, Bach, and Justo, the driver, and Art.[4]

Bach, Jensen and Art at Banuae rice terraces

"The road was one-way-controlled part of the way, and we stared straight down over the retaining wall a few thousand feet. It was too early to stop in Bontoc, as originally planned, so we headed over to Banaue in the Ifugao country, home of the world-famous rice terraces. It took two hours to do 48 kilometers over a road about the same as the Baguio-Bontoc road except for even steeper grades. Banaue is something to see! The Ifugaos have built rock terraces as high as 75 feet up the sides of the mountains in order to grow their rice and *camotes*, a kind of sweet potato. From the government rest house, where we spent the night, the view was spectacular when the moon came up and reflected off the rice paddies below. If you squinted, it looked like swirling swaths of silver sequins."[5]

Bach, Jensen, and Art posed for this picture with the terraces in the background. The picture doesn't do them justice—the terraces, that is.

"On Tuesday morning we got back to Bontoc about mid-morning and decided to sneak on up to Lubuagan in the Kalinga country. This was a trip I'll never forget! The road was so narrow it left only a foot of clearance between our outer wheels and the edge. And no retaining wall! The drop varied from two to three thousand feet, and the road twisted and turned constantly. It took us four hours to go 68 kilometers, about 42 miles.

"The women we saw were all bare-breasted, and I wanted to get some pictures. The natives don't like having their picture taken—they think it's the equivalent of having their soul taken from them—and even those who were agreeable wouldn't do it for free. When I gave one maiden a peso to pose with me, Jensen didn't click the shutter fast enough and she walked away, peso and all!

"Calvert was determined to get a picture with some of the native girls. These two gals were quite good-looking, and he offered them each a peso if they would pose. They giggled and chattered and feigned all sorts of modesty, but wouldn't come out of the water, so I took the shot anyway. I decided to call this picture, 'No, no, no, you cannot buy!'

"Then we headed back to Bontoc. That night we hired a kid to show us the oolongs. Oolongs are the huts where

girls go to live when they reach marriageable age. Any boy can come and stay all night with a girl. If she doesn't like him, she merely sleeps with her back to him, but if she does, well…! When a girl gets pregnant, a marriage follows quickly. If a girl can't get pregnant, no man wants her, and, once married, if a wife doesn't bear children

Parker Calvert with topless Filipinas

regularly, her husband can get himself a new one and demote her to the role of a menial servant.

"Each oolong was about four feet high and wide and six feet long. Our guide said a few words at the narrow doors, followed by conversation and commotion inside, and finally out came a dozen girls, ages fifteen to twenty, and five or six of the boyfriends. They sat around in a circle and giggled, and we offered them matches. One of the girls played a nose flute for us, a long, skinny wooden instrument they play by sticking the smaller end into one of their nostrils, producing a haunting, low tone. The Bontoc girls would have been quite attractive if they'd had a few baths and kept their mouths shut to conceal their betel-nut-stained teeth. Betel nut makes them look like they have a mouth full of blood, and it rots their teeth horribly.

"The next day Jensen and I went up to the Episcopal

Mission School, where I bought some native weavings as Christmas gifts for your mother and sisters. We got back in about 6 p.m. and headed for dinner at the Officers' Mess.

"Some fellows from Clark Field told us that a military force of considerable size was being assembled there. Tanks and anti-aircraft planes and several dozen Flying Fortresses have been brought in. It's supposed to be augmented by an infantry division from the States in a month, and the mission of this force is *not* the defense of the Philippines! But as far as we're concerned, the war is as near and as far away as it's been for months. If it weren't for newspapers and radios or a visiting pilot, we'd be completely unaware there's a war at all."[6]

On November 12, Art wrote again:

"Yesterday, Armistice Day, the American enlisted men had a party down at Long Beach and invited the officers. I went down, drank some beer, ate some lunch, took two rolls of pictures, and did some swimming. The water was perfect. There's a reef 250 yards out that keeps most of the waves and all the sharks out, so you can just paddle around or sit on the raft and admire the scenery. Toward sundown, while everybody else was drinking beer, I swam out to the raft and watched the sunset and thought of you. It was gorgeous. Billowy clouds of all colors dotted the sky. In the distance native boats were sailing out for the night's fishing, while on the shore I could see coconut palms and little *nipa* huts. Farther back the mountains disappeared into dusky purplish clouds. There I was, alone, separated from all the petty trials of life, surrounded by a perfect peace. I cannot help loving this country, honey. I know that it keeps me away from you and our babies, but it has a charm and beauty I find irresistible. I don't want to come home; I just want you to come here. When I leave, I fear my thoughts are going to often stray far, far away across the Pacific, *for the wind is in the palm trees, and it's there that I would be*….

"Kipling had something when he wrote *The Road to Mandalay*. If you ever come over, you'll understand. I hope you will.

"Good nite, my beloved. Art."[7]

And a few days later:

"I got a new job today. Twice a week I go down to three springs located on the mountainside along the Kennon Road, carrying along a five-gallon can and a stop watch. I stick the can under the spout, see how long it takes to fill it up, and record the result. It's to measure flow rates for an auxiliary water supply. And the Army pays me nine bucks a day to do things like that!

"I'm leaving tomorrow morning on that mountain trip about which I spoke a few letters back. Captain Giitter, Lieutenant Justo, and I and nine enlisted men are going via truck south, east, and then north to Aritao, a town on the Cagayan Valley road. It'll take all day. The next day we start hiking over the mountains back toward Baguio. There are no roads in this area, only trails. I'll have to carry three days' worth of food—that is, my *cargadore* will have to carry it, if I can get one. I hope I can as my pack weighs over 80 pounds.

The trip will take about three days, which will get us back here Thursday. Yes, there are headhunters up there, but they won't bother white men or soldiers. Besides, we have nine Garand rifles to argue with. I'll tell you about it when I get back.

"Once again, the hour grows late, and this letter must go out at 5:30 a.m. So *au revoir*, my dearest darlings. I love you so much. Art."[8]

He followed up on Saturday, November 22:

"Sweetheart, this is another blackout letter, written from my little darkroom while my photos are washing. I got back from my trip yesterday about noon, but your letter was locked up in Headquarters, it being Thanksgiving weekend, so I didn't get it until this morning. I enjoyed it so much. I can't imagine what all these Christmas presents are you're talking about. I hope one of them is the filters I've been wanting!

"Now about my trip. We left here last Monday morning

 and went by truck over Balete Pass (jungle, hardwood trees, orchids, etc.) down to Aritao in the upper end of the Cagayan Valley. We slept that night in the public market on split-bamboo

platforms the vendors display their goods on during the day. Quite uncomfortable, I assure you. The mosquitos made a meal of me too.

"The next morning we started up a 1,500-foot ridge toward Kayapa, 23 kilometers distant. It was here I discovered that my two brother officers, Captain Giitter and Lieutenant Justo, were slightly out of condition. When we'd discussed the trip, I'd mentioned hiring *cargadores*, but Giitter said he could never look his men in the face again if he had to have somebody carry his pack. Anyway, there were no *cargadores* available in Aritao, so that settled it. We hadn't gone a mile before Justo practically passed out. They had to take most of his pack and distribute it among the men. As we climbed, Giitter stopped 15 minutes every kilometer 'to let the men get a rest.' By the time we'd gone 15 kilometers, Giitter was trying to hire *cargadores*, horses, or anything else he could find. We missed Kayapa by 11 kilometers and had to sleep on the ground next to a little creek in the mountains.

"The next morning we tackled the 11 kilometers to Kayapa plus 18 kilometers more to Lusod, where a sawmill run by a man named Jorgensen was supposed to be our next night's camp. Right away my companions—the officers, not the soldiers—began stopping every kilometer in spite of the fact we'd just had 10 hours' sleep and it was the cool of the morning. After two of these stops, I made a remark that I guess had a little gravel in it, whereupon Giitter snapped that if I thought I could make better time, to go right on ahead. That challenge got my Irish up a bit, so I kept right on going. At Kayapa I asked the way to Lusod, but no one knew of the place. Then I tried asking for Jorgensen's sawmill, whereupon they answered, 'Oh, Bobok, Bobok,' and pointed up the trail. I figured maybe the name of the town had changed or something, so I kept going. After crossing two more mountain ranges—the last hour and a half on a trail eight inches wide cut into the side of a 60-degree slope—and hiking a total of about 22 miles, I arrived at Jorgensen's sawmill at Bobok.

"Ken and Roxy Jorgensen invited me to stay the night, fixed me up with clean clothes and a nice, cold glass of beer. I learned there *is* a Lusod sawmill 15 miles west of Kayapa, reached by just as difficult a trail, run by Ken's father, Emil Jorgensen. I also learned there's a road from Bobok to Baguio. The Jorgensens invited me ride with them to Baguio on their regularly scheduled supply run two days later. We called Lusod that night, but there was no sign of Giitter and the rest of our party.

"Ken gave me a tour of the mill the next day. It was quite impressive!

"The following morning we again called Lusod and got no news so started for Baguio on a paved road, but twisting and narrow, arriving about 12:30. We called Lusod a fourth time and finally got word of the boys. They'd arrived at Lusod, seven kilometers less distance than what I'd come the day before, at 11 a.m.! And with a dozen *cargadores* carrying their luggage! I had a lovely Thanksgiving dinner. At 7 p.m. Giitter and Justo got in, two of the saddest specimens you ever saw. So I'm now 'the mountain man' with everybody in camp except two certain officers, whose list I am on, without a doubt! It was fun anyway. Ken Jorgensen has asked me to climb Mount Pulag with him sometime. I plan to keep in touch with them as they're very swell people.

"It's now midnight and I have to get up and inspect the guard at 5:30, so nighty nite.

I love you. Art."[9]

November 27th was Art and Lillian's fourth wedding anniversary. He found it hard to believe that for nearly a quarter of their married life they'd been separated, with no end in sight. He wanted to take her in his arms and tell her how important she was to him and how much he loved her, but the best he could do was a telegram. Personal messages were no longer allowed, only essential business items, so he had to get a bit clever about how he phrased it. He knew she'd understand.

Telegram re 4th anniversary (installment)

His letter of November 30 was a short one:

"My sweet. I'm once again in Dutch with the Clipper, having waited until the last day to start a letter. I have an excuse, though. I've been away climbing Mount Pulag! I happened to mention to Colonel Horan that climbing Mount

Pulag would make a nice reconnaissance, and he ordered us to start two days later. Mount Pulag isn't really anything to brag about climbing, only 9,613 feet high, but it's the highest peak on Luzon, and you get a swell view from the top. I now have quite a reputation as a mountain climber!

"Lars Jensen took this photo at the summit. The wind was blowing like the devil and my shirt was full of air. I'm not really as rotund as this shot makes me look. In fact, I'm not rotund at all! These days, my sweet, I have muscles even you wouldn't recognize!

"Saturday evening after we got back, Lars and I hung around at the Officers' Mess and ended up solving all the world's problems over drinks and dinner with a couple of fellows we've gotten to know, Captain Russell Volckmann and Captain George Pinnel. They were both instructors with the 11th Infantry, Philippine Army, at Camp Holmes, a

Art atop Mount Pulag

primitive training camp about five miles northeast of here. They've now been moved down to a camp on the beach at Dagupan, where it's hot as the devil, so every chance they get they're up here for a weekend of golf.

"I'm sorry, my darling, but I've got to get some sleep, so must say good-bye. I love you. Art."[10]

CHAPTER 9

WAR BEGINS
AT CAMP JOHN HAY

December 8 to December 24, 1941

EARLY ON SUNDAY, NOVEMBER 27, a general alert was called. All leaves were canceled and all officers ordered back to their posts.[1] Russ Volckmann and George Pinnel joined Art and Lars for breakfast. All voiced disgust as they'd planned on making it a foursome on the golf course later in the day. They agreed to try again in a week.

The following days were quiet. Art turned in figures gathered on another trip down to measure water volumes at the springs along the Kennon Road.

Otherwise, he drilled his soldiers and followed a limited routine. The high point of each day was a contest between the men to see who could take their weapon apart, oil it, and reassemble it in the shortest amount of time. Sometimes they did this blindfolded. The Scouts were proud of their weapons and took excellent care of them.

Actually, being confined to the post wasn't so bad. Art spent the evenings developing, printing, and sorting his photographs, planning to combine the pictures and other little souvenirs into a travel album, a great conversation piece to show guests someday when he and Lil entertained in their "Philippines Room."

The next weekend Volckmann and Pinnel didn't make it back, but Art had his best game of golf ever when he shot an 82!

MONDAY, DECEMBER 8, STARTED OUT like most days—cold, with low-hanging, misty fog. Art and Lars were up by six, showered, dressed, and ready to jump in their jeep and go to breakfast when the phone rang. It was Captain Calvert, telling them to report to Major Giitter's office promptly at eight for an important briefing.

At the Officers' Mess they were greeted by Lieutenant Bach, the assigned mess officer. Other than Bach, a non-com named Sergeant Bland, and two Filipino desk clerks, the place was nearly deserted. A couple of the British wives huddled over in one corner while at another table a young mother was coaxing her toddler to swallow his scrambled eggs. Art and Lars ate quickly and headed over for the meeting in the Headquarters building across the street.

Aside from Major Giitter, they were the first arrivals. Giitter looked as though he'd seen a ghost but didn't say a word, not even *good morning*. In minutes the room filled with a dozen more officers and non-coms. Once the usual buzz and chatter died down, in a tense voice Giitter gave everyone the news: *The Japs have bombed Pearl Harbor*. For a moment there was silence, a sea of stunned faces. No one figured Pearl Harbor would be the first target. And if Pearl Harbor had been hit, the Philippines might well be next. Then the room erupted. Some expressed incredulity, some fired questions and clamored for additional information, but there were no answers, no further information. Major Giitter demanded silence and barked instructions for the officers to gather their units on the double and assemble back at Headquarters at nine for Colonel Horan's further orders. Art and Lars Jensen were the first ones out the door, running for the jeep. Not far away, the young mother and her little boy were taking a leisurely post-breakfast stroll.[2]

Overhead, a dull roar canceled out all ground noise. Airplanes, obviously, but nothing yet visible through the overcast. When the first of them broke through the clouds, a big two-engine job, flying lower and lower, Art knew instantly it wasn't American, not with wing markings resembling fat blood-orange slices. The planes came in three perfect V-formations, eighteen in all, like Canada geese heading south for the winter. Art slammed on the brakes, yelled back in the direction of the woman and her baby to *take cover, for God's sake, take cover*, and then he and Lars did just that. They dove into the ditch at the side of the road, wrapped their arms over their heads, and folded up like sow bugs. The rat-tat-tat-tat-tat of machine gun fire pierced the air, then a high-pitched whine, then the sound of the first bomb exploding back in the direction of the Officers' Mess and Headquarters buildings. Another whine and another hit, then other, more muffled explosions from the direction of the golf course. Black smoke and dust swirled overhead, blotting out the light. Their hearts stopped. They couldn't breathe. They hunkered down in the ditch for an eternity—probably no more than a couple of minutes—until the explosions stopped. Then they jumped back in the jeep and drove like hell toward the barracks to gather their soldiers.[3]

The place was chaos, panicked men streaming out the doors, running everywhere and yelling, some shouting orders, others just screaming. Firing his .45 into the air, Art finally got their attention, assembled his group into some semblance of order, and herded them at a trot through the black smoke.

At Headquarters the scene was even more chaotic. Air raid sirens blared. Other Scouts came running, tripping over fire hoses that were spewing water onto the flames. Ambulances clogged the road. Medics raced around, gathering the dead and wounded. Rumors were already flying. One bomb had hit the central section of the Officers' Mess, and someone said that Sergeant Bland had been killed, Lieutenant Bach had caught shrapnel, and one of the young desk clerks had had his leg blown off. Art watched Filipino medics load the young mother and her baby into an ambulance and haul them away. Another bomb had exploded near Major Giitter's office, blowing five non-coms to bits and ripping off the legs of two others, while Giitter himself had been slammed against his office wall by his own desk and was stunned but otherwise uninjured.[4]

Form up, form up, Art hollered as zigzagging emergency vehicles repeatedly scattered the men—his throat now raw, his voice reduced to a croak from inhaled smoke and grit.

When he finally appeared, Colonel Horan appeared dazed, in shock. At first he just stood there, gawking in disbelief at his staff car, which hadn't taken a direct hit but had been badly damaged by shrapnel.[5] Finally, the colonel mumbled something to the effect that he knew the version of War Plan Orange he had was outdated, but he didn't have the new revision and hadn't heard from MacArthur's headquarters, so he'd just have to wait until new orders arrived.

Version 3 of War Plan Orange called for both companies of the 1st Battalion, 43rd Infantry (Philippine Scouts), to proceed down the Kennon Road and defend sections of beach west of Rosario near Dagupan. By December 8, USAFFE Headquarters had ordered that those beach positions be taken instead by the Philippine Army units commanded by Major Martin Moses, his subordinate, Lieutenant Donald Blackburn, and Captain Russ Volckmann. Additional Philippine Army units, commanded by Lieutenant Colonel Donald Bonnett and Major Arthur K. Noble—both of whom had earlier come up from Fort McKinley to serve as trainers and then been hastily converted into infantry commanders—would spread out along the beaches farther north toward San Fernando.[6]

What are we supposed to be doing? Art wondered. *Standing around twiddling our thumbs?* Finally, when pressed, Colonel Horan assigned them to guard the utilities and communications facilities[7]—Company B on the post and Art's Company A in downtown Baguio—just in case the Japanese began dropping soldiers in by parachute. Then they were dismissed.

Art sprinted over to the office of Sergeant William Bowen, the post radio operator, to send Lil a telegram and let her know he was okay. Bowen said his radio had been cutting in and out, but he'd do his best. Art scribbled a few words and raced back to the jeep.

Passing the golf course, smoking pits dotted the hillsides, like the giant Gulliver himself had played eighteen holes, leaving behind huge divots. Just outside the main gate, another bomb had struck a couple of houses and several cars, reducing them to smoldering, smoking ruins.[8]

Though news of Pearl Harbor had begun to spread, the local citizenry appeared nonchalant. After all, Hawaii was a long way from Baguio. Even the sounds of the explosions hadn't been unusual; early morning explosions often took place at the nearby Cal Horr Mine. It was the Feast of the Immaculate Conception, and worshippers thronged the Catholic cathedral above the business district. Parents dropped their children off at the prestigious Brent International School, where the offspring of local miners, businessmen, and politicians attended classes. In the central market area, shopkeepers went about their normal activities, opening up for the day's business, greeting one another. Natives spread their wares along the curbs. Everyone apparently assumed at first—as Art had for a few brief moments—that the planes were American bombers, sent aloft from Clark Field, perhaps to attack Tokyo or, at any rate, to make sure nothing bad happened to the citizens of Baguio.[9]

Art assigned his men their positions. They'd been in place only a few hours when more two-engine bombers roared overhead, this time from the northwest, again flying in perfect Vs. By now the mist had lifted, though, and they had only to look skyward at the big orange-red circles on the wings to know the planes weren't American. Art hollered for his men to take cover, and most civilians did the same, crowding into buildings or diving under cars. But they heard no whine, no explosions, and no machine gun fire. The planes continued south toward Clark Field and Fort Stotsenburg, or perhaps Manila or Nichols Field. They couldn't tell, but it was pretty certain someone else was going to get it this time.

DURING THE FIRST WEEK OF DECEMBER, half the B-17 bombers based at Clark Field had been moved to the Del Monte airfield on Mindanao, the large southern island, to eliminate any risk the entire fleet might be lost at once in the event of trouble. Right after news broke of the Pearl Harbor attack, the remaining two squadrons at Clark, along with their supporting fighters, had been ordered into the air. If they were aloft, they couldn't all be annihilated on the ground. By 11:30, however, the all-clear had been sounded and the pilots had returned to base for refueling and some lunch. Their planes were parked neatly, wing tip to wing tip, when the second wave of Japanese bombers showed up at 12:45. Within an hour, all but seven of the American aircraft, along with hangars, barracks, and warehouses, were reduced to a mass of smoking rubble. Seventy-seven men were killed, more than a hundred wounded.[10]

The news from Nichols and Nielson fields wasn't much better. When the damage was tallied, MacArthur's Air Corps, the vaunted protector of the Philippine Islands, had in the course of a few hours been reduced by more than half.

BEFORE THE DAY WAS OVER, COLONEL HORAN implemented some provisions of War Plan Orange 3 he was sure hadn't changed. He notified the managers of the nearby mines to prepare to evacuate their women and children to Manila on one hour's notice. He ordered the local civilian police—the Philippine Constabulary—to round up all adult male Japanese nationals and escort them to Camp John Hay, to be held as potential spies. Local businessmen and storekeepers, along with dozens of other Japanese—employees of gold mines as far away as Itogon, Tuba, and La Trinidad—were locked up in an unused barrack that had sustained only minor damage in the morning bombing. The internees were outraged and demanded that they be allowed to place the Japanese Rising Sun flag on the roof because they feared the barrack might be hit again by Japanese bombs. Colonel Horan at first acquiesced but later changed his mind and ordered the flag removed. He ordered all Japanese women and children confined to the Japanese School in Baguio, and kept under surveillance by the Constabulary.[11]

The only good news Art heard concerned the lady and her baby who'd been at the Officers' Mess. Somebody said her husband worked down at Cavite Naval Base and had sent his family up to Baguio, thinking it would be safer. Anyway, when they got to the hospital, covered in blood, the mother was whisked off in one direction and the baby in another, into the care of a doctor and one of the American nurses, Ruby Bradley. The baby's kneecap was shattered, his face blue. They tried oxygen and mouth-to-mouth resuscitation, but the baby didn't respond. Meanwhile, additional casualties were flooding in through the emergency entrance, all requiring immediate attention, and the doctor turned away. But Ruby didn't give up. Remembering a flask of whiskey in a nearby cabinet and knowing liquor was a stimulant, she grabbed a wad of gauze, soaked it in the booze, sprinkled on a little sugar, and stuck it in the baby's mouth. At first the baby didn't respond, but gradually he started to suck a little, then more, his color began to return, and soon he was yelling bloody murder. One of the mother's legs had to be amputated, but both she and the baby survived.[12] Art remembered telling Lil about Ruby in a letter, describing her as *too old*, but he vowed that if he ever saw her at a social gathering again, he'd dance with her and get to know her. She was one impressive gal!

At Camp John Hay, when later that afternoon the full extent of the damage was tallied, at least 125 bombs had been dropped, though not all had exploded. Eleven people had been killed and another twenty-two injured. Had the Japanese had better aim, things could have been much worse.[13]

DURING THE EARLY MORNING ON DECEMBER 10, the Japanese again attacked northern Luzon from the air. Two locations were hit simultaneously, followed by the landing of the first waves of their infantry.

One landing took place at Aparri and nearby Gonzaga on the north coast of Luzon. Several thousand Japanese, later dubbed the

Tanaka Detachment, came ashore virtually unmolested. They quickly occupied the local airfield and set crews to work lengthening and enlarging it to accommodate their fighter planes. Part of the Tanaka force split off and, unopposed, moved west along Coastal Highway 3. The rest of the Tanaka force moved south down Highway 5 to Tuguegarao, where they met some resistance but soon had another airfield in their pocket.[14]

Concurrently, a second landing, later named the Kanno Detachment, took place near Vigan on the west coast of Luzon. Although a few American planes inflicted some damage, it wasn't enough to prevent the Japanese from gaining a foothold on the beach. Once ashore, the Kanno group also split. The smaller segment headed unopposed north up the coast road to meet the Tanaka force. The balance of the Kanno group pushed south down Highway 3 through the narrow coastal plain toward the Lingayen Gulf, where the main landing of Japanese troops and tanks was anticipated.[15]

At the Baroro Bridge just north of San Fernando, La Union, Philippine Army infantry units under Lieutenant Colonel Donald Bonnett and Major Arthur K. Noble were positioned to repel the enemy. A third Philippine Army unit, commanded by Major Martin Moses, had been moved north from the Lingayen Gulf to help Bonnett's and Noble's men meet the advancing Japanese.[16]

Japanese planes, by now virtually unopposed in the air, repeatedly bombed and strafed the beach positions, inflicting heavy casualties.

The Philippine Army reserve troops had had minimal training, most only a month or two. Some had never even fired their weapons. Badly outnumbered, with minimal artillery and no air support, some of them broke ranks, threw down their rifles, and deserted the beaches, leaving their frustrated American commanders screaming in vain for them to stop.

Those who didn't run could do little more than slow the enemy advance and gradually retreat. The defenders held for a few days, but they were no match for the well-equipped Japanese. The Bonnett-Moses-Noble units were flanked on the south and cut off by the advancing Japanese. Following War Plan Orange 3, the Bonnett-Moses-Noble group retreated inland a few miles to the town of Naguilian, regrouped, and waited for further orders from Colonel Horan.[17]

AROUND DECEMBER 16, seven Japanese bombers again visited Baguio. They didn't do much damage, but they scared the devil out of the local citizenry, some of whom called MacArthur's headquarters and raised hell. *Where were their bomb shelters? What was the plan?* They were bitterly critical of poor old Colonel Horan, accusing him of cowardice, incompetence, and inefficiency. The callers were assured that Japanese ground troops would never reach Baguio, and that, in any event, Colonel Horan had his well-armed Scouts in place with orders to stay and protect them until reinforcements arrived. This was enough for some civilians, who began hoarding food, cigarettes, and liquor. Others, more skeptical, packed up their families and headed higher into the mountains.

Colonel Horan decided that since no parachutes had shown up and since Baguio now appeared more vulnerable to attack by enemy ground troops from the coast, there were more important things for the Scouts to be doing. He ordered Captain Calvert to take Company B down and prevent the Japanese from coming up the Kennon Road. He told Major Giitter—hastily converted from adjutant to company commander—to take Company A and defend Naguilian Road, the more northerly of the two steep, winding roads connecting Baguio with the coast. Art and the men were instructed to mine the bridges and road culverts and then stand by, ready to blow them and retreat if the Japanese started up the mountain.[18]

They had had little demolitions training, but some of the local miners helped out. A group of them had already tried to enlist but had been told by Horan that without specific orders from Headquarters, he had no authority to induct anyone and wouldn't know what to do with them if he did. Undaunted, these fellows beat it back to the mines; rounded up compressors, drills, dynamite, blasting caps, and fuses; then followed the men of Company A down Naguilian Road and provided some quick lessons on how it was done. Once they got the hang of it, the miners moved on down to the coast to see where else they could assist.

When the explosives were in place and each squad positioned and assigned its night watch schedule, Art settled in to wait, only marginally aware of events unfolding a dozen miles below along the coast, just the sporadic muffled sounds of war. He was positioned below one of the bridge spans, next to a small waterfall. Just above the bridge, the road widened out into one of the few turnarounds along Naguilian Road. His thoughts turned to Lil. He wondered if she'd gotten his telegram. He wondered what kind of news she was hearing of events in the Philippines. He wondered if she'd gotten any of the packages of Christmas gifts he'd mailed. He watched as a rainbow-hued sunset painted the sky over the Lingayen Gulf and thought how incongruous the whole thing was—all this incredible natural beauty, an oblivious and uncaring backdrop to the unfolding madness. He ate his dinner ration, rolled up in his sleeping bag, and tried to imagine that Lillian was lying, soft and warm, in his arms.

As Art slept, the main Japanese landing force silently dropped anchor in the Lingayen Gulf, a vast fleet of some eighty aircraft carriers, transports, cruisers, and destroyers, strung out like beads up and down the coast. At dawn, in the distance, Art watched dozens of landing craft busily ferrying vehicles, tanks, big guns, and the first of 43,000 enemy troops from the transports to the beach.[19] The sheer size of the force was unbelievable, beyond imagination. It sent shivers down his spine.

Once ashore, it took a day or so as the Japanese met some resistance, but, like the earlier landings farther north, the Philippine Army units were no match for the onslaught and soon fell back to defensive positions at Rosario.

Rosario was a crucial junction, to be held at all costs, in order to keep the Kennon Road open as an escape route to Manila for those at Camp John Hay, Baguio, and the surrounding mountain communities.

On the morning of the 22nd, Colonel Horan's pockmarked staff car passed Art, heading down Naguilian Road, but within an hour it passed him again, speeding back up to Baguio, making good time on the narrow, twisting road.

Shortly after noon, a whole column snaked its way slowly up the mountain. In the lead came a bus carrying Majors Moses and Noble and a group of their men, followed by Lieutenant Colonel Bonnett's car, then an old, battered Plymouth with Lieutenant Donald Blackburn and several others. Behind them stretched the dusty convoy, a fuzzy caterpillar crawling slowly up the mountain and away from danger.

The bus stopped when it reached Art's position. Everyone piled out. They were a mess. Some sported blood-soaked bandages. As they doused their grimy faces and filled their canteens at the waterfall, Art learned something of what was going on. Apparently Bonnett and Noble had orders to retreat to Baguio, while Moses and Blackburn had no further orders at all. Colonel Horan was to have returned to Naguilian with new orders for the latter, but when the colonel hadn't shown up, Moses and Blackburn had opted to accompany Bonnett and Noble on up the mountain.[20]

Colonel Bonnett ordered his men to break for chow, jumped in his car, and proceeded on up to Baguio to find out what was going on. When he hadn't returned by eleven, the rest of them packed up and moved out too, leaving the demolition crews alone in the night, their last orders to *stay put until told otherwise*. At that point Art was beginning to wonder if anyone in the whole damned Army knew what they were doing.

Also on the 22nd, the Japanese again bombed and strafed Baguio and Camp John Hay, but did little damage.[21] A thousand Philippine

Scouts had congregated on the post, some having hiked more than a hundred miles in from Ifugao Subprovince, augmented now by the Philippine Army troops that had trudged up the Naguilian Road. Most had orders to proceed down the mountain via the Kennon Road, through Rosario, and south on Highway 1 toward the Bataan Peninsula.

Obviously travel on foot would take too long, yet Camp John Hay had nowhere near enough vehicles to transport all these troops. Horan sent Sergeant Emilio Velasco, one of the 43rd Infantry Philippine Scouts, to contact Bado Dangwa, president and general manager of Dangwa Tranco, a local transportation company. Fiercely loyal to the Americans, Mr. Dangwa immediately turned every operational vehicle in his fleet over to the military, more than 170 American-made buses, trucks, and cars, along with gasoline, oil, spare tires, and parts. He then mustered his drivers, conductors, and mechanics from their homes and placed them at Colonel Horan's disposal. The commandeered vehicles were loaded with soldiers and driven at daredevil speeds down the steep, zigzagging Kennon Road to Rosario. After depositing the first load, the Dangwa Tranco employees raced back up to Baguio for another. They repeated the procedure again and again.[22] Meanwhile, Colonel Bonnett's men, along with those of Moses, Noble, and Blackburn, waited at Camp John Hay for further orders. It was a very, very confusing day.

COLONEL HORAN ALSO ALERTED the local mine managers to send their families to Manila while they still could. At the Itogon mine, twelve miles east, the women and kids and their luggage were hastily loaded into pickup trucks and cars. They followed their usual route down through the gorge, up into Baguio, and then started down the Kennon Road, the most direct route to Manila, where they hoped to book passage on a ship and get out of the Philippines. Within a few hours, though, they were back at the mine, reporting that Rosario was so congested they couldn't get through.

Lewis Robinson, the Itogon manager, implemented his own backup plan and ordered the families up to Emil Jorgensen's Lusod sawmill, accessible only by hiking east for eight or ten hours up a steep, narrow trail.

This wasn't a spur-of-the-moment action. The Itogon routinely kept in their warehouse a six-month supply of food for each resident family. Beginning right after the first bombings on the 8th, Robinson's people had moved these stores by tram up to Lusod. They had quietly scooped up additional supplies in Baguio and sent those up too.

But some of the women were older or pregnant, and there were several toddlers. *How were they to manage?* In the end, native *cargadores* were hired. The Igorots tied the corners of blankets to bamboo poles, loaded up the children and weaker folks, and hoisted the contraptions onto their shoulders, the same way they habitually carried trussed pigs to market.[23]

ON THE 23RD, THE JAPANESE STARTED UP the Naguilian Road. When they approached Company A's first hidden platoon, the men lobbed a couple of grenades to try and blow one of the Japanese trucks and block the road. The Japanese returned fire and kept coming. Almost immediately Major Giitter ordered the men to complete their assigned mission and withdraw. *What a pitiful, disgusting end to the American defense of Baguio*, Art thought, but he relayed the order down the line. Then, starting from the bottom, fuses were lit, and the platoons blew a lot of mighty expensive engineering to kingdom come. When the last of the culverts and bridges had been destroyed, Art and the rest of the men skedaddled as fast as they could back up to camp.[24]

COLONEL HORAN STILL HADN'T RECEIVED any new orders from MacArthur, but directed the companies to pack up and be prepared to move. Art stopped briefly at the Headquarters building and poked his head into Sergeant Bowen's office to see if he'd gotten Art's wire out. Bowen was busily boxing stuff up but said he'd relayed it to the telegraph office in Baguio and they'd take it from there.

When Art reached their quarters, Lars Jensen was already there. Art poured himself several fingers of scotch and then tried to formulate a plan. With no idea if they were actually moving out, how long they'd be gone, or if they'd ever be back, he did what the scotch told him was logical. First, he packed all his treasured bolos but one, his Philippines album keepsakes and photos, and as much darkroom equipment as would fit, into his three footlockers, carefully cushioning the fragile stuff with extra clothing. He snapped the padlocks shut and shoved the footlockers out of sight under his bed. In the dry closet, he pushed their dress uniforms to one side, stuffed in more camera equipment and books, and relocked the closet.

Then he emptied his knapsack and started over. The footlocker keys, along with his packet of letters and photographs of Lillian and the babies, he placed in the bottom. He'd never used a red leather pocket diary Lil had given him a year earlier, so he threw that in too. Then came changes of underwear and socks, extra shorts, a couple of shirts, extra eyeglasses, a tablet, a fountain pen and a couple of pencils, his mess kit, nail clippers, extra razor blades, matches, the rest of his cigarettes, a bar of soap, and a towel. When the pack wouldn't close, he tore it apart again and reduced the clothing by half. As an afterthought, he threw in a roll of first aid tape from the bathroom. Jensen pretty much followed his lead. Then both took a hot shower, hit the hay, and tried to catch a few hours of sleep.

On the morning of the 24th, Art shaved and added his razor and toothbrush to the pack, along with his comb, a flashlight, and some spare batteries. With his sleeping bag and an extra blanket, his .45, M-1, and canteen, he figured he was ready to go.

Eggs, bacon, toast, and coffee were being served at the mess, from the only portion of the kitchen left intact. On the surface everything appeared normal, but it wasn't normal. The tenseness in the air, you could have cut with a knife.

Colonel Horan held a short briefing. He'd finally made early morning contact with USAFFE Headquarters in Manila, urgently requesting permission to move his forces out via the Kennon Road, *before* the enemy overran the junction at Rosario. He was told to stay put and not to worry.[25]

A few hours later, *after* Rosario had been overrun by the Japanese, Headquarters finally realized the precariousness of the situation and radioed new orders:

SAVE YOUR COMMAND; USE MOUNTAIN TRAILS[26]

Colonel Horan held another briefing of officers and laid out a plan. They would proceed east over the Cordillera Mountains and hopefully reach Highway 5 ahead of any Japanese coming from the north. At Highway 5 they would turn south over Balete Pass, and, if everything worked perfectly, they'd join the rest of the USAFFE forces retreating to Bataan.[27] Everyone was hastily issued a steel helmet, a gas mask, and three days' worth of canned rations.

The colonel split the troops into two groups so if the Japanese caught up with one, the other might still make it through. The Bonnett-Moses-Noble-Blackburn (and Jensen) group were to go out immediately in Dangwa Tranco buses and trucks and take the more northerly route, travel via the Baguio-Bokod road (Mountain Trail), take the cutoff to the Bobok sawmill, and from there proceed to Bambang and on to Aritao. This route had been checked with Ken Jorgensen at Bobok, who'd advised by phone that yes, the horse trail beyond Bobok could be made passable and vehicles could make it over the Cordillera Mountains to Highway 5. No one had thought to ask him how long such road work would take.[28] Art, who had hiked this route only a month earlier, volunteered that although there was a trail beyond Bobok, it certainly wasn't one that could ever accommodate buses or trucks. His input was ignored in favor of the advice from Jorgensen.

The second group, of which Art was a part, would be led by Colonel Horan himself. They would go out in the last of the Dangwa Tranco vehicles, take a more southerly route up to Twin Rivers, the terminus of the road, and from there proceed on foot up to the Lusod sawmill, then over the mountains to Imugan, and from there to Santa Fe on Highway 5.

Colonel Horan's last acts were to declare Baguio an open city and turn jurisdiction of the Japanese internees over to the former mayor, E. J. Halsema, along with the rest of the food supplies in the warehouses. The local citizenry was outraged, but with their protection detail heading out, many more of them packed up and joined the exodus.

At mid-afternoon on Christmas Eve, 1941, they loaded up and hit the road. With a heavy heart, Art bade a silent farewell to lovely Baguio.

CHAPTER 10

WAR COMES TO BERKELEY

December 1941 and January 1942

O N SUNDAY, DECEMBER 7, 1941, Lillian was in the kitch-en fixing sandwiches. The radio was on, tuned to NBC, some-thing about Canada. Abruptly, around 11:30, the regular program-ming was interrupted:

> From the NBC newsroom in New York: President
> Roosevelt said in a statement today that the Japanese
> have attacked Pearl Harbor, Hawaii, from the air. I'll
> repeat that: President Roosevelt says that the Japanese
> have attacked Pearl Harbor in Hawaii from the air.
> This bulletin came to you from the NBC newsroom in
> New York.[1]

Lil stood motionless, trying to digest what she'd just heard. Her knees felt weak. Only a few minutes later the program was inter-rupted again:

> From the NBC newsroom in New York: The White
> House also reported today a simultaneous air attack
> on Army and Navy bases in Manila. This report follows
> the president's declaration that all Army and Navy
> bases on the island of Oahu in Hawaii are now under
> air attack. This bulletin came to you from the NBC
> newsroom in New York.[2]

The rest of the day was a blur. Report after report came in, many of them contradictory. By mid-afternoon one announcer said the earlier report about Manila being bombed was a mistake, and Lil's heart soared. But other reports came in of Japanese planes being sighted near San Francisco and of submarines surfacing off the coast at Santa Barbara. There was talk of Clipper (air-mail) service being suspended. Somehow the children got dinner and baths and went to bed.

When Lillian Sr. arrived home, she was terribly upset. They remained glued to the radio. Late in the evening an announcer said it hadn't been Manila that had been bombed, but rather Clark Field, north of Manila, resulting in extensive casualties and widespread damage; *also Baguio and Camp John Hay, where dozens were killed.* Lil was numb, unable to really comprehend.[3]

At 12:30 a.m., despite reports about the Clipper service, Lil closed herself in her bedroom and began a letter to Art. She filled several pages, but when she read them over, much of it was only trivia that meant little.[4] She concluded by telling him how much she loved him, went into the closet and retrieved his favorite V-neck sweater from a storage box, put it on, and went to bed. She may have dozed for an hour, certainly no more.

ON MONDAY, PRESIDENT ROOSEVELT appeared before a full session of Congress:

Mr. Vice President, Mr. Speaker, Members of the Senate, and of the House of Representatives:

Yesterday, December 7th, 1941—a date which will live in infamy—the United States of America was suddenly and deliberately attacked by naval and air forces of the Empire of Japan. The United States was at peace with that nation and, at the solicitation of Japan, was still in conversation with its government and its emperor, looking toward the maintenance of peace in the Pacific. Indeed, one hour after Japanese air squadrons had commenced bombing on the American island of Oahu, the Japanese ambassador to the United States and his colleagues delivered to our Secretary of State a formal reply to a recent American message. While this reply stated that it seemed useless to continue the existing diplomatic negotiations, it contained no threat or hint of war or of armed attack.

It will be recorded that the distance of Hawaii from Japan makes it obvious that the attack was deliberately planned many days or even weeks ago. During the intervening time, the Japanese government has deliberately sought to deceive the United States by false statements and expressions of hope for continued peace.

The attack yesterday on the Hawaiian Islands has caused severe damage to American naval and military forces. I regret to tell you that very many American lives have been lost. In addition, American ships have been reported torpedoed on the high seas between San Francisco and Honolulu.

Yesterday, the Japanese government also launched an attack against Malaya. Last night, Japanese forces attacked Hong Kong. Last night, Japanese forces attacked Guam. Last night, Japanese forces attacked the Philippine Islands. Last night, the Japanese attacked Wake Island. This morning, the Japanese attacked Midway Island. Japan has, therefore, undertaken a surprise offensive extending throughout the Pacific area. The facts of yesterday and today speak for themselves.

The people of the United States have already formed their opinions and well understand the implications to the very life and safety of our nation. As commander in chief of the Army and Navy, I have directed that all measures be taken for our defense. But always will our whole nation remember the character of the onslaught against us.

Roosevelt addressing Congress Dec 8, 1941

P351 MacArthur photo: This image is a work of a U.S. Army soldier or employee, taken or made as part of that person's official duties. As a work of the U.S. federal government, the image is in the public domain.

No matter how long it may take us to overcome this premeditated invasion, the American people in their righteous might will win through to absolute victory. I believe that I interpret the will of the Congress and of the people when I assert that we will not only defend ourselves to the utmost, but will make it very certain that this form of treachery shall never again endanger us. Hostilities exist. There is no blinking at the fact that our people, our territory, and our interests are in grave danger. With confidence in our armed forces, with the unbounded determination of our people, we will gain the inevitable triumph, so help us God.

I ask that the Congress declare that since the unprovoked and dastardly attack by Japan on Sunday, December 7th, 1941, a state of war has existed between the United States and the Japanese Empire.[5]

So it was official. The U.S. was at war with Japan. Next, black-outs were ordered in British Columbia and from Los Angeles south to San Diego. Air raid warden squads were hastily organized and placed on 'round-the-clock duty. Radio station KFI in Los Angeles signed off the air at the request of military commanders, but, at least during the morning, the Bay Area stations continued broadcasting.[6]

Lil wondered if there wasn't some safer place she could take the children, someplace outside the congested Bay Area, where there weren't so many shipyards and vital defense industries. With all the rumors flying about, it seemed Berkeley could very well be bombed at any second. She tried to remain calm, but she was having a hard time.[7]

Radio station KGEI called to say that their shortwave programs had been canceled until further notice. It was just one more disappointment. Lil and Roberta had had their names on the list for weeks to talk by radio broadcast to Art and Brew in the Philippines. It was a nice service that KGEI provided, and they'd hoped it would be a special Christmas present for their men. Lil wondered if Art would get any of his Christmas presents, then thought how silly that was, for Christmas presents would be the last thing on his mind.[8]

The afternoon mail brought Art's half-page letter telling about climbing Mount Pulag and enclosing a picture, but that letter was dated November 30, and so many things had happened in the eternity since then.

By evening all West Coast stations were off the air except one broadcasting from Washington State. That newscaster reported that a number of people in Seattle had received radiograms and cables from relatives and friends in the Pacific to the effect that they were safe. At the end of the broadcast, the airways went silent. Lil went in and kissed the sleeping children, put on Art's sweater, and went to bed. She felt sure she'd have a radiogram the next day.[9]

Tuesday, the 9th, came and went, and there was no word from Art. Lil did get a note from Roberta saying she so much wished Lil and the girls would move back to Pacific Grove, that she missed them terribly. Lil missed Roberta too. They'd had only one disagreement in all the months they'd shared a house, and a few hours later they'd laughed about it. They had so much in common, especially now. But it was too late to go back.

The next day Lil moved the girls' beds from the sun porch into Cecil's old bedroom—figuring they'd be safer there—remade the beds, and put them down for their naps.

She took advantage of the interlude to add to her letter. She kept telling herself that no news was good news and that events in the Philippines had quieted down. A few radio broadcasts were saying everything was *well in hand*. But by evening there was still no word from Art.

On Thursday, the 11th, Germany and Italy formally declared war on the United States, so America was now in it all over the world.

Lil worked hard to keep her mind occupied, caught up on the laundry and housework, and got a wonderful lift when the afternoon mail came and there was a box from Art. In it were Christmas presents for her family, mostly brightly colored woven things made by the Igorot mountain people. It was comforting to think of Art shopping. Nothing was wrapped except a small jewelry-size box with Lil's name on it, so after the girls were in bed, she wrapped the rest and stowed the packages in her closet. Then she added the day's events to her letter to Art, affixed a Clipper stamp, and tucked it into her purse.

Blackouts happened nearly every evening. For the most part, everyone seemed calm and optimistic, although some people advocated for instantly pounding the devil out of the Japanese. They didn't seem to care so much about Europe. Military enlistments skyrocketed. Lil's brother Cecil decided he'd rather not be a foot soldier and instead went down and joined the Navy.

The Rose Bowl Game (Oregon State versus Duke) was canceled. Cal versus Georgia Tech, scheduled for Berkeley on December 27, was canceled too. Still there was no word from Art.

On Saturday, December 13, Trisha said her first sentence. By now she could repeat almost any one-syllable word and many simple two-syllable words. She could say "box" and enunciate the "x" very clearly. When asked if she was hungry, she'd reply "no" and mean it, or "hungry" or "eat" and then dash for her highchair.[10] These are the little details Lil put into the letters she continued writing to Art. He was missing so many milestones.[10]

She also told him how unsettled Eleanor was. At three and a half, she sensed something ominous was going on, but Lil had no idea what to tell her. At the end of their bedtime prayer ritual, Eleanor often asked *Where is my daddy?* or *Why doesn't my daddy come and see me?* Heartbreaking. Her way of coping was to get into mischief. She got into everything she knew she shouldn't be into. And it didn't do a bit of good to punish her. She'd go right back and do it again the next day. Lil got very discouraged sometimes, but deep down she knew Eleanor was only trying to deal in her own way with the anxiety and uncertainty that plagued them all.

That evening Lil got a phone call from Roberta, who was so excited she could hardly speak. She'd received a telegram from Brew, from Manila, saying he was safe and would soon be returning to Corregidor. Lil honestly shared her joy, but could feel a small black knot forming in her stomach. There was still no word from Art.

On Sunday, the 14th, it rained hard all day. Lil worked on Christmas cards. She sent a card to Myrtle Jensen with a nice note, but was afraid to ask if she'd heard from Lars. Lil also received Art's updated Theta Chi roster so she could finally address a number of cards she'd been holding. Many of his fraternity brothers were in the service and already overseas, so she filled her next letter to Art with this news.

That night they decorated the tree. Eleanor helped for the first time.

After the children were in bed, Lil continued her letter, adding in the tree-decorating. Alone in her room, she found it difficult to maintain her composure, for another day had passed with no word from Art.

By Monday all radio stations were back on the air, many broadcasting twenty-four hours, a couple carrying nothing but war news. A lot of it was repetitious, saying that things were *well in hand* or *under control* in the Philippines. On the other hand, the full story of Pearl Harbor broke, with graphic descriptions of the massive damage and loss of life. They also reported that Congress was proposing an amendment to extend the draft to all men from eighteen to sixty-four, with those between twenty-one and forty-five eligible for active military duty.

President Roosevelt released a statement giving the complete history of Japanese-American relationships from 1885 up to December 7. Lil cut it out to save in a scrapbook for Art because she knew someday he'd be interested in seeing what was being reported at home and comparing it with what he knew firsthand. But maybe he'd never see the scrapbook. Maybe the scrapbook would end up hers alone, a vivid reminder of these awful days. There was still no word from Art.

Tuesday, the 16th, dragged interminably even though Lil stayed busy with the usual housework. She tried not to listen to the news, but then couldn't stand it and turned the radio back on and listened all day long to the continued reports of war. Still there was nothing from Art.

On the 17th, she took the girls to visit Santa Claus at Capwell's. The line was much shorter than usual. In fact, in downtown Oakland there was little of the hustle and bustle of a normal Christmas season. Even the department store windows, with their colorful lights and elaborate animated scenes, weren't drawing a crowd. After Santa, they went down to the lunch counter in the basement for hot chocolate and then headed home. Lil didn't feel very Christmassy. At 4:45, though, all that changed when she received a phone call from Western Union.

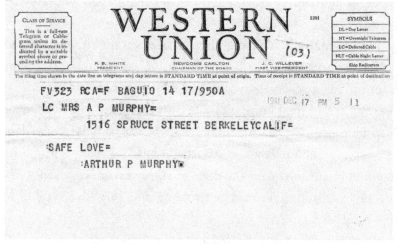

Telegram from Art "Safe Love," Dec 17, 1941

When they read the brief message, she was thrilled and ecstatic, so relieved that she started crying and couldn't stop for a long time. All of a sudden, the Christmas carols on the radio sounded wonderful. They didn't listen to any war news the whole evening. Jane brought over a bottle of champagne saved from their wedding, and they all celebrated. It was the best possible Christmas present.[11]

A few days later, censorship of all mail was formally established.

On Sunday, the 21st, Lil tried to send a Christmas message to Art by cable. She was told they couldn't accept it because the cables were too crowded with business. Instead, she wrote another letter to Art and put a Clipper stamp on it.

Roberta drove up on the 23rd. Lil was thrilled to see her. They talked quietly over early morning coffee, wondering what their men were doing, how they would be spending Christmas. Bert had heard the Army was hiring over at Fort Mason, with starting pay for a clerk-typist at $120 per month. The salary was astronomical when compared to Holman's, and it would be so much more satisfying to work closely with the military. Both women decided to apply. With Roberta, Lil didn't have to pretend. They understood each other's anxiety without having to put everything into words. Lil shared her room with Bert, who knew exactly why Lil wore Art's sweater to bed.

The girls were excited to see Scratty again, and between the three of them, and the cat, there were few quiet moments. The culmination came late in the afternoon when Trisha tried to pull an ornament off the tree and ended up pulling the whole tree down. When Lil got there, Trisha was kicking and struggling and yelling at the top of her lungs. The animals thought it was a big game and were tearing around in the debris. The tree was a sorry-looking thing when they finally got Trisha untangled, but they all laughed, put it back together as best they could, and this time they fastened it to the wall with a wire.

Roberta Gallup with dog Scratty taken Christmas Eve.

On Christmas Eve Roberta and Lil helped her mother stuff the huge turkey that was her gift to the family. Later they went to Charlotte and Bryce's for

Tom-and-Jerrys, then came home and put the girls to bed. When certain they were asleep, they filled the stockings and distributed the rest of the presents beneath the tree.

Charlotte and Bryce and Jane and Cecil arrived to watch the Christmas morning fun. The girls had plenty of presents as boxes had arrived from Art's Uncle Lock and Aunt Dink and from Art's old boss at the Los Angeles Newspaper Bureau. Lil's gift from Art held a beautiful silver brooch. She couldn't decipher the markings on the box, but Roberta said it was from Bali. They kept themselves busy so they wouldn't have too much time to think. At 4:30 they had a traditional Christmas feast. The whole family was there—everyone, that is, except Art and Brew. It was a nice, but not happy, Christmas.

On the 26th, Lil and Roberta drove over to Fort Mason and filled out employment applications.

Afterward, they had dinner at the Hostess House. The first evacuees from Hawaii had arrived and the Hostess House was full. Everyone had a different story to tell about their experiences on December 7, and although some of the accounts were quite frightening, most were simply interesting. While there, they heard over the radio that Baguio had fallen to the Japanese. Lil promptly lost all interest in the stories about Pearl Harbor.

New Year's Eve came and went without much fanfare as all noise was banned.

On January 3, 1942, Lil reported to the Post Intelligence Office at Fort Mason for her interview. Major Robert A. Gillmore, who reviewed her application and conducted the interview, had returned from the Philippines only ten months earlier. He outlined her privileges as a potential employee and suggested some financial arrangements he thought she should be making. He recommended she get a power of attorney from Art and also have Art change his allotment so that as much of their money as possible remained in the United States. Lil reminded the major that Baguio had fallen and she didn't know exactly where her husband was, but he suggested she at least try. She took careful notes and added these requests to her next letter to Art.[12]

Lil scored only thirty words a minute on her typing test, but Major Gillmore said that if she could get her speed up to fifty, she'd be hired. She rented a typewriter on the way home, and in the evenings practiced furiously. When her speed improved to forty-two, she called Major Gillmore to update him on her progress. On the 7th, he phoned and left a message with Lillian Sr., asking if Lil could report for work the next morning.

The new job meant commuting to San Francisco six days a week, leaving at 7:30 in the morning and not arriving home until 6:15 in the evening. It occupied her mind every minute of the day and yet involved no problems to be carried home at night, leaving her free to concentrate on the girls. She found the commute across the Bay Bridge enjoyable too, whether the day was sunny or shrouded in fog.

Lil immediately filed to take the Civil Service exam to become a regular Junior Clerk-Typist (CAF-2) and had no qualms about passing because her typing speed was now well over fifty.

The only problem—and it was a daunting one—was finding someone to care for the girls when Lillian Sr. had to return to her job on January 16. First Lil hired a middle-aged woman, who phoned after two days to say that an old case of housemaid's knee had flared up. Lil was frantic and spent her entire first Sunday off making calls. Finally she found a black woman named Mildred Thurman who was willing to start the next day, when Lillian Sr. would still be available to show her the ropes. When Lil got home after Mildred's first day, dinner was ready, Trisha was in bed, Eleanor was orderly and quiet, and the house was spotless. Lillian Sr. said the girls were awed by her, especially Trisha, who mostly stood and stared. When Mildred had scolded Eleanor for sliding down the banister, Eleanor actually listened. Lil felt sure Mildred was just what she'd been looking for.

A letter arrived from Myrtle Jensen in Minneapolis, saying she hadn't heard from Lars since December 12 and was awfully worried.

In Lil's reply she asked Myrtle to please share any news she got, and agreed to do the same.

Lil began another letter to Art, telling him about Christmas, her new job, all about Mildred, and more of the little everyday tidbits about the girls. Mildred even made notes of daily events at home so Lil could relay them to Art.[12]

It had now been a month since Art's telegram of December 17. Lil hoped that soon he'd have an opportunity to get in touch somehow, even if only another word or two, to let her know he was safe.

CHAPTER 11

RETREAT

December 25 to February 1942

THE DUSTY ROAD LEADING EAST OUT OF BAGUIO was jammed. Some native families traveled on foot, big bundles strapped on their heads and backs, their dogs trotting behind. A few led small horses, loaded to capacity. Others crowded into wooden-wheeled carts, pulled by lumbering *carabao*, and still others into ancient pickup trucks and cars. All were frantic to escape the invading Japanese. At first the Dangwa Tranco drivers honked loudly and forced slower traffic off to the side, but soon they were stuck in line with the rest. They proceeded at a crawl. At the cutoff leading south toward Itogon, more vehicles wedged their way into the procession. It took all afternoon to cover the fifteen miles to Twin Rivers, and there the road ended abruptly.

Once the buses emptied, Art watched a riveting spectacle. On the south side of the road, the steep precipice dropped 300 feet to the Agno River. One by one, more than two dozen Dangwa Tranco vehicles were backed up, repositioned, and driven toward the edge. The drivers jumped out at the last moment while the vehicles careened off the cliff. Some struck hillocks or huge boulders partway down, flipped, and bounced ten, twenty, thirty feet into the air before crashing back to earth, only to smash onto the jagged rocks below. Several nearly new 75-millimeter guns mounted on half-tracks followed, along with dozens of cases of ammunition. The machine guns and ammunition flew in every direction.[1,2] Fascinating to watch, but the magnitude of the waste was appalling. Bado Dangwa, had he been present, would have seen the achievements of a lifetime destroyed in moments. The soldiers couldn't carry any of it on their backs, though, and leaving anything behind for the Japanese to use against them was not an option.

From Twin Rivers, the narrow trail to the Lusod sawmill crossed two rivers and then twisted up the side of a steep mountain. Already it was jammed with the same assortment of refugees as had accompanied them all the way from Baguio. The soldiers lined up smartly and at first kept a steady pace. They hadn't gone more than a couple of miles before stragglers began to drop out of line to rest or relieve themselves. They covered a couple more miles before the sun began dropping swiftly toward the horizon.

There's an odd phenomenon in the mountains of North Luzon. It doesn't get dark gradually. It can be light one minute and then, when the sun drops from sight behind a ridge or peak, almost immediately there is total darkness.

When they came to a stretch where the trail widened out a bit, the commanders ordered a halt for the night. Captain Calvert assigned the watch schedule, and, with the mountainside as a backrest, they wearily sank down on the trail, opened their canned rations, and had Christmas Eve dinner. Even as they spread out their bedrolls, the last of the refugees, a group of miners from Itogon, climbed over them and, with a quiet *Merry Christmas*, disappeared up the trail into the darkness.[3]

Christmas Day dawned bright and beautiful. Despite Art's earlier title as the mountain man, now every part of his anatomy creaked, groaned, and complained. Progress was slow as they stopped often to rest. The trail continued climbing steeply, in places a sixty-degree slope. The sun climbed also, and soon they were all dripping with sweat and cursing audibly under the weight of their packs. When they reached a spot identified as Station 4, they were ordered to make camp for the night, having covered only six or seven miles.

Christmas dinner was nothing to write home about, and neither were the sleeping accommodations.

On December 26, they hit the trail early. The terrain wasn't as steep, and the weather was cooler. After covering another few miles, the last of them through tall, spreading pines, the column approached Lusod.

The sawmill occupied the only level spot of any size for miles, much of it bulldozed from the mountainside. The officers introduced themselves to the sawmill manager, Emil Jorgensen, who didn't look a bit like his son, Ken, the manager at Bobok. About fifty-five, Emil was tanned and fit, with chiseled features and a muscular body. His wife was a tall woman, blonde hair cascading down her back.[4] Several dozen Igorot laborers and their families lived in a barrio to one side. Now, Lusod's normal population was bloated by the arrival of the miners' families and a number of single miners. The Itogon people were crowded together in a couple of small houses, three or four families under each roof, and the miners occupied the bunkhouse. The officers in the Camp John Hay contingent were assigned spaces in the bunkhouse or the main staff house, while the men spread their bedrolls in the recreation hall or out under the pines. The Jorgensens served them a sumptuous post-Christmas dinner—turkey, dressing, potatoes, fresh mangoes, and coffee—but right afterward Art and the others returned to their quarters and fell, exhausted, into bed.

The next morning Emil Jorgensen called Baguio to check on the situation there. He talked to an official of the Heald Lumber Company, owner of the Lusod mill, who advised that everything was under control in Baguio, that the sawmill would continue to operate if the Japanese took over.[5] But news about how far the enemy had advanced or exactly where the American lines were located was much less clear.

Mr. Jorgensen was asked about the trail to the east: *How far was it? How long would it take to reach Highway 5? Was there a guide available?* There was a lot of jawboning, but few concrete answers. Jorgensen seemed to think it was forty or fifty miles, as the crow flies, but others claimed it was closer to seventy-five. Art thought Giitter should have had a pretty good idea inasmuch as he had hiked from Highway 5 to Lusod only weeks before, but Giitter didn't have much to say. The only thing Jorgensen seemed certain of was that they could make it to a place called Dyaka in one day.

The soldiers hit the trail in the morning coolness and continued climbing until they reached the summit of Mount Lusod. The view to the east was incredible—green and lush and undulating. Had they been eagles, it would have presented a welcome prospect. Each of those undulations was another tall mountain, though, and their objective lay on the far side of them all.

From the summit, the descent was steep and covered with grass, now wet and trampled flat by earlier travelers. Their Army-issue boots had leather soles, and they began to slip and slide. When one of them lost his footing, inevitably he'd take out the fellow ahead, sometimes two or three of them. The Scouts didn't have any problem, though, and they were pretty good about keeping a straight face.[6]

After a few hours on the trail and several rest stops, they rounded a curve and far off in the distance spotted a building, sunlight glinting off its corrugated metal roof. Must be Dyaka. Though clearly visible, getting there wasn't easy. Over and over the trail wound steeply uphill a mile or so, then back down hundreds of feet to a stream, then uphill again, twisting and turning all the way. Finally, in late afternoon, they reached the main building and a smaller shack, the nucleus of an abandoned mine. There was no machinery, and from the level of deterioration, the operation had been shut down for years. Thick undergrowth had reclaimed much of the level pad. With darkness fast approaching, they ate and bedded down for the night, the officers on the floor of the smaller building while the soldiers crowded into the larger one.

The 28th began with another bright, sunny, exhilarating

morning. Over breakfast some of the senior officers got into a discussion about how heavy mining equipment could have gotten in and out. Figuring there had to be a road somewhere, everyone wasted a couple of hours hacking through underbrush, trying to find an easy route to Highway 5. All they found were trails, not just one but several, all heading in different directions. Finally a couple of natives wandered up the trail. No, they weren't available to act as guides, but when Colonel Horan asked about Manila, they were all smiles and pointed out one of the trails. Everyone loaded up and headed out.

They'd only gone a mile when the trail split. Jorgensen had advised they'd come to a fork, but nobody was sure if this was the right one. The colonel conferred with Giitter, they both conferred with another native, and after considerable chatter and gesturing, it was decided. They took the left fork.

From there, the climb wasn't as steep, but Art's feet blistered as they covered eight or ten miles of the twisting, heavily forested trail. A couple of times he suspected they were going in circles and had been over a particular section of trail previously. There had been jokes and frivolity along the line earlier in the morning, but now everybody was dog-tired and concentrated on placing one foot in front of the other. Late in the afternoon, they reached the top of a ridge. Art recognized the area immediately, and now realized why parts of the trail had looked familiar. He'd hiked this way weeks earlier when he got lost and ended up at Ken Jorgensen's Bobok sawmill. With all the tact he could muster—which wasn't much—he tried to tell Horan and Giitter they'd just hiked all day long in the wrong direction. The top brass didn't want to hear it. Nerves were beginning to fray, so they decided to stop right there, eat supper, have a smoke, and hit the hay.

The next morning Art fished out the roll of tape from his pack and taped the more tender spots on his feet before pulling his boots back on. Captain Calvert, who'd bedded down next to him, watched with covetous eyes, so Art tossed the roll to him.

The officers in charge huddled among themselves and again consulted with some natives who happened along the trail, finally admitting they'd made a mistake. Art was sorely tempted to gloat but then thought better of that idea and kept his mouth shut. They retraced their route of the day before, all the way back to the fork where they'd taken the wrong turn in the first place. Heading off on the other trail, they made only a mile or two and crossed a river before stopping for the night. After a dinner of Spam and saltines, Art noted his stash of food was dwindling fast, so he decided to eat only half as much. They still had a long, long way to go.

On the 30th, they passed through Kayapa, and the going got easier as they descended into the Cagayan Valley. The trail followed a river, and on both sides, as far as the eye could see, stretched a patchwork of rice paddies, varying in color from green to tan to brown. Native barrios dotted the land, and cattle, chickens, pigs, and *carabao* roamed at will. No more mountains lay ahead, but their route presented a new challenge when the trail began following the tops of the dikes separating the paddies. The dikes were muddy and slippery as a toboggan run. Captain Calvert gave a holler and landed, arms flailing, in eight inches of water amid the rice seedlings. When he regained his footing, he started jumping around like a crazy person, yanking slimy leeches off his arms and flinging them in every direction, leaving behind open, bleeding sores. Everyone had a good laugh. At that point Calvert, normally mild-mannered and even-tempered, let loose a string of profanities that would have done a longshoreman proud.

By mid-afternoon, Imugan came into sight, a small village a few miles west of Highway 5. A couple of natives lounged alongside the road, but when asked about USAFFE soldiers, they shrugged, smiled agreeably, and went to find someone who could speak English. While they waited, Horan turned on his radio, hoping to have some reception now that they were out of the mountains. The news was terrible. The Japanese had marched into Baguio on the afternoon of the 27th, and on that same day had begun bombing raids over Manila.

The natives returned with the local mayor. Asked about retreating soldiers, he waved in the direction of Balete Pass—*yesterday, twenty-four hours*—which Horan interpreted to mean the Moses-Noble-Blackburn group had beaten them to Santa Fe and had already headed up over the pass.

The colonel decided they were too close to their objective to quit, and instead ordered an all-night march, hoping to catch up with the main body of the USAFFE forces on the other side of the pass. Some of the men were out of food and refused to go on, so Horan disbanded a number of the Filipinos, instructing them to hide their weapons and uniforms and go home. The rest headed off once more, moving at a brisk pace. Art's feet screamed in pain with every step.

At Santa Fe, they turned south and within a few miles began the steep climb over Balete Pass, the junction between Nueva Vizcaya and Nueva Ecija provinces. They reached the summit around midnight and stopped for an hour's rest, in complete darkness, and then started down the other side. It was midday of the 31st when they finally emerged from the mountains, but there were no USAFFE troops on the other side. They learned they hadn't even beaten the Japanese, who'd also cleared the pass ahead of them and were now as far south as San Jose and Muñoz, chasing the Americans toward Bataan.[7] Completely spent, they ate their meager chow, those who had anything left at all, and bedded down for some much-needed sleep.

Their last hope of catching the retreating American forces was to flank the Japanese on the east, so the next morning they continued south on Highway 5 to a road junction and there turned east. After plodding another eight or ten miles, by early afternoon on New Year's Day they came to Carranglan, where the road ended abruptly. The brass conferred with the locals, but learned there was nothing more to the east except obscure trails into the Sierra Madre. The colonel simply gave up. He decided to take the rest of the native soldiers back to their homes in the northern mountains and wait it out until American reinforcements arrived. At that point everyone still expected General MacArthur would get help to the Philippines within a few short months.

Colonel Horan then made a tantalizing offer: *If any of you want to continue trying to reach the American lines, I'll place you on detached service, and you can give it your best shot.*

For Art, it didn't require much thought. He was exhausted and so was his food supply; his feet were a mass of bloody blisters; the soles of his boots were in tatters; and he'd had about enough marching for a while. Also, to his way of thinking, the officers who were planning to return to the mountains had become a real pain in the neck. He stuck up his hand. Within seconds, Captain Calvert raised his hand. A young private named Grafton Spencer spoke up. A fellow named Tom Jagoe raised his hand too. He was a civilian, a sort of world-roving adventurer who'd been tagging along with the military ever since Baguio. They waited for other takers, but that was it, just the four of them.[8,9] That settled, everyone shook hands, wished one another good luck, and parted ways. The colonel turned the rest of the column around and headed back to the west, toward Highway 5.

ART AND THE NEWLY FORMED CADRE scrounged around Carranglan in search of some food, some horses, and, if they were really lucky, a native guide who knew the trails beyond the end of the paved road and could guide them around the Japanese and toward Manila. They were eventually successful on two of the three counts. They didn't find any horses, but they did find the Orozco family, who provided shelter for the night and a hot meal of chicken, rice, and vegetables. Mr. Orozco even came up with a jug of *tapuey*—wine made from rice—with which they toasted their hosts, toasted America, toasted the Philippines, and toasted in the New Year of 1942. It sure beat hell out of hiking back over Balete Pass on an empty stomach!

At sunup, they doctored their mangled feet as best they could, gratefully accepted a small supply of canned food, packed up, and were ready to go. With the four of them hobbling along behind, their guide, Feliciano Orozco, moved slowly south, inquiring about horses at each barrio. At the fourth stop, he parked the Americans out of sight in some trees, disappeared for fifteen minutes, and came back with four horses and their owner in tow. The price had already been negotiated, so they paid the fellow and shook hands before he disappeared.

Their new horses were scrawny, sad-looking critters about the size of a donkey, nothing like you'd see in an old western. There were no saddles, and when Art quieted his down enough to climb on its back, his feet dangled to within six inches of the ground. Hanging onto the horses' manes, they took off toward the south with Feliciano trotting on foot in the lead, no problem as the ponies had a top speed of about two miles an hour.

Feliciano led them on obscure trails through barrio after barrio, roughly paralleling Highway 5 but farther east. By noon, it was evident their four-footed friends had definite limitations where comfort was concerned. Art christened his "Rocky" and decided to split his time, half aboard and the other half on foot, leaving Rocky only his pack to carry. The others soon followed suit. At each barrio, their guide asked about Japanese troops, and, when the way appeared clear, off they went again. They covered probably fifteen miles before stopping at an abandoned conversion mill. Feliciano had promised them only one day, so this was the end of the line for him. He inquired around and, when he couldn't find a replacement, taught the Americans to ask for a *giya* or *patuto*. Before leaving, he also rustled them up an empty native shack to sleep in and another very welcome hot meal. They were sure sorry to see him go.

Captain Calvert had a tattered Standard Oil map and a small shortwave radio given to him by Colonel Horan, so they spent a couple of hours that night listening to the news from KGEI in San Francisco. It wasn't good. The Japanese were bombing Manila nonstop.

During the night, they learned their shack wasn't empty after all. Rats, some as big as cats, scampered over them and nibbled on their packs and shoes, even checked out the tips of their ears. Lesson learned: Never, ever leave your boots unattended at night; either tie the laces together and hang them over a bamboo rafter or stringer, shove them into the bottom of your bedroll, or simply wear them. Filipino rats would eat anything, but leather was for them the *pièce de résistance*.

On January 3, they moved slowly from barrio to barrio, pulling Rocky and his friends along by their ropes. By now they'd become more valuable as beasts of burden than as gallant steeds. They weren't overtly stubborn or uncooperative; rather, they offered a sort of passive resistance and slacked off every moment they could, like union workers during a slowdown. At each village, Calvert asked about the Japs. Even natives who couldn't speak a word of English seemed to know what "Jap" meant. They solemnly wagged their heads from side to side. When Calvert tried *giya* and *patuto*, though, the response was giggles and more wagging of heads. The four didn't cover many miles that day and ended up camping out under some trees well off the road. Supper consisted of crackers and canned tuna. All afternoon they'd listened to the rumble of heavy bombing to the south. On the radio that evening, it was confirmed that Manila, along with the U.S. naval base at Cavite, had fallen. The Japanese were swarming into the city—raping, looting, and pillaging every step of the way.

They moved cautiously, staying well to the east in the foothills of the Sierra Madre as they worked their way south, sleeping on the ground and not hesitating to stay put if everything didn't look just right. By January 5, though, they were out of food, so they approached a couple of natives working their rice fields. At first the Filipinos were wary and avoided eye contact, but eventually they took the Americans into their home for a meal. Several of the family daughters cooked up a big pot of rice, scrambled eggs, and vegetables. They allowed the Americans to spend the night, but insisted they sleep in a small shack hidden in a field some distance away and move on before daylight.

During the morning of the 6th, they skirted around small barrios and fields and then stopped for a meager lunch in a grove of tall mango trees. The horses began to graze, and soon several chickens emerged from the underbrush, darting about and pecking at the ground. In a flash of inspiration, Jagoe drew his .45 and fired. Not only did he miss his target, but the horses bolted. They spent the rest of the afternoon looking, but ended up with only three. Benibay, the bay horse, was nowhere to be found. After that, Jagoe traveled on foot, and carried his pack too.

They spent the night of the 8th at a little barrio called Bayabas, and on the 9th arrived at the eastern edge of the municipality of San Miguel, just over the provincial line in Bulacan. The first natives they saw became very excited, jumping around like kids at Christmas, pointing off toward the mountains to the southeast and exclaiming over and over, *Americano! Americano!* When Art nodded enthusiastically, the natives led them to the Salacot mine, a hike that killed the rest of the afternoon and most of the next day.

ART AND HIS COMPANIONS were warmly greeted by two captains, Godwin and Lockridge, and a Lieutenant Russell Barros. They had plenty of food, provided by a wealthy benefactor near San Miguel, and invited the four to stay as long as they wanted. Art's first order of business was peeling off his bloody boots and scrubbing through layers of filth in the nearby stream. It took the last of his soap, but it was worth it.

After dinner that evening, as everyone swapped yarns, Lieutenant Barros said that the three of them had been cut off just before Christmas while serving with the 91st Infantry, Philippine Army, at

Pozorrubio, a town twenty-five miles south of Rosario in Pangasinan Province.

Art promptly asked about Earl Hallgren, his housemate from Fort McKinley. The last Art had heard, Earl had been assigned to that unit as an instructor. Russ Barros then told the awful story. He said the natives of Pozorrubio had already fled, and on the night of December 23 the 91st occupied a string of abandoned houses along the main street. Colonel James D. Carter was in command, Earl Hallgren served as adjutant, and the two had established unit headquarters in the largest of the houses. They waited silently in the dark as they expected a column of Japanese tanks to come through, proceeding south, followed by infantry troops. The Americans had no artillery, so they planned to allow the tanks to pass and then go after the foot soldiers with rifles and grenades.

The Japanese tanks arrived, but instead of rumbling on through the town, the last two stopped squarely in front of the house occupied by Carter and Hallgren. It was obvious they'd been tipped off. A Japanese officer stepped down from the last tank and, accompanied by two soldiers, coolly walked up to the front door and knocked. Barros said he was less than fifty yards away, hidden in another house, and watched as Earl opened the door. The Japanese soldiers shot him in the face at point-blank range, killing him instantly. Colonel Carter escaped out a window at the back and disappeared into the darkness. The ensuing battle was a disaster for the Americans as the Japanese tanks fired on one house after another and reduced them to rubble.[10] Those few who escaped fled into the countryside. Lockridge, Godwin, and Barros had eventually found their way to the remote Salacot mine and planned to stay until they could come up with a better plan.

The news hit Art like a ton of bricks. This was the first casualty who'd actually been a friend of his. He kept thinking of the wedding photograph he'd seen of Earl and his wife, Florence. Art thought also of Lil and their babies and what might lie ahead for them. He slept only fitfully that night, haunted by the specter of Earl's shattered, bloody face.

The Salacot mine proved an excellent hiding place. They took turns standing watch, and their wealthy benefactor, some sort of public servant named Francisco Delgado, was faithful in sending runners up with food. With no great sense of urgency, the four decided to hole up for a while and allow their feet to heal. After all, infantrymen wouldn't be of much use to the Army if they couldn't walk. They had blisters on top of their blisters, and many of the lesions were deep, pus-laden, gooey, and very painful. Someone suggested a poultice made of mashed papaya, which stung like fury. The best treatment, though, seemed to be regular washing and leaving their feet exposed to the air. While they weren't using their boots, they trusted Delgado's native runners to take them away for resoling. The boots came back with thick soles made from old tire casings, thick enough to protect against rocks on the trail. A vast improvement, Art thought.

January 20 came and went without fanfare, other than Art noted in his diary that it had been exactly one year since he'd kissed Lil good-bye at the pier at Fort Mason. He silently reread her letters, but didn't mention the anniversary to the others. They'd already learned that talking about such things only worsened the pain.

The days stretched into weeks. They ate, slept, and gradually regained their strength. But their feet were very slow to heal. Rocky and his buddies grazed nearby, begging for food like domestic dogs and enjoying the occasional scratch behind the ears—really quite friendly as long as no work was expected of them.

The men continued following the news broadcasts from radio KGEI in San Francisco. According to those reports, although Manila had fallen and was crawling with Japanese, the USAFFE forces were consolidating on the Bataan Peninsula and holding their own against the invaders. General MacArthur appeared optimistic in his public assessments and said nothing to discourage the notion that they'd soon be receiving reinforcements and supplies.

In the meantime, Art's group tossed around all sorts of ideas, the most promising of which was to try and get to Bataan by boat. He'd seen the guns on Corregidor, though, and remembered the fate of native fishermen who ventured too close to The Rock. *What if they got all that way only to be blown out of the water by their own military?* Day followed day, and they continued to debate their options.

BY THE END OF JANUARY, with their feet much improved, it was time to get serious about rejoining the Army. Godwin, Lockridge, and Barros favored staying put, so Art and his companions made plans to leave. They planned to hike through Bulacan into Rizal, give Manila as wide a berth as possible, and proceed to Cavite Province. If they crossed Cavite and could get to the coast of the South China Sea, they hoped to hitch a ride on a native fishing boat north across the mouth of Manila Bay, staying well to the west of Corregidor to avoid the cannons, and finally get ashore around Aglaloma Point on Bataan. It was an ambitious plan, but seemed the only one with a prayer of success. They made arrangements with Delgado's Filipino runners for a supply of canned food, loaded up, shook hands all around, and early on the morning of Sunday, February 1, headed out.

Over the next week they moved cautiously, checking the map and asking directions as they proceeded toward Rizal. Eventually they had to leave the mountains and head southwest, toward what was left of Nichols Field. Manila was clearly visible in the distance, and the closer they got, the more apprehensive the natives were and the harder it became to find a hiding place at night. At one point a guy who spoke fair English warned them that the Japanese now patrolled every street in Manila and would shoot a uniformed American on sight. The Japanese had also established garrisons in the outlying areas, and regularly sent smaller armed patrols out to search house to house. When asked about the possibility of hiring a fishing boat, he told them they were nuts, that the waters of Manila Bay had been heavily mined by the Americans, as had the waters west of Corregidor, and now even the Filipino fishermen weren't venturing out. Not anxious to get caught talking to Americans, their new friend turned and quickly disappeared.

Around February 10, they heard something very exciting on the radio. There had been a guerrilla attack on the Tuguegarao airfield in Cagayan Province. Some Japanese planes had been destroyed. It was only a brief report, providing few details, and no names were mentioned, but it meant *something* was going on up in northern Luzon.

They hashed over their next move. *Should they continue to try for Bataan or head back north?* Captain Calvert reiterated that their standing orders were to join the USAFFE forces consolidating on Bataan. The rest weren't so sure. There simply didn't seem to be any way to get there in one piece.

They backtracked to the Salacot mine, arriving around the middle of February. Godwin, Lockridge, and Barros were still there. Art told them about the guerrilla activity up north and tried for a week to convince them to accompany his group into the northern mountains. But they had other ideas. They'd decided to go straight south, toward Antimonan, and find a boat to take them to Cebu.[11]

Lieutenant Barros suggested that they contact Mr. Delgado personally and ask his help. He might know of the guerrilla activity, or might have other ideas about how to get to Bataan.

ON THE MORNING OF FEBRUARY 22, the foursome rounded up their ponies and headed back toward San Miguel.[12] They promptly got onto a wrong trail and wasted the entire afternoon tramping in circles in the mountains, stopping only when the trail petered out at the edge of a cliff overlooking a raging river far below. In disgust, they tied up the ponies, ate some chow, and prepared to spend the night, taking turns keeping watch.

During Jagoe's watch, Rocky began making a fuss, straining at his rope and whinnying. Instantly they were on their feet, anticipating the worst, but no Japanese appeared. Grabbing his flashlight, Art tried to see what Rocky was so excited about, and at the same moment Spencer began yelling, *Snake! Snake! Snake!* Swinging the flashlight in the direction he frantically pointed, Art saw the problem. Coiled up on the foot of Spence's bedroll was a huge snake, its head in the air, ready to strike. Reacting instinctively, Art threw his own bedroll on top of the snake and began beating as hard as he could with the flashlight until finally the thing quit moving. When certain it was dead, Art pulled his bedroll off and took a look. The beast was at least two inches in diameter and three or four feet long. A boa, probably, a young one. He tossed the carcass off to the side of the trail.

The next morning, feeling quite cocky and proud of his kill, Art decided to have a little fun. He gathered twigs and leaves and got a small fire going. It was chilly, and the others thought the fire a swell idea. They huddled close, briskly rubbing their palms together. Nonchalantly Art reached over, grabbed the snake carcass by its pulpy head, and with his bolo slit straight down its belly, just like cleaning a rainbow trout at Yosemite. He cut several chunks, found some larger sticks, pointed the ends, stuck the snake chunks onto the sticks, and began roasting them like marshmallows. Art's companions were aghast, but it wasn't long before the meat began to sizzle and give off a nice aroma. In ten minutes, his feast was ready. It was delicious! Halfway through his second chunk, lips smacking noisily, Spence got brave, so Art cut him off a sample. It wasn't long before all of them were roasting their own snake chunks and enjoying *boa mignon*.

With the frustrations of the previous day forgotten, they hit the trail as happy and confident as Boy Scouts. After backtracking for several hours, they found the right route. Soon they were out of the mountains and into farming country—rice paddies amid cane fields and orchards of tall mango trees. By late afternoon they approached the outskirts of Sampaloc, southwest of San Miguel, where, after a few discreet inquiries, they turned up a family willing to take them in. The Avila family shared their dinner and then showed the four to a small outbuilding normally used to shelter livestock. The floor was covered with a thick mat of well-trampled straw, and though they were grateful to have any padding at all, by now they knew that where there is straw, there are also big, fat rats, and probably fleas and lice as well. They kept their boots on.

On the radio that evening, they picked up an address by President Franklin Roosevelt. What they heard was unbelievable. He cryptically described the Bataan fighting:

> For forty years it has always been our strategy—a strategy born of necessity—that in the event of a full-scale attack on the Islands by Japan, we should fight a delaying action, attempting to retire slowly into the Bataan Peninsula and Corregidor. We knew that the war as a whole would have to be fought and won by a process of attrition against Japan itself. We knew all along that, with our greater resources, we could ultimately out-build Japan and ultimately overwhelm her on sea and on land and in the air. We knew that, to obtain our objective, many varieties of operations would be necessary in areas other than the Philippines.

> Now, nothing that has occurred in the past two months has caused us to revise this basic strategy of necessity—except that the defense put up by General MacArthur has magnificently exceeded the previous estimates of endurance, and he and his men are gaining eternal glory therefor.

> MacArthur's army of Filipinos and Americans, and the forces of the United Nations in China, in Burma, and

the Netherlands East Indies, are all together fulfilling the same essential task. They are making Japan pay an increasingly terrible price for her ambitious attempts to seize control of the whole Asiatic world. Every Japanese transport sunk off Java is one less transport that they can use to carry reinforcements to their army opposing General MacArthur in Luzon.

It has been said that Japanese gains in the Philippines were made possible only by the success of their surprise attack on Pearl Harbor. I tell you that this is not so.

Even if the attack had not been made, your map will show that it would have been a hopeless operation for us to send the fleet to the Philippines, through thousands of miles of ocean, while all those island bases were under the sole control of the Japanese.[13]

Art's jaw dropped! It took a while for the full impact of the president's words to sink in. *A hopeless operation to send the fleet to the Philippines? Had it all been lies? Was their own government simply going to abandon the thousands of troops on Bataan? Had they all been expendable from the beginning?* Art's first reaction was disbelief—he must have heard it wrong—but his next reaction was visceral rage. *We are Americans! Our government doesn't do things like that! Or do they?* They listened another hour, hoping for something more, but there was nothing. Ashen-faced, they reconsidered their options. Captain Calvert again reminded them that their orders were to proceed to Bataan. With Roosevelt's words echoing in his ears, it didn't take long for Art to decide. He certainly wasn't going down without a fight, nor was he going to risk his neck any further to join a lost cause on Bataan, *eternal glory* be damned. If there was guerrilla action happening in northern Luzon, that was the only place to be. Art finally got everyone on the same page. They all had lived at Baguio. They knew the healthy climate up there, knew the terrain, knew the fierce loyalty of the Igorot natives, and knew they'd stand a far better chance in the northern mountains.

CHAPTER 12

BACK TO THE NORTH
March 1942

O N THE MORNING OF FEBRUARY 24, the Avilas fed them breakfast and sent them on their way with their son Lorenzo[1], who spoke a fair amount of English. Larry Avila was a congenial, pimpled fellow of fourteen or fifteen who had the biggest ears of any Filipino Art had ever seen. Delighted to guide them for a day, Larry also knew horses. He made a soft clucking sound, and the ponies picked up their pace without complaint, docile as lambs.

Russ Barros had said Francisco Delgado lived in Sibul Spring, a few miles east of San Miguel.[2] They hoped for additional guidance from him or, better yet, a two-legged guide who could lead them through the unfamiliar central valley and on toward the north.

The weather was beautiful, dry and invigorating. Rather than using the traveled road north to San Miguel and turning east to Sibul Spring, Larry claimed, *I know much better way. Much safer.* Off he went, leading the horses on a diagonal to the northeast, the four of them following behind. At first the going was easy, tramping along a well-worn dirt path, but within two miles they were slogging through knee-deep rice paddies, with no villages in sight, not even a lone *nipa* hut. An hour passed, Larry becoming more perplexed with each step. Finally, he halted the horses, shook his head, and sheepishly offered, *Sorry, so sorry, but I think I am lost.*

Damn, Art muttered under his breath. *What the hell are we supposed to do now?*

Larry scratched his pimpled chin and then led them over to a little rise and some trees. As he tied up the horses, he said, *You sleep here. I go ahead, find better direction. Then I come back. I come back before morning.*

They didn't find the plan very appealing, and told him so: *Listen, kid, you'd better not let us down. We know where your parents live.* But Larry swore on his mother's good name that he wouldn't abandon them.

Wary of building a fire and attracting unwanted attention, the four dined that night on cold chipped beef and a handful of saltines. Taking turns on watch, they bedded down close together for warmth as it turned downright cold once the sun disappeared. Surprisingly, Art slept soundly.

Just before dawn, Larry showed up, beaming broadly and anxious to get them on the trail. *See, I told you I come back. My mama told me never lie. God does not like liars.* He'd even rustled up a dozen bananas for breakfast. True to his word, the kid now knew exactly where he was going, and they made good time.

By mid-afternoon on February 25, they approached the southern outskirts of Sibul Spring, where they sheltered in a bamboo thicket alongside the road while Larry again ventured ahead to check for Japanese. In twenty minutes he was back, a wide grin stretching from one big ear to the other.

Following a circuitous route around the town to the north side, Larry pointed out the ornate iron gate of a fine villa, where a pair of heavily armed guards eyed them with suspicion. Larry spoke to them in Tagalog, and Captain Calvert mentioned the names of their American friends at the Salacot mine. One of the guards disappeared, returned a few minutes later, and sullenly unlocked the gate. They handed Larry five pesos for his services, shook his hand, and said good-bye. His parting comment: *Someday I too will be a brave soldier and will fight devil Japs and chase them out of my country.*

Inside the villa grounds, a servant boy took the horses away, indicating he would unload their packs and deliver them inside. A uniformed servant girl greeted them at the front door and led the way upstairs. Over one shoulder she advised: *Mr. Delgado in mountains. I call him on telephone. He come down to meet you for supper, two hours.*

They could hardly believe their eyes! The place was like a fine hotel: clean white sheets on real mattresses atop real beds, a western-style bathroom with hot and cold running water, soap, and fluffy white towels. They stripped, shaved, showered, and scrubbed fingernails and feet. An hour and a half later, the servant girl returned with their clothing, freshly washed and ironed. They felt like kings!

At six o'clock they were led to a drawing room on the ground floor, where Francisco Delgado greeted them with outstretched arms. His English was impeccable and his demeanor impressive. In his mid-fifties, he had graying hair, nice features, and a restrained smile. A pretty young Filipina, well-dressed and obviously not a servant, appeared with a bottle of scotch on a silver tray, ringed by delicate crystal glasses. Mr. Delgado introduced her as Constancia, his daughter.

The daughter smiled and offered her hand. When she got to Spencer, her eyes dropped demurely as she murmured, *Please, call me Connie.*

Hello, Connie, he answered, blushing from his cheeks to his hairline. *I'm happy to meet you.*

Soon they were all seated and getting acquainted. They learned Delgado was born in Sibul Spring in 1886, the son of an aristocratic family. Among the first Filipinos to study in the United States, he'd attended Compton High School in the Los Angeles area, gone to college and law school at the University of Indiana, and had topped that off with an advanced law degree from Yale. He was the first Filipino admitted to the American Bar Association. After returning to Manila, he'd worked in the office of the governor general until he'd been elected a member of the Philippine House of Representatives.

From 1934 to 1936, he'd served as a resident commissioner to the United States House of Representatives in Washington, D.C., a non-voting seat, before returning once again to the Philippines.[3,4]

I loved living in America, Connie volunteered, *and I wanted to return there for college, maybe at Georgetown University. I wanted to become a lawyer like my father. But with the war and everything, now that's impossible.* Turning to Spence, she inquired, *And where are you from, Grafton?*

Spencer dropped his gaze. *A little place called Kenmore, near Buffalo, New York.*

Connie pressed on. *Tell us about your family.*

My mom died when I was two, and when my dad remarried a couple of years later, my older brother and I went to live on the farm with Grandma and Grandpa.

Spence was squirming in his seat, bashful under her penetrating gaze. Relief came when the servant girl announced supper. Not to be deterred, Connie led the way into the dining room, indicated where each of them should sit, and boldly took her seat next to Spence.

After a sumptuous supper, Delgado shooed his reluctant daughter off to her room while the men retired to the drawing room for brandy and a smoke. The conversation turned to more pressing matters. Delgado, too, had reacted with incredulity to Roosevelt's speech and empathized with their decision to avoid Bataan and head instead back to the northern mountains with the hope of joining the American guerrillas they'd heard about on the radio. Delgado had no more information than they did; however, he expressed a willingness to help.

Captain Calvert spread his map out on a low table. With the bulk of the Japanese forces now concentrated around Manila or on the Bataan Peninsula, if they were careful, Delgado felt they could head northwest, skirt the eastern flank of Mount Arayat, and proceed up through the central valley and into the mountains south of Baguio. They'd have to avoid the main roads, and the route wouldn't be without challenges as they'd have to travel through swampy, mosquito-filled lowlands for the first couple of days, and might well encounter Japanese patrols even along the secondary roads. Delgado speculated, however, that their chief obstacle would be the Hukbalahaps, a formidable group of well-armed Communist guerrillas organized in 1913 by a fellow named Luis Taruc. For years dedicated to improving the lot of the poor Filipino tenant farmer, they were now directing all their energies into harassing the Japanese. Delgado could provide only sketchy information about the group's current status, and although it was possible they might be friendly to American fugitives, he felt it more prudent to avoid them altogether. The Huks were headquartered on top of Mount Arayat and purportedly controlled much of the surrounding countryside, exactly the areas they'd have to travel through. Delgado agreed to furnish a native guide for the first day. He also invited them to stay another night to rest and prepare for the journey, an invitation they gladly accepted.[5] Their plan decided, Captain Calvert proposed a toast to thank and honor their host.

Over breakfast, Delgado advised that if they wanted to try and get word to their families, he could perhaps smuggle their letters out of the country on a commercial vessel. Art spent several hours composing a long letter to Lil. He enclosed his chronicle of events and drew a rough map to make it easier to follow. Calvert wrote a letter too, but Tom spent his time exploring the grounds. He never spoke of having a family. As Spence tried to compose his letter at Delgado's mahogany desk in the study, Connie flitted about, peppering him with questions, all the while batting her eyelashes outrageously.

That evening they again enjoyed fine scotch, a sumptuous meal, and animated after-dinner conversation in the parlor. At one point Connie coaxed Spence to accompany her out to check on their horses. The two were gone for an hour. Toward midnight Delgado advised he'd be leaving on business before dawn the next morning and so wouldn't be available for their official send-off; however, a guide and their ponies, along with a cache of supplies, would be available whenever they were ready to go. As a final measure of his hospitality, Mr. Delgado strode over to a glass-fronted cupboard, unlocked it, and returned with two cartons of Chesterfield cigarettes. Again they shook hands all around and said a grateful farewell to this noble man who had given so generously of his time and resources.

The next morning Art took another hot shower and changed into fresh clothing. Connie herself prepared their breakfast of scrambled eggs, fried rice cakes, fruit, and coffee, plus two quinine pills. She also assembled four lunch packets of meat and potatoes wrapped in banana leaves. With no further reason to delay, it was time to tackle the next leg of their journey. Everyone was optimistic, everyone except Spence, who wasn't feeling well. Downright frisky after two days of good food and loafing, the ponies whinnied and high-stepped as they were led out of the barn. The four loaded up and said their good-byes. As they trotted out the gate, their guide in the lead, Spence turned back for one last glimpse of Connie waving her red handkerchief in farewell.

NORTHERN LUZON'S RAINY SEASON lasts half a year, from May through October, with heavy downpours nearly every afternoon and the occasional severe typhoon. The dry season, from November through April, though hot and dusty in most areas, had no impact on the Candaba swamp, a vast marshland stretching from San Miguel on the east to Mount Arayat on the west. After a few hours on the trail, they crossed into Pampanga Province and were soon slogging through murky water and deep mud that sucked at their boots with each step. The horses began to balk and had to be tugged along by their ropes, no doubt thinking the humans were nuts to trade the Sibul Spring comforts for a swamp.

By mid-afternoon Spence was vomiting and running a high fever, so the guide found them a place for the night, settled them in, and then left to rustle up a doctor. Several hours passed, but no doctor appeared. Before dark an old native woman came to the door and shoved in a bamboo tray of foul-looking rice mixed with small chunks of putrid-smelling fish. They opted to open a can of corned beef for themselves and fed the rice mixture to the ponies. In lieu of dinner, they fed Spence more quinine and put him to bed in one corner. They never saw the guide again.

The next morning the old woman reappeared with a dozen bananas. Though much improved, Spence was still not up to wading, so they loaded him onto Rocky and distributed their packs between the other two horses. To the northwest, off in the distance, Mount Arayat loomed above a wreath of clouds, dark and sinister, a perfect volcanic cone rising from the flatlands. They set a course almost due north, hoping to avoid the Huks and get through the marshlands as quickly as possible.

The swamp deepened. At one point they were struggling through waist-deep water, the ponies were in it up past their bellies, and the leeches were indiscriminate in choosing victims. Miserable as it was, they managed to avoid Japanese patrols and the mysterious Huks, and after a few hours reached dry ground.

Proceeding north a few miles, they crossed into Nueva Ecija Province and reached Sinipit, in the municipality of Cabiao. Here their luck held. The first natives they saw led the way to the home of the town mayor, a Mr. de la Cruz, who greeted them warmly and offered a place for the night. Of modern frame construction, his house had a corrugated iron roof and several rooms. Half a dozen children scampered about. The mayor's very pregnant wife cooked a big meal of roast pig, rice, and vegetables. Afterward they spent a couple of hours listening to KGEI. The news from Bataan was positive: MacArthur's troops were holding their own as they awaited the arrival of the U.S. naval fleet with supplies and reinforcements. Of course, the four knew better, but said nothing and in fact encouraged their host by telling him the Americans would soon be back and everything would be just fine.[6]

Mr. de la Cruz suggested they continue avoiding the main high-way from Manila as he'd heard there were regular enemy patrols up and down that route, and the towns of La Paz and Victoria were crawling with Japanese. Then he came up with the best idea they'd heard in two months. He knew a rice farmer who had a truck; if they were willing to leave their ponies behind, this man would probably take them on north and get them there much faster. After two days of slogging through the swamp, they jumped at the plan. Mr. de la Cruz agreed to contact his friend first thing in the morning and negotiate a trade arrangement for the ponies.[7]

The four crowded into a small room at the back for the night. The excitement began in the wee hours of the morning when Art was awakened by loud moaning and heightened activity in the main room. He jumped up, grabbed his .45 from its holster, cocked it, and peered out. As Mr. de la Cruz looked on, an old woman squatted beside Mrs. de la Cruz, who was lying on a mat on the floor, knees akimbo, moments from giving birth. Art could see black, glistening hair as the baby's head crowned. The mother bore down hard and gave one last wail as an infant boy slithered into the waiting hands of the midwife. She hoisted him up by his heels and tapped gently on the soles of his feet until he gave a lusty wail of his own, ran two fingers through the baby's mouth to ensure his airway was clear, then deftly tied off and snipped the umbilical cord. Finally, she swabbed at the baby with a rag, wrapped him in a clean blanket, and gently placed him on the mother's belly.[8] It was all so marvelously simple.

By now Art's companions were awake and on their feet, wide-eyed and self-conscious. None of them had children and had never seen a human birth. The proud father brought out a jar of *basi*, and soon everyone was smiling and laughing and marveling at the new arrival.

Art thought back to Eleanor's birth at the hospital in Los Angeles, with its white-gowned doctors and nurses and sterilized instruments and bright lights. Lil had spent several days in the hospital following the birth, and, weeks later, when Eleanor reached five pounds, they'd brought her home with a mountain of instructions and supplies. What a contrast to this birth! By sunup Mrs. de la Cruz acted as though nothing had happened. She fed the older children, shooed them outside to tend to the chickens and pigs, and then cooked a big breakfast for the guests while the mayor went off with their ponies to find his friend and make arrangements for their transportation. And aside from a chicken or two for the midwife, none of it had cost a single centavo!

A COUPLE OF HOURS LATER, Mr. de la Cruz returned, riding in the passenger seat of a ramshackle vehicle. Originally a Ford pickup chassis, the bed had been extended at both rear and sides with crude slats, converting it into a flatbed truck, though without cab doors. Sacks of rice stacked ten high lined the perimeter, leaving an opening in the center. Taken aback, Art glanced at his companions, but neither de la Cruz nor the driver took any notice. At this point the ponies were gone and the die was cast. They crowded into the hole. The driver produced a piece of tattered canvas, threw it over the top, and tied it down, but the mayor assured them that measure was only temporary, until they got out into the countryside. The entire de la Cruz family, including the newborn cradled in his mother's arms, gathered to see them off, and soon they were bumping their way toward the outskirts of Sinipit. They pulled the canvas up a few inches to take a peek and get some air.

At the Pampanga River, the driver turned onto a graveled washboard road heading north, parallel to the shore. Whenever an oncoming vehicle approached, he slowed and hollered a few words, evidently asking about Japanese. Then he hit the gas and off they went again, bumpity, bumpity, bump, the ride even rougher than had been the bony backs of Rocky and his pals.

Some miles farther on another truck approached, barreling along at a good clip. It slowed only briefly as its driver hollered *Nippon!*

Nippon! and pointed north. Their driver panicked. He slammed on the brakes, yelling at them in broken English to get out; that he'd come back for them once the way was clear. Adrenalin pumping, they threw their packs onto the ground, leaped down themselves, scurried across the road, skidded down the steep bank sixty or seventy feet, and hunkered down in the thick undergrowth that lined the shore.

The Japanese convoy approached—two truckloads of soldiers in full battle gear, rifles and bayonets silhouetted against the blue sky. They slowed to a crawl, scanning both sides of the road. The Americans froze, hugging the ground and barely breathing while the convoy inched its way along. When they were perhaps a hundred feet away, both trucks ground to a halt. Several Japanese soldiers hopped down and strode up and down, eyeing the irrigation canal on the opposite side of the road, hurling rocks into the brush. Next they crossed the road and stared down the bank, parting the tall grass with their bayonets. They fired half a dozen random shots. One missed Captain Calvert's head by inches and thunked into a tree trunk behind him. No one moved a muscle. Finally the Japanese climbed back into their trucks, and, as quickly as they'd come, they were gone, churning up big clouds of dust as the convoy disappeared off to the south.

Badly shaken, the foursome remained motionless a long time before daring to lift their heads and look around. They felt sure the soldiers had been tipped off as to their whereabouts. *But by whom? And where was their driver? Was he the culprit?* They couldn't believe de la Cruz had betrayed them, but one never knew about his friend, the rice grower. They waited all afternoon, but their driver never showed up.

THEY OPTED TO TRAVEL BY NIGHT and rely less on strangers. Once it was pitch dark, they crawled back up to the road, trudged a mile or so farther north, and spent the night in thick undergrowth.[9] They'd been very, very lucky.

Deciding to cross the Pampanga into less-populated territory, two miles up the eastern bank they found a likely-looking spot. The main channel spread wide, but a couple of sandbars in the middle suggested it wasn't too deep. One by one, balancing their packs on their heads, they waded into the water.[10] Once across, they back-tracked southwest to the point where the *Rio Chico*—the Little Pampanga—emptied into the main river from the north, figuring they could follow the Little Pampanga forty or fifty miles, all the way to Pangasinan Province.

By March 3 they reached the municipality of Nampicuan, Nueva Ecija, not far from the Tarlac border, nearly halfway to the mountains.[11] At that point Calvert became violently ill, and there wasn't much they could do except stay put a couple of days and hope like hell they didn't get whatever it was he had.

As soon as Calvert improved, they pressed on. By the 6th the volcanic cone of Mount Amorong loomed to the east, signaling Pangasinan Province. Growing more confident with every mile, when they came to a barrio identified as Buenavista,[12] they stopped to get information and, hopefully, a hot meal and a place to spend the night indoors for a change.

They weren't disappointed. Someone recognized Americans, the word went out, and half the town gathered. They felt like the grand prize at a county fair as people vied for the privilege of hosting them. That night the townsfolk threw a big party—barbecue beef with all the trimmings, and plenty of *basi*.

Basi is made from sugarcane. The natives crush the cane to get the juice, add flavoring made from a tree bark called samak, boil it in huge vats, and allow it to ferment in earthenware jugs. When ready, it looks more like syrup than wine, but the effect is the same. After a couple, everyone feels great and the world is a rosy place.

After dinner they brought out the radio to see what KGEI had on the news. It was devastating. President Roosevelt had ordered General MacArthur to leave the Philippines for Australia, his command assumed by General Jonathan "Skinny" Wainwright. In a flowery radio address, MacArthur spoke to the people of the Philippines and made them a solemn promise:

> "The President of the United States has ordered me to break through the Japanese lines and proceed from Corregidor to Australia for the purpose, as I understand it, of organizing the American offensive against Japan, a primary object of which is the relief of the Philippines. I came through and I shall return."[13]

Their hosts got pretty upset. Douglas MacArthur, as far as most Filipinos were concerned, had a personal seat at the right hand of God; that he would abandon their country was unthinkable. Calvert assured them the general was only going to Australia to gather supplies and reinforcements and would soon be back to rescue the Filipino people from the Japanese.[14]

They hit the trail. To the north rose the majestic Cordillera Mountains, drawing them like a magnet. The mountains meant cold, mosquito-free nights and warm days, the air filled with the scent of fragrant pine and hibiscus. The mountains also meant the Lusod sawmill, where there might still be Americans and all that wonderful stored food!

The going was easy. Word of their coming spread rapidly, and impromptu welcoming committees formed. People handed them bananas, mangoes, or a hardboiled egg. Each time they left a barrio, the children scampered along behind, waving and calling *Mabuhay, Joe* until they were out of sight.

Climbing into the foothills, they arrived at a little village in the municipality of San Manuel. There was no evidence of a war. Nobody had seen any Japanese, and the mood was festive. They were led to the home of an old Filipino sergeant who lived down along the Agno River. His house bustled with activity—women cooking in big pots, other women chopping vegetables, and youngsters cutting and stacking banana leaves in piles. Sarge said they'd arrived in time for a *cañao* the next day and insisted they attend as there would be a big feast, dancing, and lots of *tapuey*. The townsfolk already knew the Americans were in the area, and if they didn't attend, it would be a terrible insult. They couldn't refuse.

If they were going to a party, they figured they'd better clean up and so went down to the river's edge and stripped. The water was ice cold, and they didn't have any soap, but they did the best they could and felt better for the effort.

The next morning, they followed Sarge back into town. Behind them came the female members of his household, each carrying a huge basket of food on her head, and kids and assorted dogs brought up the rear. Sarge escorted them to a prominent table. Apparently they were to be the guests of honor. Steaming plates of food appeared—barbecued pork, beef, and chicken along with vegetables, fruit, and the usual mounds of rice. The mayor gave a flowery speech, frequently waving over at them. They could understand only *Americanos*, but the people clapped and roared their approval, so the speech must have been a good one.

The music and dancing began. Their *tapuey* cups were kept filled, and after a while they got into the spirit of things. When pretty young dancers beckoned them to join in, they did, and if they made fools of themselves, nobody cared. They clapped and cheered. In the end, they all got quite drunk, apparently, because none of the four retained any memory of the rest of the evening or making their way back to Sarge's place by the river.

When they awoke, the activities of the household were in full swing. Over a late breakfast, Sarge reminded them that they'd accepted an invitation to spend a night with the minister of Flores, another barrio a few miles distant. Art couldn't remember talking with a minister, but Sarge assured him they were expected. They would rather have continued north, but they'd evidently acquired social obligations they couldn't ignore without causing hard feelings and loss of face among the locals. In the early afternoon, they again followed Sarge into town, where he rounded up some native *cargadores* to carry their packs on the three-mile hike to Flores.

Art never got the name of the minister in Flores or his church affiliation. He remembered him, though, as a middle-aged Filipino who spoke English and had a houseful of attractive daughters. The minister wanted to discuss the war and what it might mean for his congregation and his family. They told him what they could and then turned on their radio so he could listen to the war news from San Francisco. Incredibly, San Francisco still claimed the fighting on Bataan was going well.

The minister asked about their plans. Upon hearing they were headed north, his next comment grabbed their attention. He knew of an abandoned gold mine, the Lone Star mine, where Filipino soldiers had safely hidden in the past. It was located on the other side of the Agno River and a good day's hike into the mountains of northernmost San Manuel, close to the border of Benguet Province. He drew a detailed map, noting exactly where they could cross the river on a bridge and describing landmarks along the way so they could find the mine without a guide. Then he retired for the evening while they bedded down on the floor in his main room.

AFTER BREAKFAST ON THE MORNING of March 8, the minister wished them well and sent them on their way with a burlap sack full of food. The daughters lined up alongside him, smiling and waving.

Studying the map, the four followed the river north a few miles until they came to the bridge—nothing more than a couple of heavy cables strung across a narrow, deep section of the river gorge, long, loose strips of split bamboo laid lengthwise onto a series of hammock-like vine supports suspended from the cables. White knuckles gripping the cables, stomachs churning, they gritted their teeth, made it across, and were soon climbing steeply into the mountains.

By mid-afternoon, they approached the Lone Star mine—two small, ramshackle frame buildings set in a small clearing bordering a stream. Tangled piles of rusted metal filled one building to the rafters. The second had a door on one side and a large window on the opposite wall, its filthy glass shattered and lying in heaps on the ground. It would do for the night.

Art peeled off his boots to reveal feet disgusting, putrid-smelling, and infected. After sloughing the worst gunk off in the water, he taped up the deepest ulcers, dug down in his pack for his spare socks, and pulled his boots back on. Finally he rinsed out his bloody socks and spread them on a bush to dry.

Tom took off to investigate on up the trail, but Calvert, Spence, and Art stayed put, enjoying the sunshine. Art dug out pencil and paper and added more details for Lil, describing the fiesta, the minister's daughters, and the precarious bridge crossing. When Tom returned, it was time for chow. They tried the radio, but couldn't get any reception so decided to turn in for the night.

Art drew the first watch and positioned himself on the bank where he could see both trails, coming and going, his loaded M-1 cradled in his lap. A clear night studded with stars, it soon turned damned cold. Art was glad when his shift ended and he could wake Spence to take over. Curled up in his bedroll next to Calvert and Tom, he fell asleep in no time at all.

Japs! Japs! Japs! Japs! Art was awake and on his feet in an instant! *Japs! Japs! Japs!* Spencer yelled at the top of his lungs. In the blackness, Art tripped over one of the others, went down in a heap, and scrambled up again, heading toward the corner where their rifles leaned against the wall. He lost his bearings in the dark, stumbled again, and ended up next to the window. The sound of rifle fire was everywhere. *Run! Run!* Spencer hollered. Instinctively, Art put one hand on the sill, vaulted through the window onto the ground below, and sprinted as fast as he could toward the edge of the clearing.

Feeling cold water over his boot tops, he slogged upstream, simultaneously grabbing his .45 from its holster, clicking off the safety, and pulling back the slide. Fifty yards farther on, slipping and sliding, he dove off into the brush and flattened himself against the ground. Yelling and rifle fire filled the air, and then gradually petered out. Art lay silent in the dark for hours, nerves on edge, but he gradually relaxed and even dozed a bit, until rustlings in the brush nearby yanked him back to reality. Aimed and ready to fire, he heard a familiar, high-pitched sneeze.

Calvert, is that you? he whispered.

Yeah, Murph, it's me. You okay?

Yeah, I'm okay. How 'bout you?

Yeah, I'm okay too.

The two of them lay there until the first light of dawn and then moved on, following the trail paralleling the creek. Several hours later they warily approached a village. A young native came running, waving his arms and yelling. Though they couldn't understand a word, when he grabbed Art's arm and tugged, they followed. A crowd had gathered in front of the church. Something important was going on. As they approached, the crowd parted. There stood Tom and Spence, filthy and scratched up but otherwise unhurt. It was a miracle! The natives slaughtered a pig and prepared a *cañao* to celebrate. They brought out the now familiar gongs and drums and jars of *tapuey*. The four toasted the villagers and toasted each other, jubilant to be alive.

Later that evening, stuffed full and exhausted from the events of the day, they were shown to the local schoolhouse and given woven mats to sleep on.

Finally Spence told them what had happened. He'd been sitting in the same spot as Art had, where he could see both trails, and around midnight had picked up faint clomping noises coming from the direction of the Agno. Creeping over to investigate, he'd seen a string of bobbing torchlights moving up the trail, and that's when he'd begun hollering. Still yelling, he'd run just as the first intruder reached the clearing and opened fire. He'd crashed into the brush and kept going until he tripped and fell flat on his face. As he'd scrambled to his feet, Jagoe had run headlong into him in the darkness. Together they'd kept going until they were exhausted. At dawn they'd found the same trail Murphy and Calvert had, and they'd arrived at the village less than twenty minutes ahead of them. The whole thing was pretty incredible.

Art had a hard time getting to sleep that night. The excitement of their narrow escape gave way to more somber thoughts of what he'd lost. Not only did he no longer have his rifle and clips of ammunition, but that backpack held everything he owned. He had no clothes except those on his back—no razor, no toiletries, not even a toothbrush. He had no flashlight, no first aid supplies, nothing to write with. Well, yes, he still had the little diary in his breast pocket, but that was it. Most devastating, and what cut like cold steel into his heart, all Lil's letters and the photographs of his family were in that pack. He'd never felt so vulnerable and alone.

The next morning, Art decided to go back to the mine to see if anything had been left behind. Maybe they'd just taken the rifles, ammunition, and the radio. Art had to find out. Nobody wanted to accompany him. Not far from the village there were some warm springs with reported medicinal qualities, and the rest of them were anxious to spend the day soaking. Art found one young native willing to go, so they set off right after breakfast. Within a few hours they were back at Lone Star, but nothing was left, not one goddamned thing.

THE FOUR TOOK A VOTE AND ENDED UP spending another week in the village. Each morning they hiked to the springs to soak and then spent the evenings filling their bellies, watching the natives dance, and listening to indecipherable speeches by the village elders.

They speculated for hours about who might have given them up at Lone Star. None of the local natives had heard of Japanese patrols coming anywhere near the area. They finally concluded the attack must have been the work of bandits and was somehow connected with their night at the minister's house in Flores. The fact they'd been given such specific instructions on finding the bridge and the mine and such great assurances that it was a perfect hiding place supported that theory.

When the Japanese first overran the country, scattering Philippine and American military units in every direction, here and there enterprising opportunists had come out of the woodwork, posing as guerrillas. While a few of the bastards were admittedly rogue ex-soldiers, most were simply very bad apples who'd formed marauding bands, armed themselves with discarded Army weapons, and were terrorizing their countrymen, murdering defenseless civilians, and taking whatever they chose, including the young daughters of their victims.

THE COMPANIONS SORELY MISSED their radio and news of the war, and that was the catalyst that got them moving. On the morning of March 17, they thanked the people once more and headed north. By late afternoon on the 18th, they arrived at the Itogon mine. Across the gorge to the northwest, a dozen miles away, the setting sun glinted off windows in Baguio, looking serene and unchanged and giving no evidence of the Japanese, who now had the city in a chokehold.

Itogon hadn't been bombed. Moving cautiously, guns drawn, they approached the residence compound. The buildings weren't locked, so they investigated each one. Trash was strewn everywhere, nothing of value left except a few iron bed frames. There was no power. They picked their way through the recreation hall and the big building that had housed the single miners and found the same conditions. Convinced the place was deserted, they decided to spend the night, choosing a house from which the whole area could be watched. After a cold supper, Calvert assigned the watch schedule, and they hit the sack.

The next day they continued snooping around, speculating about the former residents.

The third morning, while hashing over their next move, they were startled by a loud voice shouting in English, *Who's there? Come out with your hands up.* With .45s drawn, they peeked out a window. *Who's there?* they heard again. The voice was clearly that of an American, so Captain Calvert called back, *We're Americans. Don't shoot.*

Soon they were shaking hands with a fellow named Sagar, who identified himself as the mine's assistant superintendent. He said that when the rest of the mine employees left for the Lusod sawmill in late December, he and another miner, Richie Green, had remained behind and for three months had been living deep in the bowels of the mine. They knew the labyrinth of tunnels like the backs of their hands and had stored ample food within the mine to last a year.[15,16]

Sagar led the four down into their lair. It was actually quite comfortable. They'd dragged down a couple of beds, a table and some chairs, along with mattresses, blankets, pillows, a few cooking pots and pans, and water buckets. They'd even put together a small library, with a kerosene lantern to read by. They had rifles and a good supply of ammunition that Sagar said had been provided to the miners by Colonel Horan right after the war started. They also had an ample supply of scotch and were eager to share, scotch that had been left behind by the Itogon families in favor of hauling cases of canned milk up to Lusod for their children.

Sagar and Green felt perfectly safe at the mine and invited them to stay. The four exchanged glances. It seemed obvious the Japanese would be thrilled to get hold of a producing gold mine and, when they did, they weren't likely to keep Sagar on as superintendent or Richie Green on as a shift boss. But one never knew.

Sagar also had a radio, and they caught up on two weeks' worth of news from San Francisco, most of it innocuous and sugar-coated. Sagar and Green hadn't listened to Roosevelt's Washington's Birthday address in February, and they shook their heads in disbelief when they heard about the promised supplies and reinforcements. *What the hell?* Sagar muttered. *What the hell is going on?*

The best news, though, came from a former mine employee, a young Igorot who wandered by. There were still Americans at the Lusod sawmill, perhaps even soldiers! Tempting as Sagar's generous hospitality was, the four were excited and anxious to be on their way.

CHAPTER 13

A HOMECOMING, OF SORTS
April 1942

THE NEXT MORNING THE FOUR followed the gravel track north a few miles to the intersection at the Baguio-Twin Rivers road. Though the narrow bridge over the Agno had been destroyed, the river level was low now during the dry season. They scrambled down the steep bank and waded across, skirting the rusting hulks of the buses and trucks they'd scuttled three months earlier. Much of the debris was already gone, scavenged by natives, a few of whom were at that moment crawling through the wreckage, picking up anything that might bring a centavo or two.

By mid-afternoon, after a steep, exhausting six-hour hike, Lusod came into view. They halted to rest and assess the situation, and then approached cautiously to within a hundred yards, remaining out of sight in the trees. Men were lounging about outside the bunkhouse, talking and laughing among themselves, evidently the soldiers the Igorot at Itogon had mentioned. A Filipino woman exited Emil Jorgensen's main staff house, walked to the barrio, and five minutes later retraced her steps. Taking no chances, the four drew their .45s and slowly approached the clearing.

Americano! Americano! shouted one of the native soldiers, jumping to his feet and waving his hands.

The four smiled and waved back, holstering their weapons.

Seconds later an American came bounding down the steps of the main staff house and introduced himself.

Lieutenant Al Hendrickson, a member of the Signal Corps, was in his late twenties, a big, strapping fellow from Montana, tanned and rangy, clad in faded denim overalls, a khaki shirt, and an Army-issue steel helmet. An old Enfield rifle was slung over one shoulder, a nickel-plated .45 strapped in its holster at his side. He invited them inside and, in a slow, easy drawl, related the story of how he'd come to be at Lusod.

A private at Nichols Field, he'd been with a six-man crew laying communication wires when the first bombs fell. They'd been sitting ducks. Everybody but Hendrickson had been blasted to smithereens. He wasn't hit, but he couldn't hear and could barely see. He'd staggered into downtown Manila, gotten hold of a quart of whiskey, and had drunk himself into a stupor. Coming to a few days later, he'd heard about the main Japanese landing up at Lingayen Gulf and had hiked up there just in time to join Major Moses and his boys defending the beaches at San Fernando. Hendrickson said he'd done a bunch of different jobs, and when one of the radio guys was killed, he'd taken over operation of the switchboard until Japanese artillery wiped it out.[1,2]

Art and his companions glanced at one another. Hendrickson's timetable didn't make much sense unless he'd had wings or a vehicle, but they didn't challenge him. Based on their experience, to have covered that distance alone on foot in less than ten days, with Japanese swarming up and down all the main roads, would have been quite a feat.

Overrun on the beaches, Hendrickson said he'd retreated with the rest of Colonel Moses's men up Naguilian Road to Baguio and then had gone out east over the mountains with Colonel Bonnett's group. The trip had been a fiasco. Bonnett had finally turned his native soldiers loose and told them to go home. At that point Hendrickson had ducked into a little dive in Aritao for a drink, maybe a couple, and the next thing he knew, Bonnett, Moses, Noble, and the rest of the Americans were gone.

Hendrickson said he'd hooked up with Major Everett Warner, the provost marshal of Camp John Hay[3], who'd also come over the mountains on foot but then concluded the defenders of Bataan could get along without his services. Warner had a transmitter and had contacted Allied headquarters on Corregidor. He'd fed General Wainwright a good story and had been given a promotion along with authorization to form a guerrilla group from remnants of the disbanded Filipino soldiers and Scouts now wandering around in the area, wondering what to do. This new group had been designated the 14th Infantry (Philippine Army). Headquartered at Jones in Isabela Province, it was one of the earliest official guerrilla outfits in North Luzon.

Warner hadn't remained in charge for long. As the tide of war turned against the Fil-Americans defending Bataan and Corregidor, Warner had again radioed Wainwright's headquarters and asked that a naval destroyer be dispatched to the east coast of Luzon to pick him up, to which Wainwright had replied something to the effect that *We don't have any destroyers, and even if we did, you wouldn't get one! Get the hell back to your command*[4]! By the second week of May, following the fall of Bataan and Corregidor, Warner had surrendered to the Japanese. He died not long afterward in a stinking cell at Bayombong, purportedly from food poisoning, though Hendrickson speculated alcohol withdrawal was the cause. The 14th Infantry soldiers refused to surrender, however, and command of the outfit was assumed by two much abler subordinates, Guillermo Nakar and Manuel Enriquez.

Hendrickson claimed that early in February Jack Pearson, a civilian mining engineer from Itogon, had hiked over the mountains to Isabela and begged Warner for some military help. Old friends from Baguio, Pearson had told Warner the Itogon mining families holed up at Lusod were being terrorized and held hostage by an armed group claiming to represent the Japanese forces now occupying Baguio. Major Warner had ordered young Hendrickson to take another private and several Philippine Scouts and accompany Pearson back to Lusod, promising Hendrickson an officer's commission if he was successful in regaining control of the mill. In mid-February the group had arrived back at Lusod. Using clever surprise tactics and a good measure of guts, Hendrickson had convinced the bandits they were surrounded and outnumbered, and had finally forced them to flee back to Baguio.

As word of Hendrickson's arrival spread, Philippine Army soldiers and Philippine Scouts had begun popping up at the mill—a few still in possession of their rifles and ammunition, but most with only the will to fight—until now there were a couple dozen in camp, itching for some action. The miners' families, spooked by the dust-up with the bandits and not pleased with the rowdy new soldiers, had hauled several loads of food from the Lusod *bodega* up to the abandoned mine site at Dyaka, twenty miles east, and at the end of February the Itogon folks had packed up and cleared out.

Hendrickson now referred to himself as Lieutenant Hendrickson—but with nothing in writing to substantiate his promotion—and was in charge.[5]

Murphy told Hendrickson how they'd come to their own decision to give up on Bataan, paraphrasing Roosevelt's broadcast about the troops being a lost cause. Hendrickson had some salty words for the government and the apparent double-cross. Finally, when Captain Calvert mentioned the four might hang out at Lusod for a while, Hendrickson's brow furrowed briefly, but then he said he'd be happy to have additional officers in camp. There was plenty of room and plenty of food, and with more armed Americans, it was less likely the Japanese surrogates from Baguio would try and return.

Hendrickson then related another fascinating story. He'd been at Lusod only a few days when a barrio native had come rushing in with the news that an armed Philippine Army officer was coming up the trail. When the fellow appeared, he was holding up two fingers, loudly proclaiming *V for Victory* and *God Bless America*. He'd given his name as Captain Rivero, produced papers showing he'd fought in World War I, and claimed he was still serving with the Philippine Scouts. He claimed he'd been sent to assess the situation at the mill and had asked to be shown around. After the tour, Hendrickson had given him lunch and talked more about the war, but just couldn't pin the guy down. All of a sudden, Rivero had jumped up and said he had to get going.

That evening some of the civilian miners, discussing Rivero's visit over dinner, had voiced serious doubts about him and about his purported mission. After all, who would be interested in the situation at Lusod except the Japanese? The miners had taken their concerns to Hendrickson and soon convinced him the man must have been a spy.

Hendrickson had taken off after Rivero and had finally caught up with him three days later near Aritao. When Hendrickson had cozied his .45 up behind Rivero's ear and accused him of being a spy for the Japanese, the little fellow had readily admitted it, pulling out a bunch of papers and handing them over. The papers showed the layout of the buildings at Lusod and even named names. Hendrickson said he'd felt like killing the son of a bitch right there, but then had thought better of that idea. Now that he was an officer, he'd figured he'd better go by the rules and see that the man got a trial. Hendrickson had confiscated his gun, tied his hands, and marched him all the way back to Lusod.[6]

Where is he now? Calvert asked.

Locked up in one a them sheds behind the mill building.

Calvert and Murphy glanced at one another. They weren't certain how many officers were needed to conduct an official court martial, but it was clear Hendrickson expected them to handle the matter.

The next day Hendrickson conducted a tour of the camp, beginning with the bunkhouse where the Filipino troops were billeted. When they were introduced to the men, an awkward thing happened. Always hyper-conscious of rank, they promptly saluted Captain Calvert. This abrupt change in allegiance was nothing Calvert had asked for or even suggested; rather it was a reflexive response on the part of the men. But it certainly wasn't lost on Lieutenant Hendrickson. Though he dutifully led them around the rest of the camp, his demeanor had changed. Where he'd been chatty, smiling, and full of stories, now his expression was deadpan and he provided information in brusque grunts.

Two days later several of the Itogon miners came up the trail from the east. Art and his companions were formally introduced to Herb Swick, Enoch French, Ted Lawson, and Bill Moule. Moule told Hendrickson to unlock the *bodega* so they could collect more supplies for their camp at Dyaka. Murphy tagged along. When he saw Moule taking sacks of rice, he mentioned to Hendrickson that the rice should probably be saved to feed the growing group of soldiers in camp.[6]

The comment hit a nerve with Moule. He said, *Look, I've got a wife and three little kids to feed—*

Murphy cut him off. *It's not my problem you've got your family over here. We're in a war now and we've gotta keep the soldiers fed.*

Moule got really indignant. *Lieutenant, the Itogon miners are responsible for nine-tenths of the food stored up here. I sent a truckload up from Baguio even after the Japs got there. You officers had the same opportunity at Camp John Hay and you didn't even have the good sense to pack enough for the trail. If you guys starve to death, it won't hurt my feelings one damn bit.*

Murphy came right back. *Look, we were ordered to retreat over the mountains and were issued rations for the trip. We had no control over what happened to the rest of the food at the camp.*

As long as I helped rustle up this food, I'll take it! Moule snapped.

By now they were nose to nose, two temperamental Irishmen with clenched fists, ready for a fight. Murphy backed down. If the food had come from Itogon and Moule had been responsible for getting it up to Lusod, he was entitled to enough of it to feed his family.

Over dinner that evening the conversation was all about the war, and at one point things got a little heated again. Bill Moule wanted to know why the military hadn't stuck around to defend Baguio. Not raising his voice, Captain Calvert patiently explained Colonel Horan's dilemma and the mix-up in orders from Manila. Then Moule wanted to know why they weren't down on Bataan fighting the Japanese. Again Calvert explained.

Well, you guys have got yourselves a pretty nice little war going on, it seems to me, replied Moule.

Art couldn't keep his mouth shut. *Listen, Moule, we're in the Army, and when you're in the Army, goddammit, you obey orders, whether you agree with them or not!*

Diplomatic as always, Calvert jumped back in and smoothed things over.[7]

Later, stomachs full and tempers under control, Bill Moule and Art buried the hatchet. Moule told Art how he'd come over on a wing and a prayer, how he'd bluffed his way into the shift-boss job at Itogon, and how his wife Margaret and their two babies had come over a few months later. Everything had been great for a while, until the war started. Margaret was pregnant with a third child, and Bill was scared of what would happen to her in a concentration camp. He described their hideout over at Dyaka and how they were coping. Moule could tell a good story and had a great sense of humor. Though the events he described were serious as hell, he made the stories light and funny. Then Art told him how badly he missed his own family, how he'd schemed to get Lillian and the babies over to the Philippines, and how he'd lost all his letters and photos in the attack at the Lone Star mine. Grinning, Bill said Art ought to come over to Dyaka and babysit for a couple of days while he and Margaret took a little vacation. Art could jounce the kids on his knee and play with them all he wanted, and he could also wash dirty diapers, feed the baby, chase little Billy all around the mountain, try and keep the kids clean, and experience again all the joys of fatherhood. In the end, they couldn't decide whose situation was worse, Moule's in being responsible for his young family holed up in the mountains or Art's in being separated half a world away and having no idea what was going on back home.

The situation with Hendrickson didn't improve. He announced one morning that he'd decided, if it was okay with Captain Calvert, to head back east over the mountains to find Major Warner's outfit. Calvert didn't object. Private Mangemelli, who'd come over from Isabela with Hendrickson, left that afternoon also, as did a couple of the Filipino soldiers. But the majority, now numbering several dozen, stayed put.

WITH HENDRICKSON GONE, Calvert and Murphy moved into the main staff house. The servants reported for duty.

It was time for some organization within their new little army. The first item of business was assigning a 24-hour watch schedule so they wouldn't be caught by surprise in the unlikely event some Japanese from Baguio wandered up the mountain. Their second priority was inventorying the weapons in camp, and the available ammunition. Calvert ordered that all guns be cleaned and thereafter kept in tiptop condition. Art inventoried the food in the *bodega* and set up strict rationing. They organized some exercise for the restless men, even if it was only calisthenics and jogging in circles around the camp for an hour each day. Usually the Americans joined them.

Lastly, Calvert and Murphy questioned the captive, Captain Rivero. Before leaving, Hendrickson had turned over the papers confiscated from Rivero, so they had the evidence against him, but they were anxious to know who'd sent him up to Lusod in the first place. The only thing they could get out of him was his assertion that *I'm loyal to my country. I'm a good soldier. I'm not afraid to die.*

Occasionally, Igorot natives hiked up the trail from Baguio, and the sentries brought them in for questioning. One native said he'd heard about some guerrilla attacks on enemy work crews repairing roads up along the Mountain Trail, the steep, narrow road leading north out of Baguio and up through the Lepanto mining region to Bontoc. In retaliation, Japanese patrols had been sent out to hunt down those responsible. They'd interrogated and brutally murdered a number of natives suspected of aiding the guerrillas. Calvert and Murphy were anxious to learn who'd pulled off these feats. *Where were they? Did the Japs catch them?* Other stories they heard, though, were pretty farfetched. It wasn't easy to figure out what to believe.

AROUND APRIL 1, THEY WERE ALERTED that some American and Filipino soldiers were coming up the trail from the east. As they approached, Captain Calvert called out, and soon they were introducing themselves and shaking hands with the shorter lead man, Captain Robert Arnold, and his taller, older companion, Lieutenant Herman Kluege. Six Filipinos accompanied them. They were a ragged, underfed-looking bunch. They'd just spent several days over at Dyaka, where Doc Biason, the former camp doctor at Itogon, had operated to remove a piece of shrapnel from Arnold's leg. The leg was still bandaged and swollen.

Hey, you fellows wouldn't be the ones who ambushed the Japs up on the Mountain Trail, would you?

Yeah, I guess that'd be us, Arnold replied.

They had a million questions for Arnold, but first they led the officers over to the guest house and showed the men to the bunkhouse. That evening their cook prepared quite a feast, and they continued trading information far into the night.

Lieutenant Arnold had arrived at Fort McKinley in 1941, a specialist in the new field of radar. In early December, he'd left Manila with a crew and a ton of technical equipment to establish a radar station on the northwestern tip of Luzon. On the afternoon of

December 6, they'd reached Cape Bojeador and begun reconnoitering the area for a suitable spot. By the morning of December 8, construction was nearly complete and initial tuning of the radar was underway when aircraft appeared over the South China Sea. Arnold had counted thirty-five planes and said he knew instantly they were Japanese. He'd radioed an urgent warning back to Fort McKinley and sent another a few hours later when a second group of Japanese bombers flew over. Evidently his warnings had been ignored or hadn't arrived in time to do any good.

When the Japanese landed at Aparri and Vigan, Arnold's group had been cut off. After repeated attempts to contact MacArthur's headquarters in Manila, a response arrived: *Destroy your secret equipment.* There was nothing to do but dismantle the radar station, crush the secret components, hide the rest in the jungle, and head back south through the mountains.[8]

Arnold's group had made their way into Abra Province, where they came across Walter Cushing, co-owner of a local gold mine, who suggested they join forces. Cushing had already blown the entrance to his mine to keep it from falling into enemy hands and was ready to get even with the Japanese for causing him so much trouble. He had plenty of dynamite, was anxious to use it, and had already destroyed a bridge or two along the coast highway to thwart Japanese movements. Cushing and his miners had also raided a Philippine Constabulary ammunition depot at Bengued, the provincial capital of Abra, so had rifles, machine guns, and ammunition. With this bountiful supply of arms, Cushing and Arnold had recruited additional men and led a successful ambush on a Japanese troop convoy at the coastal town of Candon, killing dozens of the enemy and burning their trucks.

At this point Arnold's tale got complicated. He claimed that as the group was returning to their mountain headquarters after the Candon raid, Cushing had gone on ahead by himself. When Arnold and the men arrived at camp, they discovered Cushing had gone to

Bontoc to find Colonel Horan, then commander of all resistance forces in North Luzon. Cushing had regaled Horan with exaggerated stories of his exploits, claiming Arnold's boys had been half-starved when he found them but that he, Cushing, had fed them and soon whipped them into shape. He claimed full credit for planning and carrying out the recent raid at Candon, assisted only marginally by Arnold and his men. Colonel Horan, mightily impressed with Cushing's stories, contacted MacArthur's headquarters, passed the good news along, and received authorization to offer Cushing a captain's commission and also promote Arnold to the rank of captain. Still not satisfied, Cushing had allegedly claimed he couldn't be an effective commander unless he was the ranking officer in the outfit, so Horan had capitulated and made him a major.

When Cushing returned to Del Pilar, he'd advised Arnold of the promotions, and then triumphantly assumed command. To make the coup complete, Cushing had ordered Arnold to make a reconnaissance trip south into Benguet Province to gather intelligence, effectively eliminating any confusion about who was running the show. Taken aback, Arnold had obeyed. Picking up Kluege along the way, he had planned and carried out the two raids on the Japanese road-repair crews along the Mountain Trail above Baguio, suffering his leg wound in the process.[9]

Murphy and the others had no reason to doubt any part of this fascinating story, but Captain Arnold obviously harbored a great deal of resentment about the way things had turned out.

Later accounts of the above events differed markedly from what Captain Arnold told them that day. Some claimed the Candon raid was jointly planned and carried out by Walter Cushing and Candonino Gaerlan, manager of the Candon Electric Company, with Arnold and his men playing a secondary role at best.[10] Others tempered the circumstances under which Walter Cushing assumed command over Arnold's men.[11] Whatever the truth, the accepted historical account credits Walter McKay Cushing as the first, the most flamboyant, and the most effective of the early guerrilla leaders in North Luzon.

Herman Kluege had managed another sawmill on the Mountain Trail fifty miles north of Baguio. When the enemy landed at Vigan, he'd joined the war effort, traveling with a group of Baguio area miners up the Mountain Trail toward Bontoc, blowing bridges as they went.[12] They'd found Colonel Horan in Bontoc awaiting MacArthur's promised supplies and reinforcements. Horan had commissioned all the miners, and thus Kluege had become a second lieutenant in the United States Army. Kluege and his miners had moved west to Cervantes, where he was located when Captain Arnold had come through. Impressed with Captain Arnold's tales, Kluege had requested and been granted permission to join Arnold's group.[13]

OVER DINNER, MURPHY AND CALVERT told the visitors about Captain Rivero. They appreciated the dilemma and agreed to help. As the only one with any pre-war legal experience, Murphy was selected to organize the court martial and assign the roles. He designated Captain Calvert as judge and Captain Arnold as prosecutor. Murphy would represent the interests of the defendant. Kluege would be responsible for recording the proceedings, and Spencer and Jagoe would act as observers. The evidence was turned over to Arnold, and he studied Rivero's handwritten notes and drawings before agreeing it was clear what they represented. Murphy set the proceeding for the next morning at nine at the small office in the sawmill building.

They assembled as scheduled and had Rivero brought from his cell. Captain Calvert explained he was being charged with spying for the Japanese and asked him if he understood. Rivero merely grunted and glared sullenly at Calvert. Captain Arnold showed him the notes, and Rivero readily admitted he'd written them. When Arnold asked him directly if he was a spy for the Japanese, he answered with a nod. Arnold pressed him for an audible answer. *Yes*, the man hissed. The prosecution rested. Murphy took over and asked a few questions about why he'd been sent up to Lusod and had he understood at the time what he was being asked to do. Instead of answering, Rivero just repeated what he'd said a few days before: *I'm loyal to my country. I'm a good soldier. I'm not afraid to die.* The defense rested. Calvert rendered the verdict—*Guilty as charged*—and pronounced the sentence: *Death by firing squad.* The whole proceeding took less than twenty minutes.

Four natives dug a rectangular pit behind the sawmill building. Rivero was blindfolded and led over to the hole. He stood in silence, his five-foot frame stretched to its fullest, head thrown back and chin jutting out in defiance. Four Filipino soldiers lined up ten feet away. Captain Calvert barked the orders: *Ready! Aim! Fire!* The crack of four rifles shattered the morning calm. Rivero crumpled in a heap. The men removed his boots, pushed his corpse into the hole, and shoveled the dirt back in. The Filipinos appeared unfazed by the execution, but the rest of them were rattled. They rehashed the details all evening in order to fully digest what had happened. They agreed it was an ugly, distasteful, but necessary thing they had done.

MOST EVENINGS THEY LISTENED TO KGEI on Emil Jorgensen's radio. The news had turned ominous. The Japanese had mounted an all-out offensive against the starving, disease-ridden soldiers on Bataan.[14] It was so depressing that they began listening instead to a Japanese program from Shanghai that played American big band music.[15] On the evening of April 9, the bad news was confirmed: Brigadier General Edward P. King, commander of the eastern-sector defense forces on Bataan, and Brigadier General William E. Brougher, commander of the western sector, had surrendered their 70,000-plus Fil-American troops to the Japanese, the worst defeat in American military history.

ON APRIL 10, BOB ARNOLD AND HERMAN KLUEGE and their half dozen men prepared to leave, planning to hike back east over the mountains into the Cagayan Valley, where they hoped to gather intelligence.[16] Then they'd try to find Colonel Horan and get current orders. Art's feet were in pretty good shape, so he decided to tag along as far as Dyaka. He was anxious to see Bill Moule's hideout and meet the other Americans over there.

They approached Dyaka in late afternoon, as the sun painted the western sky in brilliant shades of red, orange, and purple. Bill came out to meet them, but immediately they were surrounded by excited kids. Bill introduced Margaret and their two older children, Billy and Eileen. Ted Lawson introduced his wife, Ruth, and their little girl, Janie. Inside, Margaret Moule proudly showed off the newest addition, three-month-old Linda, roly-poly and cute as could be. Janie and Eileen crawled all over Art, giving him a taste of what his own little girls must be like.

Margaret and Ruth cooked a hot meal, and over dinner they regaled everyone with their own adventures since the start of the war, including their trek over the mountains to Aritao right after Christmas in the vain hope they could get through to Manila.

Art admired the Itogon crowd, an amazing, high-spirited bunch, but tough and adaptable too. Through hard work and ingenuity, they'd transformed a couple of decrepit, abandoned mining shacks into cozy homes.

Art asked about Doc Biason and the rest of the group and was told they'd moved a few miles north to Oding, another abandoned mine.

Hey, Bill said, *I'm ready for a little hike. What say we head up there tomorrow morning for a visit?*

That night Art lay awake a long time. Margaret had described how, whenever they were on the trail, she and Bill would curl up facing one another, knees touching knees, with the unborn baby, Billy, and Eileen nestled in between, snug and protected. The image made Art long for Lil and his own babies until his whole chest ached.

Shortly after daybreak, they all said good-bye to Arnold, Kluege, and their men as they headed east toward Aritao, and then Bill and Art hiked up to Oding. The families there were divided up between two buildings that had once housed mine employees. Mom and Pop Pearson, Jack and Sally Pearson, their son Butch, and Virginia and Johnny McCuish lived in one, while Doc and Daisy Biason, their little girl Joan, Doc's sister Betty Biason, and Harry Barz and his pregnant wife Edna crowded into the larger one.

Below the two houses, a stream tumbled over a twenty-foot waterfall. They'd scrounged enough parts from Itogon, Lusod, and Bobok to build a small Pelton wheel that, through a system of shafts, pulleys, and a fan belt, turned a generator, also salvaged from one of the mills. Art had never heard of a Pelton wheel. The contraption looked like an oversized wagon wheel mounted on an axle, with iron scoops bolted along the outside. When installed in a sturdy log framework next to the waterfall, the falling water hit the scoops and caused the wheel to spin, turning the axle and powering the generator. Using wiring and headlights salvaged from destroyed vehicles at Twin Rivers, they'd installed lights in the two houses. They'd even rigged up hot and cold running water in the larger house, the hot water provided by a pipe run along the back of the woodstove they used for cooking. Art could hardly believe all they'd accomplished.[17]

After dinner everyone crowded around their shortwave radio. Following the news, KGEI sometimes ran a segment allowing stateside wives or parents to deliver messages to their men fighting in the Pacific. The announcer began: *This evening we have Lillian Murphy with us. Her husband, Lieutenant Arthur P. Murphy, is with the Army somewhere in North Luzon, and she'd like to say a few words.*

Art couldn't believe his ears. *That's my wife! That's my wife!* he shouted.

Then he heard the voice he knew so well: *Hello, my darling. I hope and pray you're staying safe over there while you do your job with the Army. Don't worry about us. We're just fine. The girls are growing like weeds and have certainly changed. Eleanor is so grown up now, and she's a big help with the everyday chores. Trisha not only walks, but she runs through the house like a whirlwind, talking nonstop all day long in a voice loud enough to command her own little army. I keep your picture right next to their beds, and I tell them about you all the time. Eleanor says a little prayer for you each evening, and Trisha chimes right in too. I'm now working full-time over at the place where we last said good-bye, if you remember. Well, I have to go now, my darling, so that Bert can talk to Brew. Don't ever forget that I love you with all my heart.*[18]

Everyone was grinning at Art. He sat in stunned silence and didn't hear anything that Bert may have said to Brew. Later that night, bedded down on the floor next to the stove at Oding, he had exquisite dreams.

The next morning Bill and Art hiked back to Dyaka, where Art stayed just long enough to tell that group about the radio broadcast. They were thrilled for him, and the women gave him big hugs. Margaret packed him a sandwich and some cold coffee for the trail, and he headed back to Lusod.

CAPTAIN CALVERT AND ART DISCUSSED the matter of rank. Every other American officer loose on Luzon had been promoted, and dozens of miners had been commissioned too. Their little army now numbered nearly a hundred, so they promoted themselves one notch and congratulated each other on their new status: Major Parker Calvert and Captain Arthur P. Murphy, commander and adjutant respectively of Detachment, 1st Battalion, 43rd Infantry (Philippine Scouts). They had no official military insignia, but their house girl obligingly embroidered the appropriate embellishments on their shirts. The men noticed the change immediately and saluted with increased respect.[19]

A WEEK LATER SEVERAL IGOROT NATIVES came into camp with a prisoner, a Japanese national they'd found operating a salt mill some miles down the mountain. They had the man's hands tied with vines and were guarding him with spears and bolos. They turned him over to Calvert and Murphy and washed their hands of the matter. *But what were they supposed to do with him?* He hadn't really committed any crime, apparently, other than being Japanese, but they couldn't let him go without risking their own necks if he revealed their whereabouts to the enemy garrison in Baguio. They placed him in the same cell that had held Rivero. That night they hashed the matter over, made a collective decision, and the next morning Calvert ordered him shot. He was buried in a shallow grave next to Rivero.[20] It was easier this time.

THEY WERE CRITICALLY SHORT OF GUNS and ammunition. Their most recent recruit had come to them by way of Ansagan, thirty miles south of Baguio in the municipality of Tuba, and he had arrived fully armed. He told them the natives at Ansagan were hoarding many rifles and lots of ammunition scavenged from the wreckage at Twin Rivers, so Art decided to make a trip down there. Herb Swick volunteered to go along. With half a dozen volunteers and their newest soldier as their guide, they set out around April 15 and hiked two days up and down mountains, asking about the enemy as they went. A native along the trail warned about one Japanese patrol, allowing them plenty of time to hide in the bushes and let the patrol go by. At Ansagan, their guide told the head man they were guerrillas and needed all the arms his people were hiding in order to attack the Japanese at Baguio. The fellow was hesitant at first, but when Murphy removed his .45 from its holster, he nodded and bowed. He said he'd need a day to get the job done, and in the meantime they could stay at his place. By mid-morning two days later, they had accumulated seventeen rifles and several thousand rounds of ammunition. Dividing the load evenly, they thanked the head man and headed back for Lusod. The return trip required three days because of the added weight.[21]

THE NEW RIFLES WERE DISTRIBUTED to the men who had none, and at that point Art figured they were ready to tackle some Japanese patrols and garrisons. Major Calvert, ever mindful of military protocol, decided the proper move was to find Colonel Horan and attach their unit to his new guerrilla outfit, the 121st Infantry Regiment. Calvert left Art in charge. If he and Spence weren't back in a week, or if Art encountered any trouble from the Japanese, he was to destroy everything at Lusod, along with a few bridges the Japanese had rebuilt between Baguio and Itogon, and then follow them north to Bontoc. On the morning of May 1, Calvert and Spence took off, and the rest sat back to wait.[22]

They didn't wait long. That same afternoon three enemy bombers flew over, dropped half a dozen eggs, then turned around and made several strafing runs over the sawmill before disappearing back to the west. Their aim was incredibly poor because no one was hurt, although several buildings were damaged. Art decided it was time to implement Major Calvert's orders.

Jagoe objected vehemently. Art told him those were Calvert's orders and they had to obey. Jagoe snapped back, *I'm not in the goddamned Army and I don't have to obey anybody, least of all you!*

Well, suit yourself, Tom, but I'm carrying out my orders whether you like it or not.

Jagoe and Enoch French, another of the Itogon miners, packed up as much stuff as they could carry and sauntered off south down the trail toward Dalupirip. They subsequently joined a guerrilla group in Pangasinan led by Charles Cushing, a brother of the legendary Walter M., and were commissioned as second lieutenants.[23]

Gathering the remaining men, Art explained what they had to do. Over the next week he and Herb Swick took a crew down the trail toward Baguio and blew three small bridges. They also destroyed several miles of telephone wire connecting Lusod with Baguio and Itogon. Lastly, they set dynamite charges in the main sawmill building and the machine shops and lit the fuses. Art admitted to feeling quite a thrill, watching the explosions. The dynamite did its job pretty well, and the resulting fires did the rest.

Art fashioned a backpack from a burlap sack. He *borrowed* Emil Jorgensen's binoculars, flashlight and spare batteries, his best bolo, and the rest of his matches. He also took stationery and a couple of pencils from Emil's desk. He found a comb and another roll of adhesive tape and stuck those in, along with a matched set of playing cards. You never knew when you might rustle up a game of bridge between guerrilla attacks! After turning over the rest of the food to the barrio natives, he and Herb set fire to the *bodega*, the guest house, and the bunkhouse.

When it came to torching the main staff house, Art couldn't bring himself to do it. All the Jorgensens' treasured furnishings were inside, including a piano, a beautiful Chinese rug, and a couple of fine paintings. With nothing of military significance left, he hoped the servants could maintain control of the place until the Jorgensens returned.

On the morning of Saturday, May 9, they were ready to march. Herb Swick took the lead as they headed out, leaving what little was left at Lusod for the Japanese.[24]

CHAPTER 14

THE DILEMMA OF SURRENDER

May and June 1942

ART PLANNED TO STOP FIRST AT BOBOK, the other Jorgensen sawmill run by the son, Ken, the fellow who grew orchids. He hoped the Japanese hadn't yet sent patrols as far as Bobok because they were too busy trying to catch the guerrillas who'd ambushed their road-repair crews up on the Mountain Trail.

Herb Swick was the epitome of a college football player—tall, dark-haired, well-muscled, agile, and good-looking. With several years of mining experience, he had a wealth of practical knowledge and was also a very congenial fellow, always ready to pitch in and help wherever needed.

Making good time, around noon they came to the now-familiar fork and turned north on the old horse trail that wound its way around a couple of mountains. The going was easy, and by mid-afternoon they approached Bobok, deserted now except for an Igorot named Chunuan, who'd been Ken Jorgensen's assistant at the sawmill and was now acting as caretaker.[1] He remembered Art and greeted him warmly. After directing the men to an outbuilding, Chunuan escorted Art and Herb to the main staff house. The place was unchanged—the orchids still beautiful, the Delco generator still chugging along, supplying power for electric lights and hot and cold running water. There was no sign at all of a war.

Chunuan cooked them a hot meal. Then they listened to the news. It was terrible! Corregidor, the last American stronghold on Luzon, had fallen on May 6. The details were devastating. The Japanese refused to accept General Wainwright's surrender unless he surrendered not only the troops on Corregidor and the other fortified islands in Manila Bay but *every last one* of the USAFFE soldiers in the Philippines. If he didn't comply, the Japanese threatened to slaughter 11,000 American and Philippine Army troops trapped on Corregidor as well as the tens of thousands of prisoners already taken on Bataan. General Wainwright felt he had no choice: "This decision on my part [to surrender], you will realize, was forced upon me by means beyond my control."[2, 3]

Herb looked at Art. *Are you gonna take these men to Baguio and surrender?*

Hell, no, Art replied. *No one has ordered me to surrender. My orders are to take these men and join Major Calvert, who should by now have found Colonel Horan. We need to keep moving, and our next stop is Bokod. Are you willing to take us that far?*

Sure, said Herb. *Be glad to.*

On the morning of May 10, they headed northwest through heavy, mossy forest. Reaching the Agno, they followed it to the fork of the Bokod River. After two nights on the trail, they approached Bokod, a small village dotted with coconut palms and spread out along both sides of an unpaved main street.

The municipal officials said Calvert and Spencer had spent a night there a week earlier, so they knew they were on the right track. The mayor had Art divide the men into four smaller groups and arranged with the locals to house and feed them.

Art and Herb were introduced to Father Robert Gellynck, a Belgian priest who headed up the local Catholic mission, and he invited them to share his small house. After a fine meal that evening, they hashed over the war news with the good padre. He felt there wasn't much he could do about the Japanese invasion except look after his people, keep a low profile, and hope for the best. When Art broached the subject of guerrilla action, though, he said he'd do everything in his power to help.

The next morning, Art tried to convince Herb to accompany him the rest of the way to Bontoc, but Herb knew nothing about the trails beyond Bokod, and he felt duty-bound to return to Dyaka and Oding to look out for the mining families there. Reluctantly, Art shook his hand, they wished each other luck, and Herb left right after breakfast. Art was on his own.

ART DECIDED TO LEAVE THE MEN AT BOKOD and head north by himself to find Calvert and Spencer. The mayor found him a guide who spoke some Pidgin English. In the interest of speed, Art stripped his burlap knapsack down to the bare essentials and left the rest of his stuff with Father Gellynck for safekeeping.

At mid-morning on May 16, Art and Tomas headed toward Mount Pulag. Tomas set a blistering pace. Art had to scramble to keep up. It began raining, lightly at first, but all afternoon they slogged along in a heavy downpour. Thick, sticky clay sucked at Art's boots with each step.

As darkness fell, Tomas hacked brush and boughs to fashion a lean-to. Still, small rivulets trickled down the back of Art's neck as they ate their supper of dried meat and cold rice. As he stretched out, the oozing mud gave under the weight of his body. Shivering cold and soaking wet, he dozed fitfully. Tomas slept like a baby.

The 17th dawned sunny and beautiful, and soon they were climbing steeply through rice paddies along the east flank of Mount Pulag. Art's clothes dried quickly, only to be wet again by perspiration. After a while, the trail dropped hundreds of feet to a river, and they followed the bank north for several miles, high mountains rising vertically on either side

Covering about twenty miles, they came to Tinoc, where Tomas inquired in dialect about Japanese and about Calvert and Spencer.

The natives hadn't seen the enemy and knew nothing of the two Americans. Tomas negotiated for a hot meal and a dry place for the night. As they ate, the locals stood and stared. Tomas explained that many of these natives had never seen a white man. Filipinos don't have much facial hair, and they were fascinated by Art's bushy, reddish beard.

On the 18th, they continued northward, hugging the bank of the river. After clear skies in the morning, it rained cats and dogs all afternoon and into the night. Art's feet were blistering again, and his burlap pack had rubbed one shoulder raw. They shared the last can of corned beef. It was another cold, soggy night.

On May 19, they reached the Hungduan Valley and pushed on toward the main village, where Tomas felt they could find hot food and shelter for several days. Art was really hobbling now. Again, the local officials had seen neither Japanese nor Calvert and Spencer, but they'd heard there were lots of Japanese farther north, and guerrillas too. They had to be getting closer.

Starting out again on the 24th, they climbed a couple of mountains, dropped into another valley, and followed it all afternoon north toward Banuae. On the outskirts, Tomas asked about Japanese, and when the way appeared clear, they proceeded to the government guest house. Again, no one had seen Calvert or Spencer, but the guest house was still offering food and accommodations, so they checked in.

Art's feet were in such rough shape that he decided to remain at Banuae and send Tomas on ahead to Bontoc with a message. For more than a week, he heard nothing. When Tomas finally returned, he brought more awful news. Not only had he not located Calvert and Spencer at Bontoc, but on the way back he'd heard that some American guerrillas farther north, up around Lubuagan, had surrendered to the Japanese. *What guerrillas were these, Colonel Horan's 121st Infantry or someone else? Had Calvert and Spencer surrendered? If they hadn't, where were they?* Tomas had gotten his news from an old American in a barrio five or six miles to the north. With his options dwindling, Art decided to check out the rumor for himself.

It took two days to locate the old American, an ex-lumberman surnamed Fish whom Colonel Horan had commissioned a second lieutenant in the 121st Infantry. He said Colonel Horan and his guerrillas had retreated to Lubuagan, in Kalinga Subprovince, where Horan had been contacted by a personal emissary from General Wainwright, bearing written orders for Horan to surrender.[4] Horan had immediately surrendered himself and several American officers, but had received little cooperation from his Filipino soldiers, who refused to obey the order and scattered into the mountains.[5, 6]

When asked about Calvert and Spencer, Fish had never heard of them. Pressed about what he intended to do, he merely shrugged and said, *Since the guerrilla commanders have all given up, I'll probably just head back to my old mill in the Lepanto area, dig in, and wait for MacArthur to get his ass back here and put an end to this stinkin' war.* As an afterthought, he added, *You're welcome to come along.*

Art was in a quandary. He had no idea where Calvert and Spencer were or if they were even alive. *What had happened to Bob Anderson and Herman Kluege? Were they still holding out with the 14th Infantry over in Isabela? What about Al Hendrickson? Herb Swick, Jack Langley, and the other civilian miners might still be down around Baguio somewhere, and it's tempting to hunt for them. But I'm not a civilian; I'm an officer in the United States Army and am supposed to obey orders. If I don't, if I continue to resist and am ever captured, it'll mean certain torture and death at the hands of the Japanese. On the other hand, if MacArthur miraculously returns and defeats the Japs, will I be court-martialed, labeled a deserter, or convicted of treason? No matter which side prevails, will I be tried as a war criminal for ordering the killing of the Jap civilian at Lusod? And what about the soldiers waiting back at Bokod?* Finally Art made a decision: Hell would freeze before he surrendered, only to rot in some godforsaken prison camp. He wasn't going down without a good fight. Lil and his two little girls back in California deserved better than that.

With that hurdle resolved, Art and Tomas headed south again, right into the teeth of a full-fledged typhoon. The wind blew so fiercely they had trouble standing. Tomas lashed together another rough lean-to between the trunks of three huge trees, and they hunkered down for protection. The rain slashed down in sheets. Soon eighty-mile-an-hour winds carried off their flimsy shelter, leaving them clinging to exposed roots and praying the trees didn't come down and squash them like bugs.

The typhoon kept them pinned without food for three miserable days. Eventually, it blew itself out, and on a Wednesday during the third week of June, Bokod finally loomed ahead, a welcome sight indeed. Tomas was anxious to get home, so Art paid him twenty soggy pesos and headed straight for the Catholic Mission, hoping to find a shower, a drink, and a hot meal.

Father Gellynck's face lit up like a Christmas tree. He threw his arms around Art's shoulders and pulled him inside, fairly bursting with news. He knew nothing of Calvert and Spencer, but he'd heard there were Americans camped a few miles east in the little barrio of Benneng. Father Gellynck said he'd have his houseboy take Art there, but first they had to celebrate his safe return. The old padre brought out a carefully hoarded bottle of scotch and had his cook prepare a barbecue beef dinner with all the trimmings. He listened intently as Art described the events of the past several weeks, clapping his hands together with glee when he heard the part about not surrendering.

The next morning Father Gellynck's houseboy escorted Art to Benneng, an hour-long hike east into the mountains. At the outskirts, they were stopped by a town official, who took down Art's name and told him to wait. It began to rain. Twenty minutes later he came back, nodding and motioning for Art to follow him up an obscure path to a well-hidden wooden hut on stilts.

With no idea what to expect, Art was surprised and delighted to find two senior officers he'd met at Fort McKinley: Majors Martin Moses and Arthur "Maxie" Noble. Art had known them as majors, but both now wore shiny silver lieutenant colonels' leaves on their shoulders.

Their officers' insignia may have been shiny, but they were not. Their tattered uniforms hung limply on bony frames. Both looked sallow and drawn, particularly Marty Moses, who appeared depressed, as though he'd been through a terrible ordeal. A patch covered Maxie Noble's left eye. Their hideout had a corrugated metal roof and several tiny rooms equipped with shabby *bejuco* furniture. A houseboy brought cold drinks, and as the heavy rain kept up a steady beat on the roof, they sat around all afternoon, listening to each other's stories.[7]

Maxie Noble did most of the talking, describing their futile defense efforts on the beaches when the Japanese had first come ashore in December, how much of their ammunition had proved defective, how dozens of their green troops had panicked and fled, and how they'd finally been forced to withdraw to Baguio, where they found only confusion and garbled orders. With the Kennon Road closed by Japanese advances, 2,000 of them, led by Colonel Bonnett, had piled into buses, trucks, and half-tracks and pulled out of Baguio a couple of days before Christmas on what they thought would be a fairly easy trip to Bobok and over the mountains to Aritao to hook up with the rest of the USAFFE boys retreating to Bataan.

Maxie Noble's voice was bitter as he detailed how the whole column had reversed course on the narrow, twisting road and headed back to Baguio when Colonel Horan radioed that the Kennon Road was open again to Rosario, then reversed course a second time when that information proved false. He described Colonel Bonnett's outrage upon reaching Bobok and discovering the road to Aritao wasn't a road at all but rather a foot-wide dirt track, forcing them to scuttle their vehicles and proceed on foot. The trip over the mountains had been a nightmare, like herding lizards. Their men couldn't understand the urgency and stopped whenever they felt like it. Well behind schedule, Moses and Noble stayed behind to keep things moving while Colonel Bonnett raced on ahead to Aritao to catch the USAFFE boys. At Aritao, he'd found the Japanese had already cleared Balete Pass, chasing the Americans toward Bataan. Bonnett telephoned with the bad news and told them to disband the Filipino troops and send them home, that he was trying to get help from Corregidor and still hoped to make it south to Manila and from there to Bataan.

When Marty Moses ordered the soldiers to disband, some had obeyed, but most refused and tagged along with the officers all the way to Aritao. There, to their complete surprise, they'd met a north-bound convoy of trucks, dispatched by General Wainwright's head-quarters to pick them up and deliver them to Bataan. Their ragtag forces had piled aboard and been hustled off to Manila for new uniforms and new assignments.[8]

Moses and Noble had ended up commanding adjacent regiments of General Bill Brougher's 11th Division in the western sector of Bataan, and for several months they'd held off the Japanese. But it was sheer hell—food rations cut in half, then halved again; ammunition so scarce that each man carried fewer than fifty rounds; black clouds of mosquitos; no more quinine. Men dropped like flies from malaria and dysentery. Toward the end, the starving men were eating anything they could find—worms, beetles, lizards, and even bark and leaves.

By April 9, their situation was hopeless. They were ordered to lay down their arms and prepare white flags. Colonel Brougher had gathered his officers for a final briefing on the surrender time-table. In the group were Moses and Noble, Russ Volckmann, and Don Blackburn. Appalled at the thought of surrender, they'd asked Brougher if they could try and sneak through the Japanese lines and escape north into the Zambales Mountains. With Brougher's okay, the four of them gathered some supplies and watched for their chance. The emaciated soldiers hung around in groups, forlorn and beaten, waiting for the Japanese. Late that afternoon, bonfires were built to illuminate the surrender flags.

Despite the white flags and the fact that everyone had their hands in the air, the Japanese burst out of the jungle with rifles and machine guns blazing, mowing down hundreds of panicked, screaming soldiers. At that point, Moses and Noble scrambled into the jungle, dropped to their knees, and began crawling. They lost sight of Volckmann and Blackburn, and only heard screams, the rat-tat-tat-tat of machine guns, and sporadic crashing noises in the jungle. If the noises got too close, they lay motionless on their bellies, faces pressed into the muck. When the danger passed, they crawled on silently. Gradually, the sounds of war became muffled in the distance. They traveled only at night, often navigating rocky streambeds on their bellies. Twice, the Japanese passed within yards of where they lay, but their luck held, and after a while there were no more Japanese. By the time they reached the mountains, both were covered with cuts and scrapes that became oozing tropical ulcers. On the fourth day, Noble had caught the thorny leaf of a rattan vine in his left eye, ripping the cornea, and now that eye was worthless.[9, 10, 11]

Picking up the narrative, Colonel Moses told Art how they'd run into some other fugitives who'd laid down their arms on Bataan but then escaped later. They said the guys who survived the initial slaughter were marched east across the Bataan Peninsula to join General King's surrendered troops. Then 70,000 prisoners were marched north in columns, one on either side of the road, more than sixty miles under the blazing sun, without food or water. If a man stumbled, he was bayonetted and left to die. Some guards used their rifle butts to knock lagging prisoners onto the road, where they were plowed over by Japanese trucks and tanks barreling down the center, until nothing remained but a smear of human matter. Others were even more sadistic. When one poor fellow, sick with dysentery, stepped out of the column to relieve himself, a Japanese guard kicked him to the ground, sliced his genitals off, and shoved the bloody mass into the screaming man's mouth before bayonetting him in the gut. Some horrified Filipino civilians along the route tried slipping water or a piece of fruit to the suffering soldiers. When a guard caught one prisoner frantically shoving hunks of mango into his mouth, the son of a bitch hacked off the poor guy's hands and left him gushing blood in agony alongside the road.

The revolting atrocities just didn't stop. At San Fernando, Pangasinan, the prisoners had been packed into sweltering, unventilated railroad boxcars and taken to Capas, then forced to trudge another seven miles on foot to Camp O'Donnell, a filthy, disease-ridden, incredibly crowded prison camp. Thousands didn't make it.

When he finished, Colonel Moses dropped his head into his trembling hands and was silent.

Art asked about other men he knew, and they were able to provide some answers. One of Art's fraternity brothers from UCLA, Adolph Meyer, had been killed early in the fighting on Bataan, but when last seen just before the surrender, Lars Jensen was still alive. No one knew what had happened to Archie McMaster.[12]

The next day, it poured furiously as they continued to talk. Art told the colonels what he'd learned about Horan and his guerrillas up north of Bontoc, again broaching the subject of surrender. Despite their West Point training and vastly greater military experience, Moses and Noble, too, had opted to escape rather than give up. They felt General Wainwright's blanket order had been given under duress, after his own surrender, rendering the order invalid. As to the Japanese threat to kill *all* their prisoners if every last USAFFE soldier didn't surrender, Colonel Moses said he thought it was a bluff. Art was glad to have his own decision reinforced.

But what were they to do now? What if they undertook guerrilla raids like those Cushing or Arnold and his boys had pulled off? Would that make them criminals or heroes? Here the colonels were less sure of their ground and admitted they'd be more enthusiastic if they had some further direction from MacArthur's headquarters in Australia.

Those decisions could be postponed for a while, though. Food was plentiful at Benneng, and the locals were glad to have the Americans. It was unlikely the Japanese would venture that far into the mountains before the end of the rainy season, and, in the meantime, the colonels planned to rest, put on some weight, and regain their strength.

S EVERAL DAYS LATER, THE SAME LOCAL OFFICIAL came up the hill, announced the arrival of two more Americans named Calvert and Spencer, and requested permission to bring them in. Art took off on a dead run down to greet his old buddies. After jubilant bear hugs, Art led them up to the hideout. The five of them spent the afternoon deep in conversation, often everyone talking at once, catching up on all the news.

Major Calvert told his story. He and Spence had gotten as far north as Natonin, in Bontoc Subprovince, by May 29, and there learned Colonel Horan and his officers had surrendered. News of their presence traveled like wildfire. Two days later Calvert got a message from Major Giitter, ordering him to surrender too. He stalled for time by requesting permission to delay so he and Spencer could go back to Lusod and round up their companion, Art Murphy, and the rest of their soldiers, all of whom he promised to surrender at Dalupirip at the end of June. Permission was granted. On the way south, they ran into a Philippine Scout sergeant who'd been at Camp John Hay. He told them he knew of at least sixty others in Ifugao who still wanted to fight. Calvert ordered him to tell those men to keep a low profile and await instructions from him regarding Major Giitter's surrender order.[13]

Major Calvert had every intention, at least at first, of keeping his promise to surrender all of them at Dalupirip. Art strongly disagreed, and now he had the backing of two other West Pointers, high-ranking lieutenant colonels at that. They debated for several days, but the argument was heavily one-sided, and in the end Calvert gave in. Spencer, who'd sat listening quietly through it all, heaved a sigh of relief.

WITH FIVE MEN, THE HUT was overcrowded. The helpful barrio official found Calvert, Spencer, and Art another place about a mile away. Some miners had built it, but hadn't used it in months. Entrance was by a hole in the floor, reached by a rickety bamboo ladder. It was equipped with beds, a table, and some chairs, all made of split bamboo lashed together with vines. It suited them fine. They worked like beavers, digging a trench latrine, patching thin spots in the thatched roof, gathering and stacking a supply of firewood, and scrounging some additional supplies to make the place more livable. Their prize was a large water bucket provided by the locals.

With the work done, Art settled down in a corner and, with the last of Emil Jorgensen's stationery, brought Lil up to date. He didn't mention names or anything of military significance, and only provided vague generalities as he described his travels in the mountains. There was always the chance his letters might fall into the wrong hands, and the last thing he wanted to do was give away their position. He had no way to mail his letters, but Father Gellynck at Bokod had offered to keep them and mail them if an opportunity presented itself.

Nearly every day, despite heavy rains, they hiked over to visit with the colonels and listen to the news. Most of it was discouraging. Even Doolittle's bombing raid over Tokyo shortly after the fall of Bataan seemed to have been done purely for show as there hadn't been any follow-through. It appeared the U.S. government's strategy was to simply wait until Japan exhausted herself. But listening to the news was something to relieve the monotony of the days. They also made good use of Emil Jorgensen's bridge cards as the two colonels knew the game and were always happy to join Murphy and Calvert to make up a foursome.

THE INCREDIBLE EFFICIENCY of the bamboo telegraph made it impossible to keep their whereabouts a secret. One day in late June, they were alerted that another American was asking about them, and soon Major Leo Giitter appeared at the hut in Benneng. They welcomed him at first, until they learned the purpose of his visit. He handed Major Calvert a letter.

"Dear Calvert. I know just how you feel about surrendering. I felt the same way at first. I love the hills, the mountains, the trees and freedom as much as you do. But I am a soldier! I ought to obey the orders of my Commanding General.

"When I decided to obey the order, I surrendered at Lubuagan, was taken first to Bontoc and then here [Santa Maria, Ilocos Sur]. At Baguio, General Homma, Imperial Japanese Army, said that he respected our group as a fine aggregation of soldiers; that we had been a thorn in his flesh for five months; that the men had fought like real soldiers and should be respected as such; but now that both Corregidor and Bataan had fallen, and that General Wainwright's surrender was on condition that I also surrender, that there was just one thing to do, to also surrender. He assured me that any actions that we have taken in conformity to International Law would be respected by him. We will all be assured of the privileges of prisoners of war.

"On about May 2nd, we had dispersed our forces. But General Wainwright agreed to surrender our personnel and equipment as part of the terms. He sent an old friend of mine on his staff, Colonel Galbraith, to me to give me my orders. He left yesterday for Manila. As a result of our conference, I am touring the west coast to induce my troops to surrender, hence my presence here.

"I am not a fifth columnist. I am not pro-Japanese! I am a soldier obeying the orders of my general. These are about the first words of every talk I give. The Japanese are paroling all troops that voluntarily surrender to either the barrio mayor or the Japanese commander. The men have to take no repeat no oath of allegiance to the Japanese. They merely surrender, their addresses are taken, and they are sent home.

"Lt. Ponces twice refused to surrender to Colonel Galbraith after personal contact. He was later caught, decapitated, and his head displayed in the plaza at Candon until it smelled too badly. This should be a warning.

"It is not expected that the American Army will again land in Luzon. The fate of the Philippines will be settled in other sectors and by naval warfare! It will be a long time before the Americans will have a chance to leave the Islands by regular boat. Those who now hide out will have to hide out for a very long time, constantly beset by fifth columnists and bounty hunters working for the Japs.

"Even now negotiations are underway for the exchange of prisoners, as you have probably heard over KGEI! We expect that we will all be exchanged by September 1st. But those of you who refuse to surrender will not only be tracked like beasts in the field, but will have no chance to be exchanged. And if the fates decree that the Islands should be held by the Japs, it will be mighty hard for one of you to get away later.

"Even though you American officers refuse to surrender, you have no right to subject the American enlisted men to this probable end. Your Americans, unlike your miners, have been members of the Regular Army. By failing to respect General Wainwright's orders, they are guilty of willful disobedience of orders, subject to court martial, will be deserters, will lose all pay and allowances due, and will lose the rights as a prisoner of war.

"If you do not care to surrender on the west coast, it is suggested that you surrender at Lubuagan, Bontoc, or Isabela.

"If there were any chance of an expeditionary force coming here, it would be different! But that is out. Two out of every three boats trying for Bataan and Corregidor were sunk! We can expect to have no expeditionary forces! We all respect your courage and fortitude in holding out, but we deplore your judgment. Use your head.

"You may think you are not subject to General Wainwright's orders as he is a prisoner. But you are all wet. General Wainwright expects you to obey orders.

"Inform the rest of the group of this information! If you want to see me personally, name the time and place to the Mayor of Burgos or Santa Maria and I will try to get there. I have no Japanese guard, having been paroled to General Wainwright.

"Best regards to the others.

"Sincerely, John P. Horan, Colonel, 121st Inf. (PA)"[14]

Giitter even claimed the Japanese were training a bunch of Filipino mercenaries to send into the mountains after un-surrendered Americans. They told him the Japanese might find some lowlanders they could dupe, but they certainly were *not* going to find any mercenaries among the loyal Igorots in the mountains!

The exact words they exchanged with Major Giitter are best not repeated. Basically, they told him to go to hell and take Colonel Horan and the insulting letter right along with him; that they had no intention of surrendering. Giitter ranted and raved some more but finally ran out of steam and got up to leave. But they had a problem. Giitter now knew their exact location, and they figured he wouldn't hesitate to share it with the Japanese. They considered shooting him, but he begged for his life and swore he'd keep their whereabouts a secret, so they let him go. A couple of days later, they wished they hadn't been so soft when it was reported back that Giitter had stopped in Bokod, confiscated arms and ammunition from their native soldiers camped out there, and delivered the weaponry to the Japanese.[15]

CHAPTER 15

GUERRILLA ACTION BEGINS, FIZZLES

July through December 1942

WHEN COLONEL MOSES LEARNED Calvert and Murphy had promoted themselves, he was in full support. He knew Colonel Horan had issued blanket promotions to everyone in his command effective February 24, and Calvert and Murphy would have been promoted, too, had Horan known where to find them. With the surrender of Horan and the growing shortage of officers, Colonel Moses also felt it was time for Spencer to have an officer's commission. The colonels had gotten a typewriter and a few office supplies from the locals, so Major Calvert drew up a formal document dated July 1, 1942. Art typed it, and it was endorsed by both the colonels.

On July 22, Art wrote to Lil:

"My dearest. Well, I'm now a captain, or at least semi-officially a captain! I can't tell you the circumstances, but please drink a little toast in my honor.

"We're still safe in our mountain retreat. The rains haven't let up; in fact, today is the first dry day in a week. But the Japs moved their outpost to the outskirts of Baguio, which is even farther from us. It's hard to keep from getting restless, especially since the news is no better. I think Japan is starting to retrench following the great damage to her fleet. If only the U.S. would start doing something somewhere! Sporadic air raids don't count unless followed by other action.

```
                HEADQUARTERS DETACHMENT 43rd INFANTRY (PS)
                     In the Field
                                              July 1, 1942

Subject: Promotion and appointment of men mentioned below

To: Commanding Officer, United States Army Guerilla Forces
     Northern Luzon, P.I.

1. Request that the promotions and appointment of the following
named men of this organization effective February 24, 1942 be
recommended for approval by you to higher headquarters:

                     TO BE MAJOR
        Captain Parker Calvert, O-30794, 43rd Infantry (PS)

                     TO BE CAPTAIN
        1st Lieutenant Arthur P. Murphy. O-334755, 43rd Infantry (PS)

                APPOINTED SECOND LIEUTENANT
        Private First Class Grafton Spencer, 6976817, Air Corps
             attached 43rd Infantry (PS)

2. Each of the above named men has been sworn in as Major,
Captain and Second Lieutenant respectively on this date by
personnel of this headquarters subject to confirmation and
approval by higher headquarters and has been furnished a
certificate to this effect.

3. The circumstances for the action taken in Paragraph 2, this
letter are as follows:
    a. On January 1, 1942 the above mentioned men were under
    Lieutenant Colonel John P. Horan's command. They were placed
    on detached service on this date at Carranglan, Nueva Ecija,
    P.I., for the purpose of attempting to rejoin United States
    Army Forces in the Far East.
    b. These men made their way south as far as Montalban, Rizal,
    P.I., but were unable to rejoin USAFFE as by the time they
    reached montalban, these forces had already retired into
    Bataan.
    c. Above mentioned men made their way North into the Mountain
    Province again. They attempted to find Colonel Horan by going
    further north, only to learn that he and a part of his
    command had surrendered to the Japanese on about June 2, 1942.
    It was also learned that blanket promotions and appointments
    had been made in Colonel Horan's command effective February
    24, 1942 and that apparently the above men had been overlooked
    for these promotions and appointments.
                     (over)
```

Promotion Orders, July 1, 1942 (Page 1)
"To Be Captain: 1st Lieutenant Arthur P. Murphy. 0-334755, 43rd Infantry (PS)"

d. The appointment of Private First Class Spencer as a
Second Lieutenant is necessary due to the shortage of officers
in the 43rd Infantry (PS) at this time.

(Signed) PARKER CALVERT
(Typed)   PARKER CALVERT
          Major, 43rd Infantry (PS)
          Commanding

1st Ind.

July 1, 1942

Headquarters, United States Army Guerrilla Forces
Northern Luzon, P.I.

To: Commanding Officer, 43rd Infantry (PS)
    Northern Luzon, P.I.

1. Recommend approval as of February 24, 1942 by higher headquarters subject to confirmation of statements made in basic
communication. This office was not in being on this date.

2. Promotions and appointment of officers recommended in basic
communication approved as of this date (July 1, 1942) by this
headquarters.

3. These officers urgently required at this time to carry on
activities.

(Signed) MARTIN MOSES
(Typed) MARTIN MOSES
         Lt. Colonel, U.S.A.
         CO. U.S.A. Guerrilla Forces
         North Luzon, P.I.

Witness:
(Signed) ARTHUR K. NOBLE
(Typed)   ARTHUR K. NOBLE
          Lt. Colonel, U.S.A.
          CO, 2nd PC Regt.
****
I certify that the matter appearing above and on the reverse
of this sheet is a true and correct copy of the original.

PARKER CALVERT
Major, U. S. Army

Promotion Orders, July 1, 1942 (Page 2)

"We've made credit arrangements with a storekeeper
in a nearby town. By giving him I.O.U.s, we get such luxuries
as sugar and soap. He gets his supplies via *cargadore* all the
way from Baguio. If anything happens to me, he'll send you a

bill after the war for my one-third share of the total. Please pay it.

"Every once in a while, I realize how you must feel. You cannot know whether I'm dead or alive, much less that I'm free and well. Sometimes at nite I try to send you a thought message that I'm okay. Other times I dream of coming home to you and the babies someday, but that's so hard when I can never be sure that I *will* come home. I dream of the wonderful things that have happened during my life, of which you and the babies are such a tremendous part. But this thing is so big that individuals have no right to stand against it. There are things bigger than men and women and their individual loves. I only hope that if I have to get mine, I get it in the last big finale, when it really counts. I often feel I have an appointment with destiny sometime during this show and that the way I meet it is going to be very important.

Good nite, *mon amore.*

Love, Art." [1]

The natives brought news that the Japanese were again sending patrols up into the mountains.

"My darling. Never a dull moment! The day before yesterday, we were warned the Japs were crossing the Agno River, so we hastily packed and hiked to another hideout almost on top of the mountain. That night the Japs moved into the town near our old residence. Yesterday we heard machine gun and mortar fire from the town, but learned later that the Japs were just showing off. Next we heard they went back toward the river. Then this morning we learned they retraced their steps during the nite and are now in a valley in back of our mountain. If the heat doesn't let up pretty soon, we're going to have to move even higher into the mountains. That's why I'll 'mail' this letter as soon as I can. If we get out of this present spot okay, there are lots of mountains left, though this is lousy weather to move in. It rains almost continuously, and on the trails it's all mud and mire. But if the Japs can move in it, I guess we can too.

"Whenever we get a scare like this, where I'm in danger of losing my life, my only desire to live is for my family. That's all I want out of the rest of my life, just to be with you again, to hold you all so close in my arms. If I don't come back to you, know that my last thought was of you and the babies. I love you. Art."[2]

On August 3, Art added a little more to his letter before sending it down via runner to Father Gellynck in Bokod:

"P.S. Just before the excitement about the Japs, we heard MacArthur sent a code message over KGEI releasing all un-surrendered troops from Wainwright's command and hence obedience to his surrender order. So I guess I won't get court-martialed after all. Hooray!"[3]

Because of increasing Japanese patrols, all five of the Americans moved to another well-hidden place near the little barrio of Karao[4], not far from Benneng.

ON SEPTEMBER 30, a fellow named Dennis Molintas was brought in by one of the guards. A tall, well-educated Igorot, he'd been a schoolteacher before the war. Molintas knew of several resistance outfits headquartered in the mountains around Baguio, one organized jointly by him and his fellow Igorot, Bado Dangwa. Though a longtime reservist in the Philippine Army, Molintas had not been called to active duty, so Colonel Moses promptly activated him with the rank of first lieutenant. Bado Dangwa reported in at Karao a few days later and was commissioned by Colonel Moses as a third lieutenant.[5] The joint Molintas-Dangwa unit was designated by Colonel Moses as M Company, 12th Infantry (Philippine Army), consisting of forty to fifty men, most of them reservists or former Dangwa Tranco employees.

A second unit was headed by Sergeant Emilio Velasco, who'd been with then Captain Calvert's Company B, 1st Battalion Infantry (Philippine Scouts), at Camp John Hay. According to Molintas, Velasco had several dozen armed men at the barrio of Sagpat in the municipality of Kibungan about twenty-five miles north of Baguio.[6, 7]

A third group was led by Lieutenant Rufino Baldwin, who'd fought and surrendered on Bataan, escaped the Death March, and made his way to eastern Pangasinan Province, where he'd joined Charles Cushing's guerrillas. After Baldwin regained his health, Cushing had sent him to operate in Benguet Province, where he now commanded 300 men. Baldwin's unit, designated the 2nd Battalion, 11th Infantry (Philippine Army), was headquartered at the barrio of Tocod in the Itogon mining district southeast of Baguio.[8, 9]

Colonel Moses immediately dispatched coded messages via runner to the various leaders, asserting his command over all guerrillas in North Luzon. He requested information as to troop strength, areas controlled, number of weapons, rounds of ammunition, and any other information germane to the launch of raids and ambushes against the Japanese. He also sent messages to the mayors of the barrios, ordering them to round up all arms and ammunition being hidden by civilians under their control and turn it over for use by the guerrillas.

As information and munitions came trickling in, Moses began formulating plans for coordinated attacks against enemy garrisons and patrols throughout Benguet Subprovince, to be launched on October 15, as soon as the rainy season ended and the trails dried out.[10] With each passing day morale improved. They were looking more and more like a real army.

D URING THE FIRST WEEK OF SEPTEMBER, a runner from Lieutenant Baldwin's unit came in with news of the arrival in the mountains of two more escaped American officers, Major Russell Volckmann and Captain Donald Blackburn. Two more old friends from Baguio resurrected from the dead! Colonel Moses sent word back, ordering them to report to Karao for a meeting. They arrived a few days later, guided by Herb Swick and accompanied by two Filipino sidekicks.

Colonel Moses took the opportunity to commission Swick a second lieutenant.[11] Herb had been operating for many months as a guerrilla in Pangasinan Province, in the area controlled by Charles Cushing, and his formal induction was long overdue.

Volckmann and Blackburn were skinny and emaciated, and Don was suffering the latest in a long series of debilitating malaria attacks. Health issues aside, they all had a grand reunion and swapped stories.

After becoming separated from Moses and Noble on Bataan, Volckmann and Blackburn had also traveled by night and eventually reached the Zambales Mountains and a refugee camp set up by two American sugar plantation owners, Martin and William Fassoth. The two had spent weeks there, receiving rudimentary medical attention and regular food. They told interesting tales about the Fassoth camp, about constant quarreling and dissention between the American enlisted men and the few officers there, but the place had provided a welcome sanctuary while they recovered enough strength to move on.

They'd been aided by the Huks, the communist guerrilla organization headquartered on Mount Arayat in the central plains, the same organization Calvert, Murphy, Spencer, and Jagoe had so carefully avoided on their trek north. They'd also gotten help from a group of guerrillas put together by Lieutenant Robert Lapham around Umingan in Pangasinan Province. Finally, they'd spent time at Charles Cushing's guerrilla camp near San Nicolas. It had taken them five months to get back to the northern mountains, but they were very grateful to have made it.[12, 13]

Volckmann and Blackburn reported to Colonel Moses for duty, but their immediate concern was their health. Lieutenant Swick led them over to Oding for treatment by Doc and Daisy Biason. Volckmann was in better shape than Blackburn, and as soon as he was back on his feet, Moses made him a liaison officer, in charge of coordinating the intelligence and guerrilla activities of the units commanded by Rufino Baldwin, Charles Cushing, and Robert Lapham. As he became able, Blackburn was assigned to assist.[14, 15]

TO PREPARE FOR THE COMING OFFENSIVE, on October 1, Colonel Moses ordered Calvert, Murphy, and Spencer, along with the men of their Detachment, 43rd Infantry (PS), to move forty-five miles west across the Mountain Trail and into Kibungan and Kapangan, assume command of Sergeant Emilio Velasco's group at Sagpat, and further plan and coordinate the upcoming missions with the unit of Lieutenants Bado Dangwa and Dennis Molintas.[16] They accomplished the move in three days, successfully avoiding a snoopy Japanese patrol on the Mountain Trail and inducting a few new recruits along the way.

The guerrilla attacks had several objectives: to raid a few specified targets in Baguio where informants had advised that arms and ammunition were being stored; to destroy again the roads and bridges the Japanese had repaired around Baguio; and to knock out a number of garrisons in the surrounding mountains in order to capture more badly needed arms, ammunition, and explosives.

ART'S TURN CAME ON OCTOBER 21. Major Calvert ordered him to assemble a platoon and take out the Japanese garrison at Kilometer Post 21, thirteen miles north of Baguio along the
Mountain Trail. Art's plan was simple enough. With eighteen men,
he would approach the garrison in the early morning hours and
remain hidden in the thick brush across the road until the Japanese
awoke and came outside for their morning exercises. Then, upon his
order, they would open fire.

Just after midnight, with one of Velasco's men acting as guide,
they followed an obscure trail and arrived at their destination around
4 a.m. on the 21st. Once the men were in position, they crouched
silently and waited.

The garrison consisted of a rectangular frame building with a
long porch across the front and a single door at its center. Wide windows flanked the door, and several more windows were spaced evenly along the rear wall. A lone Japanese guard dozed in his chair to the
right of the entrance, his rifle languishing in his lap. Everything was
quiet. Then one of the men sneezed. Instantly, the guard jumped to
his feet, hollering to his comrades asleep inside the building. At the
same time, one of Art's men panicked and opened fire. The guard
dropped in his tracks, but the unmistakable rat-tat-tat-tat-tat of machine gun fire erupted as the Japanese inside the building returned
fire through the open windows.

Realizing the entire operation was going to hell, Art took off at a
dead run to his right, crossed the road fifty feet beyond the garrison,
and then circled back through the darkness until he was behind the
building. He inched forward on his belly until he could make out
a window, grabbed one of two hand grenades attached at his belt,
jerked the pin, threw it as hard as he could, and dove for cover behind a downed tree. The grenade smashed a window and exploded
inside. In moments, the entire building was engulfed in flames.

A number of Japanese came running around the garrison, and
Art picked them off, one after another, while his men wiped out the

rest. The whole operation took less than fifteen minutes. Then, save for the crackling of the flames, it was quiet. They gathered as much booty as they could carry and melted back into the forest. They came away with a dozen rifles and numerous ammunition clips. Unfortunately, the machine guns were lost in the fire. Other than two superficial wounds, they didn't lose a single man.

Several days later, after local natives stacked the corpses of the dead Japanese, Art was given credit for seven bodies at the rear of the garrison. He was later awarded a Silver Star for the operation.[17]

AFTER THE WAR, considerable armchair quarterbacking took place in Washington and elsewhere regarding the October offensive. It wasn't that the attacks hadn't been effective, for they certainly had been; rather, the critics claimed the entire operation was ill-timed and premature. Perhaps they were right, because almost immediately the Japanese brought in 6,000 reinforcements, as well as a formidable array of tanks and armored vehicles, and began an intensive retaliatory operation aimed at tracking down and eliminating all guerrilla resistance. They gave up trying to curry favor with the natives and instead got very tough.

By offering sizeable rewards, the enemy was able to recruit barrio natives as spies, and through them determine which barrios had provided guerrilla support. Time and again, a spy-led Japanese patrol entered a suspected barrio and ordered the inhabitants to assemble. The spy, wearing a burlap-sack hood with small eye slits, sat in a chair, and as the inhabitants were paraded before him, fingered those who had helped the guerrillas. The alleged culprits were lined up, brought to their knees, and summarily beheaded as their horrified neighbors and family members looked on. To drive the lesson home, the Japanese confiscated their livestock and burned the village to the ground as the rest of the hapless natives scattered.

In other cases, where they obtained the identity of a particular guerrilla but were unable to track him down, the Japanese grabbed the man's family and starved and tortured women and children in an effort to gain further information. Kicking and punching were common, as was burning them with live cigarettes.

In cases where a guerrilla was captured, he or she was tortured in the most hideous ways imaginable to obtain information. A favorite method of the Japanese was the water cure. Tying their prisoner down, gallons of water were forced down the throat until the abdomen was distended to a grotesque degree, whereupon the ruthless captors stomped on the prisoner's stomach until the water ruptured interior organs and forced its way out through the eyes, nose, ears, anus, and bladder. Another method involved tying a prisoner's thumbs together behind his back with a rope, which was then threaded over a tree limb or a hook in the ceiling. The loose end of the rope was pulled slowly, lifting the screaming man gradually until his shoulders dislocated. He might then be lowered just until his toes touched a stool, momentarily relieving some of the pressure, but if he still refused to talk, they'd kick the stool out from under him, causing agonizing pain and doing irreparable damage to the prisoner's shoulders.[18] Sometimes they used a knife to scrape the skin from the bottoms of a man's feet and forced salt into the wounds.

THE NATIVES WERE TERRIFIED, spies were everywhere, and it became virtually impossible for guerrillas to obtain food or shelter. Hundreds were caught and killed. Others scattered and fled higher into the mountains.

Just as they had done nine months earlier, Calvert, Murphy, and Spence traveled only at night, dodging frequent Japanese patrols. They ended up during the second week of November in a primitive barrio high in the mountains of western Ifugao Subprovince, where they finally found sanctuary in a filthy *nipa* shack built over a stone-walled pig pit. The stench was incredible. There were no windows, only a small opening in one wall and a crude bamboo ladder. They were provided a wooden bucket in which to relieve themselves. An open fire smoldered on a dirt-and-rock foundation in one corner, but there was no way for smoke to escape except through the low doorway. A layer of gooey soot coated the walls and ceiling thatch. The air was barely breathable. Lungs burned. Eyes watered. They couldn't show their faces during the day. The place was so offensive that even rats and vermin wanted nothing to do with it.

Twice each day an old man delivered a tray containing chunks of boiled pork, heavy with grayish, translucent fat, and a few *camotes*, also boiled. They were provided an earthenware jug of opaque, fetid water for drinking. Major Calvert got very sick, while Art and Spence suffered to a lesser degree.[19]

At first, Art just clenched his teeth and tried to get through the long hours and days. Then he came up with an idea, a sort of psychological approach. Sitting on the floor, his back against the filthy wall, he closed his eyes and concentrated on draining his mind of every notion he'd ever acquired about what was normal or proper or expected. Visualizing a blackboard covered with jumbled writing, he slowly wiped the blackboard clean. He felt new, reborn, unfettered by what had gone before. As he breathed, he inhaled the smells as not revolting, just ordinary. The grimy appearance of the natives became ordinary, their habits ordinary, to simply be observed and accepted without judgment. He paid closer attention to their language and made an effort to learn. Later, he even tried chewing betel nut in place of craving cigarettes. Betel nut produced interesting, pleasant sensations in his body, and the blood-red stains on his lips and mouth brought roars of laughter from Calvert and Spence when he'd give a wide Cheshire-cat grin. In this process of mental reorganization, a curious thing happened. The cold knot of fear deep in Art's belly slowly evaporated, as did any fear of pain or death. In the coming months and years of the war, he repeated this mind exercise whenever uncertainty or depression threatened to swallow him. He convinced Spencer to try the method, but Calvert thought they were both nuts.

MAJOR CALVERT SUFFERED from constant diarrhea. After six weeks he'd had enough. Japs or no Japs, he decided they were going to get the hell out of their hole and head back to the lovely country north of Baguio, where fresh vegetables and even strawberries were grown, where the natives were more civilized and more familiar with the ways of Americans. Art and Spencer wholeheartedly agreed. Japanese patrols were everywhere, though, clogging the roads and barrios along all established routes. This time they'd have to hike south-southwest down the lofty spine of the Cordillera Central, give the mining district and Baguio a wide berth, and then circle their way back north to Kapangan. Perhaps Emilio Velasco, Bado Dangwa, or Dennis Molintas were still alive and loose somewhere in that area.[20]

It was a nightmare of a trip, especially for Calvert, who often vomited. For two days, they ate cold *camotes* and shriveled pork. When that was gone, they existed on roots and berries, although Art and Spencer did catch one fat lizard, which roasted up nicely. Even the persnickety Calvert didn't grumble and ate as much as he could keep down.

Finally, they approached the outskirts of Santa Maria, then moved west through familiar territory, ultimately reaching Ansagan, the barrio where Art and Herb Swick had successfully commandeered rifles and ammunition many months before. The diminutive old barrio chief remembered Art, and although the poor man trembled and was obviously scared to death, he provided a hot meal and a place to sleep.

By late afternoon of the following day, they had worked their way to the top of a ridge overlooking the Bued River and Kennon Road, a Japanese checkpoint clearly visible at a bridge crossing below. Two armed guards loitered a while and then disappeared inside. The three watched until dark, then made their way cautiously down the brushy hillside, waited a while longer, and then silently crept past the checkpoint, across the bridge, and melted into the under-growth on the other side. The two guards didn't stir.

The next day's hurdle was Naguilian Road, the second of the Baguio access roads. Here there was plenty of traffic. Huge open trucks rumbled in both directions, moving copper ore down to the port at San Fernando. Again, they hid in the brush, waiting for darkness and a break in the traffic. When finally there was a stretch with no headlights visible in either direction, they slipped noiselessly across and disappeared into the night.

Having covered 140 miles of rugged mountains, by late after-noon on the eighth day they dropped down into the municipality of Kapangan with its beautiful rice and vegetable terraces. In the middle of a field, several women chopped their way up and down bright green cabbage rows. After watching them for half an hour, the men cautiously approached.

Mabuhay, Art called out softly.

Momentarily startled, the eldest broke into a broad grin, hop-ping over a dozen rows, scrubbing her muddy hands on her skirt. *Hello*, she replied. *You American, yes?*

When Major Calvert explained they were looking for some hot food and a place to stay, her smile widened. *I know safe house. My tio have safe house. You come.*

Twenty minutes later, they were introduced to the woman's un-cle, her *tio*. His lip curled as he explained that before the enemy came, he had for years sold his cabbages to the military at Camp John Hay, but now the Japanese grabbed most of his crop and paid him nothing. *America our friend*, he said. *Jap is devil.*

After a generous hot meal of rice and cabbage, the men fell asleep, exhausted, and dreamed that 1943 would bring better times, perhaps even an end to the wretched war.

CHAPTER 16

BUCKLING DOWN IN THE BAY AREA

January through December 1942

LILLIAN'S NEW JOB PROVED A BOON in many ways. Roberta Gallup was hired too. Often they ate their brown-bag lunches on a bench overlooking the three bustling Fort Mason piers, the sparkling San Francisco Bay, and the beautiful Golden Gate Bridge. Bert hadn't heard from Brew either, and though they both lived with the same gnawing fear, they concentrated on each day's news and tried to cope with their daily challenges.

Major Gillmore took a special interest in the women whose husbands were still in the Philippines. He tacked a map up on his office wall. Often, during morning coffee breaks, he called them in to explain and interpret the current war news, pointing out specific locations on the map. Lil and Bert became familiar with the geography and with the progress of the war. The broadcasts reported the American forces were bravely defending the Philippines, though from time to time Major Gillmore expressed concern that they weren't getting the whole story. As the months went by, his skepticism proved well-founded.

Bert continued attending the Philippine Wives' Club meetings, and Lillian went when she could. After work one evening each week they rolled bandages for the Red Cross. The camaraderie among the wives was uplifting, and they felt they were doing all they could to help the common cause. Most of these women lived nearby, though, and many didn't have children. Lillian envied their freedom and flexibility.

Mildred Thurman proved worth her weight in gold, and for a while things went along smoothly. But it was too good to last. Lillian had known she was married, but not that she was already several months pregnant. On February 1, her husband received orders to ship out, and Mildred decided to move back to her mother's home in Texas, leaving Lil with the same problem: *Who was going to care for the girls?* It had become nearly impossible to find women for in-home child care. She finally convinced Mildred to stay through February, and Lillian Sr. agreed to quit her job at the girls' co-op and take over on March 1. With Lil's salary and Art's allotment as their sole support, they'd have to find a less expensive place to live.

They settled on a two-bedroom stucco bungalow on Spaulding Avenue in Berkeley. The location was good because Lucille could continue attending University High School, where she was a sophomore. They moved in on March 1. Lil and the girls shared the larger of the bedrooms, and Lillian Sr. and Lucille shared the smaller one.

Lil continued writing to Art, placing Clipper stamps on her letters and dropping them off weekly at the post office for delivery as soon as mail service resumed. She hadn't heard anything more, but told herself that Art was right in the thick of the war and would answer her letters when he could. Then, in late March, the mailman returned all her letters, stamped RETURN TO SENDER, SERVICE SUSPENDED. Lil felt a terrible sense of finality in those words. She began keeping a notebook for Art, describing local events and how the girls were growing and changing.

One of the first entries wasn't such a happy one. Just home from work one night, Lil was appalled to find the girls covered with bruises. Eleanor had decided she wanted something from the top drawer of the tall dresser in the bedroom, and she'd dragged a little wooden chair over so she could reach it. Trisha wanted to help and tried climbing onto the chair too. The chair tipped, Eleanor grabbed for the open drawer, and the heavy dresser came down on top of them both. Only the sturdiness of the chair prevented more serious injuries, but both girls had cuts and scrapes and were badly bruised. Though it wasn't her fault, Lillian Sr. felt terrible about not keeping a closer eye on them.

Lil recorded other observations, including the cost of food. Only days after Pearl Harbor, prices began to skyrocket, and by spring everyone was reeling. Eggs went from a quarter to forty-nine cents a dozen, butter from a quarter to forty-four cents a pound, milk from less than a dime to fourteen cents a quart. Vegetables were very high. Most fresh vegetables in California had been grown by Japanese farmers, and because the government had frozen the assets of all Japanese, they no longer had the money to plant their crops. Even canned goods doubled in price because of the drain on the supply. Lil and her mother did everything they could to stretch their food dollars.

The government established the Office of Price Administration (OPA), which instituted a rationing plan to curb runaway inflation and ensure that items in limited supply were distributed equitably. Sugar became the first item rationed, followed quickly by meat, butter, fats, oils, and most cheeses. Each man, woman, and child was issued a weekly War Ration Book containing numbered stamps that could be used at any store to buy different commodities at a set price for a week. Even if stamps remained unused at the end of the week, the entire book had to be turned in before a new book was issued, thereby discouraging the stockpiling of scarce items. It wasn't long before clothing, shoes, coffee, gasoline, tires, and heating oil were rationed too. Gasoline allotments varied based on how far one commuted to work, but in all cases it left very little extra for personal excursions. Bicycles became a valuable form of transportation.

The government strongly encouraged the planting of "victory gardens" to alleviate the vegetable shortages, and most families began growing their own tomatoes, cucumbers, carrots, corn, zucchini, and potatoes so the commercial canned supplies could be shipped to the troops overseas. Lil and Lucille cleared the weeds and planted a small garden in the back.

The War Production Board was established, which in turn instituted a nationwide propaganda campaign to encourage every American to support the war effort without complaint. A scrap-metal program got underway to gather enough raw materials so the country's steel plants could produce at full capacity. School, church, and scouting groups went door to door to collect everything from extra coat hangers to unused garden implements and kitchen utensils. Newspapers and rags, too, were collected and recycled.

In a further effort to curb inflation, as well as fund the massive costs of the war, the government issued War Bonds in denominations ranging from $25 to $1,000. A public-relations campaign urged every citizen to participate. Rallies featuring Hollywood stars provided entertainment along with encouragement to buy bonds. War Bond stamp albums were issued, and the little red stamps were sold everywhere, including at the

War Bond stamp album

schools, at ten cents apiece. It took $18.70 worth of stamps to fill an album. Then a nickel was placed in a slot to bring the total to $18.75, and the album was then exchanged for a $25 War Bond maturing in ten years. The rate of return on these bonds was below market, but nearly everyone felt it their patriotic duty to buy them. Millions were sold.

In mid-March, Roberta came to work bubbling with the news that radio station KGEI was resuming their morale-boosting broadcast segment. Once a week, following the evening war news, they allowed wives and mothers of soldiers serving in the Pacific to send on-air greetings to their loved ones. Lil and Roberta promptly signed up. They got a call to appear at the station at two o'clock on April 10. At the station they were given instructions as to what they could and couldn't say on the air. After jotting down their messages, station personnel reviewed them and eliminated anything deemed inappropriate. They were allowed one minute each. Lil finished her message with an unscripted *I love you, my darling*, and then her time was up and it was Roberta's turn. As they drove back to work afterward, they crossed their fingers that somehow Art and Brew would hear them.

Shortly after the KGEI broadcast, news broke of the surrender of the American forces on Bataan. The civilian community was stunned. Major Gillmore had speculated about this eventuality, though, and now he continued to make educated guesses as to what would happen next. The last Roberta had heard, Brew was still on Corregidor, where General Wainwright's forces were holding out in spite of the fall of Bataan. As for Art, there were only more questions. Major Gillmore said that some of the troops at Baguio had escaped east over the mountains, and some had made it to Bataan while others had not. If Art had been with those who made it, and *if* he was still alive, he was probably now a prisoner of the Japanese. The major also pointed out the towering mountain ranges north and east of Baguio and speculated this would be where stranded Americans would likely hide out if they'd never reached Bataan.

On May 6, General Wainwright surrendered on Corregidor, America's last stronghold in the Philippines. Major Gillmore explained that now *all* American forces were being ordered to surrender.

The Japanese had given verbal assurances that they would abide by the Geneva Convention regarding the treatment of prisoners of war and that lists of their prisoners would soon be provided via Geneva to the American government. All they could do was wait.

In the meantime, activity escalated everywhere. The government expanded the military draft. All men between the ages of eighteen and thirty-five were required to register, and those between eighteen and twenty-five, without dependents, were eligible for immediate call-up. Around the country, factories converted from peacetime manufacturing to the production of planes, tanks, trucks, guns, and ammunition. Women who'd never held a paying job went to work in offices and factories, replacing men now on the battlefronts.

In the Bay Area, the mood of the people was serious and busi-nesslike. Nearly everyone understood the challenges facing the country and stepped up to do his or her share. Art's younger broth-ers both suffered from ulcers and were classified 4-F, physically unfit for active military service. They were machinists and promptly went to work retooling plants around the country for aircraft production. Lil's brother Cecil shipped out before the summer was over. Her sis-ter Charlotte's young husband, Bryce, fresh out of high school, went to work at Mare Island Naval Shipyard in Vallejo.

The Women's Army Auxiliary Corps (WAAC) was formed, and on May 15, the first West Coast contingent was assigned to the San Francisco Port of Embarkation. The WAAC sounded more exciting than typing, so Lil tried to join. While being married wouldn't have rendered her ineligible, having two young children did, so she had to be content with office work.[1]

Major Gillmore began delegating more responsibility to Lillian.

Because all new-hires would be involved in the top-secret pro-curement of war materiel and the shipping of Army personnel and cargo to highly strategic locations all over the Pacific, each had to undergo rigorous security screening. Lil conducted these interviews, prepared the reports, and then followed up with letters to former employers and police agencies in the hometowns from which the employees had come to ensure they'd never been involved in any questionable activities. The reports were forwarded to the Provost Marshal's office, the San Francisco Police Department, and the Federal Bureau of Investigation. She kept all parties abreast of new developments, and followed each case until the applicant was either hired or rejected. She also counseled new employees as to the need for absolute secrecy about every facet of their work, a policy commonly called "Zip Your Lip."[2]

Lillian generally worked without supervision and made many of her own decisions. Lieutenant Colonel Gillmore was so pleased with her performance that in June he recommended that she be promoted to assistant clerk. In July the promotion was confirmed, and her salary increased to $135 month.

The first good news on the Pacific war front came on August 7, 1942, when U.S. Marines landed on the beaches at Guadalcanal in the Solomon Islands. Bay Area radio stations made a big fuss over it, but Colonel Gillmore advised confidentially that he thought it would take many months and heavy casualties before the island could be secured.

A FTER EIGHT MONTHS OF LIL'S SIX-DAY-A-WEEK routine, everyone at home was feeling the stress. She left for work before the girls were up in the morning, and they were asleep when she arrived home. Although she didn't complain openly, Lillian Sr. looked haggard and was exhausted most of the time. The only way

Oakland Army Base panorama

Lil could think to improve the situation was to reduce her commute time and help out more at home.

In addition to its Fort Mason location, in 1941, the Port of Embarkation had begun planning a huge new branch on the Oakland waterfront. By the fall of 1942, it was nearing completion and hiring was underway. Lil applied for a transfer and within weeks was scheduled for an interview at the Intelligence, Security, and Technical Information Division at Oakland Army Base.

On the day of her interview, publicity photos were being taken. Cynthia, Lil's black 1934 Dodge sedan, can be seen parked fourth from the left in the line of cars at the bottom.

Her interview went well. With Colonel Gillmore's superb recommendation, and pending further checking of her references, she was hired effective November 1. As the new job would entail working with highly classified documents, she underwent additional in-depth background security checks, including fingerprinting. Lil and her new boss, Captain Francis Joseph Dillon, got along well from the start.

The overall mood in the new office was serious, with very little small talk and virtually no joking or teasing among the employees. Each employee worked long hours.

Everyone seemed to have a case of spy jitters and was constantly on the alert for possible arsonists, saboteurs, or enemy agents. When any unusual incident occurred at the base, no matter how insignificant it might appear, Lil compiled a confidential report covering the investigation, which, after review by Captain Dillon, was placed in a locked file cabinet.

She also supervised completion of government-required loyalty investigation forms for all civilian personnel, both old and new, at Oakland Army Base and the Army Air Forces Terminal in Oakland. She worked without supervision, and before long other intelligence units around the Bay Area began sending their clerks to Oakland Army Base, where Lil conducted day-long training sessions in the proper methods to be used in completing the forms.[3]

She kept classified documents covered and out of sight on her desk, and all such documents were locked up in Captain Dillon's safe at night. The reports she typed required many copies. Even if a piece of carbon paper had been used multiple times, she couldn't throw it in her wastebasket. It had to be burned in Captain Dillon's presence at the end of each day.[4]

The "Zip Your Lip" policy presented her biggest challenge. Even though most of her waking hours were spent at her desk, she couldn't discuss her job with Roberta when they'd talk by phone, and even her mother had no idea what Lil did all day. If she ran into problems or had questions, the only person with whom she was permitted to confide was Captain Dillon himself.

At home, while things improved a bit for Lillian Sr., they still had no time for relaxation or entertainment. Lil's twenty-eighth birthday passed unnoticed in early October, as did Art's and Lil's fifth wedding anniversary on November 27.

In December, with the success of Operation Watchtower, the Japanese finally began withdrawing from the Solomon Islands[5], and General MacArthur's troops were making inroads into parts of New Guinea, finally recovering some of the territory lost to the Japanese.[6] When Lil checked the map on their office wall, though, it was evident the Solomons and New Guinea were more than 2,000 miles from the Philippines and even farther from North Luzon.

Lil had continued wearing Art's sweater to bed at night and for nearly a year had carefully hand-washed it. One day it got tossed by mistake into their old wringer washer and shrank to the size of a doll's sweater. It was a small thing, but Lil shut herself in the bathroom and wept over its loss. There were so many little losses.

Christmas of 1942 was subdued, only a small tree and a few toys for the girls. Lil worried ceaselessly, for it had been more than a year since she'd heard from Art and nearly two years since he'd sailed off on the USAT *Grant*.

CHAPTER 17

___

GUERRILLA ACTION RESUMES

January to March 1943

WHILE ART AND HIS COMPANIONS may have dreamed the year 1943 would bring better times, perhaps even an end to the war, the next morning snapped them back to reality. As the uncle talked, it was evident they had plenty of catching up to do.

Their host advised that Sergeant Emilio Velasco was still loose and holed up a few miles to the north. Calvert immediately sent him a message.

The next night, under cover of darkness, Velasco appeared at the door, accompanied by a couple of armed bodyguards. He appeared in good health, and also brought good news. Although many guerrillas had surrendered or been caught in the Japanese mopping-up operation, Bado Dangwa and Dennis Molintas were still alive and free, along with five dozen of their men. Calvert ordered Sergeant Velasco to inform Dangwa and Molintas they were back and were ready for some action. The outlook, although tentative, held promise.

Sergeant Velasco also described the current political setup. The supreme Japanese commander in the Philippines, General Masaharu Homma, was headquartered at the General Hospital in Baguio[1], and now a thousand troops occupied the city. The Japanese had also established garrisons in the municipalities of Kapangan and Kibungan to the north and Atok to the east. A local garrison numbered thirty to forty men, comprised of enemy-controlled Philippine Constabulary or regular Japanese soldiers, or a combination of the two. Smaller outposts, manned by two or three armed guards, were spaced every few miles along major roadways, and all vehicles had to stop and present papers verifying their identity and mission. Ten-man patrols routinely fanned out from the garrisons to search for guerrillas or citizens suspected of aiding guerrillas. Many local civilians had been rounded up, brutally tortured, and murdered. Whole families had been wiped out, even whole villages.

The provincial towns and barrios had been subdivided into neighborhood associations controlled by an overseer, a Filipino citizen who'd been coerced or bought off by the Japanese. The overseer wore many hats, from census-taker to tax-collector to spy to administrator, and was answerable to his local garrison commander for the conduct of every person in his area. The Japanese now maintained iron-fisted control of food and consumer goods of every type. Ration books had been issued to each civilian, but the rations were meager, the bulk of all goods diverted to support enemy troops. Strict rules of conduct governed the everyday actions of the natives, and infractions were dealt with swiftly. Something as innocuous as failing to bow properly to a Japanese soldier on the street brought vicious kicks and slaps.

The only monkey wrench in this grand plan of the Japanese to subdue and control the Philippine people was that many of the natives maintained a fierce loyalty to the United States and were willing to feign allegiance to the Japanese while simultaneously doing whatever they could to help the resistance. Already a fledgling network of spies was in place in Baguio. Some worked for the Japanese directly while others worked in local shops and businesses, always alert to pick up information.

Not all remained loyal. Some collaborated with the enemy, and it was a tricky business to know for certain who was on which side at any given time. A wrong guess or assumption could result in—at this point, Sergeant Velasco made a graphic motion with his hands to portray his head being severed and rolling onto the floor.

Under these circumstances, Velasco cautioned that it would be dangerous to remain in the densely populated areas of Kapangan. He would find the three Americans a more secure hiding place farther up in the mountains. It was already common knowledge that there simply weren't enough garrison soldiers to cover every inch of the rugged territory, and the enemy patrols had yet to penetrate the higher elevations.

They thanked Sergeant Velasco and their hosts for their help. Calvert said they'd be ready to move as soon as they got the signal.

THREE DAYS LATER, IT WAS TIME. Before dawn, in a heavy mist, the uncle loaded them along with two bundles of supplies into his rusty pickup. The rutted dirt road wound north-northwest through vegetable terraces for ten miles, gradually gaining elevation. It was still dark when the uncle turned off his headlights, veered into a thick grove of trees, and stopped. Sergeant Velasco was waiting. He was accompanied by Private Amando Bolislis, a young Igorot who had been inducted into the Detachment, 1st Battalion, 43rd Infantry (Philippine Scouts), several months earlier. Rounding out the escort party, two native *cargadores* effortlessly hoisted the two supply bundles onto their backs. Calvert thanked the uncle for his help and promised to stay in touch. He hopped into his truck, executed a fine three-point turn, and disappeared into the night.

Sergeant Velasco—or Emilio, as he asked to be called—cautioned that the local Japanese garrison wasn't far, so they needed to hurry, while the fog was still thick. He took the lead, followed by Calvert, Murphy, Spencer, and Bolislis. The cargo-bearers brought up the rear.

After half an hour, the gentle trail became a steep, rocky ascent. The path zigzagged frequently, tracking a stream churning furiously down through a narrow canyon. Ragged pine trees and tangled undergrowth vied for limited light. In five miles, they gained 6,000 feet, nearly straight up from the valley floor. It was a tough climb, but they didn't complain. By now they weren't strangers to the steep mountains of the Cordillera Central.

As suddenly as the climb had begun, it was over. They found themselves on a broad plateau well above the valley mist. In all directions, the morning sun illuminated spectacular vistas as tier upon tier of sharp peaks stretched away to the north and east. To the west were low, rolling, thickly forested hills, and, farther west, a glimpse of the shimmering South China Sea. Back in the direction from which they'd come, the Amburayan River sparkled far below, flanked by the terraced fields and scattered enclaves of *nipa* huts they'd passed earlier. It felt like the top of the world.

After a brief rest, they veered into the hills to the west. Emilio steered them across a *camote* patch and up to a typical Igorot mountain dwelling, elevated several feet off the ground on thick wooden posts. Their new benefactor was waiting outside to greet them, clad only in a G-string and smiling broadly, exposing stained, picket-fence teeth. He carried an infant in a sling on his back. A young boy, perhaps seven or eight, peered tentatively from behind the man, his eyes as big as saucers. Emilio performed the introductions. The old man's name was multi-syllabic and unintelligible to their ears, but his handshake was warm and his smile engaging and genuine. After a short conversation, punctuated by gestures and pointing, Emilio and the old man led them a couple of hundred feet farther into the trees.

Their new headquarters was a freshly constructed, larger version of the old man's hut, elevated on posts and roofed in tightly woven thatch. Two unscreened windows provided cross-ventilation. Inside, several native-style beds and a long table and benches lined the woven-grass walls. Emilio untied the first bundle and produced towels, a bar of soap, matches, a hatchet, a shovel, two cooking pots, bamboo cups, a bucket and ladle, and several woven hemp mats. The second bundle held writing tablets, pencils, and a Spanish-language lesson book along with smaller packages of dried meats, mangoes, and bananas. Emilio explained that while their host family would cook their regular meals, these were for snacks. He led them another hundred feet to a sheltered spring where sparkling water gushed from a fissure between mossy boulders, spilling into a rock-ringed pool below. Brilliant red blooms decorated the overhanging foliage. After their recent accommodations, this was truly the Ritz!

At sundown, their hosts staged a *cañao* to celebrate their arrival. All the neighbors turned out, drawn by the irresistible aroma of a fat hog spit-roasted for hours and now dripping clear juices onto the hot coals, nearly done. They watched as the sizzling meat was carved into hefty chunks and spread native-style on the ground atop a thick mat of freshly cut banana leaves. Fried *camotes* and cabbage, boiled carrots, both fresh and fried bananas, pineapple, and mangoes surrounded the succulent meat. After a long day, they were starved, but Emilio raised a hand and cautioned them to wait.

Separately, the people had prepared a special offering of food. Emilio explained this was for the god *Kabunian*, the chief god of the Igorots. Two holy men chanted prayers to *Kabunian* and asked for his blessing on the newly arrived guerrillas.

Finally, it was time to eat, and eat they did, until they couldn't hold another morsel.

After the feasting, several men brought out platter-sized, hammered metal gongs and began beating rhythmically with hide-wrapped batons. Others pounded stretched-leather drums. Then the dancing began. Most of the dances were slow and graceful, almost melancholy, while a few were strenuous and warlike, reminiscent of dances performed by the American Indians of Arizona and New Mexico. Emilio said the dances represented centuries of proud Igorot tradition. Harvests, marriages, births, deaths, departures, homecomings, and even illnesses each called for a different combination of dances. The Igorot god *Kabunian* always figured prominently.

Though coaxed to join in, the Americans were self-conscious and declined. Throughout the wonderful, relaxed evening, the war seemed a million miles away.

Because they couldn't pronounce his name, in time Art and his companions came to call the old man KB, an abbreviated version of *kaibigan*, the Filipino word for "friend." They called his wife *Ina* simply because that's what her family called her. By the time they learned the term meant "mother," it was too late to change. She didn't appear to mind. Their hosts had three daughters, close in age from about fourteen to seventeen, and an older son who had already become active in the guerrilla resistance and was based in Baguio as a spy.

The young boy became Art's special friend. His name was Tuaddy, but they called him Kiddo. With large, expressive brown eyes and a ready smile, he was hard to resist. He hauled fresh water from the spring several times each day, and then simply hung around the headquarters, anxious to perform any menial chore they could think of.

Several days later, Emilio Velasco and his *cargadores* returned with more food, some English-language magazines, and another, very special bundle. He delivered an old Royal typewriter he said had been *borrowed* from a business concern in Baguio. Art knew the touch system, and Calvert and Spencer wanted to learn. They took turns as Art began conducting daily lessons and practice drills.

Thereafter, Emilio and one or more *cargadores* came weekly, each time laden with food and supplies. They brought more paper and pencils, books, a razor and blades, toothbrushes, ground coffee, sometimes a pack of Filipino cigarettes, and occasionally even some American candy bars or Coca-Colas. When asked where he was getting all these items, he merely shrugged his shoulders, held out his hands, palms up, and grinned. Before long they quit calling him Emilio and began calling him Robin Hood, a nickname that stuck.[2]

Calvert and Spencer shaved off their beards, but Art decided to leave his alone. Although useless as camouflage for his whiteness, he rather enjoyed his long, bushy, reddish beard in spite of the occasional lice that made it home. Art told Calvert he'd shave when General MacArthur re-took Bougainville Island in the Solomons. Calvert just shook his head and didn't press the issue.

Kiddo had had no formal education but was fascinated by the typewriter. He draped himself over Art's shoulder, insisting on hearing each letter spoken aloud. He had a phenomenal memory, and before long he could point to any letter Art asked for, often more quickly than either Calvert or Spencer could find it. To divert his attention from the typewriter so they could get on with the lessons, Art printed the alphabet on a piece of paper for him to copy. The little guy had never even held a pencil, but he learned quickly and recited and copied the letters over and over. Then Art drew simple images and printed the English word for the object, and Kiddo copied not only the words, but the images too. He was proud of himself and never squandered an opportunity to show off in front of his family. He'd throw his shoulders back, jab his thumb into his bare chest, and declare, *Me read. Me guerrilla boy.*

Art taught Kiddo the concept of numbers by writing them on paper and laying out the appropriate number of small twigs. Pretty soon Art could say any number from one to twenty and Kiddo would repeat the number and count out the twigs himself. He loved pointing to his sisters as a group and announcing *three* or to his baby brother while proclaiming *one baby.*

Kiddo, in return, taught Art words in the local dialect by pointing to an object and saying the word, which Art wrote down phonetically but routinely mispronounced, causing Kiddo to dissolve in fits of giggles. He was a delightful addition to their new household.

I T WASN'T ALL PLAY AND FEASTING. Word of their arrival had spread like wildfire up and down the valley below, to Baguio and beyond, causing members of the Detachment, 1st Battalion,

43rd Infantry (Philippine Scouts), to come out of hiding, climb the mountain, and report for duty. In addition, every able-bodied native who'd attended their welcome *cañao* now wanted to become a guerrilla. By Art's best count, they had accumulated a force of about 150 men. With so many unfamiliar natives milling about, security became an issue. To establish control, they set up a system of lookouts along the three trails coming up the mountain. High in the trees and well hidden in the foliage, the natives constructed bamboo perches from which an armed sentry could see in both directions and demand a password. Should a passerby fail to answer correctly, he was apprehended and brought in for questioning. In the unlikely event an enemy patrol ventured up the mountain, the sentry was to fire three warning shots in quick succession, giving the Americans time to hide. The perches were manned in shifts around the clock, and the password was changed at unpredictable intervals.

While the traditional bamboo telegraph had served well enough in the past, speed of execution had never been terribly important. News-bearers often stopped to visit family or friends, or perhaps hunt a wild pig, pick some fruit, or even take a nap. A tighter, more professional network became their second priority. Their new plan called for dedicated runners to cover specific distances within given time frames so they could maintain regular contact with their unit commanders—Rufino Baldwin at Dalupirip, Dennis Molintas and Bado Dangwa at Atok—and with their agents in Baguio.

They devised ingenious ways for the runners to hide sensitive messages. Most wore only G-strings, and sometimes messages were simply folded into a man's G-string. Igorots rarely wore hats, but messages could be concealed in the folds of a dirty headband without arousing suspicion. In the colder months, the natives wrapped themselves in colorful blankets woven by their women, who now sewed nearly invisible patches behind which papers or other small items could be concealed. For generations, the natives had made water-carrying vessels from segmented lengths of mature bamboo. Now, using the same technique, they carved longer lengths of bamboo into multi-compartmented walking sticks. Art was particularly proud of one idea. Since nearly every adult Filipino in the mountains smoked homemade cigars, it was a simple matter to roll a message up inside several tobacco leaves. If a runner found himself in a precarious situation, he had only to light up, puff a few times, and send the incriminating evidence up in smoke.

News reports began coming in from Baguio. A few civilians there had managed to hide their shortwave radios, and they regularly passed KGEI war news along to secret guerrilla agents, who then passed it to guerrilla runners for transmission up the mountain. In the translation process, sometimes the reports became garbled, sometimes downright hilarious. Likewise, news items were picked up from the *Manila Tribune*, now controlled and run by the Japanese, though most of what came from that source was unreliable propaganda.

It wasn't all war news, though, and two particular reports hit Art like a ton of bricks. One of their messengers brought word that around the middle of November the Japanese had finally raided the camps of the American civilian families at Dyaka and Oding. Those at Dyaka—Bill and Margaret Moule and Ted and Ruth Lawson— had fled to hideouts higher in the mountains just before the Japanese came, and they avoided capture. Whether those at Oding had attempted to flee wasn't known; what was clear was the extent of the Japanese hideous brutality. A few days after the raid, some natives found the bodies of Daisy Biason and Betty Biason. The pretty young women had been stripped naked, savagely beaten, and raped before being bayonetted and left for dead not far from their cozy hideout at Oding, now reduced to charred, smoking ruins.[3] The rest of the Oding residents had last been seen, hands securely bound, being marched by Japanese soldiers east toward Bayombong.[4] Art was sickened by the news.

The second report said that in mid-December their old friend Herb Swick had been captured down in Pangasinan Province, jailed at Binalonan, and tortured for weeks.[5] Now, in late January, no one knew whether he was alive or had been executed. They hoped against hope that he'd somehow found a way to survive.

WITH SECURITY AND COMMUNICATIONS issues dealt with, it was time for more direct action. Status reports now arrived regularly from Rufino Baldwin, Bado Dangwa, and Dennis Molintas, giving head counts of their men, weapons, and rounds of ammunition. Calvert put out the word that they needed additional rifles and ammunition in order to arm their many anxious volunteers. Productive raids began taking place all over their jurisdiction: perhaps a small enemy truck convoy waylaid on the Mountain Trail; perhaps the innocuous theft of a rifle or two from a Japanese installation in Baguio; perhaps an unexpected night raid on one of the smaller Japanese garrisons. These were small-scale operations, but they energized both the guerrillas and the local population. The frustrated Japanese labeled the guerrillas "bandits" and howled for their apprehension or surrender.

To further bolster morale, Art sat down at the typewriter one day and worked out a parody of a little poem that had appeared originally in the *Manila Tribune*, referring to those poor unfortunates trapped on Bataan without enough food, water, or ammunition.

> *We're the battling bandits from Baguio,*
> *Feared yet revered wherever we go,*
> *The eyes and ears of our Uncle Sam,*
> *Harassing the Japs whenever we can,*
> *Brave and fearless to a man,*
> *We hope somebody somewhere gives a damn!*[6]

Things were going well. Calvert, Murphy, and Spencer were living in better conditions than they had in months, and now they were actually giving the Japanese serious enough pinpricks that they dared not reduce the size of their troop concentration in the Baguio area. The Detachment, 1st Battalion, 43rd Infantry (Philippine Scouts), was becoming a force to be reckoned with.

CHAPTER 18

MACARTHUR'S
"LAY LOW" ORDER

January and February 1943

THE EARLY MONTHS OF 1943 brought about a series of events involving one Ralph Burton Praeger, events that ultimately led General Douglas MacArthur to issue an order from his headquarters in Australia that greatly restricted guerrilla activities all over the Philippines.

Ralph Praeger was a six-foot-four, muscular Kansas boy who had graduated from the United States Military Academy in 1938. He wasn't the typical West Pointer, though, and was never impressed with military pomp and ceremony. In July 1939, Ralph was sent to Fort Stotsenburg, near Clark Field in the Philippines, where he was assigned as regimental motor officer. He relished the hours he spent on his own at the post motor pool, doing the more complicated mechanical work none of the other available personnel were trained for.[1]

When war erupted on December 8th, then Captain Praeger was placed in charge of Troop C, 26th Cavalry (Philippine Scouts). His mounted unit was assigned to Colonel Horan's Baguio-area command and given the mission of preventing enemy movement from the Ilocos coast into the Mountain Province via Highway 4, the Cervantes Road. Praeger's unit held out for a couple of weeks, but they, too, were forced to retreat from the beaches back up to Baguio. There, Troop C joined the thousands of other troops anxiously awaiting clarification of the conflicting orders coming from MacArthur's headquarters.

When Colonel Horan's group left Baguio on December 24 to head east over the Cordillera Mountains, Praeger and his men accompanied them as far as Bambang, Nueva Vizcaya. There he received permission from Colonel Horan to leave the command and proceed north into the Cagayan Valley.[2] With two junior cavalry officers, Lieutenants Thomas S. Jones and Warren S. Minton, Praeger and his men moved north through the Cagayan Valley toward Tuguegarao, picking up a number of Colonel Bonnett's disbanded Philippine Army troops along the way.

As they approached Tuguegarao, Praeger came up with a plan. Using only rifles and makeshift hand grenades fabricated by one of the men, his guerrilla band staged a daring raid on the airfield at Tuguegarao, recently occupied by the Japanese, hoping to destroy enemy aircraft and fuel stores and slow the Japanese relentless advance toward Manila. On the night of January 12–13, 1942, Praeger and his band stealthily made their way onto the airfield as the unsuspecting enemy slept, confident there wasn't an American within a hundred miles. Praeger's boys then cut loose and did their damnedest to wreak havoc on the Japanese, although the extent to which this raid was successful would come, in later years, to depend upon who was telling the story.

News of the episode might never have spread farther than the local Cagayan Valley villages except that, following the raid, Captain Praeger sent Lieutenant Minton down to Isabela Province to round up additional guerrilla volunteers. There, Minton met up with the hapless Major Everett Warner and relayed news of the Tuguegarao raid, perhaps with some embellishment. Warner promptly radioed the tale to General MacArthur's headquarters, probably with additional embellishment. From there, the story flashed to America and around the world, bringing a ray of hope and encouragement at a time when most news reports from the Pacific front were bleak.

Captain Praeger became an overnight legend, his guerrillas credited with *destroying a large number of planes* and *inflicting many casualties upon the enemy* at Tuguegarao.[3] They were also credited with destroying enemy radios and weapons, tearing up mine wires around the airfield, and burning the houses of several Japanese officials. Praeger was ultimately given credit for disrupting for several weeks all enemy communications in the area.

From Tuguegarao, Praeger and his men marched north toward the coast, destroying bridges and culverts along Highway 5 as they went. Eleven days later they attacked the enemy-held airfield at Aparri, with equally spectacular results.[4] Again, postwar accounts of the success of this raid varied, with Lieutenant Jones claiming the Aparri raid never happened at all; that one lone Japanese plane had been shot down, and that event had been magnified by a press hungry for any shred of good news.

General MacArthur promptly radioed hearty congratulations and ordered promotions for all involved.

The newly minted Major Praeger then moved his men to the vicinity of Tuao, Cagayan Province, where he joined forces with the provincial governor, Marcelo Adduru. The two maintained a stranglehold on this area for several months, against all enemy attempts to dislodge them.

When his unit became depleted in number due to casualties, Major Praeger moved west to Kabugao, the capital of Apayao Subprovince. There were no roads in or out; the capital was reached only by horse trails or by *banca* on a swift, turbulent mountain river. Praeger was driven out temporarily in the latter part of 1942, but reoccupied the town when the enemy garrison became small enough for him to wipe it out.[5]

During this year-long period, Praeger managed to maintain a working radio transmitter and periodically sent weak messages, some of which were picked up by an amateur radio operator in California. However, the major had little, if any, communication with other guerrilla units operating in North Luzon.[6]

On January 3, 1943, he managed to get a feeble signal through to General MacArthur's headquarters in Australia:

> *AM CONDUCTING GOVERNMENT WITH UTMOST CARE LEGALLY AND MORALLY DEVOID OF POLITICS AND PERSONAL CONSIDERATIONS PD MILITARY AND CIVIL AUTHORITIES IN PERFECT ACCORD HELPING ONE ANOTHER PD I HAVE PROVIDED ALL NEEDS OF THE ARMY CMA COMPOSED OF SCOUTS CMA CONSTABULARY CMA AND PHILIPPINE ARMY IN THE CAGAYAN AND APARRI PD IF I MAY BE PERMITTED CMA I CAN ORGANIZE FIVE THOUSAND ADDITIONAL MEN PD*[7, 8]

In late January 1943, Major Praeger learned via the bamboo telegraph that Colonel Moses had officially assumed command of all guerrilla forces in North Luzon. He sent the colonel a return message by runner, reporting for duty and advising that he had made radio contact with MacArthur's General Headquarters, Southwest Pacific Area, in Australia (GHQ-SWPA).

The prospect of a working transmitter was irresistible. Moses and Noble promptly set out for Kabugao, arriving safely during the first week of February. The two colonels remained with Praeger's organization in Kabugao until late spring, taking full advantage, after several months on the run, of the relative calm and safety in the region.

Colonel Moses made maximum use of Praeger's radio. He advised MacArthur of the loyalty, bravery, and fighting spirit of the natives in the mountains; of their willingness to hide and provide food to the guerrillas, even at great peril to themselves. He proudly described the successes he felt had been achieved in the October 15th offensive. But he also warned that massive Japanese reprisals were taking a toll on the morale of the people and that local action was needed to reverse this trend. He requested that propaganda leaflets be dropped by plane, and stressed that supplies of every sort were urgently needed, particularly radios, medicine, ammunition, and money. Lastly, Moses requested and obtained authorization from General MacArthur to induct the equivalent of one regiment, roughly 5,000 men, into the service of the United States, thereby putting these new soldiers on an equal footing and pay scale with regular American troops. This latter request was a mere formality as Colonel Moses had already inducted a number of civilian miners and Filipino natives, and had sanctioned promotions for a considerable number of others.[9]

Despite the urgent pleas for help, no promises were forthcoming from MacArthur. In his terse reply, the general stressed that he was operating with a critical shortage of planes and gasoline, and it would be many months before outside aid could be provided to any of the guerrilla groups on Luzon.

Encouraged to hear of widespread guerrilla activity in North Luzon, MacArthur was also deeply dismayed to learn of the harsh retaliatory measures against the civilian population. He ordered that all guerrillas immediately cease offensive maneuvers against the Japanese; that guerrilla activity be limited to that amount necessary for their own survival and safety; that henceforth their mission be confined to the organization and training of their units and the gathering of intelligence.

Within days, what was to become widely known as MacArthur's "Lay Low Order" was condensed and put into official form by Colonel Moses. Copies were sent off by runner to all known guerrilla leaders in northern Luzon. The directive was not received in Benguet until the early part of April.

In the late summer of 1942, shortly after taking over command, Moses had adopted 777 as his personal code name, and had assigned to Colonel Noble the code name 666.[10]

```
GHL   V   RGE   NR  3/23   CK 20   UNNUMBERED

VESSEL SURFACED FOUR TIMES NIGHT OF TWO TWO NOV AT POINT ONE
PD WHAT IS DOPE ON POINT TWO RPT TWO


Time Rec'd   Ø9Ø6    Dated Rec'd   11/24/44   Sgnd CURA   Opr
```

HEADQUARTERS USAFIP NORTH LUZON
IN THE FIELD

February 10, 1943

SUBJECT: Orders from MacArthur
     TO: All Guerrilla Leaders

   1. General Policy of USFIPS in PI is to limit hostilities and contact with enemy to minimum amount necessary
for safety. Concentrate on perfecting organization and on
development of intelligence net, reporting promptly names
of superior officers and other items of military intelligence.

   2. Offensive activities are premature and will only
result in increased enemy pressure, and probable retaliation against innocent people. Therefore, until ammunitions
and supplies can be sent, which will take some months, your
missions as intelligence units can be currently of the utmost value.

   3. "Nothing is surer than our ultimate victory. I
can not just tell when it will happen but you can be assured
that it is inevitable. Keep your courage and patience. An
Almighty God will guide us to success."

(SIGND)   777

(SIGNED) 666

USAFIP-NL document dated Feb 10, 1943

Moses, Noble, and Praeger already had huge prices on their heads, and some among the natives evidently found this inducement irresistible. Word filtered in that the enemy was planning a massive three-pronged attack against the Praeger-Adduru stronghold, confident they could bag the two colonels, Governor Adduru, and Major Praeger in a single operation. It was time to head for safer territory. In the company of their cook and several bodyguards,

Colonels Moses and Noble left Kabugao and moved into the more remote mountains of Kalinga. Major Praeger struggled over whether to remain with Governor Adduru and defend Kabugao to the last man or to dismantle his bulky radio transmitter and move it farther into the mountains in the hope that contact could be maintained with MacArthur's headquarters in Australia.

CHAPTER 19

LAYING LOW
IN KAPANGAN
April 1943

U NTIL NOW, THE GUERRILLAS' intelligence-gathering had been a catch-as-catch-can endeavor, enlisting sympathetic, trustworthy civilians if an opportunity presented itself. Now their priorities changed. They stepped up recruitment of new agents, particularly among ex-Philippine Army soldiers who'd surrendered on Bataan, survived the Death March, been imprisoned at Camp O'Donnell, and been paroled on the condition that they work for the Japanese. These men underwent intensive retraining and propaganda indoctrination before being assigned to new jobs. Many were genuinely converted, but some remained secretly unconvinced[1], and these became the targets of the guerrillas' new recruitment program. Of particular value were a select few now working as clerks or interpreters in the local Japanese-controlled Philippine Constabulary garrisons. It was a slow, painstaking screening process, but, when successful, these inside men provided current information detailing what the Japanese knew about the guerrillas, their plans for tracking them down, and who among the natives was collaborating and should be marked for an *unfortunate accident* down the line.

Less exciting than recruiting spies was locating physical observation sites from which to identify and count Japanese ships, planes, and vehicles moving in and out of the port of San Fernando, La

Union, and air traffic at the grassy airstrip just south of the city. Searching the western verge of their mountaintop, Art found an ideal spot at the edge of a grove of tall pines. The site afforded a bird's-eye view of the harbor below, a fairly good view of the air traffic, and limited views of vehicular movement on the coast highway north of San Fernando. Three natives who'd accompanied him spent the afternoon hacking materials and building an elevated observation platform. He named the site Observation Post 1 and decided to man the post himself for a couple of days in order to formulate a standard, easily understood method of recording the data.

The next morning, Art arose before dawn, packed a bundle of food and supplies, and was ready to leave when Kiddo appeared in the doorway, begging to go along. *Maybe some other time*, Art told him, *when your tatay says it's okay*. Kiddo slunk into a corner, squatted down on his heels, and sulked as he watched his friend disappear into the thick morning fog.

At Observation Post 1, Art settled in to watch the events of the day. Before long, the sun's rays swallowed the mist, revealing a panoramic view of the shimmering South China Sea and the quickening activity along the shoreline below. He pulled out his tablet and pencil and dated the page; divided it into columns devoted to sea, air, and land movements; then sat back with Emil Jorgensen's binoculars and waited. A couple of freighters pulled away from the docks and headed north. The airfield remained quiet, though, and the only vehicles on the coast highway were a few heavy wooden carts pulled by lumbering, chuffing *carabao* toward the rice and vegetable paddies sandwiched between the mountains and the beach north of San Fernando. It was apparent the tough part of this job was going to be staying alert.

Art's chin had dropped to his chest for the second time when he was jolted awake by rustling in the brush below the platform. He drew his .45 and cocked it, then inched to the edge and cautiously peered over, prepared to shoot a wild boar or a stranger who couldn't instantly repeat the day's password. It was Kiddo, grinning sheepishly.

Me guerrilla boy, he said. *Me help see Japs.*

Art heaved a sigh of relief. Kiddo scrambled up the ladder and plopped down, chattering like a magpie. He pointed to the tablet, wanting to know what each entry meant. With words and simple pictures, Art explained as best he could. Kiddo had the eyes of a hawk and was soon pointing out the tiniest movement along the coast while Art double-checked with the binoculars and made appropriate notes on the page. After sharing Art's lunch, Kiddo curled up for a snooze, cradling his tousled head in the crook of his smooth, brown arm. Art was glad for his company.

As the boy slept, Art's thoughts wandered to his little family so far away, but he had trouble picturing Lil's face.

WE TRY NOT TO THINK ABOUT THAT

My buddies and I recall the day,
The Japanese landed at Lingayen Bay,
We remember the troops who ran away,
But we try not to think about that.

My buddies and I recall once more,
Their easy landing on Tayabas shore,
We remember the flight from Corregidor,
But we try not to think about that.

We're learning to forget the bombs,
That came from a Yank-less sky,
We've almost recovered from that now,
Though sometimes at night we sigh.

My buddies and I recall the day,
The transports should've taken us away,
We remember the way they made us stay,
But we try not to think about that.[2]

Art was glad to turn the long watch shifts over to natives hired under contract and trained for the purpose. Most knew nothing about the larger weapons of war, so Art made drawings of freighters, carriers, destroyers, light and heavy cruisers, and the heavy bombers, Zeroes, and reconnaissance planes they might observe in the air over San Fernando.

Soon, a dozen observation posts dotted their mountaintop. The data forms accumulated rapidly. Additional forms came in by runner from Emilio Velasco, Bado Dangwa, and Dennis Molintas, making it necessary for Art to spend most of his time consolidating them into daily and then weekly reports.[3]

The reports presented a problem. They had no radio transmitter, but the word from Baguio was that Lieutenant Robert Lapham's guerrilla group in Pangasinan had secret contacts that did. Art began smuggling his reports by runner to Lapham's headquarters in Umingan, with the hope that eventually the reports would reach MacArthur in Australia. Robert Lapham was an enigmatic, independent young fellow, however, who had in the past simply ignored the efforts of Moses and Noble to organize the guerrilla units in northern Luzon into a single command. Art had the uneasy feeling his intelligence reports were going no farther than Lapham's headquarters, or, if they were, his unit wasn't getting the credit.[4] He had no way of checking, and in the end it didn't matter. Options were limited.

Meal preparation at headquarters was taken over by a well-trained Chinese chef who had worked for years in Baguio but now wanted nothing to do with the Japanese. Art began putting on weight, so he instituted a rigorous program of calisthenics and brisk laps around the area. Calvert never made the program mandatory, but he and Spencer usually participated. Kiddo never failed to show up. He counted and recorded the number of push-ups, squats, and laps each man completed, honing his math skills in the process.

Afternoons during the rainy season often stretched out long, cold, and dreary, particularly if Robin Hood hadn't included any new reading material in their weekly supply bundle. Art hadn't written to Lil in some time. He found it hard, not only because she seemed so distant but because he didn't want to make their situation sound worse than it was. Actually, there was very little he *could* tell her without jeopardizing security. On May 29 he gave it a try:

"Dearest wife and children. The rains have started, and it looks like we're not going to be disturbed for a while. Also, we're eating the best we have since the war started. We have a new cook who's very good at roasting meat, so we have roast beef or pork in addition to the usual vegetables and rice. For fruit, we have bananas and pineapple. We have cacao for breakfast and supper; it's like cocoa, only oilier as the cocoa butter hasn't been removed. I exercise every morning to keep my waistline down.

"We got news of the American civilians who lived near us last rainy season. They're all gone now. Remember the woman who had diabetes? Well, her insulin ran out and they turned in, but she died before reaching the concentration camp. Two other families got malaria and had to turn in. Another, who had a small baby, couldn't run when the Japs came to the barrio where they were hiding.

"The Japs are collecting scrap iron and paying big prices (in Jap paper money) to the natives who bring it in. Most of the big prewar Filipino politicians are in the scrap-iron business. The Japs are also buying broken glass bottles—they use them in bombs.

"According to the Jap propaganda sheet, *The Tribune*, there's a big coal strike in the U.S. Is it true? If it is, we'd sure like to have John L. Lewis and all the strikers over here. They'd work, all right! The natives here never refuse to do anything we tell them for fear of suffering severe consequences from us or from their own neighbors. That's the way to handle strikes in wartime.

"The Tribune also says most Americans are more interested in licking Japan than Germany. I hope so. We can't continue to live out here in the mountains forever. I'll be thirty in four months. And Eleanor will be five next month, twice as old as she was when I last saw her. The years being wasted here seem so precious. There are so many things we could be doing if we were together. We'll make up for them when, and if, I get home. No longer will we live by habit; instead, we'll take the helm and make our lives go as we wish them to go. There's nothing in life we cannot do if we really want to. For instance, I'd like for us to see South America. Why not? By the way, I've reached Lesson 30 in our Spanish lesson book and can say 'Hasta donde a Buenos Aires?' and 'Quando saldia el vapor?'

"We've rigged up a telegraph code practice set, and I can send fifteen words per minute and receive about five. This is in case Mac starts sending us orders. We have a typewriter, and PK and Spencer are learning the touch system. We're doing our best to see that our time here isn't completely wasted.

"You should see my one pair of shorts! They've been patched so many times that the original cloth is no longer visible. Recently someone came up and got our measurements, saying they wanted to make us some clothes. Maybe we'll have nice uniforms to welcome Mac—or be buried in.

"The Jap propaganda is really funny. The supplies left by the Americans are running short, so now it's a virtue to live a *simple* life (go without shoes, etc.) free from Anglo-American influence. They maintain the Japs are not here to exploit the Philippines, in spite of the fact that all businesses are now run by Jap firms and they appropriate most of the output for their own war-making purposes. What a bunch of hogwash!"[5]

Art reread what he'd written. He wasn't pleased with it, but Robin Hood was due any minute, so he fashioned an envelope from a sheet of Japanese propaganda, addressed it to Lil, and had it ready for him to take away and hide.

On June 15 he tried again:

"Dearest. Two weeks have passed since I last wrote. First, Ubing, the baby, got sick, so his daddy had to throw a *cañao* to get him well. Everyone came, many pigs were killed, much *tapuey* was consumed, and we all danced and had quite a party. I don't know how this could possibly have affected Ubing, but he's fine now.

"At present there are fifteen Japs at the garrison in the valley down below us. But now the yellow bastards are lazy; they stay in the barrio and only send a few men out on three- or four-day trips to look for soldiers. They rarely catch any.

"We have some sun today after our first typhoon of the season. It rained more than a week. I welcomed the sun by taking a bath and washing my clothes. I was pretty scummy.

"I've been dreaming of you a lot the last few nights—and what dreams! Spence and PK say it looks like I'm sleeping under a tent! I only wish I could make them come true.

"I have to close now so this can go down by runner. Remember, I'll always love you and the babies. Love, Art."[6]

By now, the three men had become close friends and, except for occasions when military protocol was important, normally addressed each other as PK, Spence, and Murph.

Robin Hood's next bundle included a deck of cards, so they decided to teach Spence to play bridge. Once he'd mastered Gorham's system of counting points and the basics of bidding and trick-taking, they launched the game. With each new deal, either Art or PK would bid the fourth hand in addition to his own, and once the contract was set, the fourth hand became the dummy. The system wasn't perfect, but it was better than nothing, and Spence was tickled pink to finally learn this gentleman's game.

Parker Calvert at West Point

Often they passed rainy afternoons griping about the slow progress of the war, but such talk invariably depressed everyone. Nosy and not always the soul of tact, Art sometimes steered the conversation in a direction more to his liking. Spence was usually open and chatty, but PK was by nature quiet and reticent, so Art tried circuitous methods to get him to open up.

Hey, PK, tell us about West Point. I hear the plebes have it pretty rough, but I'll bet it wasn't any worse than my Theta Chi pledge semester.

Oh, yeah? You only had to put up with it for a semester. At the Point, it went on for a whole damn year. Then silence.

What was so bad about it? They didn't beat you every morning, did they?

No, but the harassment never let up. You had to move double-time wherever you went, salute every single upperclassman each time you saw him, and there was hell to pay if you forgot to sir them with every sentence. Silence again.

What kinda hell?

You weren't allowed to address upperclassmen directly, only stand at rigid attention while they hollered abuse an inch from your face. I'm not all that big, so they honed in on my size: How'd they ever let a wimpy little squirt like you in this place anyway? How the hell are you ever gonna carry an M-1? You musta been fed on Pablum and breast milk your whole life. They belittled everything from my mother to my manhood.

Sounds like my grandmother, Art countered. *She roared like a mother grizzly and raised all sorts of hell if anyone crossed her, especially me.*

Then PK volunteered: *I remember one big fellow had a disgusting habit of spraying spit as he yelled an inch from your face. But you'd better not wipe it off if you didn't want to spend the rest of the day doing push-ups and running laps. Geez, I hated that slob.*

What else? Was the chow okay?

Oh yeah, but the crap didn't stop. At mess hall you had to sit with your back ramrod straight, eyes forward, and eat what they termed a square meal: lift your fork straight up from the plate, then on a level plane over to your mouth, take the bite, then down toward the table, then forward until the fork was over the plate again.

Spence and Art laughed as PK demonstrated.

It wasn't funny, you jerks. There was so much tension at mealtimes that I usually ended up with a fire in my belly. Puked a few times. They had a million piddling rules about everything, and the tiniest infraction resulted in push-ups or laps, hundreds of them. There was worse stuff, too, that I've tried to forget.

Spence, intent now on hearing the finer details of life at the Point, pushed PK: *Tell us about the worse stuff.*

Well, probably the worst for me happened when the upperclassmen returned to the Point after my first plebe summer. Twice in the next month, I got back to my room in the evening and found my sheets wet.

Leaky ceiling? Spence asked, grinning.

No. Somebody peed in my bed. Really soaked it. And it stunk. Peeing your bed isn't something they allow in the Army, especially not at West Point.

Spence was doing his best not to laugh. *So what did you do?*

At first I couldn't think what to do. I was really scared. Finally, I called my mom. She listened, put her hand over the receiver, and I could hear her talking to my father. I was sweating bullets. She came back on the line and told me he said to report the matter immediately, which I did, and for a while I thought the case was closed. When it happened a second time, they scheduled a formal conference. I felt sure I was gonna get kicked out, but I guess they finally believed me. Or maybe the fact my father was a colonel and an alum helped. I'm just glad he and my mom believed me. My father was usually suspicious of people, even me, and I wasn't sure he would.

Did they ever find out who did it?

If they did, they didn't tell me. But I hope they did and I hope the bastard got thrown out on his ass. I hope his whole life got ruined.

Spence was quiet now, shaking his head.

Well, I don't know, Art said. *One time several of the Theta Chi actives drove me way the hell out into the desert, stripped me naked, gave me two bucks, and left me to get back any way I could. It was damned embarrassing, and cold too, but I got lucky and caught a ride with an old guy in a pickup. He threw me his jacket to cover up with and then drove me right up to the front door of the frat house. I got back only twenty minutes behind the actives, which galled them so bad that I got total KP for a week.*

You sure it wasn't some blonde in a convertible? Spence quipped.

I wish. Maybe then I'd have been out all night. It was all for the best, though, like boot camp, and most of those guys later became close friends.

Calvert was always reticent to talk about his family. It took weeks and was like pulling teeth, but gradually he described the structured military home in which he'd grown up. Born in New York in January 1916, he was christened Thomas Parker Calvert, the only child of older parents. His father, Colonel William Jay Calvert, was a stern and distant man, stingy with praise, and not given to overt displays of affection. PK was close to his mother, Nadine (née Parker), the daughter of an Army general. Although warmer and more approachable than his father, she was not a forceful woman and usually demurred to her husband's wishes. But she knew her military history. The bedtime stories PK heard as a child often featured the exploits of his maternal grandfather, Brigadier General John Henry Parker, widely known as "Gatling Gun" Parker because he commanded the Gatling Gun Detachment of the U.S. Army's 5th Corps in Cuba during the Santiago campaign in the Spanish-American War. This same grandfather had served again in World War I and had four times been awarded the Distinguished Service Cross for bravery in battle. He'd even written a book: *The Gatlings at Santiago*.[7] Academic standards in PK's family were high, and there was never any question but that he would follow in the footsteps of his illustrious ancestors, attend West Point, graduate with honors, and make a career in the Army. Even in his choice of a wife, PK conformed. Right after his graduation in 1937, in a traditional crossed-swords ceremony at the post chapel, PK married Rilla Frances Lane, the good-looking daughter of Brigadier General Arthur Willis Lane, West Point class of '05. These were big shoes to fill, but PK never expressed regret about the rigid path down which his life had been directed.

Spence was eager to talk, and Art soon learned the two had a lot in common. Born Grafton Jacob Christ Jr. in July 1921 in Harrisburg, Pennsylvania, he was the second son of Grafton Jacob Christ Sr. and Mabel (née Spencer) Christ. His brother Frank was a couple of years older. When he was two, his mother died. Spence wasn't sure of the cause.

Dad worked as a mechanic for Pierce Arrow and was on the road a lot, so Frank and I lived for a while with our paternal grandparents in Harrisburg. Then he remarried a young girl named Bertha, the daughter of German immigrant parents. She was only sixteen, and he was more than twenty years older. We lived together as a family for a while. Pretty soon they had a little daughter, Gloria, five years younger than me. Dad's new wife was really nice. She asked us to call her Mother. And Gloria was a cute little kid. Frank and I played with her and thought it was swell to have a baby sister.

Our new mother was great, but it didn't last. Dad got sick and had to go to the hospital, so Bertha moved all of us back to Philadelphia to live with her folks. They were really poor, and sometimes there wasn't a lot to eat. After a few months, Bertha just couldn't handle it anymore, so she called Frank's and my maternal grandparents, John and Fanny Spencer, and asked them to take us. We were put on a train by ourselves and sent from Philly to Buffalo, where they picked us up and drove us to their home in Kenmore, a northern suburb.

Were they well-heeled, like PK's parents?

Not rich, but comfortable. They had a three-bedroom house,

Grafton Spencer at Philippine Military Academy

and Frank and I each had our own room upstairs. My granddad had a steady job as a park superintendent, and there was always plenty to eat and enough clothes and stuff. They were good to Frank and me. We went to the public schools, and I did pretty well in the lower grades. But I got bored by my junior year and barely hung on till graduation. Going to college was never part of the conversation. We lived pretty much like *the other neighborhood kids. I only knew a couple who went to college, and their dads were doctors or lawyers. After high school, my brother Frank worked for an air-conditioning outfit, and I got a job clerking in a hardware store in Buffalo.*

Did you like it?

At first I was so excited at having some spending money that I didn't worry about much else. But as time went on, the job got tedious and boring too.

It was kind of the same with me, Art said. *My mother died in the influenza epidemic of 1918. My two younger brothers and I went to Maud Booth for a while. That's an orphanage in Los Angeles, but they cared for half-orphans too, and the surviving parent paid whatever he or she could afford. Pops was a boilermaker and worked for the Southern Pacific Railroad. He had to travel a lot, like your dad, and he couldn't take care of us. But then he got married again, and we went back home. I guess maybe he didn't tell his new bride he had three boys under age five, and she evidently wasn't thrilled with the idea of becoming an instant mother because she didn't hang around very long. Then we went back to the orphanage.*

One night I fell from an upper bunk and hurt my back and had to be taken to the hospital. That's how I came to live with my grandmother. Sadie was her name, but I always called her Grandmother. Very formal. She took me home and nursed me back to health. From then on, I didn't see much of my brothers or my dad, only once or twice at Christmas. My brothers were taken in by my mother's siblings, and they saw each other all the time.

Grandmother supported herself as a seamstress, barely scraping by. We moved all the time, mostly here and there in Los Angeles, one time as far away as Salinas, and we once lived in Yosemite National Park for two years. But I missed lots of school. My grandmother wasn't your usual grandmother, hugging and kissing and baking cookies or playing games, you know, encouraging me to be a kid. She made all the rules and wasn't receptive to my ideas or backtalk. I guess she did the best she knew how.

I didn't always have socks or underwear, but she encouraged me to read and made sure I had access to library books. One thing she always insisted on was that, by hook or by crook, I would go to college.

Lucky you, Spence replied.

So, Spence, what ever happened to your dad, Bertha, and your baby sister?

Now Spence was more somber. *I guess that marriage didn't work out so well because they got a divorce after a few years, and then I never saw him again. I overheard bits and pieces from my grandparents, something about he had developed serious health problems and was confined at the Norristown State Hospital in Harrisburg. Norristown was the state nut house, so maybe some of his problems were psychological. Anyway, that was when our grandparents officially adopted Frank and me and changed our last name to Spencer.*

So you're legally Spencer and not Christ?

Yeah. We didn't see my dad again, and then we were told he had died of a massive cerebral hemorrhage. That was about 1932. Our stepmother and Gloria, our little sister, stayed in touch, though, and we became pretty close. We visited them in Philly every now and then. In fact, after I enlisted in the Army and got sent to the Philippines in 1939, Gloria wrote me all the time, just family news and stuff. My brother wasn't much of a letter-writer, and my grandparents weren't either, but she wrote all the time. I loved getting her letters.

How'd you come to be a student at the West Point Preparatory School in Baguio?

I'd been over here as a doughboy for about a year and a half when I found out I could take some aptitude tests and maybe qualify for the Air Corps. Learning to fly sounded a lot more exciting than the stuff I was doing, so I signed up. I did pretty well on the tests, and that's when they sent me up to the school for a six-month crash course in the basics, you know, all that stuff I hadn't paid attention to in high school. If I completed the course and did well, then in November, when I was due for shipment back to the States, I could go to West Point and become an officer.

Lucky you, PK said wryly.

Art pressed on: *So how was school? You're pretty good-looking. Were you a ladies' man? Did you wow 'em, you know, sweep 'em off their feet?*

I was pretty shy.

No steady girlfriends?

No, never really had one of those.

You're not telling us you're still a virgin, are you?

Spence blushed clear up to his hairline and squirmed a bit, then grinned. *I'm afraid so. But I did have a girl in Baguio before the war broke out. I met her when the cadets toured the Itogon gold mine. Her dad, Lewis Robinson, was the superintendent there. He conducted the tour and then invited us to his house for refreshments. That's when I met Gerry. Geraldine was her real name. She was only fourteen, but she was real pretty and looked a lot older. You know, real curvy. She went to Brent International School in Baguio, and whenever they had dances or sports events, the guys from the academy were invited. When I saw her at these shindigs, she stuck to me like glue.*

I'll bet her dad loved that, seeing as you were a lecherous old man of nineteen.

Actually, her folks liked me. I got invited to dinner at their house a few times, and I was always on my best behavior, you know, using the right fork and everything and being real polite. If the war hadn't come along, who knows, Gerry and I might be making wedding plans by now.

So that was the extent of it, some well-chaperoned dancing and polite dinners with her parents? Art teased.

Well, we did quite a bit of smooching on those rare times we were alone together, but, no, it never went much further, if that's what you're so nosy about. She was brought up to act like a lady. Besides, I only knew her for a few months. I guess she and her family must be interned at one of those civilian camps in Baguio now.

Too bad. Virginity is highly overrated, at least for men.

Yeah, I guess so.

PK had been listening quietly, but now he came to Spence's defense. *I wasn't a playboy either, Murph, or a big man on campus like you. I didn't have girls chasing me all over. Mostly there were no girls around. Life at the Point was regimented. We were always studying hard or training, and even when we did get an opportunity to meet some girls, the chaperones were thick as flies. When I met Rilla, everything had to be on the up and up—her father would have killed me otherwise—and we were both virgins when we got married.*

They gazed at Art admiringly, and for a few moments he enjoyed being the big lover, the top dog. But his conscience got to him. *Well, I guess we're all in the same boat. Lil and I did a lot of smooching and cuddling and feeling around, but I was a virgin, too, until just a few days before our wedding. I've never slept with anyone but Lil.*

They all had a good laugh.

Each time they'd have one of these bull sessions, the bond between them grew, although they didn't think of it in those terms. They were just three young fellows, no different from thousands of others, caught up in something much bigger than any one of them, trying to make the best of a grim situation, and taking things one day at a time. In truth, Art felt closer to PK and Spence than he did to his own brothers.

A FEW WEEKS LATER, WORD CAME in from one of their lookouts that an American lieutenant was asking about Art Murphy. The man didn't know their password, but because he was an American, they had him brought in. Art recognized him immediately as Lieutenant Fish, the old lumberman-turned-officer he'd tracked down north of Bokod a year earlier.

Fish said that after he and Art had parted ways, he'd made contact with Colonels Moses and Noble at Benneng, and they had, because of his intimate knowledge of the countryside, assigned him the role of liaison officer between their headquarters and whatever guerrilla units he could find still operating in Mountain Province.

In mid-March, only a month earlier, Fish had run into Don Blackburn on the trail. Fish had accompanied Blackburn back to Volckmann-Blackburn headquarters a few kilometers west of Kiangan, capital of the subprovince of Ifugao, where they'd fled in the aftermath of the Japanese massive mopping-up campaign following the October 15 offensive.[8]

It was great to learn they were all alive, and good to reestablish contact.

Art and PK filled Fish in on their organization, their runner and coast-watch networks, and sent him on his way down to Rufino Baldwin's outfit at Dalupirip and toward the camps of Charles Cushing and Robert Lapham in eastern Pangasinan. In his pack, he carried Art's current consolidated intelligence reports as well as personal messages addressed to their old friends: Martin Moses, Maxie Noble, Russ Volckmann, and Don Blackburn.

Life on their mountaintop was settling in a good way. They went about their business more relaxed than at any time since the start of the war. They slept soundly at night, listening to the drumming of the rain and, sometimes, the muted sounds of the night birds.

CHAPTER 20

THE NOOSE TIGHTENS

May through August 1943

THE STABILITY ON THEIR MOUNTAINTOP didn't last long. When efforts to control the locals via bribes, propaganda, and sweet talk didn't produce the desired results, in May and June the Japanese brought in reinforcements and ramped up their pursuit of guerrillas. They put heavy pressure on the barrio natives to provide information and were merciless in making an example of anyone thought guilty of aiding guerrillas. As local farmers grew more terrified, the guerrillas' food supply suffered. For months, beef and pork had been plentiful; now most meals featured chicken, often not a great deal of that.

More benign but no less effective, propaganda leaflets were widely distributed, urging Filipino soldiers to surrender and join the Japanese in their efforts to vanquish all Americans from the Philippines and establish what they termed the Greater East Asia Co-Prosperity Sphere.[1]

The Japanese also stepped up reconnaissance flights from the airfield at San Fernando and patrolled the mountain trails throughout Benguet and the Ilocos Provinces. As a result, two observation posts were attacked, the men on duty bound with vines, interrogated, tortured, and left suspended from the platforms as the attackers torched the structures. Those brave men opted for a horrible death rather than reveal the location of the guerrilla headquarters. *But how could the Japanese have made their way past the lookouts? Had they parachuted*

Filipino collaborators in without being detected? Were enemy collaborators living right among them? Maybe some of their new recruits weren't who they professed to be. The Americans no longer slept as soundly as they had during the peaceful months of January, February, and March.

Japanese propaganda document

OPPRESSION vs. LIBERATION

The Filipino people's loyalty to their country is beyond question. It is a national characteristic that has manifested itself in many a critical moment in the past, and been proven in battlefield on more than one occasion.

It was this spirit of loyalty to country that has moved Lapulapu, Rizal and other Filipino heroes to fight against Spain; that has inspired Aguinaldo to revolt against America. It is perhaps the same spirit that lies behind most of the present guerrilla activities against the Imperial Nippon Army due to their having been misled by enemy propaganda.

We ask them, therefore, *to ascertain first if their present acts of resistance are conducive to the realization of their aims.*

THE GUERRILLA ELEMENTS SHOULD KNOW that Nippon is fighting this war precisely for the purpose of helping the Filipinos establish a Philippines for the Filipinos.

Since both the Japanese and the Filipinos have the same purpose in view, IT IS RIDICULOUS FOR THE FILIPINO GUERRILLAS TO FIGHT AGAINST THE JAPANESE.

In the light of the foregoing, coupled with Nippon's solemn reiteration of her ideal to grant the Philippines the honor of independence, and the Imperial Army's policy of "enlightenment rather than punishment" towards the as yet "handful of misguided elements in the Philippines", it is more logical for the guerrillas—in order to realize their purpose of creating a Philippines for the Filipinos—to cooperate with the Imperial Nippon Forces instead of fighting against them.

We, therefore, invite the Guerrillas to lay down their arms and join us in the common task of building a new and greater Philippines for the Filipinos.

"Oppression vs. Liberation" (Japanese propaganda document)

Their communications system also suffered as runners were restricted to the hours of darkness in order to avoid detection by reconnaissance pilots. Even so, one runner heading to Baguio was caught, trussed up like a pig on a bamboo pole, and roasted to death over an open fire while the man's family was forced to watch. Again, the poor wretch never divulged a shred of information. They owed him gratitude beyond measure. Art had never thought of the Japanese as particularly human; with this atrocity, he became convinced they were less than animals and deserved the worst the guerrillas could dish out. His deep-seated sensibilities, born of his grandmother's stern sense of right and wrong, were eroding. His internal calluses thickened by the day. His resolve to survive, at whatever cost, grew like a smooth, cold, granite stone within.

In early April, the rest of the American civilians from Dyaka were captured: Bill and Marge Moule and their three children, Ted and Ruth Lawson and their little daughter, and Johnny and Virginia McCuish. The only good news was that, once cornered, those folks apparently didn't resist and were now interned at Camp Holmes a few miles north of Baguio.[2] As long as the Japanese were ignorant of their guerrilla connections—Bill Moule had by then been inducted into the Army by Charles Cushing—Art and his companions hoped they'd receive humane treatment, though they already knew the internees at Camp Holmes weren't getting enough to eat. They instructed their spies in Baguio to keep tabs on what was going on inside the camp.

THEN, ONE BY ONE, the guerrilla leaders began to fall.

A runner from the Lepanto mining area claimed Lieutenant Herman Kluege had been captured near Cervantes.[3] Art and his companions hadn't heard a word about him since he and Bob Arnold had left the Lusod sawmill a year earlier to head east over the mountains to Isabela Province. Even without confirmation, the report was unnerving.

In March Charles Cushing surrendered. His Filipina wife and children had been taken into custody and were being held at Santo Tomas prison in Manila, and his wife was begging him to surrender.[4] Some of his men drifted over to Robert Lapham's outfit, but others followed their commander's lead. They gave up and went home.[5]

Another guerrilla leader gave up under similar circumstances. Manuel P. Enriquez had fought as a captain with Colonel Bonnett's 71st Infantry defending the Ilocos beaches at the start of the war and had retreated up to Baguio when those forces were overrun. He'd hiked over the mountains with the Bonnett-Moses-Noble group. When it was reported at Aritao that the Balete Pass was already closed, Enriquez was among the troops disbanded. That report proved false, but it was too late. Most of the men, including Enriquez, had already scattered.[6]

Enriquez began organizing the disbanded soldiers. When Major Everett Warner, the old provost marshal from Camp John Hay, arrived on the scene from Baguio, Enriquez, believing it advantageous to have an American officer in charge, asked Warner to assume command. A few weeks later, Guillermo Nakar also made his way over the mountains from Baguio, and these three—Enriquez, Warner, and Nakar—teamed up to run the new guerrilla group, which they had named the 14th Infantry (Philippine Army). Enriquez did the organizing and recruitment, and Nakar harassed the Japanese attempting to enter the Cagayan Valley from the south. Warner's contribution was apparently limited to consuming a quart of whiskey a day.[7]

Following the fall of Bataan in April 1942, when the enemy entered the Cagayan Valley in large numbers, the 14th Infantry split into two parts. The first, commanded by Warner and Nakar, moved into eastern Nueva Vizcaya and Isabela. After the fall of Corregidor in May 1942, Warner surrendered and a month later died in jail. Nakar assumed command. On July 10, 1942[8], Nakar got a radio signal through to MacArthur's headquarters in Australia. As a result of this contact, all Nakar's guerrillas were inducted into the United States Army, and his outfit became the 14th Infantry (AUS). For a while Nakar managed to maintain radio contact with SWPA headquarters in Australia; however, toward the end of 1942, he was captured, tortured, and eventually executed.[9]

Meanwhile, the western segment of the 14th Infantry, commanded by Captain Enriquez, moved into western Nueva Vizcaya and eastern Benguet, and subsequently reported for duty with Colonel Horan's guerrilla unit, the 121st Infantry. Over the next two months, Enriquez expanded his organization, those efforts earning him a promotion to major. When Horan surrendered and ordered his men to do likewise, Enriquez was among those who refused. He reported in as soon as Moses assumed command, and Enriquez's unit conducted several effective raids and ambushes against the Japanese during the October 15, 1942, guerrilla offensive.[10]

The Japanese then grabbed his wife and children and were withholding critical medications from the children unless Enriquez gave up. He panicked, deserted his command, and traveled to Mountain Province, where in April 1943 he voluntarily surrendered to the Japanese.[11]

The only bright spot in this report was that following Enriquez's surrender, command of his men was assumed by the next senior officer, Major Romulo A. Manriquez.[12]

While Art and his companions could perhaps sympathize with their motivations, the surrender of Charles Cushing and Manuel Enriquez did nothing to boost morale among those holed up on their mountaintop in Kapangan.

In late May, Rufino Baldwin was captured, betrayed by a former fiancée. He was taken to the Kempeitai prison in downtown Baguio, where he was tortured and interrogated every day for months.[13] He was then transferred to Fort Santiago, the Japanese dungeon in Manila, where they were keeping him bound hand and foot in an isolation cell while he awaited a so-called trial by the Japanese on a litany of charges. It wasn't clear who had assumed leadership of Baldwin's 2nd Battalion, 11th Infantry (Philippine Army).[14]

Immediately after Baldwin, news came in concerning Enoch French and their old buddy, Tom Jagoe. Both had been commissioned as second lieutenants by Charles Cushing in September 1942 and were operating out of a small guerrilla camp at San Nicolas, Pangasinan, when they were murdered by one of their own bodyguards. The episode allegedly had nothing to do with the Japanese. Instead, it involved a dispute over counterfeit money that French possessed and the bodyguard felt he was entitled to. According to the story, the primary dispute arose between French and the bodyguard, but Tom, upon hearing the altercation, tried to intervene and was also shot to death at point blank range.[15, 16]

As Art digested this information, he thought back to the last time he'd seen Enoch at Lusod. He remembered Enoch's thick Boston accent as he described his beautiful wife, Barbara, how much he missed her and how, in retrospect, he'd made a terrible mistake leaving her behind and coming to the Philippines with the hope of making a quick killing in the mines.

Though they hadn't parted on good terms, Tom had been with Art and the others during their month-long retreat toward Manila and their long, arduous trip back north in February and March 1942. Art remembered wryly how Tom had gone off half-cocked and tried to shoot a chicken, but ended up scattering their ponies. He remembered, too, how Tom had apparently had no one to write a letter home to when given the opportunity at Mr. Delgado's villa in Sibul Spring. And now he was dead. *Did anyone care?* Well, they mourned him, and PK recited the Lord's Prayer so that Tom would have a proper sendoff to whatever he faced in the afterlife.

The next guerrilla leader to go down was Jack Langley, a miner who'd come to the Philippines with Bill Moule in 1940. Langley was commissioned a second lieutenant by Colonel Horan and had subsequently become attached to Nakar's 14th Infantry. In the summer of 1943, he was based at a small camp near Aritao. The mayor of Aritao, already suspected of collaborating, learned of Langley's activities and fingered him to the enemy. The account Art heard was that following his capture Jack was badly tortured, but the Japanese couldn't break him. Finally, in frustration, they yanked out all his teeth, fingernails, and toenails and left him to bleed to death in a fetid jail cell in Bayombong.[17]

During the first week of June 1943, the old colonels, Moses and Noble, finally ran out of luck. After leaving the Praeger-Adduru headquarters in Kabugao, they, accompanied by their longtime cook and security guard, Sergeant Donato Ignacio[18], hiked high into the mountains of Kalinga. Exhausted and suffering from dysentery, the group sought refuge in a cave just south of Balbalan. When they sent Ignacio to town for supplies, the Japanese nabbed him. After hours of torture, the man broke and led them to the cave. Moses and Noble were taken without a fight. They were marched to Lubuagan, Bontoc, then taken by bus to Camp John Hay, then to the Kempeitai prison in downtown Baguio, where they were starved, beaten, and interrogated for weeks, until they feigned cooperation and agreed to deliver propaganda speeches for their captors.[19] Then Moses and Noble were trucked to Bilibid Prison in Manila, there to stand trial for their alleged crimes. Art and his companions prayed for them, that somehow they would survive.

That wasn't the end of it. A runner brought word in July that Lieutenant Fish had been caught. Because he'd so recently been in their camp, they feared the intelligence reports and personal messages they'd sent with him were now in Japanese hands. One of Art's intelligence reports reportedly was sold in Baguio for a great deal of money. For weeks, they waited nervously, anticipating the Japanese would send a massive force up onto their mountaintop to wipe them out.

To protect against such a catastrophe, they established an evacuation camp in a cave several miles away and equipped it with a month's store of food and ammunition. If they got warning the Japanese were coming, at least they wouldn't be caught flat-footed. But their sleep was no longer peaceful. Everyone was constantly on edge. Not infrequently, PK awoke in the middle of the night and went outside to vomit.

Though he had tremendous misgivings about what lay ahead, Art had no desire to put those thoughts into words. On July 12, he tried to paint a rosy picture for Lil:

"My sweetheart.

We just got in some radio news from Baguio. It looks like things are getting underway at last—advances in the Solomons, New Guinea, and Russia. We just hope they keep it up. It's the long periods when nothing is happening that get us down.

"Our little yellow bastard neighbors down below haven't abandoned us, but they don't show much disposition to climb mountains in the rain. And let me say that our mountain is a high and difficult baby! We haven't been off of it now in six months.

"We just got in a few magazines. I'm so hungry for reading

material that once I get through a magazine, I go back and read it again, including all the advertisements. The best advertisements are the ones picturing an American woman and maybe some kids. I never thought I'd get excited at the sight of a pretty housewife in an apron and high heels pushing a vacuum cleaner around the living room floor. But such are the times in which we live.

"We've now confirmed the capture of our C.O.s, but someone else will take over and the work will go on. We've concluded that when this war is over, we're either going to get medals or be court-martialed. We've had to do a lot of things on our own responsibility—killing spies, burning sawmills, blowing up power plants, enlisting men, making promotions— that some meticulous bastard of a finance officer will probably find was 'not according to regulations.' But what the hell! We're fighting a war and we believe anything that helps us win is okay. (It just started to rain like the devil!)

"One of the books we have was written by Dorothy Canfield during World War I, describing conditions in France. I guess things aren't so different in this war. Victory seems to boil down to your ability to hold out. And for us, that's exactly what it will consist of. Whenever anybody asks what we did in the war, our answer is going to be: 'We survived!'

"PK and Spence are clean-shaven these days, but I'm still the Old Man of the Mountain. I've said that I'll shave when our forces take Bougainville Island in the Solomons. I own more razor blades than anybody. I also have quite a few matches as a result of not using many *and* some judicious poker playing, so now I have to furnish matches for all. But I drew the line at my razor blades. I said I could never tell when I might run across a beautiful blonde.

"The American and British civilians have been moved

from the concentration camp at Santo Tomas University in Manila to Los Baños on the shores of the Laguna de Bay, but so far the people interned at Camp Holmes in Baguio haven't been moved. The big-hearted Japs allow 25 cents a day per person to cover food, electricity, fuel, and medical supplies. Those folks are now accustomed to eating nothing but rice.

"Did I tell you that we have two little Igorot girls in the barrio near where we live that are about Eleanor's and Trisha's ages? I see them every once in a while. Their hair is far from blonde, their skin is far from fair, and they've never worn clothes in their lives. Mostly, I watch them play from a distance because they're afraid of soldiers and run away whenever I get too close and try to make friends. But they help me to visualize how big my girls must be now.

"During a recent period of boredom and being down in the dumps, I composed the enclosed parodies. I hope you'll enjoy them.

"This is all I have to say now, except, I love you, Art."[20]

THE LAST GUERRILLAS
(Tune: "When You and I Were Young, Maggie")

I wandered today to the hill, Buddy,
To watch the bay below,
To see if our supplies had come in, Buddy,
As promised to us long ago.

The Japs, they're still down below, Buddy,
The people all speak Nippongo,
All of our friends, they are dead, Buddy,
And we haven't much time to go.

They said for the Yanks to come back, Buddy,
Would take at least fifty years,
And judging by that, I believe, Buddy,
Our stuff, it should almost be here.

So take one more notch in your belt, Buddy,
The cows, they now are all gone,
And dream of the pay we will get, Buddy,
If we ever get off of Luzon.[21]

MY IGOROT MAID
(Tune: "The Isle of Capri")

'Twas on the Isle of Luzon that I found her,
Thank God fate never meant her for me,
She had an odor offensive about her,
All her clothes were from belly to knee.

She had hair that was jet black and oily,
The lice and the fleas held full sway,
Both her legs, they were muscled and soily,
And her eyes, they were surely not gay.

Every morning she'd leave us early,
To go and dig camotes all day,
She was quite a husky young girlie,
But not the sort that I'd care to lay.

So I left her unsullied and virgin,
Tho I admit, braving my good wife's wrath,
That it wouldn't have taken much urgin',
If only she'd have taken a bath.[22]

Occasionally there was a bright spot. They got a tremendous lift when Robin Hood arrived one day with thirteen of the fourteen volumes of the Cambridge Modern History series. Volume 9 was missing. The books had belonged to some high government official who'd fled Baguio and was now hiding out with his family on Mindanao. How Robin Hood got hold of them was anybody's guess. Art promptly grabbed Volume 4 and began to read.

ART HAD NOW BEEN IN THE PHILIPPINES more than thirty months and had avoided serious illness. He'd had a few minor attacks of malaria, some nasty skin infections, and an upset stomach from time to time, but certainly nothing life-threatening. All that changed when he contracted cerebral malaria and dysentery at the same time. It began one evening with nausea and a splitting headache and quickly escalated to a high fever, vomiting, and excruciating cramping in his gut, followed by body-wracking chills and continuous explosive diarrhea. He couldn't keep anything down and was delirious by the fifth day, thrashing and screaming like a madman. By the seventh day, fearing he was dying, PK sent word to Baguio, pleading for a doctor or nurse.

Art couldn't remember the arrival of Nona[23], a Filipina Red Cross nurse, and only vaguely remembered the days that followed. Because his stench made their headquarters uninhabitable for the others, Nona had him moved to a small shack, where she ministered to him around the clock, swaddling him in wet towels during episodes of spiking fever and wrapping him in blankets and rocking him like a baby during the worst of the chills. She fed him a brackish, foul-tasting native concoction until his worst symptoms began to subside, and then added tiny morsels of mashed rice and vegetables. Each day she massaged his legs and feet until he was able to stand for short periods and finally to take a few steps. Each night she slept next to him to share the warmth of her body.

After several weeks, with Nona's encouragement, Art tried to read. When his eyes wouldn't focus, she read aloud to him, until he could see again, and then he read aloud to her. Together they learned about the Thirty Years' War in Europe and the gradual disintegration of the Spanish Empire. Under her gentle care, he improved slowly, although he lost nearly a quarter of his body weight.

As Art convalesced, he and Nona spent long hours in quiet conversation. He told her about Lil and his two little girls and how happy they'd been in America before the war.

Nona had grown up in an aristocratic home in Manila, where her doting father had made a small fortune in his import-export business. As a child she had been educated by Catholic nuns, and after high school had graduated from nursing school and gone to work for the hospital in Baguio, anticipating a bright future. When the Japanese took over Baguio, however, their guards at the hospital had ogled and harassed her. Fearful of being raped, Nona had slipped out of the hospital one afternoon and caught a bus back to Manila, where she'd worked for a while as a private nurse.

When Nona's father refused to cooperate with the Japanese, they'd arrested him, thrown him into prison, and torched the family home. Nona had escaped, but her mother had died in the blaze. A few months later her only brother had been brutally murdered by the Japanese after he was caught smuggling guns and supplies to a group of guerrillas hiding out in the Zambales Mountains. Frightened and alone, Nona had returned to Baguio, where she knew friends involved in the resistance, and now she devoted all her energies to helping the cause.

Halfway through telling her story, Nona broke down, overcome with emotion, and it was several minutes before she could continue. It was the first time she'd been able to cry for her lost family.

Gradually the friendship between Art and Nona deepened, two lonely human beings caught up in a tangled web of circumstances they couldn't control. For a time they became lovers, both recognizing their relationship had no future, and expecting none, but grateful for even a short interlude of comfort and caring and connectedness, a time for their battered souls to mend a bit.

Before Art recovered fully, Nona was called away to care for other sick guerrillas. She came back to visit from time to time, but then disappeared. He never knew if she survived the war.

"August 22, 1943

"My dearest. I'm still alive and kicking, having recovered from a recent attack of malaria that had me pretty low.

"The news leaves nothing to complain about these days as Sicily falls, the Reds push the Nazis back, and we advance in the Solomons, while at the same time bombing northern Japan. I'm not holding my breath until a second front is opened up here, but I can be patient if things keep going as they are now. Recently, several shiploads of Japs embarked for places unknown, so those Allied successes are beginning to create ripples here. Even the Jap newspaper is admitting a few losses.

"I just finished reading an 800-page volume of the Cambridge Modern History on the Thirty Years' War and am now halfway through the one on the Age of Louis XIV. Judging by them, I've concluded that wars are the rule in history, not the exception, and that we got a free ride for the 20 years before Pearl Harbor.

"I recently met an American officer who worked as a miner in Arabia before the war. He was telling me about the international mining game and similar international jobs. They seem to be a cinch after you once break into them, and the man who works for less than $250 a month is a sucker. I think, when this war is over, I'm going to hit up

Marsman & Company for a job. They're one of the biggest import-export outfits in the Philippines and also have a branch in Hong Kong, and they pay quite well. I'll try to work a deal whereby I'm hired as of about three months after I get home. I could then come home via Army transport, we could have a three-month vacation and spree, and then the company would pay our way back via ocean liner, first class. It's customary that when you've filled your two- or three-year contract, the company pays your way home again, and if you're willing to renew your contract, they'll give you a month or two of paid vacation anywhere in the world, with transportation paid both ways. Who could ask for a better deal? I'm going to give it a try, anyway, if and when this damned war is over. Love, Art."[24]

As Art reread the letter before putting it aside for Robin Hood, he knew it wasn't altogether honest and sounded far more optimistic than he felt. But Art and Lil in their early days had often talked of seeing the world. Or maybe he'd done the talking and Lil had done the listening. They'd dreamed of traveling the globe, learning about different people, different languages, and different cultures, of not being trapped in a world defined by how often the grass got mowed, what was going on in some dead-end job, or what they saw on the screen at the local movie theater. They'd never quite figured out how to realize their dreams, but there on that mountaintop in Kapangan, during the depths of the war, ruminating about the possibilities helped Art to get through the days and maintain his sanity.

CHAPTER 21

VOLCKMANN TAKES OVER
September *through* November 1943

IN AUGUST, A MESSAGE ARRIVED BY RUNNER from Major Russell Volckmann's headquarters in Kiangan, Ifugao Subprovince, advising that as the next senior officer still free in northern Luzon, he was officially assuming command of the United States Army Forces in the Philippines, North Luzon (USAFIP-NL). The Moses-Noble territory included everything from the north coast south to a line extending from the southern end of the Lingayen Gulf eastward through the town of San Jose in Nueva Ecija to the east coast of Tayabas at Baler Bay.[1] Calvert sent the runner back with a reply acknowledging Volckmann's takeover and wishing him well.

Wasting no time in exercising his authority, Volckmann first tackled what he perceived to be the major obstacle to a unified command: communications.

While Colonel Moses had attempted to maintain direct contact with each leader within his command, he had not always succeeded. Most of the scattered units had no radio, and the traditional bamboo telegraph had proven a poor vehicle for maintaining military control. Lack of communication and strong leadership had sometimes resulted in rivalries and boundary disputes among his guerrilla leaders, rivalries that had occasionally deteriorated into open warfare.

To improve communications, Colonel Volckmann devised a system patterned on the one Art and his group had established in Benguet, but he carried it several steps further. He ordered that carefully concealed centers be set up, approximately six hours' hike apart, through which messages could travel day and night from one end of the command to the other. Each center had its own chief, charged with keeping track of enemy activity in his area and apprising adjoining message centers of potential threats. Runners were stationed around the clock at each center, ready to grab an incoming message and run the next leg. If a roving Japanese patrol came too close, a trail was abandoned and a new one created. Volckmann envisioned eventually having local chiefs hire *cargadores* from their civilian populations so that supplies as well as messages, and eventually personnel and troops, might move along the message center routes with comparative safety and speed.[2]

Volckmann next tackled reorganization. Recognizing that no single commander could maintain adequate control over such a vast territory, he divided his guerrillas into seven districts, each under a sub-commander:

- 1st District—All units in Benguet, commanded by Major Parker Calvert, then existing commander of the Detachment, 1st Battalion, 43rd Infantry (Philippine Scouts).

- 2nd District—La Union and southern Ilocos Sur Provinces, commanded by Major George M. Barnett, who had inherited Colonel Horan's 121st Infantry following his surrender.

- 3rd District—Northern Ilocos Sur, Abra, and Ilocos Norte, also commanded by Major Barnett as no known guerrilla units operated there at the time and the 121st Infantry was best located to expand into those areas.

- 4th District—Apayao and Cagayan Provinces were allotted to Major Ralph Praeger. Although contact with

Praeger had been absent for months, Volckmann believed he was still operating in those areas.

- 5th District—Isabela and Nueva Vizcaya Provinces, commanded by Major Romulo A. Manriquez, commanding officer of the surviving eastern arm of the 14th Infantry (Army of the United States).

- 6th District—The parts of Nueva Ecija and Pangasinan Provinces north of the Lingayen-San Jose line were allotted to Captain Robert Lapham, who was already operating there.

- 7th District—The subprovinces of Ifugao, Bontoc, and Kalinga were initially retained under the command of Major Volckmann and his adjutant, Donald Blackburn.[3]

Each district chief was given authority to reorganize all troops within his assigned area into a unified command.[4, 5]

Volckmann also instituted a new system of code names. The first two digits, 11, identified Volckmann's overall command, followed by the first letter of the individual's last name, represented by its numerical position in the English alphabet. Thus Volckmann became 1122, with "V" being the twenty-second letter of the alphabet. Calvert became 113, "C" being the third letter, Barnett became 112, Manriquez became 1113, and so on. As Calvert's subordinates, Art was labeled 113-A and Spence became 113-B. Messages between units were thereafter sent under their code names.

Finally, Volckmann directed each district commander to draw up detailed plans for potential future action within his district: locate all Japanese telephone wires and mark them for destruction; identify enemy supply routes and select their most vulnerable spots for ambush; locate supply depots, motor pools, enemy troop concentrations, and command posts to be eliminated with explosives; lay plans to strangle the enemy by cutting off his access to food and construction materials, native labor, and all alternative modes of transportation.

A T DISTRICT 1 HEADQUARTERS, there was work to be done. Following Rufino Baldwin's capture, his unit appeared to be disintegrating, so PK and Art jointly decided that Spence would move down near Dalupirip and take over the unit. They hated to break up their longstanding threesome, but it was a necessary military decision. September 22 was set as the date for his departure.

As the first step in complying with Volckmann's directive to form a unified district command, on November 5, the Detachment, 1st Battalion, 43rd Infantry (Philippine Scouts), was renamed the 1st Battalion, 43rd Infantry (Philippine Scouts), and PK placed Art in command. The three Benguet battalions—Art's new 1st Battalion, 43rd Infantry (Philippine Scouts), Spencer's newly acquired 2nd Battalion, 11th Infantry (Philippine Army), and Dennis Molintas's 3rd Battalion, 12th Infantry (Philippine Army)—were combined into one infantry regiment. To name the new regiment, they simply added together the numbers of the existing infantry

Nowhere Yet Everywhere logo

units—43, 11, and 12—and came up with the 66th Infantry (Composite). Officers were in short supply, so PK designated Art executive officer, adjutant, and chief intelligence officer of the new 66th Infantry.[6] They named their headquarters Camp Shangri-La. To promote esprit de corps, they came up with a regimental motto, "Nowhere Yet Everywhere," while one of their more artistic soldiers sketched a regimental logo.

Volckmann was so impressed with the smoothly running intelligence operation in Benguet that he appointed Major Calvert to serve as G-2—chief intelligence officer—for the entire USAFIP-NL command. Art was appointed assistant G-2. From then on, intelligence reports from all district commanders were sent by runner to 66th Infantry headquarters in Kapangan. Art consolidated, organized, and typed them into weekly reports, then monthly, and sent those by secret agent down to Robert Lapham in Pangasinan or Bernard Anderson, operating in Tayabas. Where they went from there was anybody's guess.[7]

Promotion Recommendation for 113A

With this grand reorganization, all had greatly increased responsibilities, meriting commensurate elevations in rank. Major

Volckmann authorized field promotions for all district commanders, and called upon the district commanders to submit recommendations for promotion of subordinates. All promotions, of course, were subject to later confirmation by a higher headquarters. Volckmann became a lieutenant colonel, as did majors Calvert, Barnett, Blackburn, and Manriquez. Spence, as the newest of the battalion commanders, was promoted to first lieutenant.

Calvert's recommendation that Art be promoted to major was quite generous. When he presented Art with his copy, he smiled and pointed to paragraph 2 as he reached over and gave Art's luxurious beard a gentle tug. *Not in strict compliance with Army regulations, you know.* Art grinned and reminded him that *Mac's forces haven't yet taken Bougainville, you know.*

On September 21, he brought Lil up to date as much as he dared:

> "Sweetie Pie. It's been a month since I last wrote. Italy has surrendered, to our joy and the Japs' confusion, resulting in all kinds of explanations in the Jap *Tribune*. But we haven't had any news now in ten days. There's a concerted hunt on for un-'reconditioned' short wave radios, so they've all gone into hiding, at least for a while.
>
> "Our little yellow friends are wandering around three or four kilometers from here. I hope they'll stay there as I have no desire to sleep out.
>
> "PK recently recommended that I be promoted to major. A major gets $430.50 per month, which would be a raise of $88.50. After next March, when my next fogey is due, I would draw $443.00. As we say, 'We make lots of money, but we don't have any fun!' Anyway, if I get the majority, I can wear gold braid on my dress cap—if I ever get a dress cap!

"Spencer is leaving tomorrow to take charge of another outfit that we've fallen heir to. We're really going to miss him.

"We recently got ambitious and carved ourselves a set of bamboo chessmen. We're playing by the rules as we remember them, but we don't always agree. The winner usually depends upon who makes the fewest mistakes.

"I cannot imagine what Patricia must look like now. I'd been keeping track of her by thinking of Eleanor at the same age, but now Trisha has passed Eleanor's age when I last saw her. I read in the Jap *Tribune* that American children are being left in parked cars while their mothers work in the war plants. We got a jump on them on that score, didn't we, when we left Eleanor locked in our car so we could see a show. I also hear there's no meat left in the U.S. As soon as the war is over, let me know if this is true, and I'll try to bring home some dried *baca* (cow) meat and a *manook* (chicken) or two.

"I made you a birthday card. I hope you like it.

"The Japs are coming closer. Bye-bye and love, Art."[8]

V OLCKMANN MADE OTHER SIGNIFICANT changes. Mimicking a procedure already established successfully in Major George Barnett's 2nd District, he ordered that all individual units be removed from the barrios. Henceforth, units were to be widely dispersed, away from civilian-populated areas. The locations of individual units and the names of the officers and men were kept secret as much as possible so that, if the Japanese captured one man, the information they could elicit through torture or coercion would be limited. Strict military protocols and disciplinary standards were put in place, and regular training scheduled.[9] With the new setup, discipline improved and morale soared.[10]

Volckmann envisioned that each district would eventually have a field hospital equipped with six doctors, one dental officer, six to fourteen nurses, and seventy enlisted men to serve as orderlies, and would be augmented by civilian employees when necessary.[11] That requirement presented quite a challenge for rural areas like Kapangan, where the only medical people were native medicine men. The goal was not fully realized in Calvert's district for more than a year, and then was only achieved by kidnapping nearly all the personnel and supplies of a Baguio-area hospital.

Under Volckmann's plan, district commanders were responsible for maintaining the support of their local civilian populations.[12] The majority of the Igorots loved America and hated the Japanese; however, as food and other supplies dwindled and as the Japanese bore down harder on the locals, spies, informants, and collaborators became more numerous while active supporters dwindled in number. After all, who could expect a farmer to turn over part of his rice harvest to feed guerrillas if one of his neighbors was apt to turn him in for a small reward and he ended up losing his head? To solve this dilemma, Volckmann ordered that even *suspected* spies, informers, and collaborators be tracked down and eliminated.[13] To discourage the loss of troops and arms, he ordered that any soldier who voluntarily surrendered to the enemy or allowed himself to be captured through his own negligence would be shot on sight, and any soldier or civilian who surrendered arms or gave information to the enemy would face immediate execution, without regard to mitigating circumstances.[14]

These orders were tough to carry out but proved effective, and the evidence that the guerrillas could be just as tough as the Japanese earned them grudging respect. Word came in via a Baguio agent that the Japanese were openly telling each other, "All of the brave and worthwhile men are in the mountains."[15]

Next on Volckmann's agenda was expansion into areas claimed but not yet under the control of USAFIP-NL. Major George M. Barnett's 121st Infantry, the largest of the regiments, was ordered to expand into the 3rd District. A few months later, when it was confirmed that Major Ralph Praeger was no longer functioning in the 4th District, Major Donald Blackburn's 7th District was instructed to absorb that area. Because Lieutenant Robert Lapham tacitly refused to acknowledge Volckmann's authority, Calvert's 66th Infantry was authorized to expand southward into San Manuel and San Nicolas, Pangasinan, in order that they might draw food from those areas to feed their troops. Likewise, the 121st Infantry was authorized to expand southward into the Sison-Pozorrubio area of Pangasinan. The 121st even established, for a time, a company in the Bolinao-Alaminos region of Pangasinan, with communications being maintained with this unit by *banca* across the Lingayen Gulf.[16] Thus Volckmann's original seven districts were reduced to four: the 1st District under Calvert, the 2nd and 3rd Districts combined under Barnett, the 4th and 7th Districts combined under Volckmann/Blackburn, and the 5th District under Manriquez. Later, when Barnett's 121st Infantry grew so large it became unwieldy, the northern portion was again truncated and became the 15th Infantry, bringing the total to five.

Meanwhile, the Japanese got cocky. Figuring they'd captured and executed virtually all the major guerrilla leaders on Luzon, the commanding general of the Japanese Imperial forces declared that guerrilla resistance in the Islands had been eliminated and it was time to follow through on their promise of independence for the Filipino people. Amid much staged fanfare and celebration, Japan officially granted the Philippines its independence on October 14, 1943. However, only Japan, Nazi Germany, and Spain recognized the new regime.

On October 31, Art wrote to Lil:

"My dearest Lil. I am still among the ranks of the free and footloose. I've had a nasty cold, but I'm recovered now. The rains, which we thought were gone, have recently returned. When it's not raining, it's quite foggy around our mountain.

"Our little yellow friends haven't caused too many problems of late. They did raid the camp of one of our neighbors at 3 a.m. one morning, but without success; he'd already gotten away. Because they had such good information concerning his location, though, two local citizens were sent on 'a long vacation to Japan.' We trust this will constrain any others who may be tempted to go against their better judgment by the rustle of Jap paper money.

"One of our neighbors to the north has been on quite a spy-killing spree. He's done away with over 150 during the last couple of months. I don't believe all his victims are guilty, as evidence obtained by the third degree is not always reliable. However, that's his business, not mine.

"I just realized the other day that it's been 33 months since I last saw you and the babies. In a very short time, one-half of our married life will have been spent separated from each other. Suffice it to say, this life out here has already passed the point of being 'an interesting and valuable experience.'

"Everywhere in Luzon, the Japs are preparing for air raids by digging shelters and mounting anti-aircraft guns. We wish we could be as expectant as the Japs are of Allied planes coming soon. The only base from which planes could reach the Philippines is China. The U.S. has had an air force there for months now without doing anything in our direction, so why should they start now? We still tell the people, though, that all these preparations by the Japs are a refutation of the Jap contention that the Allies will never come back to the Philippines.

"To change the subject, they have quite a system in this country. Our host is walking around the yard with Ubing, the baby, slung over his back in a cotton shawl, while also weaving some rattan pack straps. His wife and daughters are up on the hill digging *camotes*. They went out this morning just after they fed the pigs and will get back just in time to feed the pigs this evening. The Orient is certainly a man's world!

"I wonder what grade my daughters will be in when I get home. Or will I get back in time to watch them graduate college? I certainly hope it's not that long.

"And so, until my next letter, I send all my love. Art."[17]

Calvert's regiment continued the relentless track-down of spies and informants in Benguet. No effort was spared in finding and eliminating the kingpins of every spy conspiracy they uncovered. After a few months, Volckmann's policies bore fruit as traitors began seeking cover within localities strongly garrisoned by the Japanese. Calvert's secret agents eventually caught up with many of them anyway. For instance, a sizeable number of Filipino agents working for the

Japanese in Baguio fled eighty miles north to the town of Cervantes, where they took refuge in the local Japanese garrison, a building protected night and day by lookouts dug into foxholes around its perimeter. Calvert ordered Dennis Molintas's 3rd Battalion to find and eliminate them. They raided the town under cover of darkness, pinned the Japanese lookouts in their foxholes, and then set fire to the garrison building. The few spies who managed to escape the fire were easily picked off, like shooting fish in a barrel.[18]

PK and Art whooped and hollered when news of this massacre reached their mountaintop. They brought out the jug of *tapuey* they'd been saving for Christmas and toasted Captain Molintas and the 3rd Battalion. They'd come a long way since the execution of Captain Rivero and the Japanese civilian at Lusod. Being responsible for the burning alive of a few dozen spies didn't bother them one bit.

> "Somewhere in North Luzon, November 27, 1943
>
> "My dearest. For a while yesterday, it looked like I was going to have to spend our wedding anniversary hiding in the bushes or a cave. A Jap patrol came to a nearby trail junction, but they took the wrong branch of the trail, so we're a little more at ease today.
>
> "Six years ago today you became my wife and my life. In many ways, it seems like centuries. Yet I can still remember how you looked as you came down the aisle at the J.P.'s office with that dinky navy blue hat on your head. I can still remember how I carried you over the threshold of our little bungalow, and we found ourselves, husband and wife, in our own home. I can still remember how we tied that colored bandanna around the lampshade to make it more romantic, and then fell fast asleep! All these things seem like only yesterday. Yet how much has happened since then.

"I came home one day, and you said, 'Hello, Papa.' Months later I was admitted to the delivery room as a spectator and ended up helping to hold you down. We heated the kitchen almost red-hot to give Eleanor her first bath. We made the trip up to Berkeley on the Greyhound bus to show her off to Grandma. We ditched her long enough to take a quick trip to Crater Lake and Yosemite. (Remember the parties we had with that jug of haut sauterne?) We went to the snow at Big Bear. I said good-bye to you at the Glendale station as I started for summer camp to spend our first anniversary apart, never dreaming we'd spend so many others the same way. Our threesome became a foursome. Your body so melted into mine as we embraced when I returned to move you to Carmel. You looked so alarmed when I told you I was going to the Philippines, until I said you were going too. Then you were so excited at the prospect, only to have your hopes dashed. We did our best at a gay going-away celebration, but you looked so forlorn as the USAT *Grant* pulled away from Fort Mason. And barely over three years of our life together had elapsed.

"Then you became a neatly addressed letter that came with (almost) every Clipper, and a great vacant space in my heart. After the December 8th bombing, you were the addressee of the radiogram that I sent, telling of my safety. Since then, all has been darkness except for the ray of light shed for a few brief moments when I heard you speak to me over KGEI, a darkness like exists in a long tunnel whose entrance is ever-receding and whose exit is too far away to give any light. I have such wonderful plans for the future, but I dare not as yet make hopes of them. Destiny gave me much happiness during the brief span of time we had together, and I dare not expect more, but I will be ever so grateful if she will place you in my arms once again.

"If it should chance to be that we've drained our cup of happiness, not to be refilled, let the joys we've known together fill the vacant spaces in the days to come, but don't let them crowd out the joys the future may bring. Should you meet someone who will love you as I have loved you and who will be a father to our little girls as I would have been, accept his love and know that I will bless you both. Love, Art."[19]

CHAPTER 22

THE GRIND GOES ON AT HOME

January through December 1943

WHILE 1942 HAD ENDED with a few promising developments on the Pacific war front—in the Solomon Islands and New Guinea—the New Year brought additional stress. The Port of Embarkation continued hiring at an astounding rate. Because of the lack of trained office personnel in the labor market, the government established the Port Clerical Training School to qualify less experienced women for positions on both sides of the Bay. For war purposes, typing speed requirements were reduced and new hires were given an intense one-month refresher course, including typing, filing, military correspondence training, typewriter shortcuts, stencil-cutting, business English, and shorthand.[1]

In spite of these measures, the workload in Lillian's office only increased. Employees were asked to work additional hours. Although Lil had young children, she had her mother to care for them, so she told Captain Dillon she could work Mondays and Thursdays until 10 p.m. The girls were usually in bed by the time she got home, and often Lillian Sr. was so worn out that she was asleep also. People all around Lil were testing their limits, and she could too. She didn't complain.

The next weeks became a blur of fatigue. Working nearly sixty hours a week, Lil felt like a robot, a brain-dead machine. Sensing her mounting stress, Captain Dillon asked one day how she was able to cope with the additional demands. She told him, *I pretty much just put my head down, sir, and push on.*

But everyone has a breaking point, don't you think?

I suppose so, but I've never stopped long enough to consider that someday I might reach mine.

Have you ever asked God for help?

No, sir, I haven't. Actually, I've never had any religious training. I think about God from time to time, and I've taught my children to say little prayers at bedtime, but I guess I learned as a child to rely on myself, to believe I was strong enough to handle whatever life might throw at me. I've always considered that asking someone else for help was a form of weakness.

You're a very capable woman, that's obvious, but I'm not sure that's always enough. These are demanding times we're living in, and I think everyone's limits will be sorely tested. I come from a strong Catholic background, and I have an unwavering belief in God. My faith has always sustained me through tough times, and I've never considered it weakness to ask Him for help. It's just something you might think about.

Lil thanked Captain Dillon for his concern, and she thought about their conversation as she drove home. The idea of sharing one's burdens with God doubtless had a certain appeal. But then another crisis erupted, and it took everything she had. Trisha picked up a bad cold that turned into a severe infection in both ears. She wouldn't eat, couldn't sleep, and spent all day crying pitifully and pulling at her ears. Sucking her thumb only increased the pain. Lil knew there was little a doctor could do since she wasn't running a high fever, so she and Lillian Sr. resorted to home remedies. A hot water bottle wrapped in a towel helped a bit, as did warmed camphor oil applied with a medicine dropper, but the only thing that lulled the child to sleep for even short periods was being held and walked about the house. The women alternated all night long, but by morning Lillian Sr. could do no more and fell into bed, completely spent. Eleanor awoke early. She was abnormally quiet as Lil prepared her breakfast. Solemnly watching Trisha whimpering in the playpen, she asked, *Is Trisha going to die?*

Lil was taken aback. *Of course not. She has an ear infection, that's all.*

I think she's going to die.

Lil called the office and told them she couldn't come in. One day off stretched to two, then to three, before Patricia improved enough for her to return to work.

Stacks of paperwork spilled out of her inbox. The other women had worked extra hours and tried their best to pick up the slack, but many items were marked "Top Secret" and had to be dealt with by Lil personally. She felt terribly guilty about letting her coworkers down. Several  times that morning Captain Dillon brought fresh coffee to her desk as she did her best to dig out.

The following Thursday, after finishing work at ten, Lil hurried to the parking lot to head home. Cynthia's engine turned over normally, but the gearshift wouldn't go into reverse, and she couldn't back out of her parking place. She tried several times without success, and then ran back into the building to use the phone before the office was locked up for the night. There was no answer at the first three auto shops she dialed. Just then Captain Dillon emerged from his office. *Is something wrong, Mrs. Murphy?*

Well, yes, there is, sir. I can't get my car into reverse.

The captain followed her back to the parking lot and also tried several times, but the gearshift was stuck fast. *I'll tell you what*, he said. *I'm heading out myself. I'll be more than happy to take you home tonight and pick you up for work tomorrow morning. Then we can get one of the fellows from the mechanical shop to take a look and hopefully fix what's wrong, or at least diagnose the problem.*

I couldn't ask you to do that, sir. I'll just call a taxi.

Nonsense. It's no trouble at all. I'll lock up, and then we'll be on our way.

Lil thanked him profusely, and they exchanged pleasantries on the drive to Berkeley. When Captain Dillon inquired how Trisha's ears were coming along, Lil told him, *She's much better now, sir, and thank you for asking.*

Oh, please don't call me sir. I get that all day long, and, after a while, I find it pretty tedious. Please call me Frank.

All right, Frank. You may call me Lillian.

Except for the porch light, the house was dark when they arrived. Captain Dillon waited in his car until Lil got safely inside.

She was up early the next morning, dressed, and ready to leave at quarter after seven. Lillian Sr. was up too, so Lil explained what had happened with the car and that she hoped to have the problem resolved sometime during the day. When Captain Dillon arrived, Lil was waiting at the curb. She could see Lillian Sr. peeking through the curtains in the front window as he got out and came around to open the passenger door.

As soon as they reached the office, Captain Dillon called for a mechanic, who arrived shortly and tinkered with the transmission until he got it working. Lil felt extremely grateful and thanked Captain Dillon again.

I'm happy to help, Lillian. I think God is looking out for you and knows you're more valuable here at your desk than worrying about fixing your car. And remember, it's Frank, not captain or sir.

AS THE WEEKS WORE ON, activity at Oakland Army Base continued to escalate. At all hours of the day and night, seven days a week, long freight trains that had hooted and clattered and snaked their way west from around the country converged in the East Bay to disgorge millions of tons of cargo: trucks, tanks, and jeeps from refitted auto factories in Detroit; bulldozers, cranes, and other construction equipment; rifles, bullets, machine guns, bombs, hand grenades, blankets, canteens, clothing, boots, and medical supplies from plants in obscure towns; food, oil, gasoline, and all manner of raw materials. Forklifts transferred the arriving rail cargo into dozens of multi-block-long warehouses, where it was sorted, classified, placed on a prioritized shipping schedule, and eventually loaded onto huge ships heading to designated battle theaters in the Pacific. Every facet of the work was top secret. Time scheduling had to be precise and was subject to last-minute revision as conditions on the battlefields evolved and needs changed. Small leaks or mistakes occurring anywhere in the process might have serious, far-reaching consequences.[2] Tension and urgency permeated the air.

THE ATMOSPHERE IN LIL'S OFFICE mimicked that in the warehouses, filled not with heavy equipment sounds but with the rustle of shuffling papers, the incessant ringing of telephones, the clanking of metal file drawers, and the steady staccato clatter of a dozen typewriters. Plumes of cigarette smoke curled toward the ceiling, but cigarettes weren't enough to calm her nerves. She frequently caught herself clenching her teeth as she worked, and often by the end of the day her jaw ached and her neck was stiff and sore.

Lil's car troubles weren't over either. The transmission continued behaving erratically, and on a couple of mornings she was late for work. The exhaust pipe belched black smoke as the engine burned increasing amounts of scarce, rationed oil. Her tires had almost no tread left, but under the rationing rules she couldn't qualify for new ones. Then, as she was on her way home one evening, the right front tire blew, causing her to lose control momentarily. The car fishtailed down Sacramento Avenue, and she narrowly missed colliding with an oncoming truck. *What if I had been killed?* The only new cars being produced in the country were reserved for high government officials, and people weren't parting with their used ones. At her wits' end, Lil sold Art's beloved Cynthia for scrap[3] and began taking public transportation.

What had been a twenty-minute commute of less than nine miles now required three streetcar and bus transfers and a ten-minute walk at either end. Counting the waiting time at each transfer point, it took Lil an hour to get to work, longer on rainy days, and another hour to get home. Captain Dillon offered her a ride. She refused at first but then accepted on Monday and Thursday nights to avoid waiting alone for buses on the dark, menacing streets of downtown Oakland.

As they drove to Berkeley late one evening, the conversation turned again to God. Lil told Captain Dillon, *I think I'm ready to share my burden, but I'm not sure how to begin. I've never been in a Catholic church and I wouldn't know what to do.*

Let me show you, Lillian. You won't be sorry. This coming Sunday I'll pick you up for morning mass.

When told of the arrangement, Lillian Sr. narrowed her eyes and pressed her lips together into a tight line. Her displeasure was obvious, but she said nothing.

On Sunday, Captain Dillon parked at the curb and came to the door. Lil briefly introduced her mother, her sister Lucille, and the girls, and to each he offered his hand and a nice greeting.

Captain Dillon drove to St. Joseph the Worker Catholic Church, a beautiful old building with magnificent stained-glass windows, situated only two blocks away on Addison Street. They could easily have walked. It was crowded, but they found seats in a pew toward the back. Then mass began. Lil sat quietly with her eyes closed and listened as the Latin words and the music washed over her, gentle and soothing. When it was over, Captain Dillon drove her home. They chatted for a few moments.

What did you think? he asked.

I thought it was beautiful, Lil said. *I'm so glad I went.*

It will mean much more as you begin to understand, and I can help you with that if you want.

Yes, I'd like that. Thank you, Frank.

As he drove Lil home on Monday and Thursday nights, Captain Dillon began teaching her church history and the stories of the Bible. He recited passages from memory and explained their meaning. He also told her about himself. As he'd grown up in New York City, the Catholic Church had been the solid foundation of his large Irish family, and, at his mother's urging, he'd seriously considered becoming a priest before deciding instead to enter law school. His father had been a deputy police commissioner before retiring and opening an insurance agency. After his father died of a heart attack in 1925, he'd remained at home to care for his mother until her death in 1935. Lil could identify with his deeply ingrained sense of responsibility and family duty.

She also told him about her family, about Art and his family, and the adversities both had faced growing up. He was an excellent listener and assured Lil that Art had undoubtedly developed the qualities and strength of character necessary to bring him safely through the terrible war.

After that, Captain Dillon drove to Spaulding Avenue each Sunday morning, and they walked to Sunday mass at St. Joseph's. He suggested that Eleanor, now nearly five, might enjoy attending their Sunday school program. She loved it from the very first day and could soon recite simple Bible verses on her own. Lil smiled as Eleanor tried to get Trisha to repeat them, but she could see disapproval written all over her mother's face.

One Monday night, while driving her home from work, Captain Dillon reached in his pocket, pulled out a tiny box, and handed it to Lil. *This belonged to my mother,* he said. *I'd like you to have it.* On a bed of cotton batting lay a delicate sterling silver rosary strung with blue crystal beads.

It's beautiful, she told him, *but I don't think—*

This rosary hasn't been inside a church in more than five years. My mother was a wonderful woman, a strong woman, a beautiful woman, just as you are. I think she'd be happy to know I've placed her rosary in deserving hands.

Lil made no attempt to hide the gift from her mother, and this was evidently the last straw. Lillian Sr.'s anger spilled over in a torrent of accusations and recriminations. *You're a married woman, you have two children, and your husband is away at war. You have no business cavorting around with another man.*

I'm not cavorting, Mother. Captain Dillon and I are coworkers and friends. I have to work late some nights, and, for my own safety, he's been kind enough to drive me home. As far as going to church is concerned, he's helping me discover my own faith in God, and that faith is bringing me some peace of mind where Art is concerned. It's helping me to get through these days and months of uncertainty. Is that so hard to understand?

Her mother's reply was caustic: *I wasn't much older than you are when we lost your father. And I had four children, not two. I didn't have the education or skills to get a good job like yours, but we somehow got along. It's been very, very hard for me, but I've done the best I can to teach you right from wrong. What you are doing is wrong.*

The arguments went on, neither of them willing to give an inch. In May, Lillian Sr. announced she had found another job and she and Lucille were moving out.[4] Lil tried to dissuade her, but further discussion was pointless. Lillian Sr. was adamant. When she felt she was right about something, more talk always proved futile. Never in Lil's life had she been able to change her mother's mind about anything.

Through the employment office at Oakland Army Base, Lil found another young Army wife to move in and care for the girls. She had a little girl of her own and was also pregnant, so it wasn't a long-term solution, but Lil didn't have a choice.[5] Not as capable and meticulous as Margaret Thurman had been, Lil tried to ignore her shortcomings, grateful that the girls appeared well fed and content.

I N JULY, LIL GOT A PHONE CALL FROM ROBERTA. She was so excited that Lil had trouble understanding her. She'd received a letter from the War Department advising that Brew's name was included on a list of prisoners of war being held by the Japanese. The communiqué hadn't given a location but claimed all prisoners of war were being treated humanely, in accordance with the articles of the Geneva Convention. This was the first word about Brew in fourteen months. And he was still alive! Bert was so happy that she ran out of words and finally dissolved in tears. Lil cried right along with her.

Lil immediately wrote to the War Department again, requesting information about Art, and once again her hopes were dashed. His name hadn't shown up on any of the prisoner-of-war lists provided through Geneva.

C APTAIN DILLON AND HIS ASSISTANT, Lieutenant Truax, were required by their duties to be out of their office more than half the time, and when they were both gone, Lil was left in charge. She supervised a number of junior clerks. She also received, analyzed, classified, indexed, and then filed all incoming correspondence, documents, reports, and directives, much of it marked "Top Secret." If a secret document required forwarding, she executed the complicated procedures to send it on its way. She maintained multiple filing systems and set up new ones when necessary. In his absence, she also fielded all of Captain Dillon's phone calls. It was left to her discretion as to what information could or should be divulged to a caller.[6]

Toward the end of October, Captain Dillon recommended to the head of the Intelligence Branch in San Francisco that Lil's job be reclassified. His recommendation was approved. Effective

November 1, she was officially promoted from assistant clerk-typist to clerk-typist and received a raise to $150 a month.[7]

WAR NEWS FROM THE PACIFIC FRONT picked up in late November when U.S. Marines, after a bloody three-day battle, finally took Tarawa Atoll in the Gilbert Islands. The reports weren't pretty, though. The Marines suffered more than a thousand killed-in-action casualties, almost as many as had been lost in the entire six-month campaign on Guadalcanal.[8]

Lil had never heard of Tarawa, or of the Gilbert Islands, and when she finally found them on the map, she was stunned. These little pinpricks of land in the middle of the ocean were even farther from North Luzon than either the Solomons or New Guinea. To her, this latest victory didn't represent any progress at all.

DECEMBER ARRIVED TOO SOON, and Lil's housekeeper quit early in the month because her baby was due. Though Lil tried, she couldn't find a replacement.

With so many women in the labor force, daycare centers now operated adjacent to most elementary schools, including Washington Elementary a mile from their house. Lil enrolled both girls. By getting up at five-thirty, they could walk there by seven. School-age children like Eleanor were escorted across the playground to kindergarten at the elementary school and then returned to the center for the rest of the day. Lil picked the girls up at six. By the time they got home and had a hasty dinner and a quick bath, it was bedtime for the girls, though not for Lil. Household chores had to be done. She rarely got to sleep before midnight. Then they'd get up at five-thirty the next morning and do it all again.

Mondays and Thursdays posed a problem because the daycare center closed at 8 p.m. Lil's sister Lucille came to the rescue. Out of her classes by four, she picked the girls up from daycare, walked them home, made them dinner, put them to bed, and stayed the night. Lil paid her well. At seventeen, Lucille loved the arrangement because it enabled her to buy some new clothes and other incidentals Lillian Sr. wasn't able to afford.[9]

On Saturday, December 18, Lil was baptized by Father Thomas J. Brennan at St. Joseph's. Although she barely knew them, longtime members Fred and Leonore Gutierrez served as her sponsors, and Captain Dillon provided moral support.[10]

Christmas turned into quite a family affair. Lil's sister Charlotte did the planning and shopping. While Lil was still at work on the evening of the 23rd, Charlotte brought over a tree and helped Lucille and the girls decorate it. With Cecil away at sea, his wife Jane and their baby Tommy were expected too. Lucille stayed over on Christmas Eve so Lil could attend mass with Captain Dillon, and she invited him to join them for turkey and all the trimmings the following afternoon.

Christmas morning was bedlam, but the biggest surprise came when Lillian Sr. walked in. She hadn't spoken to Lil in months, but she evidently couldn't pass up this rare opportunity to see her family gathered together at Christmastime. When presents were finished, Lillian Sr. was the first one in the kitchen. She supervised the rest of the preparations as though there had never been a problem. When Captain Dillon arrived shortly before dinner, Lillian Sr. shook his hand graciously. Lil even saw a tear in her eye when at the dinner table he suggested they all join hands as he asked God to bless their meal and to bless Art and Cecil and bring them home safely.

Despite the vacant hole in Lil's heart, it was a lovely, lovely day, the nicest Christmas she'd had in three long years.

CHAPTER 23

SOME GOOD NEWS, SOME TERRIBLE

January through July 1944

A RT FINALLY LEFT THE MOUNTAINTOP in mid-December 1943. As a newly appointed battalion commander, he needed to acquaint himself with his men and inspect their camps. His units were scattered in the mountains northwest of Baguio, in the municipality of Sablan, with one as far south as Tuba, so he probably covered fifty miles. By sticking to the well-concealed message center routes, he didn't see a single enemy soldier the entire trip.

On January 12, 1944, he brought Lil up to date:

"Dear Lillian. A belated Merry Xmas and Happy New Year! I just took a three-week trip down to visit some of my units. Did I tell you I'm now the C.O. of the 1st Battalion of the 66th Infantry? They really treated me nicely. The people hadn't seen an American in two years. On Xmas Eve, they put on a show and dance. They even had a Christmas tree. I got a decorated cake, a bunch of bananas, a bar of soap, two hankies, and some cigarettes. I lived quite comfortably less than a kilometer from the local Jap garrison. The Japs hardly come into the mountains anymore.

"On my return, I found our camp quite changed. PK has

gotten in some new personnel to help run his headquarters, and our camp has been rebuilt. Another thing new is 'Skippy,' a baby goat that wandered in from somewhere. He's quite friendly and eats up all our important papers! Just today, however, I found out he is actually a she! Perhaps we can have milk someday.

"Regarding the war, my intuition tells me that things are finally picking up. This opinion seems to be fairly general judging by the way prices are beginning to skyrocket. The price of bananas jumped from 4.50 pesos to 6.00 pesos per hundred in only three weeks. We used to give our market boy 30.00 pesos for a trip to Baguio; now we have to give him 100.00. Money is also getting easier to borrow. The people realize their Jap money will soon be valueless, so they're anxious to loan it to us so they can get its equivalent back in U.S. money after the war. But I'm afraid Manila will soon be starving due to the inflation.

"I'm well and healthy, and so is PK. By his last letter, Spence was doing okay too. Two Americans were recently captured up north, though. There aren't many of us left.

"I wish this damned war would get over with. I long for the humdrum life of peace again, though I don't know how well I'll do in peaceful surroundings with all the bad habits I've picked up. I've become accustomed to doing very little, but I've also come to appreciate the efficiency of just having S.O.B.s bumped off instead of fooling around with them. We had a case recently of a municipal mayor who was just too loyal to the Japs. Poor fellow, he died of lead poisoning.

"For weeks the weather's been pretty cold. It's now let up a little, but not before our house caught fire as a result of our building too big a fire inside to keep warm. My biggest loss was the burning of a couple of inches off the bottom of my only blanket. The house itself wasn't seriously damaged.

"Will close for now with, I love you. Art."[1]

OUR MAYOR DOESN'T LIVE HERE ANYMORE
(Tune: "Annie Doesn't Live Here Anymore")

Our mayor doesn't live here anymore,
Our mayor doesn't live here anymore,
He was a politician, should have known his stuff,
But as a politician, he wasn't good enough,
He lost his sense of duty just as things were getting rough,
Our mayor doesn't live here anymore.

Our mayor doesn't live here anymore,
Our mayor doesn't live here anymore,
He listened to the Hapons when they promised him great gain,
He helped them look for soldiers over and over again,
Of the men who serve their country, he became the bane,
Our mayor doesn't live here anymore.

It was spring, there was hardship in the air,
And everything was looking dark,
And there was he, mean as could be,
Just as we took our mark.

And that's the reason…
Our mayor doesn't live here anymore,
Our mayor doesn't live here anymore
He was given lots of warnings, should have seen the light,
Should have got positioned on the right side of the fight,
Instead he helped the Hapons 'til he disappeared from sight,
Our mayor doesn't live here anymore.[2]

ONTINUING TO MONITOR THE WAR NEWS, they learned that on February 4 "Operation Flintlock" had secured Kwajalein, a small coral atoll in the Marshall Islands where the Japanese maintained an airfield crucial to their defensive positions in the Pacific.[3] Art and PK promptly sent this news by runner over to Russ Volckmann and Don Blackburn in Ifugao and also sent along a couple of Kaywoodies, four cans of Prince Albert tobacco, and several Coca-Colas they'd received in a recent supply bundle from Baguio.[4]

Whether it was the encouraging news from the war front or the Cokes and tobacco that provided the inducement, within days they got a message back from Russ advising that he'd decided to pay them a visit, leaving Don in command of the 4th District. Aware that plenty of Japanese patrols were prowling about the areas he'd have to hike through, they advised him to stay put until things quieted down or travel only at night and sleep in the message centers during the day. Russ was in a big hurry, though, and on February 18 he arrived on their mountaintop, tired and footsore but otherwise in good shape.[5]

After a good meal and a sound night's sleep, PK and Art showed Russ around Shangri-La and gave him a full rundown on their network of secret agents in Baguio. They explained how well the three battalions of the 66th Infantry were coming along and let him examine their collection of consolidated intelligence reports, ready to be smuggled down to Robert Lapham or Bernard Anderson. They also described their efforts, so far unsuccessful, to acquire a radio transmitter, and about their idea, if they ever got one, to take a lesson from Art's old friends at Oding, build a Pelton wheel, and harness a nearby waterfall to provide power.[6]

Then Russ dropped a bombshell. *You know, I think it's likely that when MacArthur's boys finally push their way back to the Philippines, they'll come in through the Lingayen Gulf, just like the Japs did in December of '41. Benguet is a much better spot from which to direct guerrilla operations when they arrive, so I've decided to move my head-quarters over here.*

PK and Art glanced at one another, gulped a couple of times, and replied, *That's swell, Russ. Thanks. Welcome aboard.*

Russ was also anxious to visit George Barnett's territory, so he left Shangri-La on an inspection trip to La Union and southern Ilocos Sur.

After a couple of months, on March 4th, Art wrote to bring Lil up to date:

"My dearest wife. I've been a bit lazy about writing lately, chiefly because there has been little of note to write about. The Japs haven't bothered us, though they're still down in the valley.

"The Japs recently caught one of my men and tortured him pretty badly, but he kept his mouth shut and finally escaped. He was betrayed by his wife's cousin because he had knocked up his wife's sister. Unfortunately, the cousin left the company of his Jap friends and went behind a bush to urinate and never came back. The Japs are still wondering what became of him.

"The Japs have been giving the boys up north quite a bit of hell lately. One American has been captured and a mestizo killed, plus several native soldiers. After his capture, the American smuggled out a note telling about it. He and several Filipinos had been left in a barrio, sick with malaria and unarmed. A nearby pro-Jap barrio led the Japs in on them. The Japs bayoneted those who were too sick to walk. Lovely people, the little yellow bastards! Well, when our boys get their chance, they're not going to be bothered with any scruples about international law and humane treatment, either. Of course, that pro-Jap barrio will be wiped off the map at the earliest opportunity.

"The Japs seem to think there are going to be American planes over here pretty soon. Manila is holding practice black-outs, and a civilian air-raid protection organization has been organized. Food in Manila is getting so scarce that the puppet government is trying to persuade the people to move to the provinces; government employees can do so and continue receiving their salaries.

"I'm pretty well resigned to spending another rainy season out here and to celebrating my 31st birthday in the mountains, but I think Christmas will be a different story— always with the big *IF* I am still alive.

"I cannot explain how and why, but I am at present smoking a Chesterfield cigarette!

"*Au revoir*, my darling. I love you. Art."[7]

NONE OF THE DISTRICTS HAD SUFFICIENT ARMS for every man itching to become a guerrilla. Not wishing to dampen their enthusiasm, the districts organized units called Bolo Battalions, groups of able-bodied civilian men who could be called upon to perform support functions for the guerrillas. They collected food, built camps, and served as *cargadores* and runners. They were also taught how to construct roadblocks, perform simple demolitions, and collect information.[8]

Because the native women were also anxious to help, in early 1944, the Women's Auxiliary Society (WAS) was established. These all-female units provided a wide range of support services, everything from sewing and patching clothes to rolling cigarettes and administering first aid. Some were trained as espionage agents. They went to work in bars in Manila and Baguio and became extremely

proficient at extracting information from inebriated Japanese officers. They also procured desperately needed medicines. Some of the
best female spies risked their lives, riding openly on public buses and
trains, to carry intelligence reports to Manila and beyond. Still other
women provided entertainment. It wasn't unusual for these wom-
en, accompanied by a three-piece orchestra or a *cargadore* carrying
a portable phonograph, to tote fancy clothes in a bundle on their
heads and hike for hours to guerrilla camps in the mountains to sing
and dance for the soldiers. One popular orchestra played part of the
time for the Japanese in San Fernando, La Union, and the rest of the
time for the units of Barnett's 121st Infantry in the nearby mountains. Two Americans fell in love with and married Filipino girls.[9, 10]

To further boost morale and camaraderie, the Headquarters began producing a monthly newsletter. The publication detailed the
war news, especially Japanese defeats, gave pep talks, told entertaining stories and bawdy jokes, and even included poetry. The newsletters were sent to all districts, and the district commanders circulated
them among the local populace.[11]

BACKTRACKING A BIT, late in 1943, PK and Art had finally concocted a scheme to get additional food to the underfed civilians being held at Camp Holmes. Rokuro Tomibe[12], the
English-speaking Japanese commandant of the camp, had grown
sympathetic toward his civilian charges and allowed them considerable freedom as long as they didn't make trouble. When one of our
guerrilla double agents in Baguio approached him with the idea of
allowing the internees to purchase supplemental food from female
vendors given supervised access to the camp, he agreed. These vendors not only sold vegetables from baskets carried on their heads but
also smuggled in money, medicines, and tidbits of war information
to boost morale. In this way, the guerrillas learned that many of the
old Itogon crowd were still at Camp Holmes and were doing okay. It
was great news, but nothing prepared them for what happened next.

One day in mid-March their market boy was down in Baguio buying supplies when a ragged, disheveled American sidled up to him. The man was part of the lightly guarded garbage detail that daily hauled refuse from Camp Holmes and dumped it into the river.

I remember you from Lusod, the man whispered. *Where is Major Calvert?*

Momentarily taken aback, their man replied, *He's up in the mountains. I'm on my way to their camp now.*

Tell him Herb needs to see him.

They only knew one Herb, and that was Herb Swick, whom they'd months earlier given up for dead. The news was electrifying.

On the market boy's next trip to Baguio, he carried a secret message that he slipped to a member of the garbage crew, specifying the time and place for a nighttime rendezvous with PK just outside the camp. Security at the camp had grown so lax that after evening roll call a few nights later, Herb easily ducked past the guards, down beyond the rear barracks, and over a four-foot fence. Upon meeting, Herb told PK that after his capture back in December 1942, he'd been interrogated and tortured for weeks but had finally convinced the Japanese he was a civilian miner. He'd now been at Camp Holmes for fifteen months, always fearing they might discover his true identity and relieve him of his head. Herb said that Richie Green, another Itogon miner-turned-guerrilla, was also anxious to escape and join the guerrillas in the mountains. When PK learned Johnny McCuish was the resident shoemaker at Camp Holmes, arrangements were made for a second rendezvous so that their boots could be smuggled in for repair, no questions asked. Finally, April 4 at 9:30 p.m. was set for the final breakout.[13, 14]

At the appointed time, Robin Hood was waiting to lead Herb and Richie up to guerrilla headquarters. Traveling under cover of darkness, they arrived on April 8. After two days of feasting and swapping stories, it was time to get back to business. Colonel Volckmann sent Herb up to Don Blackburn's headquarters in

Apayao, and Richie Green joined George Barnett's 121st Infantry in La Union.[15]

W HILE STILL CELEBRATING their good fortune, a run-ner from Baguio brought the worst possible news. On April 8, the very night that Herb and Richie had arrived amid so much elation, Spence's camp near Dalupirip had been raided. The mes-sage said he'd been killed but contained no further details. Art just couldn't believe it. Spence was like his kid brother, and here they'd been having a party at the same time he was getting hit. Never a praying man, that night Art begged with all his soul that the report would prove false.[16, 17]

On April 15th, after more than a month, Art penned this letter to Lil:

> "My dearest wife. We just got a terrible shock. We received word that Spencer's headquarters was raided and that he was killed while trying to escape. Spencer, if you will recall, was one of our group who made the trip to Manila after the start of the war. He was with us until last September, when he went to take charge of another unit. We're hoping against hope that the report is false. The two captured soldiers that were reported to have been responsible for the raid on his camp have now appeared in our area, leading the Japs around. We've detailed men to shoot them right out from under the Japs' noses.
>
> "If the report of Spence's death is true, it means only half of our foursome is left, PK and me. Who will be next?
>
> "The Japs are really raising hell these days with the civilians. One patrol recently killed 14 civilians within

one week. Most of the civilians have been subjected to the most inhuman tortures to make them reveal the whereabouts of soldiers. In one case they chopped off the head of a man's penis, shoved a sharpened stick up his anus, rupturing his colon and intestines, and then beat him to death with clubs. Another man, they roasted alive like a pig. I'm not saying these things to shock you, I just want to make a record of what inhuman monsters these little yellow bastards are so that the world will someday treat them accordingly.

"I guess the Japs realize they don't have much time left before they have to fight U.S. landing forces with us at their backs. I don't expect anything here until the end of the rainy season. However, the radio news doesn't excite me anymore. It's all taking place in another world. Here is the world I live in.

"I had a most awful dream the other night. (I'm really in a black mood today.) I dreamed that when I got home, you were dead. I didn't dream anything about you dying; there was just the taken-for-granted fact that you were dead. The feeling of desolation was indescribable. Then I woke up. Oh, honey, I do hope you're taking good care of yourself. With all the danger out here, I've sort of forgotten that things can happen to people back home too.

"There's not much more to say except that I'm still healthy and strong and have sufficient clothes, shoes, and tobacco to do me a little while longer, and that, as always, I love you. Art"[18]

On the 20th, they got confirmation of Spence's death. Two of his men who got away provided the details. They said they got warning that a Japanese patrol was on its way out from Baguio but probably wouldn't arrive for several hours. Spence didn't evacuate right away but instead began destroying his records and rosters. As the patrol closed in, much earlier than anticipated, he ran, but it was too late. When the Japanese got him, they tortured him mercilessly, but Spence just gave them a big smile and gave up only his rank and serial number.[19] Enraged, the Japanese bastards bayoneted him to death, chopped off his head as a souvenir, and left the rest of his body for the wild dogs and pigs.

Art's dream about Lil being dead had shaken him to the core, but it was only a bad dream. This wasn't a dream. This was real. It was too much to handle. Art headed into the forest, sank down against a tree, and sobbed. His whole chest ached as it sought to fold in on itself and fill the black vacant hole pulsating there. When Kiddo slipped down beside him, tears rolling down his cheeks, and gently patted Art's hand, he hardly noticed.

But they had little time to grieve. Life had to go on.

A WEEK LATER ROBIN HOOD ARRIVED with a surprise, an inoperable short-wave radio he'd "acquired" somewhere in Baguio. PK and Art looked at each other, shrugged their shoulders, and sent for Bado Dangwa, who they knew had worked with radios before the war. Soon Bado had the unit humming, bringing in KGEI loud and clear. But they found the broadcasts from the States depressing. Two thousand miles from the nearest American forces, they found it difficult to share the announcer's enthusiasm over a paltry ten-mile advance when there were still 1,990 miles to go. Instead, they'd turn on the States for fifteen minutes to get the news and then switch to Manila, Shanghai, or Tokyo to listen to the excellent American recordings the Japanese were playing.[20]

"May 23, 1944

"My darling wife. Things are moving faster these days. We have a radio in operation now, and each news broadcast seems to bring a new development. We're expecting Allied planes over P.I. any day now.

"Things aren't quiet locally either. One of the companies of a neighboring battalion caught a spy, but he escaped to the Bakun Jap garrison, taking all the company's records with him. The company attacked the garrison in an attempt to recover the records, killed four Japs, had one man killed and one wounded, and were withdrawing when sixty reinforcements for the garrison arrived. Those Japs are now making a wasteland of the Bakun area. They're shooting everybody they see, burning houses, and destroying crops. I fear they're going to get a rude surprise in the near future if present plans carry through.

"The news of Spencer's death has been confirmed. I'm sorry to say it was due to his trying to be too brave. Despite his efforts, some of his records were captured, and, as a result, his area is also plenty hot at present. I sure miss him.

"The rainy season has begun, a downpour every afternoon. There are no takers for my offered bet that this is our last rainy season in the mountains. Every nite I dream that the war is over, but I have difficulty remembering just where I was when it started.

"It is now quite definite that any of our forces who fall into Jap hands get their heads chopped off, so if the Japs get me in a tight spot, I'll try to send as many of them to hell as possible before I put a bullet through my own head and deprive them of the pleasure of lopping it off. It's really rather comforting to have such matters settled in advance.

"Our local conditions are about the same. PK and I are both well (also Major Russell W. Volckmann, C.O. of USAFIP-NL, who has his headquarters with us at present) except for a flu epidemic that brushed us all lightly. It killed several natives. The Japs haven't visited us yet, though we went into the bushes the other day when a Jap patrol started up our mountain, only to return to their garrison after coming up halfway.

"Two Americans recently escaped from a civilian concentration camp and joined up. They're now regaining the weight they lost in there.

"Once again, I've run out of things to say except that it's wonderful to be able to look down the final stretch and realize that, if I can but live through it, I can be with my wife and babies once again. I love you, Art."[21]

AT THE BEGINNING OF JUNE, Art moved his 1st Battalion headquarters down with one of his companies so he could be in closer contact with his other company and a new company that had just been attached to him for general renovation. The new location, at a lower elevation, was warmer, had a few mosquitos, and was closer to the local Japanese garrison, but was still just as isolated. His newest charges proved to be an ornery bunch. It took a couple of weeks of hard work and discipline to settle them down.

Art's boys were itching to practice some of the theory they'd been taught, and, despite MacArthur's order, they badly needed more rifles. A joint plan was drawn up whereby at a given hour on the night of June 19 two of Dennis Molintas's companies from the 3rd Battalion would attack the Philippine Constabulary garrison in La Trinidad, and at the same time Art would lead two of his companies in a raid on the P.C. garrison at the Baguio Easter School.

What a fiasco! The raid wasn't really unsuccessful because it wasn't really a raid. Art's unit got lost in the dark and was still four hours away from the Easter School at the time set for the attack. When he heard heavy firing coming from La Trinidad, he knew something had gone wrong there and decided to get his men out of the danger area before dawn. As it turned out, one of Molintas's inside men had squealed, and the Japanese had plenty of troops hiding in wait at both La Trinidad and the Easter School. Molintas ended up losing several men and their rifles. While Art didn't lose men or rifles, his ego took a beating. This was the first offensive action his outfit had undertaken since he assumed command, and it fizzled because he hadn't allowed enough time to make a night approach march. Assured the hike would take four hours by day, he figured they could make it in five at night. They should have allowed eight or nine. Art felt like a real jackass.[22]

When Volckmann got wind of the sad story, he gave Art a royal chewing out for leading the raid. He lectured that a commanding officer's function was to lead from a command position, not do the dirty work himself. He forbade Art to repeat such a foolhardy act.

Art's chance to redeem himself came a week later when an agent in Baguio advised that a P.C. patrol was heading up into the mountains. Robin Hood had been clamoring for some action, so Art put him in charge of Company B's twenty-four men and sent them out to ambush the patrol. He hoped the boys would bring home some rifles. Maybe some badly needed clothes too.

They located the patrol in an isolated barrio, surrounded the place, and then, of all things, Robin Hood sent in a note to the P.C. officer demanding his surrender! The P.C. officer opened fire in all directions. Robin Hood hollered for his men to hold their positions, but half of them had already run away. He took off with the remaining men, was chased and fired at the next morning by the P.C., shook them, and finally came limping back to headquarters. Two of Art's guerrillas were killed, one was shot through the leg, and their only automatic rifle plus two other rifles were captured. The men were looking for sympathy, but Art sent them right back out to continue the fight. Eventually, they caught one of the P.C. fellows alone in a barrio and beat his brains out, but the rifles were never recovered. Art was thoroughly disgusted.

Volckmann must have figured Art was more valuable in a position other than infantry commander because he ordered another shake-up. He reassigned PK to the position of headquarters chief of staff. Art became chief intelligence officer for all of USAFIP-NL and assumed full responsibility for the planning, gathering, and consolidating of intelligence reports, and making every effort to get them to Australia. Major Dennis Molintas replaced PK as commanding officer of the 66th Infantry.[23]

Art packed up his gear and by August 1 was back behind a desk at Shangri-La, a move that suited him just fine.

CHAPTER 24

NOTHING COMES EASY

August through October 1944

THE WAR NEWS ON THE RADIO WAS ALL GOOD, General MacArthur and Admiral Nimitz winning one battle after another. However, their market boy picked up a rumor in Baguio that somewhere on Luzon supplies had come in by submarine from Australia, an event of far greater significance as far as the guerrillas were concerned.[1]

Desperate for more arms and ammunition, direct contact with HQ-SWPA in Australia now became their top priority. They badly needed a radio that could both receive *and* send.[2]

Russ Volckmann ordered all districts to scour their areas for radio parts, acquire them by whatever means necessary, and send them by runner to Kapangan. The pile grew quickly. He also put out the word for a radio technician. Agents in Manila found two experts, Captain Timoteo Sinay and a civilian, Crespo Hernando, and persuaded them to join the guerrillas in the mountains. The two radiomen zealously tackled the pile of parts. Sadly, quantity didn't necessarily equate to quality, and in the end they had to fabricate by hand most of what they needed. Progress was excruciatingly slow.[3]

While the transmitter work proceeded, scouts were sent out to find a new headquarters location, one near a waterfall with enough velocity for a power plant. They found an ideal spot on the next mountain to the south, above the tiny village of Liteng in the barrio of Sagubo. Several natural springs converged into a creek that cascaded down a 300-foot vertical rock face into a pool in a narrow, secluded box canyon below, just right for a couple of well-hidden buildings and a hydroelectric plant. As an added bonus, its entrance well-concealed behind the waterfall, a spacious cave afforded a perfect hiding place in the event of enemy attack.[4] Russ ordered that construction begin immediately.

When Kiddo learned they planned to move from Shangri-La, he burst into tears, stamped his foot, and begged to go along. *Me guerrilla boy. Me fight Japs.* Art reminded him that his family needed him and ordered him to continue partnering with the men manning the lookout stations above the coast, *a most important job.* He also promised to come back and visit whenever he could.

As the new buildings were going up, attention turned to the hydroelectric plant. In the town of Naguilian, George Barnett found an engineer named Ariston Huliganga. He and several technicians arrived soon after and began building the framework, using pipes and lumber scavenged from mine sites at Tublay.[5] At the mention of a Pelton wheel, though, Huliganga burst out laughing, saying their technical knowledge dated from the Stone Age. What was needed was a turbine.

Where does one acquire a turbine? Again, Russ Volckmann sent word throughout the districts. Through an agent in Baguio, they learned about Ernest Schneider, a Swiss electrical engineer who before the war had managed the Baguio Power and Ice Plant. When the Japanese took over, they'd retained him to run the place but kept him under close surveillance. When contacted secretly, Mr. Schneider agreed to cooperate and came up with a clever scheme. He disassembled one of the company turbines, telling the Japanese it needed a routine overhaul. The following Sunday, while the inebriated relief guard snored in his chair, Schneider silently smuggled the turbine parts out through a rear door, where guerrilla agents and *cargadores* were waiting to transport Schneider and the parts up the mountain.[6]

Bado Dangwa's boys came up with an inoperative 220-volt generator that had belonged to his transportation company, and within days Schneider, Huliganga, and the other technicians refurbished the generator and had the power plant up and running. They even strung stolen wire to provide electric lights in the new camp buildings.

The new headquarters of the United States Army Forces in the Philippines-North Luzon (USAFIP-NL) was formally christened Camp Utopia.

Still, they had no way of transmitting a radio signal.

BACKTRACKING TO MID-1943, at Southwest Pacific Area (SWPA) Headquarters in Australia, with his island-hopping campaign proceeding satisfactorily, General MacArthur turned his attention once again to the liberation of the Philippines. He knew the Filipino people well and was confident that with proper leadership and sufficient arms and equipment a powerful guerrilla army could be organized, powerful enough to be of significant help to his invasion force when they made it back onto Philippine soil. Toward that end, MacArthur now sought to establish an intelligence network and make contact with guerrilla groups all over the Islands.[7]

As the first step, Mac's intelligence people recruited hundreds of Filipino-American volunteers, sent them to camps in California and Oregon for several months of intensive radio, intelligence, and demolitions training, and assembled them in Australia. Submarines began putting groups of these men, equipped with state-of-the-art equipment, ashore at remote beach locations all over the Philippine Islands. Their mission: to find and make contact with guerrilla leaders, provide them the technical assistance needed to establish radio contact with each other and with HQ-SWPA in Australia, and lay the groundwork for their coordination and resupply.

One of these submarine missions began on November 25, 1943, when the USS *Narwhal*, captained by Commander F. D. Latta, departed from Port Darwin. Aboard were Major Charles M. Smith, Captain Robert V. Ball, nine enlisted men, and ninety tons of ammunition and stores. A week later, Smith and the others were secretly landed on Samar.[8] By December 20, Major Smith had set up a radio control station and was in regular radio contact with Australia.[9]

The *Narwhal* departed Port Darwin on another mission on May 14, 1944. Two weeks later, Commander Latta delivered to Major Smith twenty-three of MacArthur's specially trained Filipino-American radio operators and twenty-five tons of radio equipment, including a number of British-made radio transceivers compact enough to be carried by one man.[10, 11]

At the end of May, Smith sent Captain Ball and several radio technicians by sailboat to Dibut Bay in Tayabas Province on the east coast of Luzon. They were spotted by Robert Lapham's coast watchers and escorted to Lapham's headquarters at Umingan. Soon, the new equipment was up and running and Lapham's intelligence reports were being radioed directly to Australia.[12]

Another of Smith's Filipino-American radio teams, this one hiking north through the jungles from the southern coast of Luzon, came upon Major Bernard Anderson, the commander of a guerrilla group headquartered in the mountains east of Manila. Without delay, Anderson, too, established direct contact with Australia.[13] Some of Art's earliest intelligence reports had passed through Major Anderson's hands, and he became the first to notify HQ-SWPA that Volckmann's USAFIP-NL was alive and well in North Luzon.[14]

As a result of information provided to HQ-SWPA by Major Anderson, on August 16, 1944, the first submarine mission to North Luzon was launched when the USS *Stingray*, captained by Lieutenant Commander Samuel Loomis Jr., left Australia with ten tons of cargo and a fifteen-man radio and demolitions team headed by Lieutenant Jose Valera, alias "Captain Joe." Their destination was Pasaleng Bay along the north coast. When the *Stingray* approached her destination eleven days later, though, Loomis ran into trouble.

A Japanese tanker had been torpedoed the day before and lay incapacitated in the bay, attended by a destroyer, numerous sailboats, and a Japanese single-engine plane flying menacing circles overhead. With this landing spot compromised, Loomis went searching for another.[15]

Continuing eastward along the north coast, Loomis rounded Mayraira Point and eased into Caunayan Bay, Bangui, Ilocos Norte, at five o'clock in the morning on August 27. Though submerged, they were spotted and depth-charged around three that afternoon but remained motionless and sustained no damage. At nine that night, Loomis finally surfaced, anchored a thousand feet offshore, and began unloading his passengers and cargo into rubber boats. All went well for a couple of hours, until the sub's radar operator sounded an alarm. Three or four Japanese cargo ships were approaching in the darkness. The *Stingray* lay motionless and allowed them to pass, then resumed unloading. About midnight, though, another convoy of freighters and several escorts entered the cove. This was too much for Commander Loomis. He cut adrift two partially loaded rubber boats, hoisted anchor, submerged, and silently crept out to sea.[16]

All passengers made it ashore safely, but forty percent of their equipment remained aboard the *Stingray*. Valera and his team narrowly evaded an enemy patrol, moved swiftly into the jungle, and began wandering the mountains of Ilocos Norte looking for guerrillas.[17]

BACK AT USAFIP-NL HEADQUARTERS in Kapangan, they knew nothing of these exciting developments. During the first week of August, though, one of their lookouts intercepted a Filipino guide, a pair of Filipino-Americans, and a couple of *cargadores* coming up the trail, claiming to be from Robert Lapham's headquarters. They didn't know the current password, but the lookout's message said the Filipino-Americans' English was flawless and they wore new uniforms, carried shiny new weapons, and carried big bundles of radio equipment. Throwing caution to the winds, Volckmann shouted, *For God's sake, send 'em up.* They all raced out to meet the newcomers and were soon shaking hands and exchanging introductions with Lieutenant Carlos Ancheta and Sergeant Pete Luz.[18]

We've got all sorts of goodies for you, Ancheta told them. *Mac has sent us to put you in radio communication with other guerrilla leaders operating here in the north and into direct radio contact with SWPA Headquarters in Australia.*

Unbelievable! Of all the good news they might have hoped for, this was the best. Art felt like turning cartwheels but settled for jumping up and down like a deranged madman, back-slapping everyone he could get hold of. Finally, after three long years of anxious waiting, the veil of darkness was lifting!

It didn't happen seamlessly, though. It took several days for Ancheta and Luz to set up their equipment. They got through to HQ-SWPA once but then had trouble because of Camp Utopia's location, where high mountains blocked all but the strongest radio signals. After a week, a dejected Ancheta admitted his dry-cell battery and his spare were both dead. Unwilling to give up, they put pressure on Captain Sinay and Lieutenant Hernando, who hastily improvised a power pack, run from their 220-volt hydroelectric generator, to replace the batteries. But still there were troubles. Their weak signal didn't elicit any responses. Again, Sinay and Hernando came to the rescue. With help from Ancheta and Luz, they cobbled together a 75-watt transmitter, powerful enough to get a clear signal all the way to HQ-SWPA in Australia.[19, 20]

In his first message coded and transmitted by Lieutenant Ancheta to Mac's headquarters on August 20, Russ Volckmann described the USAFIP-NL organization and the circumstances under which he had taken command. He emphasized their need for supplies of all kinds, particularly modern rifles, machine guns, mortars, ammunition, and medicines. Anticipation reached a fever pitch as they awaited Mac's answer, but more than a week dragged by without a word.

Volckmann followed up his first message with a second one dated August 29:

> D-DAY MISSIONS HAVE BEEN ASSIGNED WITHIN THIS COMMAND AS FOLLOWS CLN TO DESTROY ALL ENEMY LINES OF COMMUNICATION CMA TO HARASS DELAY AND DESTROY ENEMY TROOP AND SUPPLY MOVEMENTS CMA TO DESTROY ENEMY SUPPLY DUMPS TRUCK PARKS TROOP CONCENTRATIONS AND COMMAND POSTS CMA TO PREVENT ENEMY FROM SECURING LOCALLY FOOD SUPPLIES CONSTRUCTION MATERIALS LABOR MEANS OF TRANSPORTATION PD UNITS OF THIS COMMAND HAVE BEEN GIVEN DETAILED ASSIGNMENTS AND HAVE ASSEMBLED MATERIALS AND TRAINED MEN TO ACCOMPLISH ABOVE ON ORDERS FROM YOUR HQ OR LACKING THESE ON ORDERS FROM THIS HQ PD REQUEST YOU INFORM THIS HQ OF ANY CHANGES DESIRED SGD VOLCKMANN[21]

Again, they waited. Two more weeks crawled by, weeks during which the only good news was a radio report that carrier-borne bombers launched from Admiral Halsey's Third Fleet were pounding strategic targets on Mindanao and the Visayas. Finally, on September 13, they got a reply. Several hours later, Lieutenant Ancheta had it decoded:

YOUR MSG OF TWENTY AUG HAS
BEEN RECEIVED BY ME WITH INFINITE
SATISFACTION PD AYE COMMEND YOU
AND THE OFFICERS AND MEN WHO
HAVE STOOD STEADFAST WITH YOU FOR
RESOLUTE AND RESOURCEFUL SERVICE PD
TELL THEM I AM FULLY CONSCIOUS OF THEIR
DIFFICULTIES AND STEPS WILL BE TAKEN TO
SUPPLY YOU AND BRING YOU INTO DIRECT
RADIO CONTACT AT THE EARLIEST POSSIBLE
MOMENT PD A DETACHMENT CONSISTING
OF AN OFFICER AND FOURTEEN MEN HAS
RECENTLY BEEN LANDED ON NORTH
COAST OF LUZON CMA WITH RADIO EQUIP
AND LIMITED SUPPLIES CMA UNDER THE
OPERATIONAL CONTROL OF THIS HQ RPT
HQ WITH THE VIEW TO ESTABLISH YOUR
COMMUNICATION NET IN NORTHERN
LUZON AND EFFECT CONTACT WITH YOU
AND MOVE NORTH [sic] ON LAND TO
FACILITATE COMMUNICATIONS FROM YOUR
AREA AND SECURE ENEMY INTELLIGENCE
PD AYE DESIRE THAT YOU CONTINUE
TO DEVELOP CHANNELS OF INFO ON
ENEMY POSITIONS AND MOVEMENTS
WITH PARTICULAR EMPHASIS ON HEAVIER
CONCENTRATIONS AND STRATEGIC
POINTS ON NORTHERN LUZON PENDING
MY FURTHER INSTRUCTIONS PD CONVEY
MY ASSURANCE TO YOUR OFFICERS AND
MEN THAT OUR CAMPAIGN IS PROCEEDING
SATISFACTORILY TOWARD THEIR RELIEF PD

TELL THEM THAT AYE AM GRATEFUL FOR
THEIR PAST SERVICE AND SHALL COUNT
FULLY UPON THEIR FUTURE SERVICE IN THE
PHASE WHICH LIES AHEAD PD MACARTHUR[22]

The message was confusing. They were *already* in direct contact. *And who was this officer with fourteen men and limited supplies who'd been landed on the north coast?* Colonel Volckmann requested clarification. Again they waited. A reply came several days later:

PARTY HEADED BY LIEUTENANT VALERA
LANDED AT MAIRAARA [sic] POINT TWENTY
SEVENTH AUGUST WITH RADIO AND OTHER
EQUIPMENT PD HE WAS INSTRUCTED TO
CONTACT YOU AND GOVERNOR ABLAN PD
HAVE HAD NO REPEAT NO RADIO CONTACT
WITH HIM SINCE ARRIVAL PD DESIRE YOU
SEND AGENT TO VICINITY OF LANDING SITE
TO SECURE INFO AS TO SITUATION VALERA
AND PARTY PD[23]

Volckmann sent a runner to George Barnett in La Union, who notified his northernmost unit to start looking for this Lieutenant Valera and the lost party. If they could be found, Russ requested that HQ-SWPA assign Valera's party to him as his organization urgently needed supplies and equipment. Barnett's boys did eventually locate Valera's party, and they were indeed assigned as requested, but they didn't arrive until November 19, more than two months later[24], just in time to help out with another major headache. But more about that later.

ONE MORNING IN SEPTEMBER, they heard the rumble of bombs to the west. The Japanese at San Fernando periodically sent planes aloft to find and attack American subs in the South China Sea, so they didn't pay much attention. But a few hours later, an excited runner brought an electrifying message from Major Barnett. American planes—a dozen mighty silver beauties sporting unmistakable red, white, and blue wing markings—had bombed the hell out of the Japanese airfield and port at San Fernando! It was too late to get a firsthand look, but Art and the rest whooped and hollered. The American boys were coming!

A S A RESULT OF THE AMERICAN BOMBINGS, on September 22, 1944, President Jose P. Laurel, head of the Japanese-controlled Philippine puppet government in Manila, formally declared war on the United States and Great Britain. It seemed a preposterous move in view of the string of defeats the Japanese armies had already suffered, but it nonetheless required action. Colonel Volckmann ordered Calvert, as his chief of staff, to draw up a warning to all Filipinos:

1. *The Puppet Government of the Philippines,
   following the orders of its Japanese masters, has
   declared war against the United States of America
   and has declared a state of martial law throughout
   the Philippines.*

2. *On or after October 7, 1944, any civilian or
   government official bearing arms for the Puppet
   Philippine Government or in any way connected
   with the enforcement of martial law, or any
   attempt to conscript men for any puppet army,
   will be considered an enemy of the United States of
   America and will be treated as such by our forces.*

3. *On or after October 7, 1944, all members of the
   Bureau of Constabulary or any other military*

Patricia Murphy Minch

*organization that may be organized by the Puppet
Philippine Government will be considered enemies
of the United States of America and will be
treated as such by our forces.*

4. *On or after October 7, 1944, all persons working
for the enemy in purely military installations such
as airfields, in defense positions, or those driving
trucks supplying troops, etc., will be considered
enemies of the United States of America and will
be treated as such by our forces.*

5. *Davao has been bombed! The Visayas have been
bombed! Manila has been bombed! Northern
Luzon has been bombed! American forces are
ready to land in the Philippines!*

   *This war declared is a last attempt of the Japanese
warlords to stave off defeat. Do not be taken in
by it! The day of liberation from the Japanese
oppression is at hand! Be sure that you are alive
when it arrives![25]*

PK sent the warning out to all district commanders with a cover
letter dated September 22, 1944:

*In view of the Philippine Puppet Government's
Declaration of War upon the United States of America
and the Declaration of Martial Law throughout the
Philippines, you are hereby directed to take the following
actions without delay: (1) You will distribute copies of
the enclosed warning throughout your area. The date
to be set in the warning will be one week after copies
of the warning are distributed. (2) After the expiration
of the date set in the warning, you will start measures*

333

to capture, kill, and disarm all persons not complying with the warning. By order of 1122. Signed 1122-113, Executive Officer.[26]

ON SEPTEMBER 21, another exciting radiogram came in from Mac's headquarters:

CAN YOU HANDLE SUPPLY SHIPMENT OF ABOUT TWENTY TONS ABOUT TWENTY SIX OCTOBER QUERY INDICATE TWO OR THREE SITES PAREN IN ORDER OF PRIORITY PAREN AVAILABLE TO YOU WHERE YOU MAY ACCUMULATE SMALL CRAFT TO EFFECT UNLOADING OF SUPPLIES WITHIN FEW HOURS PD SITE SHOULD BE REASONABLY SHELTERED FROM PREVAILING WEATHER AND WHERE VESSEL MAY APPROACH CLOSE TO SHORE WITH NO NAVIGATIONAL OBSTRUCTIONS SUCH AS SHOALS OR CORAL REEFS PD SANTIAGO COVE, DIRIQUE RPT DIRIQUE INLET CMA CURRIMAO CMA SALOMAGUE HARBOR OR SOLVEC RPT SOLVEC COVE WOULD BE SUITABLE FROM NAVIGATIONAL STANDPOINT PD PARAOIR AND DARIGAYOS INLET NOT SUITABLE PD[27]

Volckmann and Barnett discussed the matter, and despite HQ-SWPA's admonition, they chose Darigayos Cove as the primary rendezvous site. Located twenty miles north of San Fernando, with a good-sized fishing village along the shore, it had a fine harbor and provided an ideal spot to assemble several dozen *bancas* and a thousand *cargadores* without arousing suspicion. For the alternate site, they chose Santiago Cove, Ilocos Sur, twenty miles north of Darigayos, where an equal number of *bancas* and *cargadores* could be assembled. Volckmann designated Major Calvert as the contact officer for Spot One and Major Barnett for Spot Two.

A rapid-fire series of radiograms followed in which Volckmann managed to convince HQ-SWPA to approve Darigayos. The exact arrival date of the sub was set for October 25. Beginning at 6 a.m. on that date, shore signals consisting of two white rectangular panels about the size of a bed sheet—they used white Ilocano blankets mounted on bamboo poles—were to be displayed vertically and placed 200 meters apart, facing out to sea. These signals were to be displayed all day long, though hauled down temporarily in the event of an enemy patrol, until the submarine surfaced at 5:30 p.m. Once sighted, the rendezvous officer was to approach the sub in a single *banca* to finalize arrangements for unloading the men and supplies.[28, 29]

They followed every instruction to the letter. On the 23rd, Calvert hiked down to Darigayos Cove, carrying with him sensitive intelligence maps and drawings to be turned over to the sub captain. Accompanying *cargadores* carried their transceiver and the homemade power pack so PK could maintain direct contact with Australia. At the same time, Major Barnett completed his preparations at Santiago Cove. The required *bancas* and *cargadores* were ready and waiting at both locations.

The shore signals were hoisted early on the morning of the 25th. Several times they were hauled down because of nosy Japanese shore patrol boats, but those interruptions were brief, less than an hour and a half total. All day and until well after dark, PK waited. He saw no sign of the sub. When he tried to contact HQ-SWPA, the radio malfunctioned; evidently the jostling it had taken on the hike to Darigayos had loosened a connection. Unable to contact SWPA and speculating the sub must have met with some sort of disaster or had proceeded to Spot Two, the next morning PK dismissed his *bancas* and *cargadores* and climbed dejectedly back up to headquarters.

Meanwhile, at Santiago Cove, George Barnett displayed his signals all day on the 25th. No sub appeared. On the 26th, he repeated the procedure, but saw no submarine periscope. For a third day, Barnett displayed the signals. Still no sub. Finally he gave up, dismissed the *bancas* and *cargadores* on the 28th, returned to his headquarters, and reported the failure.

You can imagine their disgust when on October 30 and 31 the following two radio messages came in from Australia:

> SUBMARINE COMMANDER ADVISES NOT RPT NOT ABLE TO MAKE CONTACT WITH YOU SINCE TWENTY FIFTH AT SPOT ONE RPT ONE PD HE IS ATTEMPTING CONTACT TODAY AT SPOT ONE PD IF NOT SUCCESSFUL THEY ARE HEADING FOR ALTERNATE SITE PD ESTIMATED TIME OF ARRIVAL DAWN TWENTY NINE RPT TWO NINE PD ADVISE BY URGENT REPLY REASONS FOR NON CONTACT WITH SUBMARINE AS PREVIOUSLY ARRANGED PD[30]

> SUBMARINE REPORTS NO RPT NO CONTACT WITH YOU AT SPOT ONE PD PROCEEDING TO SPOT TWO PD ADVISE WITHIN THIRTY MINUTES AFTER RECEIPT OF THIS MESSAGE DETAILS WHY SUBMARINE WAS NOT CONTACTED AND INSTRUCTIONS WHICH MAY BE TRANSMITTED TO THE SUBMARINE IN ORDER THAT CONTACT WITH YOU CAN BE MADE PD UNLESS WE HEAR FROM YOU IMMEDIATELY SUBMARINE WILL PROCEED BACK TO THIS HEADQUARTERS PD[31]

Even had these messages been received in a timely manner, it would have been impossible to reassemble the *bancas* and *cargadores* on such short notice. The only explanation they could come up with—and it did nothing to lessen their disappointment—was that Mac's sub had somehow gotten lost and surfaced in the wrong cove on the 25th. They were where they were supposed to be exactly when they were supposed to be there. It wasn't.

IN HIS OWN LATER ASSESSMENT of the mission, Edward F. Dissette, commander of the USS *Cero*, the "phantom" submarine, claimed that although he'd arrived on time at Spot One and remained in the area three days with periscope raised, he'd seen no beach signals, no small boats, and no people other than a couple of Filipino fishermen. He did say that on the night of his approach to Spot One, he'd nearly been run over by a Japanese convoy being chased by the submarine USS *Cod*, a Pearl Harbor boat unaware of *Cero*'s presence or mission. Commander Dissette admitted spending most of that first night submerged, looking for an opportunity to launch a couple of torpedoes at the Japanese convoy, allegedly to draw them away from the guerrilla landing spot.[32] No official explanation was ever offered for the snafu, but logic dictated that Commander Dissette, after his nighttime cat-and-mouse game, couldn't find his way back to the proper cove if in fact he'd ever located Darigayos in the first place.

NONE OF THE GUERRILLA OFFICERS had the heart to label the Ancheta/Luz, Loomis/*Stingray*, or Dissette/*Cero* episodes fiascos, but each brought with it an incredible level of frustration. After waiting so long and coming so close, each day that went by now seemed like ten. Experience had taught them, though, that war isn't predictable. It doesn't come packaged neatly. It isn't a pretty business. With all the frustrations, disappointments, and heartbreak of the past three years, they'd managed to survive. They'd gotten tough. And if these supply-sub contacts weren't destined to happen without a struggle, well, it was just one more challenge they'd have to meet and overcome.

CHAPTER 25

A DAMSEL IN DISTRESS
October and November 1944

AMID THE RADIO AND SUBMARINE EXCITEMENT in October 1944, Colonel Volckmann assigned Art to devise a plan to get Mrs. Osmeña and her party out of Baguio. Who was Mrs. Osmeña? We'll have to backtrack several years, to the beginning of the war.

IN 1941, MANUEL L. QUEZON, head of the Philippine Commonwealth government, was just completing his first term. President Quezon and his family lived primarily in Malacañang palace in Manila, but they often spent holidays at their summer palace in Baguio.

On December 8, 1941, Quezon and his daughter Nini were enjoying Baguio while the rest of the family vacationed in Pampanga. When the bombing began, Quezon and Nini were whisked by U.S. Army personnel to the American ambassador's house at Camp John Hay, then escorted to Pampanga and finally to another farm in Marikina, Quezon City, which was equipped with an air raid shelter. They were confident it would be only a short stay, just until American reinforcements arrived.

A few days later, Quezon was summoned to Manila for a secret meeting with MacArthur, who urged the president to move his family to the fortified island of Corregidor. On Christmas Eve, the Quezons made the move. On Corregidor, they were joined by the

Philippine vice president, Sergio Osmeña. All were given quarters near MacArthur's own family in Malinta Tunnel and remained there for nearly two months. While on Corregidor, Quezon was sworn in for a second term.

In the damp conditions in the tunnel, President Quezon suffered a relapse of his longstanding tuberculosis. Seeking a more healthful climate, American personnel moved the family by boat to first one and then another Philippine island until finally they arrived on Mindanao, where General MacArthur informed them they were going to Australia.[1]

On March 21, 1942, even as American and Filipino troops on Bataan were suffering in the final throes of starvation and defeat, a B-17 bomber based at the Del Monte plantation on Mindanao flew the Quezons and Vice President Sergio Osmeña to Australia.

General MacArthur, ever mindful of Quezon's precarious health, next proposed sending them to the United States to establish a government-in-exile and where Quezon could receive the very latest in tuberculosis treatments. Concurrent with the fall of Bataan on April 9, the Quezon family, Sergio Osmeña, and several aides departed Melbourne for San Francisco aboard the USAT *President Coolidge*. From there they traveled by train to Washington, D.C., where they were met at the station by President Franklin D. Roosevelt.[2]

The vice president, Sergio Osmeña Sr., was born in Cebu in 1878, was schooled in Manila and the United States, and entered politics in his native province in 1904. He served as provincial governor of Cebu and later became speaker of the Philippine National Assembly. Long an activist in the cause of Philippine independence, Osmeña made frequent trips to Washington to appear before the U.S. Congress and was instrumental in the passage of the Tydings-McDuffie Act in 1934.[3]

Sergio Osmeña Sr., a widower with ten children, married Esperanza Limjap in 1920. Esperanza raised Sergio's youngest child, Sergio Jr., and bore him four more: Ramoncito, who died shortly after birth, Ramon, Rosalina, and Victor.

While the family occasionally accompanied Sergio Sr. on his trips to Washington, Esperanza more often remained in Manila with the children. She recognized her husband's devotion to public service and was content to stay behind. Following the Japanese invasion, she was not unduly upset when her husband was taken to Australia. She, too, was confident the separation would last only a few months, the type of separation she'd endured many times before.[4]

When the Imperial Japanese Army stormed into Manila in the spring of 1942, the fortunes of the Osmeña family suffered. Their home was confiscated, forcing them to move in with Esperanza's mother. Before long they were driven from that sanctuary as well, the Imperial Japanese Navy claiming they needed the waterfront location for a boat-building facility. A Manila industrialist and long-time Osmeña family friend came to their rescue by offering them a house he owned on Aviles Street.[5]

Though the Osmeñas remained in the Aviles Street home for more than two years, their day-to-day lives were not without worry. Japanese officials monitored their every move. For Esperanza, it became a test of character and strength. When she no longer had access to a car, she bought a tandem bicycle and had her houseboy pedal her to weekly beauty parlor appointments. When funds grew short, she quietly sold off some of her jewelry and formal tableware. She held her head high and maintained her dignity, confident the family was in no great danger.[6]

On August 1, 1944, President Manuel Quezon died in a tuberculosis sanitarium at Saranac Lake, New York. On the same day, Sergio Osmeña Sr. was sworn in as president of the Philippine Commonwealth by Justice Robert H. Jackson of the United States Supreme Court. Overnight, Esperanza became the first lady of the Philippines.

She now felt vulnerable, filled with a sense of foreboding. When Sergio Jr. suggested the family might be safer in the mountains,

Esperanza agreed. They arrived at the summer palace in Baguio during the first week of September. In addition to Esperanza, the party included Sergio Osmeña Jr., his wife Lourdes, then pregnant with the couple's second child, nine-month-old Sergio Osmeña III, eighteen-year-old Ramon, sixteen-year-old Rosalina, and nine-year-old Victor. A couple of servants and a female security guard rounded out the group.[7]

Within days, the Kempeitai, the dreaded Japanese secret police, came to arrest them. Esperanza was frightened, but indignant too. She called another longtime friend, Baguio lawyer Florendo Aquino, who then contacted the Baguio mayor, Ramon P. Mitra. Combining their political clout, the two men prevailed upon the Kempeitai to allow the Osmeña family to remain under house arrest at Mr. Aquino's home instead of going to jail. Armed Philippine Constabulary guards were posted at the home, two in front and two in the rear. Esperanza's hair appointments became a thing of the past. The children ventured outside only rarely, though Sergio Osmeña Jr. was permitted to take his pregnant wife to a local obstetrician for checkups. Two of the armed guards accompanied them on these outings, leaving two behind, one in front and one in back. All the detainees lived in constant fear.

The Japanese were unaware, but Florendo Aquino had long been supportive of the guerrilla cause. When Esperanza learned one of the 66th Infantry's 1st Battalion intelligence agents, Sergeant Godofredo Tacay, was scheduled to pay a secret visit to Aquino's office in late September with a list of items needed by the resistance, she gave a handwritten note to Aquino to pass on to Sergeant Tacay. In it, she outlined her family's precarious circumstances and stated she feared they would be used as hostages by the Japanese. Esperanza pleaded to be rescued and taken to guerrilla territory in the mountains.

The note was passed up the line to Volckmann, who sent a coded message to Australia, advising of Mrs. Osmeña's request and asking for instructions. At the same time, Volckmann told Art to come up with a plan.

A RT'S FIRST CHALLENGE WAS FIGURING OUT how to get all these people out of Baguio. He sent Robin Hood to Baguio to round up two cars, one large enough for seven passengers, equip both with red flags to mimic Japanese officers' vehicles, and hide them until the day of the operation.[8]

He detailed a particularly attractive female agent to impersonate a peanut peddler and begin making daily trips past the Aquino residence. Soon she was making friendly conversation and selling her wares to the appreciative P.C. guards. It wasn't long before the guards from the back began coming around to the front, one at a time, to buy peanuts and join in the fun.

As a diversion in the event the Japanese caught on, Art had another agent bribe the P.C. guards at a checkpoint on the Kennon Road so that on the appointed day they'd mark their logs to reflect that the "official" vehicles had passed by on their way to Manila.[9]

Art enlisted Captain Telesforo Pulido, commander of Headquarters Battalion, 66th Infantry, to assemble a hundred native *cargadores*. They built carrying chairs mounted on pairs of bamboo poles to transport those who couldn't navigate on foot the rugged mountain trails north of Baguio. Other natives under Captain Pulido's direction constructed three new *nipa* houses, along with a latrine and a bathing shack, near the 66th Infantry headquarters. Art felt Camp Shangri-La would be the safest and most secluded location for the anticipated guests now that USAFIP-NL headquarters had been relocated to Camp Utopia.

Art assigned Sergeant Tacay to drive the larger escape vehicle and Lieutenant Paul Velasco of Company B to drive the second car.

Finally, he assigned Captain Dominador Cepeda, one of their men who possessed a charming manner and some medical training, to accompany the rescue party and serve as Mrs. Osmeña's personal physician and aide-de-camp.

Every facet had to be coordinated with precision for the scheme to work. Art spent hours going over the timing and rehearsing each move with Sergeant Tacay and Lieutenant Velasco. They reviewed the plan with their men and with their comely peanut vender. Then they waited.

On October 16, after the groundwork had been completed, a radio reply came in from Australia:

> TO VOLCKMANN RE UR AD FIFTY TWO BELIEVE THAT MRS OSMENA SHOULD USE HER OWN JUDGEMENT BUT FROM INFORMATION AVAILABLE HERE IT WOULD APPEAR BEST FOR HER TO REMAIN WITH HER FRIENDS IN BAGUIO PD MAC ARTHUR.[10]

When this information was relayed to Esperanza, her reaction could only be described as explosive. She was adamant that the rescue take place as soon as possible.

WITH VOLCKMANN'S GO-AHEAD, Art set the plan in action. Mrs. Osmeña Jr. was advised to make an appointment with her obstetrician. The other family members were told to pack only the barest essentials and be ready to evacuate on the same day.

On October 27, Esperanza sent word that the appointment had been scheduled for 1 p.m. on the 30th.

The next few days were a time of high tension, but the plan went off without a hitch. On the 30th, Sergio Jr. and his wife left the Aquino house at 11 a.m., accompanied by two of the guards. The seductive peanut vender carried off her role perfectly. She engrossed the third P.C. guard at the front of the Aquino home in lively conversation, and before long the last guard came around to the front, not wanting to miss his share of the peanuts and flattery. Moments after he deserted his post, the first of the specially prepared vehicles, a Dodge station wagon, moved into the alleyway behind the house. Esperanza, carrying her step-grandson in her arms, her three children, two servants, and the female security guard slipped out the rear door and climbed into the waiting vehicle.

Sergeant Tacay drove swiftly through the streets of Baguio and down Naguilian Road. There was no pursuit. At Kilometer Post 4, the party was met by two well-armed platoons of Company A, 1st Battalion, and more than five dozen *cargadores*. The first lady, daughter Rosalina, and the security guard were loaded onto carrying chairs while *cargadores* hoisted the other children and the luggage onto their backs. With one armed platoon leading the way and the other bringing up the rear, the procession moved north on a steep, narrow trail and quickly disappeared into the thick undergrowth. Sergeant Tacay drove the station wagon several miles farther down Naguilian Road, sprayed it with bullets, and shoved it over the side into a deep canyon.

The second part of the operation went just as smoothly. As the two P.C. guards sat smoking and talking in their vehicle in front of the obstetrician's office, the second escape car pulled up at the back door and whisked Sergio Jr. and his wife away. It was almost an hour before the guards became suspicious, and by then it was too late.

Lieutenant Velasco also proceeded down Naguilian Road, turned north at the junction leading to Pinsao, Guisad, and delivered the Osmeñas into the custody of another fully armed guerrilla company led by Captain Pulido. Lourdes Osmeña was loaded onto a chair, and two dozen *cargadores* alternated to carry her into the mountains. Lieutenant Velasco proceeded back to Naguilian Road and disposed of the second escape car in the same manner as the first.

Exactly according to Art's plan, the two Osmeña groups arrived, several hours apart, at the home of Bado Dangwa's mother in the tiny barrio of Cadtay. The accommodations there were primitive and the food rudimentary, but no one complained.

Five more days of rugged climbing up slippery trails through dense forest brought the party to Camp Shangri-La, where they knelt together and thanked God for their safe deliverance.

Thank you from Esperanza Osmeña

A FEW DAYS LATER, TWO NOTES WERE DELIVERED to Art by Captain Cepeda, along with a fifth of Johnnie Walker Red. Art never figured out where Sergio Jr. got the scotch, but Russ, PK, and Art wasted no time in drinking a toast to the success of the rescue operation. Unlike the radio and submarine snafus, it truly had gone off without a hitch. Art folded the notes and tucked them inside his pocket diary. Over time the humidity caused the red leather to bleed onto Sergio Jr.'s note, leaving it barely legible. Dated November 3, it was addressed to "Major Arthur Murphy":

> *My dear Major: Just a word of greeting and thanks. Through your able men under Capt. Pulido, who have spared no efforts to make our trip safe and as comfortable as possible, we have succeeded in realizing our plans. For all your efforts, I wish to express my thanks. My mother has already written a separate note indicating her gratitude. When the smoke of the battle clears, which I know will not be far off, I shall see to it that all those who have contributed to the realization of our plans shall be justly accredited. Sincerely, S. Osmeña Jr. P.S. I am sending through Capt. Cepeda something which I hope will help to alleviate you from some of your strenuous work."*

RET V KAZ VIA ANA NR L/o   IN TWO PARTS CR 128 NR 29 FROM KAZ

TO VOLCKMANN

AYE COMMEND YOU AND YOUR OFFICERS AND MEN WHO PARTICIPATED IN SECURING THE SAFETY AT HER REQUEST OF MRS. OSMENA CMA FAMILY AND PARTY PD PLEASE CONTINUE TO EXTEND TO THEM EVERY POSSIBLE CARE PD DEEPLY THANKFUL FOR HELPING MRS. OSMENA AND PARTY TO REACH YOUR HEADQUARTERS AND FOR EVERYTHING YOU ARE DOING FOR THEM PD OF COURSE PRIME CONSIDERATION SHALL BE THEIR SECURITY PLEASE DELIVER TO HER THE FOLLOWING MESSAGE CLN DEAR CLN MOST HAPPY TO KNOW THAT YOU AND CHILD EN ARE SAFE IN FRIENDLY HANDS PD I HAVE BEEN PRAYING FOR YOU ALL PD TAKE CARE OF YOURSELF AND BE PATIENT PD GOD GRANTING CMA DELIVERING NEAR PD LOVE PD FROM PRESIDENT OSMENA

Time Rec'd 1505
Date rec'd No. 11/44
Opr. SC Sgnd.

Radiogram from KAZ to Volckmann

Sergio Jr. and his wife were subsequently moved over to Major Barnett's field hospital in La Union. There, on January 18, Lourdes gave birth to a healthy baby girl. They named her Maria Victoria, but everyone called her "Minnie," a nickname she carried throughout her life.

The guerrillas pulled out all the stops to make sure the Osmeñas were well taken care of. Natives fashioned soft mattresses from dried leaves and grass, tied together with vines. The guards gathered firewood in the forest and drinking water in bamboo poles from the nearby spring. The walls of their bathing hut extended out over the pool on posts to provide complete privacy; bar soap and fresh towels were provided daily. They were assigned a cook, and every week a courier delivered rice, fresh vegetables, fruit, and meat, often accompanied by current war news. At Thanksgiving, they had roast turkey with all the trimmings, and for Christmas the children received gifts of candy, chewing gum, and American magazines, all procured by guerrilla agents in Baguio.[11]

When Art finally found time to hike up to Shangri-La to meet the first family, Esperanza greeted him warmly. They sat outside on bamboo benches sipping *cala-mansi* as she and the others told vivid stories of their harrowing adventures since the beginning of the war. Tears streamed down her cheeks as she recounted the brutality of the Japanese and the suffering of the people in Manila. The children listened, wide-eyed, as Art described a couple of his own narrow escapes.

Photo of Esperanza's jewelry

They could have talked all afternoon, but Art had a two-hour hike back to headquarters. When he got up to leave, Esperanza was the last to say good-bye. As she took his arm and walked with him toward the trailhead, she reached into her bodice, retrieved a small blue velvet pouch, and tucked it into his shirt pocket. Then she took his hand in hers and spoke quietly: *I cannot thank you enough for all you have done for my family. You have told me you have a dear wife in California whom you haven't seen in more than four years. When you arrive home, please give this to her as a small token of my appreciation for her husband's bravery and devotion to his sacred duty.*

Before Art had been on the trail five minutes, he sat down on a log and pulled out the blue pouch, loosened the drawstring, and poured the contents into his hand. He couldn't believe his eyes! It was jewelry, Esperanza's jewelry: an elaborate garnet necklace with matching rings and bracelet, a natural pearl bracelet with matching ring and earrings, and a pair of delicate diamond earrings. After examining each piece, Art returned the jewelry to the pouch and tucked it back into his pocket, thrilled to have objects of such beauty to take home to Lillian.

THE OSMEÑAS HAD BEEN WITH THE GUERRILLAS only a few weeks when Art got a disturbing communiqué from their 5th District in Isabela. Colonel Romulo Manriquez, the commander, wrote that a day earlier a young stranger had wandered into their camp, wanting to join up. The stranger had given his name as Major Ferdinand Marcos and had said he'd been sent by General Manuel Roxas to make arrangements to supply arms to the North Luzon guerrillas.

Art was aware that Manuel Roxas had been an influential politician in Manila before the war, that he'd fought with the USAFFE forces on Bataan, and had surrendered to the Japanese in April 1942; but Art also knew that, following the surrender, the Japanese had elevated him to the rank of general and made him a part of the puppet government they set up in Manila. This wasn't the first time a stranger had turned up at a guerrilla camp claiming to represent General Roxas, asking all sorts of questions, and requesting copies of their rosters. In each such case, they had conducted a brief investigation, determined the stranger was an enemy spy, and had him executed.

In the present case, not only was this Ferdinand Marcos claiming to represent Roxas, he'd also told Manriquez he knew Mrs. Osmeña personally and asked where she was being held so he could send her a letter.

Manriquez wanted to know what he should do with the fellow. The fact that the president's family was at Shangri-La was top secret, so Art took no chances. He dispatched a message back to Manriquez that this so-called Ferdinand Marcos was undoubtedly a spy; that Manriquez should ostensibly accept him into the organization, make him a company commander, and then send him out on patrol, a patrol during which Marcos would meet with an *unfortunate accident*. Problem solved.

A short time later, Art mentioned the matter to Russ Volckmann. USAFIP-NL's G-3, Colonel Calixto Duque, overheard the conversation and immediately jumped in. He said he knew exactly who Ferdinand Marcos was; that he was the son of Mariano Marcos, a big shot in prewar Manila politics, and was indeed a friend of Sergio Osmeña. This still didn't explain how the fellow could possibly know the guerrillas had Mrs. Osmeña and her family in their custody, but Russ decided to reverse Art's decision. He promptly sent Manriquez another message, telling him that the young Marcos might be attached to the organization for duty but should be kept under close watch. Russ's instructions were carried out. Marcos was given a job as civil affairs officer, and he fulfilled those duties satisfactorily. Later on, Russ dispatched a liaison plane to pick Marcos up and fly him back to Darigayos. He remained attached to USAFIP-NL headquarters until the end of the war.[12, 13]

IN EARLY JANUARY, THE GUERRILLAS escorted Mrs. Osmeña and her family on horseback from Shangri-La down to San Fernando, where a PT boat picked them up and whisked them to Dagupan. There, they were delivered safely into the custody of Sergio Osmeña—husband, father, and president of the Philippines. Their ordeal was over. A job well done, Art thought to himself.

AFTER FERDINAND MARCOS ARRIVED at Darigayos, Art had plenty of opportunity to get to know him. He was quite a charming fellow and soon convinced Art his family did indeed know the Osmeñas. Trained as a lawyer, Marcos also had great political ambitions. Art followed his career with interest.

After the war, Ferdinand Marcos served from 1949 to 1959 in the Philippine House of Representatives and from 1959 to 1965 in the Senate. In 1965, with the full backing of the United States government, he was elected president of the Philippines, and was reelected four years later. Marcos and his wife, Imelda, lived lavishly, borrowed heavily, and the Philippine national debt soared. While U.S. investments and the elite in the Philippines flourished under Marcos's presidency, his people did not. As his opposition grew, Marcos increasingly violated democratic principles, jailed his political adversaries, and finally declared martial law in 1972 in an effort to keep his people under control.

Art sometimes wondered how different U.S.-Philippine relations and the fortunes of the Filipino people might have been had his original order been carried out.

CHAPTER 26

MACARTHUR KEEPS HIS PROMISE

October 1944

IN MARCH 1942, GENERAL DOUGLAS MACARTHUR was taken from Corregidor to Australia. Shortly after arriving, in a dramatic radio address to the Filipino people, MacArthur concluded with a solemn promise: "I shall return." After thirty-one months of brutal Japanese occupation, Mac made good on his pledge.

THE ROAD BACK WASN'T EASY. In Australia, MacArthur was appointed supreme commander of the Allied theater of military operations known as the Southwest Pacific Area (SWPA). His immediate assignment was to defend Australia as the Japanese Imperial Army and Navy were making unparalleled advances in the South Pacific and represented a distinct threat to overrun that continent.[1]

Rather than concentrate on defense, Mac elected to take the offense against the Japanese. His first battles were fought in the jungles and swamps of mountainous eastern New Guinea, where, despite long odds, MacArthur's forces ultimately prevailed. From there, they pushed through the northern coast of New Guinea, then the Solomon Islands, the Bismarck Archipelago, and the Admiralty Islands, seizing airfields as they went. From each newly captured airfield, supporting airpower became available for the next move forward by ground troops. With this island-hopping strategy, MacArthur's forces successfully isolated strongly defended enemy troop concentrations and seized strategic but often weakly defended areas.[2]

In the meantime, American naval forces and marines under the command of Admiral Chester W. Nimitz conducted a parallel naval offensive through the Gilbert and Marshall Islands, then through the Marianas and the Carolines, thereby depriving the Japanese of strategic airfields in these locations and unraveling their dominance of the Pacific Ocean.

So successful were these advances by General MacArthur and Admiral Nimitz that by early 1944 the American Joint Chiefs of Staff in Washington ordered two months' acceleration in the date set for the eventual invasion of Japan. Island targets previously thought essential were abandoned. A new target date of November 15 was set for MacArthur's forces to land on Mindanao, to be followed by a landing at Leyte Gulf in the Visayan Islands on December 20. This revised plan had as its ultimate objective the recapture of Manila and destruction of the central command structure and logistic support centers of the Japanese forces occupying the Philippines.[3]

These decisions were not reached easily. Sharp differences of opinion existed between the Army and Navy contingents of the Joint Chiefs of Staff, and heated debate continued through the summer of 1944. The argument centered not on Mindanao but rather on where to go from there. Navy opinion favored Formosa. General MacArthur was equally vehement in his opinion that Mindanao be followed by a landing on Leyte and then the island of Luzon in an all-out push to liberate the Philippines. MacArthur considered Luzon a superior location for the establishment of a major base from which to sever enemy supply lines and bombard and invade Japan. He insisted the United States had a *great national obligation* to the people of the Philippines and that bypassing any part of them would stain American honor and credibility far into the future.[4]

In late July, President Roosevelt flew to Pearl Harbor for a meeting with General MacArthur and Admiral Nimitz, but it was not until September 1 that the Joint Chiefs of Staff finally approved MacArthur's plan for the November invasion of Mindanao, to be followed by the Leyte assault just before Christmas.[5]

As advance preparation for the landings, during the second week of September, a carrier group of Admiral William Halsey's Third Fleet, part of Nimitz's naval command, began bombing the southern coast of Mindanao. They encountered little ground-based resistance. A few days later, another task force of the Third Fleet began bombing the Visayas. Again, enemy ground-based reaction proved surprisingly light. These successes came so easily that Admiral Halsey on September 13 recommended the invasion of Mindanao be scrapped entirely in favor of an early and direct assault on Leyte; that by concentrating Nimitz's mighty aircraft carriers, they could provide all the air power necessary to support a successful Leyte invasion. With the support of Admiral Nimitz and General MacArthur, the Joint Chiefs of Staff adopted the new plan and moved the date of the Leyte invasion forward another two months to October 20.

FOR THE LEYTE OPERATION, MacArthur's force was made up of the 200,000 infantrymen of General Walter Krueger's Sixth Army; the 2,500 carrier-borne combat aircraft of Lieutenant General George C. Kenney's Far East Air Force; and Vice Admiral Thomas C. Kinkaid's Seventh Fleet, consisting of more than 100 combat vessels, 500 transports, supply vessels, landing ships, and other support craft, in addition to 500 airplanes. Admiral Halsey's Third Fleet would provide pre-invasion airstrikes and then provide backup naval support for Mac's forces with nearly 100 modern warships and more than a thousand additional carrier-based aircraft.[6]

Japanese Imperial Army forces in the Philippines, under command of General Tomoyuki Yamashita, consisted of an estimated 500,000 men, the heaviest concentration around Manila Bay. The

Japanese Imperial Navy was based near Singapore to the south and in the northern waters of the South China Sea.

To provide a diversion from Leyte and encourage the scattering of enemy defensive forces, on October 10, one carrier group of Admiral Halsey's Third Fleet began bombing enemy air bases in the Ryukyu Islands south of Japan, then bombed Formosa and specific targets along the northern coast of Luzon. Sending hundreds of planes into the air at a time, these attacks inflicted crippling damage on enemy air power.[7]

Based upon intelligence provided by guerrillas on Mindanao, Leyte, and Samar, MacArthur's staff estimated Japanese combat strength on Mindanao at only 50,000 defenders, another 20,000 on hand to defend Leyte's half dozen airfields, while fewer enemy troops occupied Samar. Even allowing for the potential of Japanese reinforcements from Luzon, the odds favored the Americans, who hoped to utilize the element of surprise to get ashore quickly, move inland to capture crucial enemy-controlled airfields, and secure Leyte as a base from which to conduct future operations on Luzon.

The preliminaries began early on October 17 with the neutralizing of several lightly defended islands guarding the eastern approaches to Leyte Gulf. By midnight on October 19, the vast Allied invasion force lay assembled beneath a moonless sky at the entrance to the gulf, silently waiting. With the first light of dawn on the 20th, the big guns of the naval ships began pounding the shoreline. Soon, wave after wave of Admiral Kinkaid's landing craft churned toward the sandy beaches. Meeting little resistance at first, General Krueger's infantrymen successfully established beach positions. From behind logs and other cover, they attacked the dug-in enemy fortifications in the thick jungle immediately inland while overhead hundreds of fighter pilots circled and dove furiously, bombing and strafing, clearing the way as the ground troops advanced, inch by inch.[8]

In the third assault wave, one of the landing craft carried General MacArthur and Philippine President Sergio Osmeña, along with a sizeable contingent of staff and newsmen. Fifty feet from shore, the skipper dropped his ramp. The passengers stepped off into knee-deep water and waded toward the beach. Within a few hundred yards of the noise, smoke, and flames of the ongoing battle, a mobile broadcasting unit was set up, and General MacArthur, with his typical flare for drama, took the microphone:

> *People of the Philippines, I have returned. By the grace of Almighty God, our forces stand again on Philippine soil, soil consecrated in the blood of our two peoples. We have come, dedicated and committed to the task of destroying every vestige of enemy control over your daily lives, and of restoring, upon a foundation of indestructible strength, the liberties of your people.*
>
> *At my side is your President, Sergio Osmeña, a worthy successor of that great patriot, Manuel Quezon, with members of his cabinet. The seat of your government is now, therefore, firmly reestablished on Philippine soil.*
>
> *The hour of your redemption is here. Your patriots have demonstrated an unswerving and resolute devotion to the principles of freedom that challenge the best that is written on the pages of human history. I now call upon your supreme effort that the enemy may know, from the temper of an aroused people within, that he has a force there to contend with no less violent than is the force committed from without.*
>
> *Rally to me. Let the indomitable spirit of Bataan and Corregidor lead on. As the lines of battle roll forward to bring you within the zone of operations, rise and strike. Strike at every favorable opportunity. For your homes and hearths, strike! For future generations of your sons and daughters, strike! In the name of your sacred dead,*

strike! Let no heart be faint. Let every arm be steeled. The guidance of Divine God points the way. Follow in His name to the Holy Grail of righteous victory."[9]

Gen. Douglas MacArthur wades ashore during initial landings at Leyte, Philippine Islands. October 1944. This image is a work of a U.S. Army soldier or employee, taken or made as part of that person's official duties. As a work of the U.S. federal government, the image is in the public domain.

Despite the triumphant words of the general, the battle for Leyte proved neither quick nor easy. Weather weighed in on the side of the enemy. High winds and torrential rains pounded Leyte, turning the ground to mush. Thirty-five inches of rain fell in the first forty days of the campaign. Trucks, tanks, and troops on foot bogged down in the sticky mud. Engineering battalions tasked with lengthening and improving the newly captured airfields became increasingly frustrated as their heavy equipment foundered in the muck. As a result, only a few American fighters and ground-based bombers could be advanced to bases on Leyte before December, leaving the bulk of the air-support missions to Kinkaid's battered escort carriers and Halsey's tired and overworked larger ships.[10]

Imperial Japanese General Headquarters in Tokyo, over the strenuous objections of General Yamashita, abruptly reversed strategy and elected to throw everything it had against the Americans on Leyte. Thick clouds blanketed the central Philippine Sea passages, enabling Japanese convoys to ferry 45,000 additional troops and tons of supplies south from Manila to the port of Ormoc on Leyte's west coast. These reinforcements quickly moved inland and dug themselves deeply into a complicated network of mountain bunkers and foxholes, prepared to fight to the death.

Imperial Japanese Headquarters also came up with a new weapon, the suicide or *Kamikaze* pilots, dedicated young men willing to fly cobbled-together planes and give their lives in defense of their emperor and homeland by becoming human bombs. Their targets ranged from ships and airfields to troop columns and ammunition supply depots, and while not a decisive element in the campaign, these *Kamikaze* missions inflicted measurable damage and significantly prolonged the battle for Leyte.

MacArthur also sent in reinforcements, but despite the overwhelming advantage of the Americans in both men and materiel, it was not in the Japanese character to give up. Better to die with honor than surrender. Protracted battles continued along both Leyte coastal plains and on the steep ridges and mountains of the interior. It was not until the end of December 1944 that Allied victory was assured.

The Leyte campaign, including its air, sea, and land phases, resulted in 5,000 American deaths and 14,000 wounded, along with a relatively lighter toll in planes and warships. It had taken longer than anticipated, not because of the strength of the enemy defenses but because the awful weather and problematic soil conditions thwarted the Americans at every turn. On the plus side, their protracted efforts to defend Leyte had cost the Japanese a significant portion of their airpower, the bulk of their naval fleet, and a crucial segment of their army, all of which reduced their chances for success in the upcoming battle for Luzon.[11]

CHAPTER 27

A COMEDY OF ERRORS

Mid-November through Mid-December 1944

O N NOVEMBER 12, Art brought Lil up to date:

"Dearest Lillian. I am now at a different camp. Two puppet Philippine Constabulary fellows, who deserted the Japs—or so it seemed—and joined a unit adjacent to our old headquarters, ran back toward the Japs the other day. As I was engaged in getting out some very important reports that couldn't stand interruption, I had to move to an alternate camp to get them finished. Some of the boys stuck around to give any Jap visitors a warm welcome. However, later reports say the Japs, on sighting these two P.C. fellows, fired on them, killing one and wounding the other, who escaped but was later captured and executed by our units. If this report is true, I'll be back at our old camp pretty soon.

"Just as I got down here, we were hit by a late-season, 50-mile-an-hour typhoon that kept us holding onto our hair to keep it from being blown away. The weather is okay this morning, except my fingers are so cold that I can't type worth a damn.

"Life and I are pretty much the same. The Leyte landings have lost their excitement as MacArthur is still a long way from here. Allied planes are doing a little bombing in North Luzon, but I have yet to actually see one. Meanwhile, the Japs are pouring in thousands of troops that we'll have to wade through before North Luzon is truly liberated. In the occupied areas, the Japs are killing people right and left. In Bangui, Ilocos Norte, they machine-gunned 300 civilians, but the joke was that these people were pro-Japs and were fleeing to the Jap garrison for protection from our units! The coastal areas are deserted now due to Jap depredations and the fear of Allied bombers.

"Well, my darling, it's now time for breakfast, and I have a million and one things to do before the mail goes out this afternoon. So I'll say *au revoir* for now. Kiss the babies for their daddy. Love, Art." [1]

NOT LONG AFTER THE FAILED SUBMARINE supply mission in late October, HQ-SWPA promised them another, one carrying sixteen men and twenty-five tons of supplies, with an estimated arrival date of November 20. [2] The radiomen had wasted no time in repairing their transceiver, but with all the Leyte activity, no further details had come in regarding this second mission, and time was running short. Even if the next sub contact went off without a hitch, the guerrillas needed time to distribute the supplies by *cargadore* to the five districts and to get a radio net set up.

Finally, during the first week of November, HQ-SWPA inquired if the same two rendezvous spots could be used. In a coded reply, they were assured the same spots would be fine. HQ-SWPA also updated the arrival date to November 22, the day before Thanksgiving, with an exact timetable and specific shore signals to follow. [3]

Again, Major Barnett assembled the *bancas* and *cargadores*, ready to move into position at both rendezvous spots on November 21. He divided the *cargadores* into carrying parties and assigned armed escorts to each party. Combat units were briefed on what to do if an enemy patrol threatened the beach after the sub surfaced and unloading was underway. Barnett detailed lookouts to begin 'round-the-clock observation of both points beginning on November 15 to check for any unusual enemy activity at nearby Japanese garrisons. Beginning on November 18, he ordered command posts established near the rendezvous points and advance parties moved in to set up radio equipment.[4] Everything would be ready by the 22nd.

Unwilling to delegate this critical task a second time, Russ Volckmann elected to take charge of the primary rendezvous spot himself, while Barnett was assigned to Spot Two as before. Volckmann also decided to hike down to Darigayos Cove several days ahead of time so he could personally ensure that every instruction was followed to the letter. The final landing instructions would be relayed to him by radio as soon as they came in.[5]

Now Mother Nature threw them a nasty curve. By the middle of November, the rainy season should have been over, but on the morning of the 14th, the skies filled with swirling gray clouds and the wind picked up in a way they knew presaged a tropical storm. Normally, only a fool would try hiking to the coast under such conditions, but with the sub already on its way from Australia, Volckmann dared not risk another screw-up.[6]

The locals rounded up a pony for him, and shortly after dawn on the morning of the 15th, he and a small party headed out on what should have been a six- to eight-hour hike down the steep trails to the coastal plain and another four or five hours north to Darigayos.[7]

Volckmann hadn't been gone an hour when the full fury of the storm slammed ashore. Deafening typhoon-force winds buffeted Camp Utopia, sending the rain slashing down in sheets and blowing the roof off one of the storage buildings. PK and Art remained glued to the radio, anxiously awaiting the follow-up communiqué from Australia to confirm the final rendezvous time and landing instructions. Suddenly the radio went dead! As Ancheta and Luz frantically checked the wire connections, Art tried the lights. They had no power at all.[8]

Moments later, one of their native lookouts, soaking wet and out of breath, came charging in. *Carabao down waterfall,* he hollered. *Everything broke!*

What the hell? A carabao? How could that be?

PK and Art rushed out into the storm. Indeed, an adult *carabao* had evidently waded into the swollen river up on the plateau, lost its footing, been washed over the waterfall, tumbled 300 feet straight down, and landed squarely atop their hydroelectric plant, splintering the framework like so many matchsticks. The beast lay writhing on its back amid the boulders. *Of all the miserable goddamned luck,* muttered the normally reserved PK.[9]

Despite the storm, PK ordered a construction detail to begin putting things back together. Then he sent a handwritten message by runner to catch up with Volckmann and give him the awful news that they'd been knocked off the air by a *carabao* but were doing everything humanly possible to restore power.[10]

The construction crew performed magnificently. By noon on the 17th, Ancheta and Luz had the radio back up and receiving, though they still couldn't transmit. That afternoon, to their great relief, a radiogram came in from HQ-SWPA confirming the November 22 date and ordering a strange-sounding set of shore signals. Certainly, they were in no position to argue. PK sent a second runner with the detailed radiogram down to Volckmann at Darigayos. Then he and Art heaved a sigh of relief, confident the sub rendezvous was back on track.[11]

But Fate wasn't finished with them yet. On the afternoon of the 18th, a bombshell arrived from HQ-SWPA:

CONSIDER THAT YOUR NR TWO OF THE SIXTEENTH PART ONE CHECK FIVE FIVE IS READ BY THE ENEMY PD CHECK AND RECHECK

EVERY MESSAGE FOR THE ERROR OF SINGLE TRANSPOSITION PD TAKE APPROPRIATE ACTION TO CHANGE SPOTS PD BEGIN TO USE MESSAGE BEGINS PROCEDURE AS ILLUSTRATED BY THIS MSG PD[12]

They couldn't believe it! *Read by the enemy? How could that have happened?*

Lieutenant Ancheta began a systematic review of all the radiograms sent to HQ-SWPA. Sure enough, he discovered one had been wrongly coded, using single-transposition instead of the double-transposition code that MacArthur's headquarters had specified. If only they had some way to make direct contact with the sub! But that's not the way the communications worked. Everything had to go through Australia. In Volckmann's name, Art wasted no time in drafting an answer:

IMPOSSIBLE TO CHANGE SPOTS ONE OR TWO AT THIS DATE PD REQUEST YOU CONSIDER THAT ENEMY HAS NOT RPT NOT READ OUR NR TWO OF SIXTEENTH PART ONE PD BELIEVE SIGNAL SYSTEM ORDERED BY YOU GIVES AMPLE SECURITY TO VESSEL PD NOTE THAT SPOT TWO RPT TWO WAS NOT RPT NOT MENTIONED IN MESSAGE PD VESSEL CAN PROCEED TO SPOT TWO IF SPOT ONE IS COMPROMISED COMPLETELY PD HOWEVER MAILBAG CONTAINING ENEMY DOCUMENTS IS ONLY AT SPOT ONE AND CANNOT BE MOVED IN TIME TO SPOT TWO PD AGAIN STATE WE WILL BE READY FROM NOVEMBER TWO TWO RPT TWENTY TWO ON AT BOTH SPOTS AND UNDERSTAND

YOUR TWO SEVEN RPT TWENTY SEVEN PD
SGND VOLCK[13]

A S IF THEY HADN'T ENOUGH on their plates, early on
November 19, Lieutenant Jose Valera's party, the long-lost
group that had landed by sub on the north coast of Luzon the previous August, finally arrived at their headquarters, guided by one of
George Barnett's agents.[14] Valera brought a bewildering array of new
radio equipment. In view of his greater knowledge and experience,
PK placed him in charge over Ancheta, Luz, Sinay, and Hernando.

Valera first tested the power pack set-up and inspected the newly
repaired hydroelectric installation, pronouncing them adequate. Then
he set up a new transceiver dedicated exclusively to communications
with KAZ, the radio code name of MacArthur's SWPA headquarters
in Australia. With that unit operational, Valera went to work on a
plan for a communications network to tie together all of USAFIP-
NL's districts as well as several other guerrilla units farther south.[15]

As impressive as Valera's work was, PK and Art could focus only
on events they hoped were taking place at Darigayos. All they could
do was cross their fingers and wait.

On the afternoon of November 21, they got yet another
gut-wrenching scare, the sickening sound of bombs hitting their
targets somewhere off the coast. Although it wasn't unusual to hear
Japanese bombers out over the South China Sea, after the recent series
of disasters, they feared the Japanese had spotted and destroyed the
supply sub.

Worry made sleep impossible. They sat glumly in the headquarters building, Art working on intelligence reports late into the night
while PK passed the time playing solitaire. Suddenly, they heard the
measured pop-pop-popping of rifle fire, followed by the sound of
light mortar fire. Instantly, they doused the lights and hit the floor,
cocked their .45s, and waited in silence, prepared to sell their lives
dearly. Outside, the entire camp was awake, men running everywhere

and yelling. Within ten minutes, though, the furor subsided, so Art took a peek. No Japanese in sight. One of the men reported that a small fire had ignited spontaneously in the damaged storage building on the hillside above, and what they'd heard were the sounds of exploding ammunition, hand grenades, and steam-filled canteens.

PK and Art waited the rest of the night and all the next day, silent and dejected. On the morning of November 23, Thanksgiving, a message dated the 21st came in from Robert Arnold, now commanding the 15th Infantry in Ilocos Norte, describing a convoy of half a dozen Japanese ships that had passed his coast-watchers, heading north. The information was of little interest except as general intelligence, but Art incorporated it into other recent reports and readied a consolidated report for transmission to HQ-SWPA. Keeping busy may have passed the time, but it did nothing to relieve the anxiety they felt as they awaited further word about the sub.

Another short radio communiqué came in around noon, also of little consequence.

Then, late in the afternoon on the 23rd, a runner brought the following message. It had been written at four o'clock that morning:

Subject: Report
To: C.O., USAFIP-NL

1. *Made contact 7:15 p.m., November 22, 1944. They wanted to unload at Point One, so we went there. Could find no one except what we thought were Japs on the beach, so returned here. If coast is clear, we will unload tonight.*

2. *Load as reported: 16 personnel (6 Americans and 10 Filipinos) and 25 tons. If God permits, should reach you in a few days.*

3. *Best regards and good luck.*
   G. M. BARNETT, Major, U.S.A., Commanding.[16]

Eureka! The mood at Camp Utopia soared. As the news raced swiftly through camp, spontaneous cheers erupted and quickly reached a crescendo of exuberant celebration. Many of the men dropped to their knees in prayer. *Thank the Lord!* they shouted. *Hooray!* The contact had been successful after all! They still didn't know what had happened to Russ, and the supplies had yet to be distributed, but step one of their comeback was safely in the books.

Art grabbed his Johnnie Walker Red and motioned for PK to follow him into the trees. Out of sight of the others, they drank a toast to the submarine mission, swigging straight from the bottle. Art danced a little jig, and they drank another.

A BEDRAGGLED RUSS VOLCKMANN ARRIVED back in camp two days later, as dejected as they'd ever seen him. Barnett's good news hadn't caught up with him on the trail, and he was still trying to come to grips with yet another failed sub contact. At first he stood, bewildered, as PK and Art, excitedly shouting over each other, filled him in, but gradually his eyes widened and he broke into a big grin.

No kidding? he stammered. *Are you sure?*

Hell, yes, we're sure, Art told him as PK pulled Barnett's message out of his pocket and handed it over. While Volckmann stared at the paper, Art grabbed the last of the Johnnie Walker Red so he, too, could celebrate.

After a shower, some clean clothes, and a good hot meal, Volckmann filled them in on the details of his trip.

Within an hour of leaving Camp Utopia, the storm had unleashed its full fury, gale-force winds tearing huge limbs from the trees and whipping the heavy rain horizontally, slowing progress to a crawl. Several hours into the ordeal, Volckmann's pony had stumbled on the slippery trail, sending both of them tumbling down the mountainside. Fortunately, a tree had broken Volckmann's fall and he'd sustained only cuts and bruises. The pony hadn't been so lucky.[17]

Late that first afternoon, the party had approached a barrio on the banks of a normally fordable stream. Now a raging torrent, none of the frightened natives would attempt a crossing. A couple of hours later, PK's messenger had reached them with the news about the *carabao* knocking Utopia's radio off the air. A frantic Volckmann could do nothing but pace through the night, decrying their rotten luck and praying the storm would blow itself out quickly.[18]

By the next morning, the storm let up and Russ and his party crossed the stream. The rest of the trip to Darigayos had been relatively uneventful. Finding the beach preparations in order, he'd settled in with his local host, a Judge Zambrano, and waited for further word from Utopia.[19]

On the 19th, a runner had appeared with the good news that Camp Utopia was back on the air. But when he'd handed over the confirmation of the November 22nd landing date and final contact instructions, Volckmann had been as puzzled as PK and Art had been[20]:

BETWEEN 0600 AND 0800 DISPLAY ON BEACH TWO HUNDRED METERS APART TWO WHITE DISCS TWO METERS IN DIAMETER WITH A SMOKE SMUDGE FIRE MIDWAY BETWEEN DISCS PD REPEAT SAME SIGNALS FROM 1600 TO 1800 PD AT 1630 COMMANDER SHORE PARTY PUT TO SEA IN A SMALL SAILING BOAT FLYING A CHINESE FLAG PD IF NO CONTACT IS MADE PRIOR TO DARK DISPLAY THREE LIGHTS VERTICALLY FROM THE MAST OF THE SAILBOAT STOP[21]

The white discs weren't a problem. Judge Zambrano's wife rounded up a couple of white Igorot blankets, and the shore crew stretched the blankets between sets of bamboo poles so they could be displayed vertically the required 200 meters apart, facing out to sea. Even the small sailboat wasn't a problem, but PK and Art couldn't help laughing out loud as Volckmann described his reaction to the rest of the shore-signal instructions: *What? A sailboat with a goddamned Chinese flag? How am I supposed to come up with a Chinese flag? What the hell does a goddamned Chinese flag look like anyway? And lights vertically from the mast? How am I supposed to manage that? Shimmy up the mast while holding onto three lit torches with my teeth?* Volckmann and the judge had finally agreed on wide red, white, and blue stripes for the flag, and the judge's wife and daughters had raided their wardrobes for enough material to stitch together a reasonable facsimile.[22]

On the morning before the sub was due, as Volckmann watched from his observation post above the beach, he'd gotten another surprise. Several miles out to sea, he saw a dozen northbound Japanese ships and then sat spellbound as a swarm of U.S. planes attacked the ships, sending six of them to the bottom of the South China Sea. An American air strike was an electrifying spectacle, but his initial elation turned to concern when a few hours later the beach at Darigayos was crawling with Japanese patrols looking for survivors from the sunken ships. Volckmann described his great relief when they had finally pulled out at dusk, leaving the beach empty and quiet.[23]

On November 22, Russ went to his observation post before dawn. As the shore-signal detail waited, poised to light the smudge fire and display their white blankets promptly at six, suddenly a lookout flashed a warning of an approaching enemy patrol boat. The beach detail ran for cover. Volckmann described his anguish as the patrol boat headed into the cove and dropped anchor. A dozen Japanese soldiers came ashore in a dinghy and spent more than an hour searching the empty village huts before returning to their patrol boat and disappearing up the coast.[24]

Once the patrol boat was out of sight, Volckmann ordered the shore-signal detail back onto the beach, but no sooner had the signals gone up than the crack of rifle fire sent the men scurrying for cover a second time. Presently, a Japanese foot patrol emerged from the jungle carrying a dead goat. They lit a cooking fire and settled down for a leisurely meal and a nap. A frustrated Volckmann could do nothing but groan and watch helplessly as the minutes and hours ticked by.[25]

When five o'clock came and the Japanese still hadn't budged, Volckmann had concluded there could be no sub landing that night at Spot One. With no further need of *cargadores*, he had ordered the bolo units to disperse and the 1st Combat Battalion of Barnett's 121st Infantry to return to their headquarters. With a heavy heart, he and his party had trudged back up to Camp Utopia.[26]

THREE DAYS LATER, ON NOVEMBER 25, Major George Barnett led a column of American officers, enlisted men, and several hundred heavily laden native *cargadores* up the trail to Camp Utopia. Behind Barnett came Captain William A. Farrell and Captain William Vaughan, followed by two demolition experts, Lieutenants Fred Behan and Donald Jamison. Behind them were a couple of weather-station men and ten Filipino radio operators and demolitions experts. Volckmann, PK, and Art were in a jubilant mood as they formed a reception line to greet them. After several minutes of joyful hugs and handshakes, Barnett confirmed that the rest of the newly arrived personnel and supplies had been divvied up in the early morning hours of November 23 at Spot Two and were already on their way via the message center routes to the other districts.[27]

No kids on Christmas morning could have been more excited as they pried open the wooden crates delivered by the USS *Gar*. There were rocket launchers, grenade launchers, Thompson submachine guns, carbines, and plenty of ammunition. There were cases of dynamite. There was medicine, including Atabrine and Plasmoquine to treat cerebral malaria and dengue fever. There were two-way radios and a good supply of batteries. There were boots, blankets, compasses, and a supply of Ten-in-One military rations.[28]

The last crate—requiring four men to carry—was marked to be opened by Volckmann himself, but they all crowded around. When the final slat came off, they were flabbergasted! The entire contents consisted of chocolate bars, packets of Chesterfield cigarettes, matchbooks, and big rubber stamps, all bearing the slogan "I Shall Return. General Douglas MacArthur"! Accompanying instructions stated the material was to be used for propaganda purposes—the candy, cigarettes, and matches spread among the natives in the barrios, and the stamps used to plaster MacArthur's message on every conceivable surface in order to rally the people. What a joke! The morale in their district had never been higher. Every day, dozens of men were pouring in, wanting to join up. Their problem was munitions, not morale![29]

That evening Barnett told his story. After several anxious days, a runner had arrived at his headquarters with the final sub-landing instructions, and, like Volckmann, he'd managed to rig up the required shore signals and come up with a flag. On November 22, at Santiago Cove, he displayed the signals exactly as instructed. Around six that evening he spotted the periscope and went out in a small *banca* to meet the sub captain. At that point, the mission had taken an interesting turn.

Are you Volckmann? inquired skipper Maurice "Duke" Ferrara.

Nope. I'm George Barnett. Volckmann's waiting for you down at Darigayos.

You mean this isn't Darigayos?

Nope. This is Santiago Cove. Darigayos is twenty miles south.

Well, I'll be damned. We're supposed to meet Volckmann and unload at Darigayos. You'd better come aboard and take us there.[30]

An hour later, when the sub arrived off Darigayos, fires were burning on the beach, so Barnett and two bodyguards went in a rubber boat to get Volckmann. As they approached the shore, they were aghast to realize that the men clustered around the fires were Japanese, not guerrillas. They beat a hasty retreat back to the sub and returned to Santiago Cove, where the cargo was unloaded without further incident.[31] The men and supplies were divided up and dispatched to the guerrilla districts exactly according to plan.

As Russ Volckmann, PK, and Art sat around enjoying Chesterfield cigarettes and chewing the fat with the new officers, they hatched a little scheme. For General MacArthur, they scrounged up an Igorot pipe, filled it with native tobacco, and attached a tag with "USAFIP-NL" printed on one side and the slogan "We Remained" on the other. For Ferrara, they found a navigator's compass salvaged from a Japanese freighter, put it in a fancy wooden box, and attached a tag saying, "To aid you in keeping your bearings." Both "gifts" were placed with the mailbag to be delivered to the captain of the next supply sub.[32]

On December 9, Art brought Lil up to date:

> "Dearest Lillian. We've had some excitement recently. One of our units made a little raid within the Baguio city limits. We've also collected miles and miles of the Japs' telephone wire and have given them other little pinpricks. They apparently lost their temper and began burning houses and rice granaries and shooting everybody they saw. The granaries contained little rice, for long ago we had the people hide all their rice. We put up with it for a day or two and then, deciding we had nothing to lose,

we hit back. In the first ambush, we killed three. They ran back toward Baguio with our units in hot pursuit. Two rearguard actions took place before the Japs reached safety. We haven't learned their losses yet, but our only casualty was one man wounded. It remains to be seen if the Japs will return in greater numbers, thus weakening Baguio for a possible attack from another direction, or whether they will stay where they're safe—for the time being. If they return, we'll be ready.

"While all this was going on, we got a report that the Japs had learned the location of our headquarters and were coming after us, so we moved out for the nite and returned the next day. Everything is now returning to normal.

"I could tell you lots of other exciting things, but the necessity for secrecy forbids. Remind me after the war.

"I'm still quite well and healthy and have just received a new pair of shoes!

"Much love to you and the little girls. (I guess they're not babies anymore!)

Art."[33]

THEN THEY RECEIVED the following from KAZ:

CAN YOU HANDLE TWO SIMULTANEOUS SHIPMENTS TOTALING SEVENTY TONS AT SANTIAGO COVE QUERY EASY TARE ABLE TO BE NINE DECEMBER PD SECURITY SIGNALS TO BE SAME USED LAST DELIVERY PD TWO VESSELS INCLUDE SUB WHICH EFFECTED DELIVERY LAST SHIPMENT PD DESIRE YOU DESIGNATE ALTERNATE SPOT

IN CASE RENDEZVOUS SITE COMPROMISED PD REQUIRE CONSTANT REPORTS ON RENDEZVOUS POINTS GIVING BOTH POSITIVE AND NEGATIVE INTELLIGENCE INFORMATION PD DESIRE URGENT REPLY THIS MESSAGE PD[34]

A week later, another radiogram revised the plan:

SUPPLY VESSEL REVISED EASY TARE ABLE DARIGAYOS INLET IS ELEVEN DECEMBER PD ONLY ONE VESSEL NOT TWO WILL ARRIVE YOUR AREA PD APPROXIMATELY THIRTY FIVE TONS ON BOARD.[35]

This time Volckmann designated PK to meet the USS *Gar* and its skipper, Duke Ferrara, at Darigayos. The sub landing went off without a hitch, and thirty-five additional tons of guns, ammunition, and medical supplies—along with hundreds of loaves of freshly baked bread—were quickly dispersed to the five guerrilla districts. There were no more candy bars or matchbooks.[36]

CHAPTER 28

TAKING BACK
NORTH LUZON
January through March 1945

AMID THE TUMULTUOUS EVENTS surrounding the submarine landings, a runner from Major Manriquez's 5th District brought in perhaps the guerrillas' greatest intelligence find of the war. A small plane carrying several high-ranking Japanese officers had crashed in Nueva Viscaya, killing everyone aboard. In combing the wreckage for salvage, Manriquez's men had discovered a briefcase containing top-secret documents detailing revised plans for the enemy's final defense of North Luzon.

ON OCTOBER 10, 1944, just ten days before MacArthur's Leyte landing, General Tomoyuki Yamashita, a decorated veteran of earlier Japanese successes in Malaya and Singapore, was placed in command of all Japanese forces remaining in the Philippines, a force estimated at 250,000 men. Yamashita anticipated the Allies would invade somewhere in the southern Philippine Islands preparatory to an assault on Manila. Realizing his weakened forces could not successfully defend the capital or the fertile plains north of the city and knowing there was no longer any chance of air or naval support from Japan, Yamashita devised a new defensive plan that called for abandoning Manila and dividing his remaining troops. One small contingent would remain in the Zambales Mountains to control the Clark Field complex, and a second contingent would move into the Sierra Madres east of Manila to maintain control of the dams and reservoirs providing the city's water supply. The majority of his troops would pull back gradually into northern Luzon, where they would dig in deeply and prepare to defend the critical ports, airfields, mountain passes, connecting roads, and the summer capital of Baguio. Yamashita envisioned that if these defenses crumbled, his remaining forces could withdraw slowly north and east over the most inaccessible reaches of the Cordillera Central and gradually make their way down the Cagayan Valley to Aparri, where they could perhaps commandeer enough boats to reach Japan. With this strategy, Yamashita hoped to stall MacArthur's progress for months or even years, thereby preventing or at least delaying an attack on the homeland. He'd called his generals for a top-secret conference in Manila to brief them on the new strategy and then sent them back to their command posts. Finally, after wreaking maximum damage on Manila, destroying everything of strategic value, and slaughtering more than 100,000 innocent civilians, Yamashita had moved his own headquarters and the offices of the puppet Philippine government north to Baguio[1, 2]

Through guerrilla agents, Art already knew about many of these enemy troop movements. His intelligence summaries had for several months included detailed information concerning the shifting and consolidating of Yamashita's forces, along with his carefully considered, up-to-the-minute assessment of their defensive capabilities.[3] Now, though, they had the overall strategy, explicit details, and precise timing right from the source!

SINCE MACARTHUR'S LEYTE LANDING, HQ-SWPA had been soliciting their input on the optimal location for an invasion of North Luzon. Volckmann, PK, and Art now pored over the captured documents, and Art carefully compared the new information with the mountain of intelligence collected earlier from their districts. They hashed over the options and agreed that, with the Japanese beach defenses expected to be minimal, the landing could take place at Lingayen Gulf, at the same spot where the Japanese had landed three years earlier.[4]

MacArthur's headquarters accepted the recommendation and set January 9 as the date for the invasion, preceded by three days of intense naval and air bombardment.

Volckmann didn't want to miss any of the action, so he and PK and a small support group went down the mountain to one of George Barnett's training camps near San Gabriel, leaving Art in charge at Utopia. Much as he would have liked to accompany them, he couldn't afford a sightseeing trip. He was transmitting dozens of detailed reports by radio to HQ-SWPA every day, reports crucial because they pinpointed the targets to be destroyed during the pre-invasion bombing in order to minimize losses among the landing troops and maximize the chances for a successful invasion.

BACK IN AUGUST 1944, at the time of the first successful radio contact with HQ-SWPA, Russ Volckmann had informed General MacArthur of his plans to support an invasion of North Luzon.

On January 5, the guerrillas received the go-ahead to begin their pre-invasion work:

> YOU WILL PROCEED TO DESTROY TARGETS
> ASSIGNED BY THIS HEADQUARTERS UNDER
> ITS PLAN OF SABOTAGE COMMUNICATED
> TO YOU BY DISPATCH OF 29 NOVEMBER
> PD CONCURRENTLY CMA IF FEASIBLE CMA
> OR THEREAFTER CMA YOU WILL UTILIZE
> ALL OF THE MANPOWER AND MATERIAL
> RESOURCES AT YOUR COMMAND TO
> DESTROY ENEMY WIRE COMMUNICATIONS

CMA EXCLUSIVE OF MANILA CMA POWER
LINES CMA RAILROAD TRACKS CMA SPURS
CMA ROUNDHOUSES CMA ROLLING STOCK
CMA TRUCKS AND OTHER MEANS OF
TRANSPORT PD ALL POSSIBLE DESTRUCTION
OF PLANES CONCEALED IN DISPERSAL AREAS
CMA AMMUNITION CMA FUEL AND OTHER
SUPPLY DUMPS IS DESIRED PD OBSERVE
UTMOST SECRECY PD ACKNOWLEDGE[5]

All districts were ordered to mobilize to full strength. In addition to the armed units, the Bolo Battalions in each district were called to action. Within days, USAFIP-NL's numbers swelled to more than 22,000 men, including the native guerrillas and the dozen or so American officers still alive and kicking.

Beginning on the 6th, under heavy fog cover, simultaneous attacks erupted in all districts. The fury and thirst for revenge that had festered in the men during three long years of brutal Japanese occupation were now unleashed. Telephone wires were cut, hidden airplanes destroyed, convoys ambushed, bridges blown, fuel dumps set afire, sections of railroad track disabled, roadblocks set up, and landslides initiated along the mountain roads to thwart enemy movement. Thousands of Japanese soldiers were killed. Dozens of local Philippine Constabulary garrisons were surrounded and given a single warning to surrender. Some obeyed instantly; those who did not were annihilated.

Concurrent with these attacks, the first advance ships of the Allied invasion armada arrived in the Lingayen Gulf and began pounding the southern shore. A swarm of Japanese *Kamikaze* suicide planes based at Clark Field took to the air and came in low under the fog, inflicting damage to some of the earliest arrivals. One minesweeper was sunk. Two Japanese destroyers also showed up, but the American and Australian ships were able to chase them off, and planes from the escort carriers quickly rendered them useless.[6]

On January 7 and 8, the weather cleared and the heavy bombardment began.

The morning of January 9 dawned bright and beautiful. The seas were calm, with only the occasional swell breaking gently on the sand beaches. Shortly after sunup, several more *Kamikaze* planes from Clark Field put in a brief appearance. Two missed their targets and crashed into the sea while the third clipped the deck of a light cruiser, inflicting minimal damage. Then the skies were empty and all was quiet—for a while.

At 7 a.m., the bombardment resumed as naval guns and carrier-based fighters again bombed and strafed the beaches. Then the first ground troops of General Walter Krueger's Sixth Army climbed into their amphibious landing craft and headed for shore. Exactly on schedule, the first wave hit the southern beaches and moved quickly inland through flooded rice fields and marshes. They encountered virtually no opposition.

By nightfall, 70,000 men of General Walter Krueger's Sixth Army, accompanied by massive amounts of supplies and equipment, had made it ashore. Just as he had at Leyte, General MacArthur, with President Sergio Osmeña right behind him, waded triumphantly ashore.[7]

From the Lingayen beaches, General Krueger divided his forces. Some moved north to begin the tough task of clearing the coast highway, while the majority headed south down Highway 11, bent on liberating the suffering people of Manila.

At seven that evening, HQ-SWPA placed USAFIP-NL under General Krueger's command, assigned them the code name AURORA, and gave the call sign and radio frequency by which they could communicate directly with his headquarters. Though officially a part of his Sixth Army, Krueger authorized USAFIP-NL to deal directly with General David Hutchinson of the 308th Bombardment Wing and with Admiral Kenneth Royall's Transport Command for

continuing their resupply now that submarines were no longer necessary. Unbelievable! The guerrillas could now order supplies as needed, *and* they had their own personal air force!

Art finally moved from Camp Utopia down to join Volckmann and PK at Darigayos Cove. The local schoolhouse became the headquarters building. Art's G-2 section occupied the Domestic Science Building, an impressive-sounding name for a rambling, sawali-walled shack with a badly leaking thatch

USAFIP, North Luzon HQ after return of US forces

roof. Within weeks, construction crews bulldozed a landing strip on the beach just north of the town. On February 2, to honor their lost friend, they christened the new installation "Camp Grafton Spencer."

Working with the 308th Bomb Wing, they devised a plan to provide air support for their front-line guerrilla forces on the ground. The 308th based three L-5 liaison planes—Piper Cubs—at the new airstrip. VHF radios were installed in each L-5, along with sets that could communicate with radio equipment on the ground.

Here's how the plan worked: If a guerrilla unit found itself unable to advance by the enemy dug into tunnels and cement bunkers on a hillside above a crucial objective—a tactic widely used by the Japanese—the commander called Camp Spencer and requested an air strike. A liaison plane reconnoitered the area, established radio contact with the ground commander, and provided a bomber pilot with coordinates for the strike. Guerrillas on the ground placed white discs to mark their positions. During the initial phase of the assault, the bomber pilot, directed via radio by the liaison plane, thundered down over the heads of the guerrillas and dropped a 500-pound bomb and surrender leaflets onto the dug-in enemy, sometimes as little as fifty yards away. After a prearranged number of such bombing runs, the bomber pilot followed up with a series of strafing runs, also carefully directed by the liaison pilot. On a particular strafing run agreed upon in advance, the bomber pilot signaled by dipping his wings that the next strafing runs would be fake or "bunny" runs, giving the guerrillas an opportunity to advance on the ground while the Japanese were still pinned in their pillboxes. These air strikes required exquisite coordination,

(top) *Camp Grafton Spencer main flag pole with headquarters building beyond.* (bottom) *Art's home, a little shack on the beach that he shared with Major Farrell.*

and there were one or two screw-ups, but they enabled many a successful advance against the enemy.[8, 9]

Now that supply subs were no longer necessary, HQ-SWPA had another request:

> IT IS DESIRED THAT WITHIN THE AREAS SUBJECT TO YOUR PROTECTION POSITIONS BE PREPARED FOR THE AIR DROPPING OF EQUIPMENT AND SUPPLIES WHEN SUCH PROJECT BECOMES FEASIBLE PD AS FAR AS POSSIBLE CMA SEVERAL POINTS SHOULD BE SELECTED WITHIN AN AREA OF CLOSE OBSERVATION SO THAT WHEN CASUAL FLIGHTS ARE MADE OVER SUCH AREAS SUPPLIES MAY BE DROPPED WITHOUT PREARRANGEMENTS PD YOUR RECOMMENDATIONS ON THIS ARE DESIRED PD[10]

USAFIP-NL eventually established seventeen drop zones. At first, the drop zones were marked with smudge fires, but some of the Japanese caught on and built smudge fires of their own to trick inexperienced pilots unfamiliar with the topography. The Japanese did manage to hijack a couple of loads of food supplies before the smudge fires were replaced with a system of walkie-talkies. Parachutes weren't always needed for shipments of soft goods and canned food, only for the heavier and more sensitive arms and ammunition. Following each drop, teams of local *cargadores* carried the shipments to the nearest district headquarters, where the natives were paid for their services with a tall can of ham or corned beef and a supply of California-grown rice.[11]

Art devised a plan whereby the drop zones could also be utilized to pick up mail and intelligence reports. He had industrial-sized hooks welded to the undersides of the Piper Cubs. When intelligence reports and mail were ready in one of the districts, a tall bamboo pole was erected on either side of the nearest drop zone and a long rope strung between them, to each end of which was attached a section of hollow bamboo designed to hold documents, the same apparatus the guerrillas used to move sensitive information by runner. The Cub swooped low, hooked the rope, and delivered the improvised mailbags to Art at Darigayos.[12]

USAFIP-NL also needed inland airstrips to receive heavier equipment. The first of these was built near the municipality of Paykek, Kapangan, a couple of mountains southeast of Camp Utopia. With help from local civilians, the guerrillas marked out the perimeter and used *carabao* pulling improvised wooden bulldozers to scrape the area level. The airstrip was further improved once they had real bulldozers on the ground. Volckmann, PK, and Art, along with Dennis Molintas and Bado Dangwa, attended inauguration ceremonies for that first airstrip. They christened it "Dontogan Airfield," Dontogan being one of Bado Dangwa's code names.[13] The heavily used airfield later became known simply as "The Landing."

ART HAD RECEIVED NO ANSWER TO HIS LETTERS to Lil that had gone out with the submarines. On January 23, he tried once more to let her know he was okay:

"Dearest Lillian. Well, after three long years, our 'reinforcements' have finally landed. I am almost, but not quite, on the right side of the lines again. I don't find that I'm unduly thrilled or excited, principally because I'm working so hard these days. Then again, the reunion was not a sudden thing, like walking out of the dark into the light. Instead, it happened by a very gradual process, the details of which I'm not yet at liberty to describe, so that I was deprived of that burst of joy a man might experience when the door of his prison is suddenly opened.

"I've heard there'll be some mail from home within a week, and I'm anxiously looking forward to a reply to my letter sent back in December via a source that I cannot name. I only hope that, if you've moved, you left a forwarding address.

"Inasmuch as she is now on her way to safety, I guess the censor will allow me to tell you it was my soldiers who rescued Mrs. Esperanza Osmeña, wife of the president of the Philippines, from Baguio. She and her family were our guests for a couple of months. They're all very nice, and I have a standing invitation to Malacañang Palace for dinner if I ever get a chance to take advantage of it.

"I imagine you're wondering when I'm coming home. I've certainly accumulated more than the required number of points to go home on rotation right away, but I was here when this war started, and I feel duty-bound to see it through to the end. When it's all over, I'd like to look into one of the good jobs that will be opening up in this part of the world. I've already had one offer. I'll then send for you and the kiddies. The thought of ever going back to the Los Angeles Newspaper Service Bureau makes me shudder. My experiences during the past four years have taught me that I'm capable of better things than that, and I'm sure you'll learn to love this part of the world when you come to know it as I do.

"This war is really getting tough. I just got word that the Japs massacred 200 civilians in X. They killed 100 in Y and twenty in Z the other day. We are still a little ahead, however. Our boys have killed more than 2,000 Japs since the offensive started two weeks ago. In one encounter in Ilocos Norte, our boys faced an all-day attack by over 1,000 Japs and threw them back with more than 200 casualties on their side. Our losses amounted to one killed and five wounded. A few days later the same unit went in and raided a big airfield and destroyed two bombers and one fighter. These Japs are very easy to kill. The trouble is that there are so darned many of them. I used to think that wars were very complex affairs, fought by superbly trained armies. Now I find they're just two big mobs of men, neither one very expert or smart, trying to kill each other with the help of modern aids such as guns, artillery, and tanks.

"I was not privileged to witness the pre-landing bombardment of Lingayen Gulf—I was too busy in an office miles away down in a deep canyon—but I could certainly tell when the big battleship salvos went off. They shook the ground. The bombardment scared the living daylights out of the Japs, who ran into the hills like frightened rabbits. They were prepared for a landing, but not for that pre-landing bombardment and its deleterious effects on their green troops. Manila will probably fall very soon, but don't get taken in by that. The real fighting and casualties are still ahead of us, during the period that the radio calls merely 'mopping up.'

"It's ironic. The Jap bigwigs are now trapped in Baguio, just like I was at the start of the war, and it looks as though they're going to have to head out over the mountains just like I did. Most of those we take prisoner firmly believe their reinforcements are now on the way from home and will arrive soon, just like so many of us believed three years ago.

"I'm still well and healthy, though a little short on sleep,
so I'll wrap this up and close by saying I love you. Art."[14]

NOW ARMED AND SUPPLIED, USAFIP-NL's combat units proceeded with a vengeance.

1st DISTRICT—Units of the 66th Infantry, now commanded by Major Dennis Molintas, harassed the enemy daily, particularly in and around Baguio. As soon as enemy road crews rebuilt a bridge on the Naguilian or Kennon roads, their boys destroyed it again. Sometimes they ambushed the crews even as repairs were underway. If the Japanese tried to move troops, they were tracked and ambushed. If they sent out parties to commandeer food from the local farmers, those parties were wiped out.

Other units of the 66th worked the surrounding areas, including the Mountain Trail north of Baguio, keeping the Japanese road crews hopping and preventing food and supplies coming in from the Cagayan Valley.

Intelligence efforts were intensified. No matter how small a move the enemy made, Art heard about it, including the exact number of vehicles and men in a convoy, what it carried, and where it was headed. He joked that if he wanted to know how Yamashita liked his eggs, all he had to do was ask and one of their agents would find out.

In late February, units of the 66th Infantry joined General Krueger's 33rd Division in a slow advance up Naguilian and Kennon roads toward Baguio. They met stiff resistance but were able to close to within four miles of their objective. By mid-March, American artillery began carpet-bombing Baguio and drove the president of the Japanese puppet government, José Laurel, out of the city. The rest of the puppet government fled a few days later. General Yamashita and his staff escaped up the Mountain Trail toward Bambang at the end of March, leaving his chief of staff in command. For a month, the situation remained static as units of the 33rd Division were pulled off and sent elsewhere. Finally, when another American infantry division was released from garrisoning Manila and came to assist, the last push toward Baguio got underway. A six-day battle raged along Naguilian Road at Irisan Gorge, one of the last tank-versus-tank engagements of the entire Philippines campaign. In mid-April, 7,000 civilians, including foreign nationals—mainly the taciturn foreign business owners and their families who hadn't been interned by the Japanese—made their way from Baguio to the American lines, and on April 22, the final contingent of enemy troops pulled out. On April 27, after nearly three and a half years, the Americans reentered the summer capital. Two days later, the American and Filipino flags were once again hoisted over what was left of Camp John Hay.

Concurrent with the siege of Baguio, units of the 66th gradually fought their way up the Mountain Trail toward Kilometer Post 90 and the important road junction at Highway 4.

As early as the end of March, the 66th had reported the deaths of 4,000 Japanese. So mind-boggling were these figures that Krueger's Sixth Army at first didn't believe them and sent out a cadre of Army Rangers to double-check. After a few days in the field with the guerrillas, the Rangers returned to their headquarters, confident the field reports of the 66th were accurate.[15]

In late June, other units of the 66th moved into the Mankayan-Lepanto area to dig the Japanese out of this crucial mining region. The guerrillas battered the Japanese furiously for weeks. On July 20, they were finally successful. Art had followed the progress of this battle closely, and when news of the victory came in over the radio, he pounded his fist on the table and hollered, *I knew our boys of the 66th could pull it off! I never doubted them for a second!* In the process, Art also spilled a cup of steaming hot coffee in the lap of the radio operator. *Damn you*, he exclaimed, but he, too, was grinning from ear to ear.

2nd DISTRICT—The heaviest guerrilla fighting involved the men of the 2nd District under Colonel George Barnett. The Japanese had more than 8,000 men defending the port and airstrip at San Fernando. Barnett's men first eliminated the Japanese garrisons in the smaller towns of southern Ilocos Sur and northern La Union provinces. Next, they turned their attention to San Fernando, where the defenders were dug into tunnels, foxholes, and cement bunkers on Reservoir Hill to the northeast, on Insurrecto Hill to the southeast, and on the Bacsil-Apaleng ridge directly to the east, effectively blocking all approaches to the city. The defenders had stockpiled large supplies of food commandeered from the local civilians and were prepared to fight to the death. It took all three battalions of Barnett's 121st Infantry guerrillas two months of grueling work, but with daily close air support by the 308th Bomber Wing and pressure brought by units of the U.S. Sixth Army moving up from the south, they were finally able during the third week of March to rout the Japanese. The enemy lost more than 3,000 soldiers in the battle for San Fernando, the rest escaping east into the mountains or up the Naguilian Road to Baguio. Barnett's losses were limited to fewer than 900 casualties.[16, 17]

From San Fernando, the men of the 121st were given a few days' rest, then ordered to move east on Highway 4, a one-lane gravel road running east-west through the Abra River valley, to wrest the Bessang Pass and the town of Cervantes from 4,500 Japanese troops. The area presented formidable obstacles: jagged peaks, deep gorges, dense vegetation, and the unpredictable flash-flooding of swiftly flowing streams. Large swaths consisted of bare, slippery rock faces, devoid of any trails at all. Thick fog blanketed the area most mornings, reducing visibility to only a few feet and severely curtailing air strikes, followed by rain in the afternoon, and sudden landslides. During three months of heavy fighting, the 121st and the Japanese traded hilltops. Eventually, the 1st and 2nd Battalions of the 3rd District joined the fight, as did one battalion of the 66th Infantry and a battalion of U.S. Field Artillery. The enemy defenders proved stubborn and tenacious, but finally, on June 15, the objectives were secured. It was a costly victory. Fully fifty percent—more than 1,500 men—of Barnett's 121st Infantry were either killed or wounded and were awarded Purple Hearts.[18]

3rd DISTRICT—The 3rd District was commanded by Lieutenant Colonel Robert H. Arnold, the same Bob Arnold Art had met as a captain at the Lusod sawmill in late March 1942. No one had heard from him until late 1944, when HQ-SWPA advised Russ Volckmann that Arnold was alive and hiding out in Isabela Province. Wasting no time, Volckmann summoned Arnold to Kapangan and in early January 1945 placed him in command of the 3rd District, lately carved from the 2nd District because it had grown too large and unwieldy for George Barnett to handle.[19]

Colonel Arnold went to work first along the northern coast. His troops cleared the remaining Japanese from Highway 3 and destroyed all major bridges to prevent further troop movement. Next, they attacked and destroyed the Japanese garrisons remaining in the area. Then they turned their attention to Gabu, an important enemy-controlled airfield in Ilocos Norte, and the nearby capital town of Laoag. Outnumbered by a ratio of three to one, by the end of February, Arnold's guerrillas achieved both objectives. By the middle of May, they had cleared the enemy from the entire northern Ilocos coast.

Arnold then moved his battalions into Abra Province, where the defenders had dug themselves deeply into foxholes and pillboxes on Casamata Hill. Reluctant to call for air strikes because of an earlier snafu that had nearly cost him his life, Arnold finally called in the bombers and succeeded in routing the Japanese from their burrows and chasing them even higher up into the Cordillera Mountains.

Meanwhile, Russ Volckmann was getting antsy because Barnett's boys had gotten bogged down at Bessang Pass and weren't on track to meet the tight fifteen-day schedule ordered by General Krueger.

To get that operation moving, Volckmann ordered Arnold to help them out. Despite Arnold's 1st and 2nd battalions making some headway, Volckmann still wasn't satisfied and told Art to grab a jeep and a driver and head up to the front lines to find out what was holding them up. Art was glad to get away from his desk for a day and excited as they wound their way up the narrow Highway 4, passing through territory purportedly under guerrilla control. Suddenly, a sniper's bullet whizzed by Art's right ear, missing by no more than an inch. His driver stomped on the gas and quickly got them around a bend and out of range. Art was badly shaken, though, and when they arrived at Harley Hieb's 2nd Battalion command post, Art gave Hieb a piece of his mind. Hieb apologized about the sniper but said that if they spent the time necessary to kill every last Japanese straggler holed up in the mountains, they'd never take the pass. On the way back to Darigayos, Art thought how fortunate he was to be returning to his desk in the Domestic Science Building.[20]

Art reported back to Volckmann that he didn't feel Arnold's guerrillas were making enough use of air support. Volckmann had a talk with him, and once Arnold's battalion commanders began calling for more air strikes, progress resumed. On June 14, the combined efforts of the 121st, 15th, and 66th infantries, with plenty of aid from the U.S. Air Force, finally forced the Japanese to give way. Krueger's schedule had been met. USAFIP-NL had achieved its greatest single victory of the war.[21, 22]

From Bessang Pass and Cervantes, the men of Arnold's 15th Infantry were ordered to attack the important road junction of Highway 4 and the Mountain Trail, where they routed 3,000 Japanese located in half a dozen different defense pockets. For their final engagement, they turned south down the Mountain Trail to meet up with a battalion of the 66th Infantry.[23]

When the final tally came in, Krueger's Sixth Army headquarters estimated that of the 10,000 Japanese troops that had faced Arnold's 15th Infantry, seventy percent had been successfully eliminated.

4th DISTRICT—USAFIP-NL's 4th District was commanded by Colonel Donald D. Blackburn, Russ Volckmann's old friend from Bataan. Blackburn's 11th Infantry area included Cagayan Province and several lightly defended subprovinces east and north of Benguet. Geographically, Blackburn's was the largest district in Volckmann's command, requiring careful strategic planning and judicious use of his guerrilla forces.

A few companies of Blackburn's 1st Battalion went to work in western Bontoc and Ifugao Provinces to eliminate widely scattered garrisons and blast roads and bridges.[24]

Other units of the 1st Battalion moved to eliminate all Japanese forces remaining west of the Cagayan River in order to cut off the primary food source of the enemy consolidating on the east side of the river. By the middle of March 1945, aided by Sixth Army infantry, artillery, engineering, and medical units, they accomplished their goal, except for the nearly impregnable stronghold of Babayuan near the northern port of Aparri.

Babayuan, manned by 700 Japanese determined to hold onto their last outpost in the western Cagayan Valley, was protected by natural caves, dug-in artillery pieces, machine guns, and trench mortars. Again, the 308th Bomber Wing provided close air support, and on June 19, Blackburn's 2nd Battalion succeeded in driving the last of the enemy out of Babayuan and east across the Cagayan River. With Babayuan cleaned out, two days later Blackburn's guerrillas easily occupied the northern coast port of Aparri, from which point HQ-SWPA planned to launch the final attack on the Japanese homeland.[25, 26, 27]

Blackburn's units then moved south up the Cagayan Valley toward the 37th Division of U.S. forces coming north from Manila. To provide a diversion for this strong northbound Allied force bound for Aparri, Blackburn's guerrillas attacked the main Japanese headquarters stronghold at Tuguegarao and for three days and nights held out against determined enemy counterattacks. This diversion allowed the 37th Division to reach Aparri unscathed.

Beginning on July 13, Blackburn's 3rd Battalion, along with the 1st Battalion of Manriquez's 14th Infantry based in Nueva Viscaya, was assigned to attack the last enemy strongholds dug into the ridges in eastern Ifugao and eastern Bontoc, the bulk of them concentrated at Mayayao. Beginning with a three-pronged attack, the guerrillas and the Japanese traded ground for twenty-seven days until finally, on August 8, the two guerrilla battalions succeeded in routing the enemy, killing more than 1,100 of their soldiers.[28]

5th DISTRICT—At the time of the Lingayen landings, the 5th District consisted of 2,200 officers and men under the command of Lieutenant Colonel Romulo A. Manriquez. The 5th District's territory included all of Nueva Viscaya and southern Isabela. At the time of the landings, Colonel Manriquez's forces were spread out along Highway 5 from the Isabela-Cagayan border south to Balete Pass. The least-well-equipped of USAFIP-NL's forces, and too far away to request air support, they harassed the enemy by destroying lines of communication, attacking and burning numerous garrisons and supply dumps, ambushing Japanese patrols, destroying bridges and other strategic points along Highway 5, and collecting and transmitting intelligence. They were responsible for killing more than 1,300 Japanese soldiers while keeping their own losses to fewer than 200.

Two months later, the 1st Battalion of Manriquez's regiment was attached to Colonel Blackburn's 11th Infantry and participated in the fierce fighting that culminated in the battle for Mayayao.

Finally, on July 1, Manriquez's remaining two battalions were attached to General Krueger's Sixth Infantry Division for the balance of the war.[29]

ART COULDN'T HAVE BEEN MORE PROUD. Of all the scattered guerrilla elements on Luzon, USAFIP-NL proved to be the best organized, the best trained, and the most efficient. They were the only guerrilla division recognized by HQ-SWPA as a genuine independent fighting division, not relegated to a supporting role as were so many others after the Lingayen landings. Art felt proud not only of himself and the other officers but of the front-line boys, the ones who put their lives on the line each day, prepared to die in the defense of their country's freedom. Above all, Art's heart swelled with profound gratitude for the simple, everyday Filipino people. Their support hadn't always been easy to gain or maintain, and some had become collaborators and spies for the Japanese, but the overwhelming majority of the brave men and women of the mountain tribes had from the start been fierce and unwavering in their loyalty. No challenge had been too much, no sacrifice too great. Without their devotion to duty, Art was convinced he would not have survived to tell his story.

CHAPTER 29

OUR PRAYERS
ARE ANSWERED

January 1944 through Mid-September 1945

A S CAPTAIN DILLON DROVE LIL HOME one evening right after Christmas 1943, he asked if she had plans for New Year's Eve. She answered truthfully that, as far as she was concerned, New Year's Eve wasn't any different from any other evening.

How would you like to help me celebrate? he asked.

Lil was taken aback. She couldn't think of what to say.

You've been working so hard for so long now that you need a little respite. I'd like to take you out to dinner, somewhere nice that has a good band. When did you last go dancing?

Oh, I can't even remember. It's been years, I'm afraid.

Well, then, you deserve it. Let's ring in the New Year properly.

Let me think about it. I'll let you know.

All day long, Lil wrestled with her conscience. Certainly she wanted to go. She was tired, and a bit depressed; she couldn't remember the last time she'd gotten dressed up or had any real fun. Some days, as she contemplated her looming thirtieth birthday, she felt like a middle-aged frump. And she did love to dance.

Captain Dillon brought hot coffee to her desk, but he didn't say anything more. Late in the afternoon, Lil dropped a folded note on his desk. On it she had written simply, *Yes.* That night she arranged for Lucille to babysit.

She wore her kelly-green dress, swept her hair up on top of her head, and painted her nails. Frank took her to the Claremont Hotel in Berkeley, where they had prime rib and shared a bottle of champagne. The orchestra was dreamy. Frank proved to be an excellent dancer. He knew the waltz and the foxtrot, and then shifted easily into the rhumba and samba. Midnight arrived too soon. As the orchestra played "Auld Lang Syne," Frank hugged Lil and kissed her on the lips, not passionately but warm and friendly. As the next day was a regular workday for both of them, Frank drove her home before one. It was a wonderful evening.

Otherwise, Lil's daily routine varied little. Her workload at the office only increased as the Allied advances in the Pacific picked up steam and made increasing demands on their facilities.

That summer, Lil's brother-in-law, Bryce Brooks, left for the battlefields of the Pacific, and Charlotte and her children moved in with Lil.

In September, the girls went back to school, Eleanor in first grade and four-year-old Trisha in the adjacent daycare. Each day, when her own children awoke from their afternoon naps, Charlotte walked them the mile to Washington Elementary and then escorted all four children home at two-thirty. Eleanor was indignant and complained that she wasn't a baby and could walk Trisha home without Charlotte's help. Overall, the arrangement was working well, though, and Lil felt more relaxed and confident with Charlotte in charge than she had leaving her girls with a stranger.

In October, Captain Dillon was promoted to major. He asked Lil if she'd help him celebrate by pinning his new gold leaves on his shoulder, an Army tradition usually reserved for a wife or a mother. Because of their close friendship, she agreed. After the official ceremony, they went back to the Claremont to dine and dance.

That Thanksgiving of 1944, the whole family, including Lillian Sr., gathered at the house on Spaulding Avenue. Once more Major Dillon joined the family for turkey and all the trimmings, the only man present. Again, he said grace, only this time he added Bryce's name to the list when he asked God to send their men home safely.

Eleanor continued pestering Lil about walking home alone, so right after Thanksgiving, she agreed to try a new arrangement. Beginning the next day, Eleanor would pick up Trisha at the daycare at two-thirty, and together they would walk the five blocks down Bancroft Avenue to the only stoplight on their route. Charlotte and her children would meet them there and escort them across the intersection and the rest of the way home. Eleanor was elated at being entrusted with this new responsibility. She turned to Trisha: *I'm going to walk us home tomorrow. I'm going to be in charge, and you're going to have to mind me.* Lil was too tired to admonish her about being bossy.

The next afternoon, as she waded through a mountain of paperwork at her desk, Lil's phone rang. It was Charlotte. She was crying, nearly incoherent.

There's been an accident, she blurted, *but I think the girls are okay.*

What? An accident? What accident? Lil was shaking.

The girls were hit, Charlotte blubbered.

What? Lil shrieked, verging on hysteria. Her coworkers stopped what they were doing and stared, wide-eyed. Major Dillon rushed from his office and hovered over her shoulder.

Hit by—hit by—hit by a car, Charlotte stammered. *Eleanor only g-got a scraped knee, but Trisha g-g-got a b-bump on the head, and now it's swollen and red.*

How bad a bump? Lil screamed. *Is she bleeding?*

No, there's no blood, but she did throw up a little. By now Charlotte was sobbing uncontrollably.

Lil slammed down the phone. Major Dillon grabbed her arm. *Come on*, he said, *I'll take you home.*

Trisha lay on the couch, covered with a knitted afghan, her thumb in her mouth and her glazed eyes half closed. When Lil felt the angry-looking silver-dollar-sized bump on her forehead, Trisha cried out.

Major Dillon wasted no time. He wrapped the afghan around

Trisha, picked her up, and headed for the car. *Come on, we're going to the hospital.* He drove straight to Children's Hospital and carried the child into the emergency room. After x-rays were taken, the doctor said she had sustained a moderate skull fracture. He advised that she be kept very quiet for two weeks, that the swelling would subside, and that she should be fine.

Frank drove them home, carried Trisha inside, and tucked her into bed.

Charlotte had settled down and was able to tell them what had happened. Eleanor's class had been released ten minutes early. She'd gone across the playground to the daycare and presented Lil's note authorizing them to release Trisha into her care. The girls had walked down Bancroft Avenue. At the intersection of California, Charlotte wasn't there. The light turned green. Eleanor hesitated several moments, then grabbed Trisha's hand and began to run, exactly what she was not supposed to do. Trish stumbled and fell, dragging Eleanor down also. At the same time, a driver stopped at the light on Bancroft had seen the girls standing on the sidewalk, watched them a bit, and then, deciding they weren't going to cross, began making a perfectly legal right-hand turn. It was just a terrible accident.[1]

Listening to Charlotte's story, Lil had her doubts that Eleanor had been released early, but there was no point in making accusations. It wouldn't change anything and would only make Charlotte more miserable than she was already. Lil was so relieved that Trisha was going to be okay that she let the matter drop, but that was the last time the girls walked home from school alone.

Frank insisted Lil take Saturday off and said he would phone on Sunday. If everything was going okay, he would pick Lil up for work as usual on Monday morning.

By Sunday afternoon Trisha seemed her old self and refused to stay in bed any longer. The swelling had subsided somewhat, but Lil could feel a large soft spot when she touched her forehead gently. *Ouch, Mommy. Don't do that*, Trish wailed, pulling away.

Lil returned to work on Monday, and the next few days were very busy as she tackled the mountain of paperwork that had accumulated on her desk.

TRISHA HAD ONLY BEEN BACK AT DAYCARE a few days when late in the afternoon on December 18 Charlotte called Lil again. At the sound of her voice, Lil panicked.

What is it? What's happened? Is Trisha okay?

No, no, no, it isn't Trisha. She's fine, Charlotte said, talking so fast Lil could barely follow. *But the mailman just came, and there's a letter for you from the War Department! Do you want me to open it?*

What?

From the War Department! There's a letter addressed to you from the War Department! Do you want me to open it or do you want to open it yourself?

Lil sat in her chair, dumbfounded. She couldn't say a word. For three long years, she had both anticipated and dreaded this moment. *You'd better open it,* she whispered.

Lil listened, zombie-like, to the rustling sounds as Charlotte slit open the envelope and unfolded the letter.

It's dated November 24th, she went on excitedly. *The letter, I mean. This envelope is postmarked December 7th, but there's another envelope inside that's postmarked November 24th, and that one is addressed to the old house on Spruce Street. That one's marked "Unclaimed."*

Please, Charlotte, just read the letter.

"Dear Mrs. Murphy: Word has been received from your husband, dated September 12, 1944, in which he states he is healthy and has not been wounded since the war began."

Charlotte began to cry. It was a while before she could continue.

"He stated that he is able to dodge the Japanese with very little trouble and has three meals a day. He has gained 15 pounds in weight. He desires photos of you and the children. It is permissible to send letters and snapshots once a month by addressing your letters to Military Intelligence Division, Dept. E, Room 1C744, Pentagon Building, War Department, Washington, D.C. Enclose your letter with only your husband's name on it inside the envelope having the above address. Do not write anything which would be of value to the enemy in your letters. Packages cannot be sent."

It's not even signed, Charlotte said. *It just says,* "Department E, Military Intelligence Service, War Department."

Thank you, Charlotte, honey. Please don't say anything to the children.

Lil hung up the phone and sat motionless, her mind racing in a dozen directions at once, dancing around the main thrust of the letter. *If the letter's not signed, could it be someone's idea of a cruel, sadistic joke? And why two envelopes? This makes no sense.* Gradually, she put it together. The War Department must have sent the letter to Spruce Street. She'd left a forwarding address when they moved, but that expired after a year, so the letter must have been returned to Washington. The War Department must have rechecked their files and pulled up Lil's Spaulding Avenue address, put the letter into a new envelope, and mailed it again on December 7. *But why has it taken eleven days? Oh, yes, the government doesn't use Air Mail for routine correspondence. Too expensive.*

Finally, Lil got up from her desk, went into Major Dillon's office, and closed the door behind her. He looked up and smiled. *What is it, Lillian?*

Art is alive, she said quietly. *A letter just came from the War Department. Art is alive and well in the Philippines.*

Frank rose from his chair, came around the desk, and took Lil in his arms. *That's wonderful news. I'm so happy for you, so very happy for you. Blessed be to God. He has answered our prayers.* His eyes glistened.

Then the dam broke. Frank held Lil close as she sobbed, tears rolling down her cheeks and onto his khaki uniform blouse, even as the shiny gold major's leaves on each shoulder twinkled in the glow of the overhead fixture.

Would you like me to take you home? he asked.

No. I'm fine. I'd like to go at the regular time.

At home that evening, Lil discovered a form document had come with the letter, setting forth more explicit instructions on how to write to Art. She could only write once a month, on Air Mail-weight paper, two pages maximum, and was permitted to send three small photographs each month, but no packages. The document was adamant about the need for secrecy, both for Art's safety and for the safety of those serving with him. It threatened that if she told anyone Art was alive, she would no longer be permitted to contact him at all. Of course, Charlotte already knew, as did Major Dillon, but Lil swore them to secrecy. The hardest part was keeping the secret from the girls. She wanted to shout from the rooftops, but she'd learned the extreme importance of every one of the government's security measures.

The days flew by in a blur. Charlotte did the Santa shopping, bought them a Christmas tree, and decorated it with help from the children. Lil asked Major Dillon to join them for Christmas dinner, but he declined, saying his sister Grace back in New York was begging him to come for the holidays.

Lillian seated with Patricia and Eleanor

It took Lil several days to get over her initial shock and compose a letter to Art. She began again and again, trying to condense three years of their lives onto two pages. She finally finished on December

21 and found a photograph to enclose, not a recent one but one taken in 1943. She didn't want to shock Art all at once with how grown up his daughters were. When it came to mailing the letter, she followed the War Department's instructions precisely.

Lil waited anxiously for her first real letter from Art.

Though good used ones were nearly impossible to find, Lil began shopping for a car. It was unfair to impose any longer on Frank Dillon, and she could tell it was difficult for him too. Her neighbor, Norman Bradley, located a 1936 Plymouth Deluxe four-door sedan in reasonably good condition, and Lil bought it for 500 dollars.[2]

L ILLIAN WAS AT HER DESK ON JANUARY 8 when Major Dillon burst out of his office carrying a radio. The news anchor began:

> The largest invasion force ever assembled in the Pacific landed today in western Luzon, driving a great steel wedge between Japanese forces defending the biggest and most important of the Philippine Islands. American doughboys riding in amphibious tanks began their race across the sand bordering the bottom half of Lingayen Gulf at 0927 hours. Long amphibious columns poured thousands of yank infantrymen ashore, and within a few minutes, the last great battleground of General MacArthur's liberation campaign took outline on a beachhead fringed inland by the Lingayen rice fields. Soldiers from Ohio, California, and many other states landed a few hundred yards from the Lingayen Airdrome which borders the beach area. Observers reported no immediate opposition and said the troops were pushing forward standing up, under cover of naval gunfire which began shortly after dawn. A half hour

after the initial landing, the troops were reported 300 yards inland and still largely unopposed.[3]

They were jubilant! Everyone hugging everyone else. Many of them couldn't keep from crying. As they spilled outside, from all over the base came exuberant shouts and whistles as personnel from other offices and warehouses emptied into the streets. The loudspeakers played "The Star-Spangled Banner" and followed up with "America, the Beautiful." For more than an hour, the celebration continued. Then they went back to work. The war wasn't yet over, and there was still much to be done.

That evening, Charlotte cooked a special dinner. By combining three ration books, she bought a big pot roast and had it simmering in the oven. The Bradleys came. Lillian Sr. and Lucille came too. Everyone assumed the party was simply a celebration of the Lingayen beach landings. When Lillian Sr. commented how nice it was that the Americans were finally achieving these successes, Charlotte and Lil exchanged glances. They didn't say a word about Art.

AROUND THE 15TH OF JANUARY, another envelope arrived from the War Department. Charlotte called Lil at work, but Lil told her to put it aside, that she wanted to open it herself. All afternoon she fidgeted, anxious to get home. What a disappointment! The envelope contained a brief note from Art, much of it clipped out by the censor, an Officers' Mess dinner menu dated October 12, and a duplicate of the previous government form setting forth instructions about how she could write to Art and admonishing her about the need for secrecy.[4]

On January 21, Lil wrote Art another two-page letter, enclosed another photograph of her and the girls, and mailed it in the same manner as before.

A week later, she got a long-distance call from Art's Uncle Lock. He was so excited she couldn't understand him and had to ask him to start over. He had just received a letter from Art, enclosing another letter addressed to Frankie and Charlie, Art's brothers. The letter hadn't come through the War Department. It had a regular A.P.O. return address. *But how could that be?* Lil listened as Lock read her the letter. Basically, it said Art was alive and well and had never been captured or wounded. There was no mention of keeping his whereabouts or the fact he was alive a secret. Lock promised to send Lil a copy the next day. Now thoroughly confused, she wrote another letter to the War Department, explaining her husband's family had heard directly from him, whereas she had not, and asking for clarification.[5]

The copies of Art's letters arrived from Uncle Lock. Still, she dared not disregard the explicit instructions from the War Department. She wrote another two-page letter to Art on February 21 and mailed it through the War Department channels.

In early March, a large manila envelope arrived containing six long letters from Art: one dated October 4, the others dated October 20, November 12, December 3, December 9, and December 21. The letters were accompanied by a brief, businesslike note from the War Department providing an A.P.O. address at HQ-SWPA through which she could now write to Art directly.

Finally, that evening, Lil told Eleanor and Patricia. She read to them portions of Art's letters, describing some of the guerrilla activities in the Philippines. Eleanor listened intently, but not Trish. She began to laugh.

What's so funny?

Gorillas, she replied.

What's so funny about guerrillas?

I know about gorillas 'cause they're in a book we have at school about Africa—

Oh, no, no, no, honey. Not gorillas. Guerrillas. It sounds almost the same, but they're two different words. Daddy doesn't mean gorillas like the ones in Africa. He's talking about the thousands of Filipino men who have formed a big army up in the mountains of North Luzon and are fighting against the Japs who invaded their country and have been treating the people very badly.

Are the Japanese the same as the Japs? Eleanor wanted to know. *There's a girl at my school whose daddy was killed by the Japs, and now everybody hates them.*

Yes, Japanese and Japs are the same thing. Lil was beginning to regret having read the letters to the girls.

What does Daddy look like? Trisha wanted to know.

Well, he used to look like the picture next to your bed. I'm not sure how he looks now. Remember, he's been away in the Philippines for nearly five years, ever since you were a little baby.

Maybe the Japs will kill our daddy too, Eleanor volunteered.

No, no, honey. Our daddy is safe and very much alive. He says so in these letters.

Feeling she was losing control of the situation, Lil changed the subject by offering the girls a cup of hot chocolate with marshmallows. After that it was time for bed.

ON JUNE 9, LIL SUBMITTED AN OFFICIAL LETTER of resignation effective July 15, 1945. She explained that she needed time to prepare for her husband's anticipated homecoming around October 1.

On her last day of work, she made the rounds, shaking hands and telling her coworkers again how much she appreciated their hard work and dedication. Then she stepped into Major Dillon's office to tell him good-bye.

You know I'll never forget you, Lillian, he said quietly.

I'll never forget you either, Frank. You've been my rock through all of this. I don't know what I would have done without you. I wish you all the luck and success and future happiness the world can offer.

He folded Lil into his arms and gave her one last hug. *I know in my heart that God will take care of us both.*

IN AUGUST, CHARLOTTE HELPED LIL REPAINT the interior of the Spaulding Avenue house. They pulled weeds in the yard and planted bright red geraniums in the bed beneath the front window and in flowerpots on the porch. Charlotte began scanning the newspaper for another place to live.

Art and Lil wrote once a week. Their letters were very different from those of years past. They contained no wild declarations of passion, rather a gradual catching up and getting to know one another again. They were both a little apprehensive. After all, they were vastly different people now, and the dynamic of their relationship would have to be forged anew, with new parameters and new priorities. Where once Lil might have feigned neediness or incompetence in the interest of appearing feminine and attractive, she knew she couldn't go back to that. She sensed Art, too, had grown in self-confidence. In every letter, he voiced his desire to explore the world, learn about different cultures, and experience new things.

The last item on Lil's to-do list involved shopping. She bought each of them a new outfit to wear when they welcomed Art home. She had her hair trimmed and got a new permanent wave. Charlotte trimmed the girls' hair.

Art had talked in several letters about coming home by ship, sailing in August, and having a long, leisurely voyage to rest and recuperate—and get a tan. Then his plans changed to coming home by air, something about his commander needing him at least until the second week of September.

At last the date was set. September 17, 1945. Nearly five years of separation were coming to a close. They would be ready.

CHAPTER 30

STACKING ARMS

February through September 1945

FINALLY, ART HAD AN OPPORTUNITY to fly down and meet General Walter Krueger at his headquarters at Dagupan—Art's first view of the new American Army. It certainly wasn't the Army he remembered. The soldiers were different, the equipment was different, and the things people talked about were different. He felt like a total stranger in the Army of which he was supposed to be a part, reinforcing his nagging doubts about how well he'd fit in back home. Also, he wore shorts—which is all he had at that point—not knowing that General Krueger hated them and that it was a court-martial offense in the new American Army to expose bare arms or legs to those wicked malaria mosquitoes! Art had to inform five different M.P.s that he was *not* a part of General Krueger's Army and that he was wearing exactly the same clothes he'd worn during three long years in the jungles and mountains, when the U.S. Army wasn't furnishing him any clothing at all. He did break down, though, and draw a pair of trousers before returning to headquarters.[1]

AT LONG LAST, ON FEBRUARY 8, the first of Lil's letters arrived. Art answered it immediately.

"Dearest Lillian. Your letter dated 21 December 1944 arrived today—my first letter from you in over three years. The bridge back to civilization has been rebuilt.

"You didn't say which of my letters you received. I assume it was the one in which I said I was sitting at my desk in the headquarters, etc., etc. I thought that one went out by sub around the end of October, but judging by when you got it, it must have traveled on the slowest boat the Army has, and gone through a couple of shipwrecks, to boot! Also, how much was the letter censored? I'm curious to learn the ways of censorship, being unfamiliar with such matters. One of the boys who recently visited us told a story about one wife who received the following note: 'Dear Madam, your husband still loves you, but he talks too much.' It was signed by the censor. Your letter was uncensored except that it was put in a new envelope, probably because Higher Headquarters doesn't like our organization's name to appear in letters.

"Yes, I got a promotion to lieutenant colonel a couple of days ago. Like my other promotions, I'm not quite sure what

it amounts to. Based on a recent pronouncement by President Osmeña, it's good in the Philippine Army, with pay 'similar to that of the American Army.' My U.S. Army standing will have to wait on Higher Headquarters having time to worry about such trivial matters, and will probably also involve a special act of Congress.

"Perhaps you'll be interested in my reactions to

Art in front of HQ building at Camp Spencer

your letter. When you wrote, you noted the businesslike tone of my letters. I noted the same thing in yours. I guess it isn't possible for two people to undergo more than four years of separation and still be an excited bride and groom. I suppose there's also a difference between married twenties and married thirties. Well, the loss of four years out of those inexperienced, passionate, and marvelous twenties is something we'll have to chalk up to this war that has occasioned so much loss around the world. No one can reimburse us for that loss, so we'll just have to write it off and try to get that much more out of the next chapter of our lives.

"My wife seems to be quite a businesslike, capable little woman. You used to be not very self-reliant. I had to make the decisions, though I now suspect a lot of that was a concession to my ego. Now I realize you're quite able to take care of yourself and the children, and even hold down a job. I was afraid, when you didn't know if I was alive or dead, you might have become a nun or a morbid case of nerves. But just as I have done, you seem to have settled down to living and working the war out. Though I'd rather we'd have aged these past four years together, I'm very pleased with the sort of wife it seems I have the prospect of returning to. I must add 'if I return' as this war isn't over just yet. Though I'm now eating bread instead of rice, I'm not a 100-percent insurance risk.

"I'm pleased to hear I have such intelligent daughters. I will puzzle my brain to see if I can't rustle up a little present to send them. Also, I have accumulated a few souvenirs lately which I will ship home as soon as I learn what the score is on such things. (No Jap skulls or thighbone letter openers included!)

"I was really glad to get the photo. Did I tell you that the Japs captured all my photos of you (including the nude) and the kiddies when they ambushed us in March 1942? We recently borrowed a camera and I had the enclosed picture taken. Now you can see that extra 15 pounds for yourself!

"I know you can't cover three years in one letter, but I'd like you to describe my status, as far as you were concerned, throughout the period. In other words, what word or news, official and unofficial, did you hear about me after the last letter you got? Did you think I was dead? Did you think I was on Bataan? Were you ever informed I was loose? I'm curious to know in view of certain efforts I made in order to let you know my status. Did you get the radiogram I sent you right after Camp John Hay was bombed? (Incidentally, the bombing CJH has been getting during the past four weeks makes that 1941 bombing look like a gentle rain!)

"Regarding present news, there's not much that I can report. We've moved twice since my December letter, and each move has meant more heat and more mosquitoes and more civilization, i.e., fewer G-strings. I'm now shaving and bathing daily. I'm still working hard, and my job is getting bigger and bigger as there's a shortage of capable assistants. You work six days a week; I work seven days and seven nights. Our little army continues to cover itself with glory. The details are still not for publication, but they are amazing.

"My sweetheart, the closing words of your letter were beautiful. There was no fuss, just the honest, simple, brave statement of your love. I guess that love in this form is the one thing that years of separation cannot change. The past four years have obliterated all the fancy trimmings of my love for you, leaving only the pure essence deep within. I'll be honest and admit that days and weeks have gone by when I have not consciously thought of you, but you were there in my heart all the time.

"I'm so glad the lost years have made you the person you seem to have become, for I want to try to do things right when and if we start anew. Our love has always been fine, but the arrangements have often left much to be desired. We built our life like a patchwork quilt, adding a bit here and a bit there until we had a quaint, lovable structure, but one in which there were drafts and in which the plumbing didn't work very well. We would never have willingly torn down the old structure, but the flames of war have burned it down, and we will soon collect the insurance. We can now build a new structure with all the fine things but without the imperfections of the old one.

"As I said in an earlier letter, I'm through with the Newspaper Service Bureau. There are lots of opportunities in this part of the world. I'd like to get your ideas on future plans. You said you were ready to settle down to being a wife and mother, but I'm sure you want more than that. You always seemed much happier when you were working than when you were tied to nursery, kitchen, and laundry. In this part of the world, there's a cook for the kitchen, a *lavandera* for the laundry, and an *amah* for the nursery, leaving you free to pursue such other interests as you might wish. Also, unless you've changed a great deal, you like to be out in 'society.' Here, we'd always be welcome at the very best country clubs and the most boring of formal social functions. And, always, waiting for as much attention as you're willing to give them, are some of the most fascinating country and people in the world.

"Enough of my sales talk. When you write, tell me about your ideas for the future.

"Until we meet again,

Sit a while upon the daisied grass,
Hear the larks, and see the swallows pass.

"I love you, Art."[2]

As Lil's letters trickled in, Art got a little burr under his saddle. He'd thought all along that he'd been checked in to Corregidor early in 1942. He was pretty sure he'd also been checked in to GHQ-SWPA in February 1943 when Moses and Noble first made contact using Ralph Praeger's radio. In early September 1944, he'd sent Lil a letter that was supposed to have gone out by submarine via Captain Ball down at Lapham's headquarters in Pangasinan. Later that same month, right after direct radio contact with Mac's headquarters had been established, he was positive he'd been checked in again. He'd sent another letter in late November about having gained fifteen pounds and still another one shortly after the Lingayen landing. Yet, in all this time Lil hadn't received a thing. He was pretty burned up at the thought that the big brass at Higher Headquarters were so concerned about keeping the guerrillas a secret—the Japanese knew all about 'em; they just couldn't catch 'em!—that they couldn't even bother to let a wife know whether her husband was dead or alive.[3]

In April, Art made a quick trip down to Manila. The city was a wreck, to say nothing of the hundred thousand civilians who'd been slaughtered before Yamashita pulled out. Nice places they'd once gone to for fun were nothing but piles of debris. It was obvious that reconstruction would be a long, drawn-out affair, and Art began to suspect the good jobs he'd heard so much about weren't going to be in that part of the world anytime soon.

On the way back from Manila, Art's jeep hit a soft shoulder and went into a ditch. Luckily, they were prevented from rolling by another bank on the other side of the ditch, so the only casualty was a cracked window and torn top on the jeep.[4]

When the Japanese were finally driven out of Baguio, Art went up to take a look. It was just as bad. The little house Art and Lars Jensen had lived in was nothing but a gaping bomb crater. So much for carefully packed camera equipment.[5]

May 27 was a tough day. Grafton Spencer's older brother Frank, a sergeant in a Signal Corps unit recently arrived in the Philippines, came up from Manila to Camp Spencer to try and find out what had happened to his kid brother. Art told him most of the details, but omitted the goriest parts. He was pretty distraught when Art told him the chances of recovering Spence's remains were just about nil.[6] Frank said that his folks had only recently received the letter Spence had written to them from Francisco Delgado's house at Sibul Spring back in February 1942, and it had come with a personal cover letter from Connie Delgado, who seemed to be unaware that Spence had been killed in 1943.[7]

On June 6, Art wrote again:

"Dearest. Last nite was weekly report nite, so I worked late and slept in this morning. I've just finished checking over the morning reports, so this afternoon I have some free time.

"War can be a boring thing. The trouble is you don't have an opportunity for any other interests, so when the fighting isn't exciting—which it is *not* most of the time—I'm like a fish out of water. I'm afraid that when I get home, I'm going to have to learn to have fun all over again. Sometimes, when I think of living back home with no war to engross me, it seems an incredibly boring prospect, and that scares me. You see, this war has calloused over many of my tender spots. When one learns to look at destroyed towns and cities without emotion, when one learns to give information to the Air Force for the wholesale destruction of others, when one learns to have little regard for the uniqueness of human life—'We took hill X cheaply, only ten men killed' or 'In town Y are 100 Japs and 100 civilians; recommend bombing and strafing'—in the process, one becomes hardened. During the occupation, many of our soldiers surrendered to the enemy because their families had been imprisoned or tortured. We regarded them as traitors and, if we caught them back in our area, we shot them on sight. Cruel and tough, it's true, but that's the reason we survived and grew while other units failed. The worst thing about the war is not the destruction and death that men have accomplished but the indifference with which they've had to learn to accomplish it in order to stay alive. Sometimes I think of the damage and destruction these years of war have done to the world and I shudder.

"But I'm getting morbid. This is not the first war in the world's history, and it probably won't be the last. I suppose death and destruction will always be just another aspect of living. I only hope that when I come home, I can learn again to do the everyday, inconsequential things and get a bang out of doing them. Right now that's hard to imagine.

"We got some P.X. supplies in the other day. I splurged

and bought a new fountain pen and pencil and a wristwatch, only I can't wear it on my wrist due to prickly heat. Instead, I strap it through a buttonhole of my shirt.

"We've just had a little excitement. This afternoon, the Air Force sighted two downed and possibly injured U.S. airmen on a Jap-held island near Luzon. A PT boat will pick up some of our men who know that island and take them there tonite and put them ashore in the dark. They'll try to locate the pilots and deliver them back to the PT boat in the morning. We've rescued more pilots than you can count.

"Well, I hear the orchestra at the Officers' Mess playing, so it's time to go wash my face for supper. I meant to do better than these few pages, but there just isn't any more. I love you. Art."[8]

And on June 20:

"My dearest wife. It's like spring today, and I feel quite good. Our first typhoon of the year is over, after doing a great job of clearing the air. I've just recovered from a cold, I'm caught up on my work, and the war in the Philippines is getting over faster every day. Why shouldn't I feel good? The only sad thing is that I haven't heard from you in more than a week. I can't understand why your letters to me take so much longer than the ones I write to you.

"Now for a little surprise! For a while now, PK has been chomping at the bit to get out from behind his desk, so now Russ [Volckmann] has made him an infantry brigade commander, in charge of all USAFIP-NL forces in the field. I'm replacing him as chief of staff in addition to my duties as head of intelligence. My new position carries the rank of colonel, so Russ has recommended that I get my 'chickens.' I don't know if I'm capable of acting like a colonel, though. Colonels are supposed to be old, fat, and grumpy!

"By the way, if you see Calvert's wife, tell her that he's okay and being a good boy, but working too hard to find time to write. He hasn't written her in two months.

"Our troops are going through the Cagayan Valley like a dose of salts. At last word, they were already north of Ilagan, Isabela, and seem set to clean up the whole valley all the way to Aparri. Of course, back in the hills there are bound to be pockets of Japs that will take months to completely eradicate.

"Aside from the Cagayan Valley, the only sizeable bunch of Japs left is in central Mountain Province. Our troops just made a big dent in this pocket by taking Cervantes, Ilocos Sur, after finally smashing enemy resistance at the 6,000-foot-high Bessang Pass. Once these Japs in Mountain Province are eliminated, the North Luzon campaign will be over except for mopping up, and when the North Luzon campaign is over, I should be able to come home. An August date is looking better all the time.

"As the day when I can start home nears, I'm actually beginning to think about it in concrete terms, about how much luggage I'll have, about taking sun baths on the ship—if I come home that way—about how the Golden Gate Bridge will look, about how Fort Mason will look from the seaward side, about whether I'll recognize you (and vice versa), and about where we'll eat lunch. I have a premonition that I'll arrive in the morning. I had planned on Fisherman's Wharf, but I hear it burned down, or was it only part of it that burned? I think about whether you'll have a new hat for Annie. Better make it two. Love, Art.

"P.S. I'm enclosing some pictures taken by a friend of the C.O.'s. You'll see that nearly all our buildings have tarps draped over the thatched roofs. They leak like sieves."[9]

(Top L) Camp Grafton Spencer main flag pole. (Top R) Chapel. (Bottom) Post Exchange.

Just a week later, General MacArthur went on the air and declared the North Luzon campaign over. The USAFIP-NL newsletter for Thursday, June 28, 1945, printed the news, titling it "MacArthur's Communiqué":

> " 'Except for isolated operations, this closes the major phases of the Northern Luzon campaign,' reported General MacArthur's communiqué issued today. Describing the North Luzon operations as 'one of the most bitterly fought and the most savage in American history,' the communiqué added: 'No terrain has ever presented greater logistical difficulties and none has ever provided an adversary with more naturally impregnable strongholds.' The losses inflicted on the enemy were heavy, 113,593 dead, with the graves of many other thousands located but uncounted, and several thousand prisoners. Our own losses were 3,793 dead, 34 missing, and 11,351 wounded, a total of 15,178. Our troops comprised the I Corps and the North Luzon guerrillas, all of the Sixth Army, closely and most effectively supported by the Far Eastern Air Force and the Seventh Fleet. The entire island of Luzon, embracing 40,420 square miles and a population of 8,000,000, is now liberated."[10]

But of course it wasn't over. Yamashita still had a sizeable force squirreled away in caves and bunkers in the mountains, and they certainly weren't going to walk out with their hands in the air. The guerrillas were going to have to dig them out of their holes, and many more enlisted men, and probably some officers, too, were going to lose their lives in the process.

Art continued to write to Lillian, though most of his letters contained nothing of significance beyond housekeeping details—insurance premiums, back pay, accrued vacation time, that sort of thing—and speculation about when he might be ready to head home. He wanted to be home in time to celebrate Lil's and his birthdays during the first week of October and their eighth anniversary on November 27. If he went home by ship, he'd have to leave Luzon no later than the first week of September. He submitted a formal request to that effect.

Then a momentous event occurred that practically guaranteed Art's departure date. On August 6, 1945, an American B-29 bomber, the *Enola Gay*, dropped the first atomic bomb on the Japanese city of Hiroshima. The bomb wiped out ninety percent of the city and instantly killed an estimated 80,000 people. When the Japanese still refused to surrender, three days later, on August 9, another American bomber dropped a second atomic bomb on Nagasaki, killing an estimated 40,000. Many thousands more died in the days following.

Art lost no sleep over the devastation in Japan. On August 16, he wrote to Lil:

> "Dear Lillian. Well, the war is finally over, but the Japs haven't started to surrender yet. The radio says the Emperor's order to cease firing and surrender will be given sometime today. Just yesterday we had four men killed and twenty-one wounded up on our front, and last nite a lone Jap was killed trying to attack PK's command post. But there's a general feeling that the big show is over. Anything after this will be an anticlimax. Not that the news caused any big celebrations here. Our principal reaction is that of a plow horse when his harness is removed at the end of a long, hot afternoon. He just feels like having some chow and resting in his stall, not going out and kicking up his heels. We'll leave that to the

people back home who can muster the necessary excess energy in spite of the privations they've endured.

"Prompted by some of your comments, I've been thinking a lot lately about our marriage, and I'd like to run some of it by you. The years I've been away have taught me that there's much more to marriage than physical attraction, or even companionship. There's something bound up in it as an institution, a duty—although not an unpleasant one—a *must*, a meaning that the words *husband, wife,* and *family* have aside from the particular individuals who bear those titles. Please don't feel hurt if I say it is not *Lillian* and *Eleanor* and *Patricia* that I'm coming home to. It is to my *wife* and my *family*. I'm going to have to recreate the *Lillian, Eleanor,* and *Patricia* all over again, just as they're going to have to recreate me. It's nothing to be afraid of. In fact, it has an element of fun and novelty about it. Don't you think it'll be interesting to have an ever-so-moral and legal affair with a very strange man? As for any sadness or loss in it, shrug your shoulders and blame it on the war, just as we have to do when someone we knew well turns up on a list of those killed in action. Love, Art."[11]

Headquarters got in the first draft of a thick document entitled "Guerrilla Resistance Movements in the Philippines," written by the Intelligence Section at GHQ-SWPA, asking them to review the USAFIP-NL section for accuracy. That little chore got dumped in Art's lap. He found it interesting reading, but full of errors and inaccuracies, and he had to write a lengthy treatise to straighten things out.[12] Russ also asked Art to tackle a portion of the "After Battle Report," so he spent a couple of days writing the chapter covering the 66th Infantry.

Robin Hood brought Art the letters he'd been hiding for him, but Art couldn't locate Father Gellynck to retrieve the ones he'd left with him for safekeeping. An agent in Bokod said Father Gellynck was chased into the mountains by the Japanese in late 1944, and nobody had seen him since.

Otherwise, Art attended to administrative matters: his pay data card, identification card, immunizations, mailing a couple of boxes home, things like that. He got a haircut and noted that his hairline had receded more than an inch. He was also missing some teeth, but dentistry would have to wait. He hoped Lillian wouldn't be too shocked when she saw him.

At night, Art found himself dreaming of eating nice, cool, crisp green salads and crunchy French rolls with butter and lots of milk, the genuine kind, not powdered or out of a can. In his dreams, the salads were served on a table covered with a clean, freshly ironed white tablecloth.

Now that the fireworks were over, the AP press corps arrived at Camp Spencer to document USAFIP-NL's story for posterity. The officers got all dolled up and posed for official photographs. The top photo (pg.419) depicts Art and Calixto Duque waiting for the radio operator to decode a message from GHQ-SWPA. But don't be fooled. The fancy maps on the wall were brought in as props. The guerrillas never had anything like that. In bottom photo (pg.416), Russ Volckmann, Art, PK, and Bado Dangwa are admiring a samurai sword confiscated from one of the surrendered Japanese officers. After the picture was taken, Art packed up that sword and shipped it home. The main headquarters building appears in the background.

On September 6, Art wrote one last time:

"My dearest Lillian. Well, there's no longer any censorship, so I can tell all—only there's not an awful lot to tell. As you can see from the letterhead, our headquarters is in Barrio Darigayos. It's about 25 miles north of San Fernando, La Union, on the shores of Darigayos Bay, a few miles south of the town of Luna.

"USAFIP, North Luzon, at present has about 20,500 officers and men and has functioned like a regular Army division during most of the Luzon campaign, the only guerrilla unit to be treated as such. Other guerrilla units to the south were attached to U.S. units, who used them to guard bridges and supply dumps or as *cargadores*. We have had our own sectors of action. At the start, our sector was all of North Luzon because the U.S. forces didn't have enough men to tackle the area. Our forces have killed about 53,000 Japs since 4 January, which is about one-fifth of all the Japs on Luzon at the time of the landing. We have also taken 472 prisoners. As of August 29th, we have suffered 1,290 men killed, 3,236 wounded and 149 missing. We have at present several hundred men with missing arms, legs, and other permanent injuries.

"We smashed the enemy's 79th Brigade and left the enemy's 19th Tora Division but a bunch of remnants. After June 1st, they actually attached American artillery units to *us*, placing them under *our* command, which was never done with other guerrilla units. When the war is over, we are to be organized into the 2nd Philippine Army Division, one of two divisions on Luzon.

"We're still waiting for the Japs to come out and surrender. They have ceased firing, and there is frequent interchange of emissaries across the lines, but they say they're not going to come in until they get General Yamashita's order. Yamashita surrendered the other day in Baguio—Russ [Volckmann] sat at the surrender table—but we couldn't immediately get that order to the Japs up on the Mountain Trail. They should start coming in tomorrow. Incidentally, they took two hand grenades off Yamashita's surrender party—'Sooo solly, please'—and a nice, long Batangas knife off the old lad himself. They're now talking about air-dropping food and medicine in to the Jap sick and wounded in the mountains. That was *not* what the Japs did to our boys on Bataan. They told the sick to get up and walk and bayoneted those who couldn't.

"I'm prepared for the pajama shortage you told me about. I just had our tailor make me two pair out of a damaged silk air-drop parachute. They're a perfectly gorgeous red! Otherwise, my entire wardrobe consists of four white undershirts that were in a freak Army issue, a couple of long-sleeved khaki shirts, a pair of often-patched khaki shorts, and the one pair of trousers I drew down from Supply at Krueger's headquarters. You'll just have to use your imagination to figure out what I wear under those shorts!

"By the way, have you bought Annie a nice new hat yet? If not, better hurry.

"I'm beginning to get a few butterflies in my tummy, though after the above remark, you'll probably say they're not in my tummy! I'm scheduled to leave Camp Spencer on the 12th of this month and will report in to the 29th Replacement Battalion in Manila on the 13th. If I get out on the 15th and the trip takes 61 hours, I should be in California on the 18th, that is *if* I get out on the 15th. The 18th is but eleven days from today—only now it's nite. Wait a minute! I'll be in on the 17th. I forgot the International Date Line.

"I'm very, very sleepy, so I'm going to bed now.

Love, Art."[13]

Headquarters threw Art a rousing farewell bash at the Officers' Mess.

On the 10th, he attended a second, even more rousing send-off in San Fernando, a typical native *cañao* with roasted pigs, *camotes,* and all the trimmings. For more than an hour, Art scoured the crowd, hoping *somebody* might have brought Kiddo down for the festivities, but he didn't find his young friend. Natives Art had never seen before danced for him and kissed his hands. Art had prepared a speech, but when it came time to deliver it, his emotions got the better of him and he messed it up. Guerrilla colonels are not supposed to cry.

On Wednesday, the 12th, a jeep took Art to Manila. His driver, a young, wide-eyed American G.I. who had only been in the Islands a month, chattered like a magpie. He wanted to know every little detail of what it was like to be a guerrilla, how many times Art had been shot, and how many Japanese he'd killed. The kid's face fell when Art told him that he'd *never* been shot and that officers generally just gave the orders and left the dirty work to someone else.

You must be the luckiest guerrilla of them all, the driver marveled.

You may be right, Art said.

Shortly after dawn on September 15, another jeep ferried Art over to Nielson Field, where a C-54 Skymaster was waiting on the runway. He climbed the metal stairs, stepped into the belly of the plane, found a seat just ahead of the wing, and stowed his duffel underneath. The plane filled and the door slammed shut. One by one, the engines began to roar and the four propellers started to turn, slowly at first, then faster and faster. The pilot taxied to the end of the runway, turned around, and prepared for takeoff. Within moments, they were airborne. The sun, just clearing the horizon, painted brilliant orange and pink splotches on the undersides of the clouds over Manila.

Finally, it was over.

The staff officers of USAFIP-NL: (L to R) Lieutenant Colonel Froilan Maglaya (Adjutant General), Lieutenant Colonel Calixto Duque (G-3 Operations), Lieutenant Colonel Emmanuel Cepeda (Engineer), Colonel Russell William Volckmann (Commanding Officer, USAFIP-NL), Colonel Thomas Parker Calvert (Infantry Commander), Colonel Arthur Philip Murphy (Chief of Staff and G-2 Intelligence), Major Timoteo Sinay (Division Signal Officer), Major Bado Dangwa (Assistant G-4 Supply), and Major Bienvenido Nebres (Chief Surgeon).

AFTERWORD

A FLURRY OF MEDIA ATTENTION followed the initial eu-
phoria of Art's homecoming. Relatives and friends dropped by
to welcome him back and listen to his stories. Art basked happily
in the limelight, telling and retelling the tales of USAFIP-NL's glory
days. After a while, the attention waned. Although in 1945 the term
"post-traumatic stress disorder" hadn't yet been invented, Art did
indeed suffer some of its symptoms, not in the form of drug or alcohol addiction, uncontrolled rages, nightmares, or flashbacks, but
in occasional bouts of deep depression and difficulty living in the
present. Art and Lillian slogged through a painstaking adjustment
period that lasted several years, complicated further by losing a son
at birth in October 1946. Gradually, they ironed out their differences and forged a new, more durable foundation for their marriage.

In late February 1946, Father Gellynck sent Lillian an envelope
containing the letters left with him four years earlier. He apologized
for the poor condition of the letters, explaining that when he'd been
forced to flee into the mountains toward the end of the war, he had
buried Art's letters in a tin can at his mission. Then he'd gotten very
sick and had barely survived. His home, mission school, and church
had been destroyed, but he wasn't giving up and was starting over.
Without discussion, Art bought a new Singer sewing machine and
shipped it, along with a generous money order, to Father Gellynck
in Bokod.

Art accepted a regular commission in the United States Army,
which entailed a reduction in his temporary wartime rank of full
colonel to lieutenant colonel. He subsequently served at such far-
flung duty stations as Berlin, Trieste, Bangkok, Tokyo, Verdun, the

usual infantry posts in the States, and in postwar Korea, usually in positions utilizing his administrative abilities and/or his knowledge of guerrilla warfare. His family accompanied him to all duty stations except Korea, a sixteen-month "hardship tour" in 1959–1960.

Before World War II, the curricula at U.S. military schools hadn't included guerrilla warfare, but they now recognized its importance. Russell Volckmann was designated by President Dwight D. Eisenhower to write the U.S. Army's first field manuals on guerrilla organization and tactics. At Fort Benning, Georgia, Volckmann had spent a year on this assignment when the Korean War broke out in June 1950 and General Douglas MacArthur was again called out of retirement to command U.S. troops. Without access to guerrilla warfare field training manuals, General MacArthur wanted the expert himself, and Volckmann was summoned to Korea. In July 1950, Art Murphy went to Fort Benning to finish writing the manuals. *Operations Against Guerilla Forces*, Field Manual 31-20, was published on an expedited basis in February 1951; Field Manual 31-21, *Organization and Conduct of Guerilla Warfare*, was published in October of 1951. Both manuals were accepted, without significant revision, by the Joint Chiefs of Staff and became the foundation upon which all later Special Forces were built. Following completion of the field manuals, Art prepared the course in guerrilla warfare required of all Army officers subsequently attending the Advanced Officer Training Course at Fort Benning.

Ten years after the end of the war in the Philippines, Art served a two-year stint in Tokyo. Art and Lillian immersed themselves in Japanese culture. Lillian took classes in *Ikebana*—Japanese flower arranging—and Art made frequent trips with his camera to *Kabuki* performances and the *Takarazuka* dance review. Both took Japanese lessons, along with lessons to learn to jitterbug to Elvis Presley's current hits. Neither harbored any animosity toward the Japanese people.

Art retired from the Army in June 1965. He and Lillian embarked on a meticulously planned travel odyssey. They went first to Australia and New Zealand, spent a year in South America, and then visited Thailand, Nepal, India, Hong Kong, and Singapore. They proceeded to North Luzon, where after a quarter century Art showed Lillian his beloved Manila, Baguio, and Camp John Hay. They hiked to the site of Camp Utopia and walked the beaches at Lingayen and Darigayos. Many things had changed.

They visited Alaska, crisscrossed Canada in an Airstream trailer, and explored the historic sites of Mexico. During the winter months, when not traveling, Art pursued graduate course work in philosophy at Arizona State University. Following two hip replacements, his passion turned to fishing, and their travels concentrated on finding the best fishing holes in Canada, the United States, and Mexico. Each summer, they returned for a month to Sandy's Resort in northern British Columbia, several times taking a grandson or nephew along.

In 1977, shortly after celebrating their fortieth wedding anniversary, Art was diagnosed with metastasized colon cancer. He underwent numerous courses of chemotherapy and three surgeries over the next five years. On May 28, 1982, at the age of sixty-eight, he died in Lillian's arms at their small home in Mesa, Arizona. He is buried at Golden Gate National Cemetery in San Bruno, California (Section E, Site 280).

Following Art's death, Lillian continued their longstanding interest in WWII history—particularly USAFIP-NL—and maintained a cordial relationship with those guerrilla officers who still survived, among them Russell Volckmann, Parker Calvert, and Herb Swick. Her primary focus, genealogy, provided the impetus for further travel as she sought source records in the dusty basements of courthouses from Texas to California to Kansas to Missouri. And, of course, she maintained close ties with her daughters and grandchildren. At age ninety, Lillian passed away on June 21, 2005, in Mesa, Arizona. She shares Art's grave at Golden Gate National Cemetery in San Bruno, California.

Art Murphy's medals and decorations:

Silver Star Medal

Legion of Merit and Legionnaire Set

Bronze Star Medal

Philippine Military Merit Medal

Army Commendation Medal

Presidential Unit Citation and Oak Leaf Cluster

American Defense Service Medal and Bronze Star Attachment (Single) and Foreign Service Clasp

American Campaign Medal

Asiatic-Pacific Campaign Medal and Silver Star Attachment (Single)

World War II Victory Medal

Army of Occupation Medal and Germany Clasp

National Defense Service Medal and Bronze Star attachment (Single)

Armed Forces Reserve Medal

Combat Infantryman Badge 1st Award

Philippine Defense Ribbon and Bronze Star Attachment (Single)

Philippine Liberation Ribbon

Philippine Independence Ribbon

Expert Badge and Pistol Bar

Korea Defense Service Medal

I N THIS BOOK, the reader has come to know some of the guerrillas who participated in the events in North Luzon, as well as a few individuals who played a role at home, and may wonder what became of them after the war.

CALVERT, Thomas Parker: After the war, PK suffered severe post-traumatic stress disorder. Receiving a medical discharge from the U.S. Army in 1948, he periodically spent time in Veterans Administration hospitals undergoing psychiatric care. In the mid-1950s, while PK was confined at the VA hospital in Battle Creek, Michigan, he and Rilla were divorced.

Unknown to PK at the time, his mother had died in May 1944 and his father had remarried a younger woman, Gertrude Hosking,

"Trudi" for short. PK's father died in 1962 in Florida. For a few years, PK continued to correspond with his stepmother but then lost track of her through the course of his many hospitalizations.

In 1987, while undergoing treatment at Brook Army Medical Center in San Antonio, PK tracked down his stepmother in Florida and called her. He discovered she had remarried, was now Mrs. George Dickman, and was living at Treasure Island, a suburb of St. Petersburg. She invited PK to come for a visit, and he said he would try. Following his release from the hospital, he caught a flight to Orlando, planning on taking a bus the last hundred miles to St. Petersburg. That night, on the streets of Orlando, he was attacked, severely beaten, stripped of his belongings, and left to die. When the police discovered him, he was taken to a local emergency room. His neurological injuries were so severe that he could not give his own name. After weeks of treatment, his condition stabilized, and the hospital, still unable to determine his identity, transferred him to a public institution in Sumterville, Florida.

When months passed and Trudi Dickman didn't hear from PK, she and her husband began a search. They eventually located him in Sumterville, established his identity, secured his release, and brought him to St. Petersburg, where Trudi found him a studio apartment in a nearby assisted-living complex. Gradually, PK regained some of his memory and recognized a few friends from his past, but he never regained the ability to speak. His arms and legs twitched so that he could walk only with assistance.

Lillian had continued corresponding with PK, usually at Christmastime. When one of her cards was returned by the post office, she contacted the Department of the Army and eventually located PK at the assisted living facility in Florida. She spread the word to Herb Swick, Don Blackburn, and a few others, who then also contacted PK. Don Blackburn visited him personally from time to time.

In 1989, PK was diagnosed with severe anemia and bone cancer. He died on March 14, 1990. Don Blackburn looked upon his death as a blessing, saying, "The poor guy has lived a life of hell ever since World War II."

For his service during the war, PK earned two Silver Stars and the Legion of Merit along with numerous other decorations. He is buried at the West Point Cemetery in Orange County, New York (Section XXIV, Row C, Grave 57).

DILLON, Francis Joseph: Frank Dillon, a lawyer by education, attained the rank of lieutenant colonel before he left the U.S. Army Transportation Corps in September 1946. He went to work as a civilian for the government. In that capacity, he traveled widely, including trips to the Philippines and North Luzon. He never married. Years later, when asked by a favorite nephew why not, he answered simply, "I came very close once, but it just didn't work out." Frank Dillon died on April 21, 1971, in Washington, D.C. He is buried at Long Island National Cemetery, Farmingdale, New York (Section O, Site 33042).

GALLUP, Brewster Garroway: Captain "Brew" Gallup, the husband of Lillian's closest wartime friend, Roberta Gallup, was on duty with the Corps of Engineers on Corregidor in May 1942 as the Japanese closed in. At one point in the fighting, the American flag was brought down in a hail of bullets. Brew retrieved it, hoisted it aloft, and gallantly urged his comrades to fight on. On May 6, 1942, his commander, General Jonathan Wainwright, ordered the remaining troops to surrender. Brew obeyed. For two years, he was held in a squalid Japanese prisoner-of-war camp near Manila, until the Japanese began shipping able-bodied prisoners to Japan as slave labor. Brew and hundreds of others were packed like sardines into the hold of an unmarked Japanese freighter. As the freighter pulled out from Subic Bay, it was torpedoed and sunk by an American submarine. Brew was among eighty survivors who managed to swim to shore, right back into the clutches of their Japanese captors.

On October 10, 1944, Brew and more than 1,700 other prisoners were loaded onto another unmarked ship, the *Arisan Maru*, bound for Japan. Two weeks later, on October 24, the *Arisan Maru* was torpedoed, again by a U.S. submarine, and sank in the South China Sea. There were fewer than ten survivors, making it the worst naval disaster in the history of the United States Navy. Brew Gallup was not among the ten. His remains were never recovered. He has a memorial headstone at the Manila American Cemetery, Fort Bonifacio, Manila, Philippines (formerly Fort William McKinley). He was posthumously awarded a Silver Star and a Purple Heart. A few years later his widow, Roberta, remarried and bore two sons.

JENSEN, Lars Chris: Lieutenant Lars Jensen, Art's friend and roommate at Fort McKinley and Camp John Hay, was married before the war to Myrtle Ovidia Olson and had a young daughter, Marjorie, nicknamed "Peachy." Lars fought on Bataan with General Brougher's forces until ordered to surrender in April 1942. He was starving and weak with dysentery when his Japanese captors ordered him to march seventy miles north under the blazing sun, without food or water, to Camp O'Donnell. When he could no longer walk, he was carried by a fellow prisoner, Sergeant Clarence Graves. Some months later, nearing death, Lars removed his wedding ring and gave it to Sergeant Graves with the request that Graves, should he survive the war, return the ring to Myrtle in Minneapolis. Not long after, Lars fell to the ground and was bludgeoned to death by a brutal Japanese guard. His remains were never recovered.

Sergeant Graves survived several years of captivity and returned home in1945. He no longer had Lars Jensen's wedding ring—the Japanese had found and confiscated it—but Sergeant Graves was haunted by the promise he'd made. He traveled to Minneapolis, located Myrtle Jensen, and gave her the tragic account of her husband's last days. Clarence and Myrtle became fast friends. They eventually married and added two more daughters to the family.

Lars Jensen has a memorial headstone at Fort Snelling National Cemetery in Minneapolis (Section C-24, Site 13995).

McMASTER, Archie Lee: Archie McMaster, another of Art's roommates in the spring and summer of 1941, upon arrival at Fort McKinley was assigned to command C Company of the 1st Battalion, 45th Infantry Regiment (Philippine Scouts), a unit later assigned to seal off potential enemy landing sites at Bagac Bay on the western side of the Bataan Peninsula. His soldiers fought the Japanese in the "Battle of the Pockets," a temporary success for the Allies, but when ordered to do so, Archie surrendered in April 1942. He spent three harrowing years in prisoner-of-war camps, where he suffered traumatic injuries, tropical illnesses, and extreme malnutrition. Finally, in early February 1945, McMaster was among those liberated from Bilibid Prison in Manila and returned to the States, where he spent several months in a hospital in Denver, Colorado. He was discharged from the Army in 1946. Gradually regaining his health, he earned both a bachelor's and master's degree at the University of Nebraska and spent the next thirty years working in the field of soil conservation in Wahoo, Nebraska.

When Archie, an Army reservist, was first called to active duty in October 1940, he left behind his pregnant wife, Aural Jacquetta (nee Rusho) McMaster, and three young children—a son and two daughters. One of the little girls died of acute leukemia in January of 1941 as Archie was on his way to the Philippines. Months later, Jacquie gave birth to the couple's second son, who was not to meet his father until the war was over four years later. During Archie's absence, Jacquie, like so many American wives and mothers, held down a full-time job in addition to raising her children.

Archie Lee McMaster died on January 25, 1992, in Wahoo, Nebraska. He is buried in the family plot at Sunrise Cemetery in that city, where he shares a joint headstone with Jacquie.

MOULE, William and Margaret: Bill and Margaret Moule and their three small children hid out in the mountains above Baguio for sixteen months following the initial Japanese invasion. During that time, Bill was inducted as a second lieutenant into Charles Cushing's guerrilla forces in Pangasinan Province and participated in several raids. Only when their son Billy contracted malaria and they were without medicine did Bill conceal his guerrilla status and surrender. They were interned at Camp Holmes, a civilian concentration camp near Baguio. Bill was repeatedly tortured by the Japanese, who suspected his guerrilla connections, but gave up no information. Later, the family, suffering from malnutrition and beriberi, was moved from Camp Holmes to Bilibid Prison in Manila, from which they were liberated by U.S. forces on February 4, 1945.

Returning to Grass Valley, California, they established Moule Paint and Glass Company, still a thriving business after seventy years. Their children eventually totaled a dozen, all respected members of their church and community.

Bill memorialized the family's wartime experiences in his book entitled *God's Arms Around Us,* first published in 1960.

In 1989, while traveling near Winnemucca, Nevada, Bill and Margaret were killed instantly in a traffic accident. They are buried at St. Patrick's Catholic Cemetery on Rough and Ready Highway in Grass Valley.

SPENCER, Grafton Jacob (Christ): After having been promoted to first lieutenant by Colonel Russell Volckmann in September 1943, Spence assumed command of the 2nd Battalion of the 66th Infantry, USAFIP-NL. He was killed in a raid by the Japanese on April 8, 1944, near Dalupirip, Benguet, Philippines. His remains were never recovered. He never married and left no descendants. He was posthumously awarded the Legion of Merit and the Purple Heart. He has a memorial headstone at the Manila American Cemetery (Plot A, Row 7, Grave 10), Fort Bonifacio, Manila, Philippines (formerly Fort William McKinley).

SWICK, Gregory Herbert: Herb Swick, sworn into the U.S. Army as a second lieutenant by Colonel Martin Moses in mid-1942, aided the North Luzon resistance movement for many months before being captured around the middle of December of that year. Thrown into a filthy jail cell in Binalonan, he was tortured repeatedly for more than a month in an effort to get him to admit his guerrilla status and divulge information about his guerrilla outfit. He refused, maintaining he was a civilian mining engineer. Eventually, his captors believed him and transferred him to Camp Holmes, a civilian internment camp located a few miles outside Baguio. He remained there more than a year, always fearful his captors would discover his true status. Finally, Swick and a companion escaped the camp in early April 1944 and rejoined the USAFIP-NL guerrillas in the mountains. Assigned by Colonel Volckmann to Colonel Blackburn's 4th District, he served admirably in the active fighting in the spring of 1945.

Herb Swick remained in the U.S. Army for seventeen years and attained the rank of lieutenant colonel, eventually receiving a medical discharge based upon petite-mal epilepsy resulting from beatings suffered while he was a prisoner of the Japanese. Herb died in Tucson, Arizona, on August 16, 1997, and is buried at Arlington National Cemetery in Virginia (Section 64, Site 3355).

ABOUT THE AUTHOR

PATRICIA MURPHY MINCH

A TYPICAL "ARMY BRAT," by age nineteen, Patricia Murphy Minch had lived in twenty homes in half a dozen different states as well as in Europe and the Far East. Because her father, a U.S. Army officer, never "wasted" accrued vacation time, she'd also traveled extensively beyond those locales. With an insatiable curiosity and thirst for knowledge, Colonel Murphy sought to experience everything he read about in his many guidebooks. And where he went, the family went too.

An avid reader from a young age, Ms. Minch absorbed her father's lust for life. In the early grades, she demonstrated an affinity for the written word and, encouraged by both parents, wrote fanciful childhood stories about the places they saw and the people they met. Imaginative and artistic by nature, she often illustrated her stories with sketches or photographs.

After spending a dozen years researching her father's World War II involvement with the people and events of the guerrilla war in North Luzon, Philippines, Patricia Murphy Minch completed *The Luckiest Guerrilla: A True Tale of Love, War and the Army.* Incorporating actual letters and documents discovered more than

two decades after her father's death, she has put together an eminently readable yet historically accurate portrayal of this fascinating
bit of World War II history.

Information regarding this book and her other writings can be
found on her website, PatriciaMinch.com. She can be contacted at
guerrilladaughter@gmail.com.

NOTES

Dedication

1. Ray Wright, "Guerrilla Lt. Made Col. in 3 Years," *The Stars and Stripes*, Ramstein Bureau, Verdun, France, 18 August 1964.

Preface

1. Mike Guardia, *American Guerrilla: The Forgotten Heroics of Russell W. Volckmann* (Philadelphia, PA: Casemate Publishers, 2010), p. 74. In the first paragraph, the author states: "Calvert and Murphy had been with Horan when he surrendered his units at Baguio." This statement is clearly misleading. Art Murphy and Parker Calvert *never* surrendered.

2. Bernard Norling, *The Intrepid Guerrillas of North Luzon* (Lexington: The University Press of Kentucky, 1999), p. 27. Though arguably the best and most detailed of the modern books about the guerrilla war in North Luzon, this volume nevertheless contains several significant errors. On page 27, Norling states: "The first small elements of Troop C, under Lt. Thomas S. Jones, arrived in Baguio about noon on December 23. The city had been abandoned by the troops stationed at Camp John Hay, and the two roads from the lowlands left undefended." This assertion is incorrect. Art Murphy's diary entry for December 23, 1941, says that he and his Company A, 43rd Infantry (PS), spent that night with the cavalry on the Naguilian Road. The last of Colonel John P. Horan's troops, including Art Murphy and Parker Calvert, did not leave Baguio until the late afternoon of December 24, Christmas Eve.

3. Ibid., p. 39. In the final paragraph, Norling states: "Colonel Horan initially divided his forces to reduce Japanese chances to destroy or capture all of them. Half of them, led by Col. Donald Bonnet [sic], were to go from Baguio to Twin Rivers, the Lusod sawmill, Santa Fe, and Carranglan. The other half, led by Horan, would take a more northerly route through Bokod, Boboc [sic], and Pampanga [sic] to Aritao." There are several problems here. Colonel Donald Bonnett

commanded the group which took the more northerly route, while
Colonel John P. Horan commanded the group which took the more
southerly route and which included Captain Parker Calvert and
Lieutenant Art Murphy. The description of the more southerly route
should not include Carranglan, which was not part of the original plan
and only became a destination after Horan's group realized the enemy
had beaten them over Balete Pass and their only remaining option
was to try and flank the Japanese on the east. The description of the
more northerly route is also garbled. It should read: "through Bokod,
Bobok, and Bambang to Aritao." Admittedly, Norling's source for these
assertions was Colonel Horan's "1960 Diary," a document about which
Norling himself expressed skepticism.

4. Ibid., p. 105. In the last paragraph, Norling states: "In June 1942,
there trickled into Benguet an assortment of footloose Filipinos and
Americans, the most notable of whom were Russell Volckmann,
Donald Blackburn, and Lieutenant Colonels Martin Moses and Arthur
Noble." Again, this sentence is misleading. While Moses and Noble
were indeed in Benguet by June 1942, Volckmann and Blackburn did
not make it from Bataan back to North Luzon until the end of the
first week of September, having spent the better part of the intervening
months after the fall of Bataan recuperating at the Fassoth camp in
the Zambales Mountains. Volckmann himself states on page 81 of his
book *We Remained*: "It was exactly five months since we had set out
for North Luzon. The way had been long, the delays heartbreaking,
and the going at times pretty rough." And on the very next page we
find: "The news of our arrival in North Luzon had preceded us by a
couple of days. On 9 September 1942 a native brought us a message
from Colonels Noble and Moses asking that we meet them at Barrio
Benning [sic]. We reached the meeting place in about half a day and
found the colonels waiting for us. It was great seeing them again
after all these months. Captain Parker Calvert and Lieutenant Arthur
P. Murphy were also there. Don and I had known both Parker and
Murphy well before the outbreak of the war, when they were stationed
at Camp John Hay near Baguio."

Chapter 1 – Humble Beginnings

1. Murphy Papers, "Statement of Lt. Col. Arthur P. Murphy," 8 August
1958, pp. 1-5.
2. Ibid., letter from Art to Lillian, 18 August 1937.

Chapter 2 – You're in the Army Now

1. Murphy Papers, letter from Art to Lillian, 22 November 1940.
2. Ibid., letter from Art to Lillian, 15 December 1940.

Chapter 3 – Change of Plans

1. Murphy Papers, letter from Art to Lillian, 29 January 1941.
2. Ibid., letter from Art to Lillian, 31 January 1941.
3. Ibid., letter from Art to Lillian, 10 February 1941.
4. Ibid., letter from Art to Lillian, 13 February 1941.
5. Ibid., letter from Art to Lillian, 14 February 1941.
6. Ibid., letter from Art to Lillian, 15 February 1941.
7. Ibid., letter from Art to Lillian, 17 February 1941.

Chapter 4 – Fort William McKinley

1. Theresa Kaminsky, *Angels of the Underground* (NY: Oxford University Press, 2016), pp. 7-9.
2. Ibid.
3. Ibid.
4. Ibid., p. 23.
5. Ibid., pp. 24-25.
6. Murphy Papers, letter from Art to Lillian, 21 February 1941.
7. Ibid.
8. Ibid.
9. Ibid.
10. Ibid., p. 2.
11. Ibid., letter from Art to Lillian, 24 February 1941, pp. 1-2.
12. Ibid., pp. 2-3.
13. Ibid., letter from Art to Lillian, 28 February 1941.
14. Ibid.
15. Ibid., pp. 1-2.
16. Ibid., letter from Art to Lillian, 21 March 1941, p. 1.
17. Ibid., p. 2.
18. Ibid.
19. Ibid, letter from Art to Lillian, 22 March 1941, p. 2.
20. Ibid.

Chapter 5 – Seeing the Sights

1. Murphy Papers, letter from Art to Lillian, 8 April 1941, pp. 1-3.
2. Ibid., letter from Art to Lillian, 15 April 1941.
3. Ibid., letter from Art to Lillian, 2 May 1941.
4. Ibid., letter from Art to Lillian, 10 June 1941.

5. Ibid.

6. Walter R. Borneman, *MacArthur at War* (NY: Little, Brown and Company, 2016), pp. 60–75.

7. Murphy Papers, letter from Art to Lillian, 29 July 1941.

8. Ibid., letter from Art to Lillian, 30 July 1941.

9. Ibid., letter from Art to Lillian, 15 July 1941.

10. Ibid., pp. 2-3.

11. Ibid., letter from Art to Lillian, 8 August 1941, pp. 1-2.

Chapter 6 – Moving, and Moving Again

1. Murphy Papers, letter from War Department to Lillian, 3 March 1941; letter from Roberta Gallup to Lillian, 26 October 1941, p. 1.

2. Ibid., p. 2.

3. Ibid., letter from Lillian to Art, 4 December 1941, p. 2.

Chapter 7 – Camp John Hay

1. Murphy Papers, letter from Art to Lillian, 13 August 1941.

2. Ibid., letter from Art to Lillian, 17 August 1941.

3. Ibid., letter from Art to Lillian, 25 August 1941, pp. 1-5.

4. Ibid., letter from Art to Lillian, 4 September 1941, p. 1.

5. Ibid., p. 2.

6. Ibid., letter from Art to Lillian, 9 September, 1941.

7. Ibid., letter from Art to Lillian, 17 September 1941, p. 2.

8. Ibid., letter from Art to Lillian, 26 September 1941, pp. 1-2.

9. Ibid., letter from Art to Lillian, 3 October 1941, p. 1.

10. Ibid., p. 2.

Chapter 8 – The Mountain Man

1. Murphy Papers, Special Orders No. 229, Manila, P.I., 1 October 1941.

2. Ibid., letter from Art to Lillian, 22 October 1941.

3. Ibid., letter from Art to Lillian, 29 October 1941.

4. Ibid., letter from Art to Lillian, 6 November 1941, p. 1.

5. Ibid.

6. Ibid., pp. 1-2.

7. Ibid., letter from Art to Lillian, 12 November 1941, p. 2.

8. Ibid., letter from Art to Lillian, 16 November 1941.

9. Ibid., letter from Art to Lillian, 22 November 1941, pp. 1-2.

10. Ibid, letter from Art to Lillian, 30 November 1941.

Chapter 9 – War Begins at Camp John Hay

1. Russell W. Volckmann, *We Remained: Three Years Behind Enemy Lines in the Philippines*, p. 9.

2. Earl C. Dudley Jr., "An Angel on Their Shoulders," *The Washington Post*, May 28, 2004, (http://www.washingtonpost.com/wp-srv/metro/specials/wwiimemorial/civilians.txt), Accessed Sept 15, 2012

3. James J. Halsema, "A Recollection of the Day after Pearl Harbor in Baguio," (http://philippinecommentary.blogspot.com/2005/12/day-after-pearl-harbor.html), p. 2.

4. Ibid.

5. Ibid.

6. Volckmann, *We Remained*, p. 11; Philip Harkins, *Blackburn's Headhunters* (NY: W. W. Norton & Company, Inc., 1955), p. 10; Louis Morton, *United States Army in World War II, The War in the Pacific, The Fall of the Philippines* (Washington, D.C.: Office of the Chief of Military History, Department of the Army, 1953), p. 131.

7. Halsema, "A Recollection," p. 2.

8. Ibid.

9. Ibid., p. 3.

10. Borneman, *MacArthur at War*, pp. 83–87; Morton, *United States Army in World War II*, pp. 84-87; Halsema, "A Recollection," p. 4.

11. Ibid.

12. Elizabeth M. Norman, *We Band of Angels: The Untold Story of American Nurses Trapped on Bataan by the Japanese* (NY: Random House, Inc., 1999), pp. 7-8.

13. Murphy Papers, letter from Art to Lillian, 4 October 1944.

14. Morton, *United States Army in World War II*, pp. 104-106; USAFIP-NL, *Guerrilla Days in North Luzon: A Brief Historical Narrative of a Brilliant Segment of the Resistance Movement during the Enemy Occupation of the Philippines 1941–1945* (Camp Spencer, Luna, La Union, North Luzon, Philippines: United States Army Forces in the Philippines, North Luzon, July 1946), p. 1; Morton, *United States Army in World War II*, pp. 106–108.

15. Ibid.

16. USAFIP-NL, *Guerrilla Days in North Luzon*, pp. 2-3.

17. Morton, *United States Army in World War II*, pp. 106-108; Murphy Papers, letter from Art to Lillian, 27 November 1944, p. 2.

18. Norling, *The Intrepid Guerrillas of North Luzon*, p. 36.

19. Frazier Hunt, *The Untold Story of Douglas MacArthur* (North Greenwich, CT: The Devlin-Adair Company, 1954), pp. 228-230.

20. Harkins, *Blackburn's Headhunters*, pp. 18-19.

21. Clark Lee, *They Call It Pacific: An Eye-Witness Story of our War against Japan, from Bataan to the Solomons* (NY: The Viking Press, Inc., 1943), p. 83.

22. Bonifacio Dulagan Marines and Caroline Marines Depaynos, *The 66th Infantry and the Igorot Diary* (West Conshohocken, PA: Infinity Publishing Co., 2010), pp. 102-108.

23. William R. Moule, *God's Arms Around Us* (Grass Valley, CA: Blue Dolphin Publishing Company, Inc., 1990), pp. 44-45.

24. Murphy Papers, letter from Art to Lillian, 27 November 1944, p. 2.

25. Norling, *The Intrepid Guerrillas of North Luzon*, p. 38.

26. Ibid., p. 39.

27. Ibid. Norling has confused the two groups. It was Bonnett's group that left first and took the more northerly route. Horan's group, including Murphy and Calvert, left Baguio in the late afternoon on December 24 and took the more southerly route.

28. Harkins, *Blackburn's Headhunters*, pp. 20-24.

Chapter 10 – War Comes to Berkeley

1. (modestoradiomuseum.org/radio%20reports%20pearl.html).

2. Ibid.

3. Murphy Papers, letter from Lillian to Art, 8 December 1941, p. 1.

4. Ibid.

5. (https://www.youtube.com/watch?v=TLM7P9fa6ww).

6. Murphy Papers, letter from Lillian to Art, 8 December 1941, p. 1.

7. Ibid., p. 2.

8. Ibid.

9. Ibid.

10. Ibid., letter from Lillian to Art, 11 December 1941, p. 1.

11. Ibid., p. 2.

12. Ibid., letter from Lillian to Art, 5 January 1941, pp. 1-2.

13. Ibid., letter from Lillian to Art, 10 January 1941, pp. 1-2.

Chapter 11 - Retreat

1. Robert H. Arnold, *A Rock and a Fortress* (Sarasota, FL: Blue Horizon Press, 1979), p. 75.

2. Moule, *God's Arms Around Us*, p. 61.

3. Ibid., p. 56.

4. Ibid., p. 50.

5. Ibid., p. 63.

6. Ibid., p. 71.

7. Murphy Papers, letter from Art to Lillian, 27 November 1944, p. 1.

8. Ibid., pp. 1-2.

9. Norling, *The Intrepid Guerrillas of North Luzon*, p. 41.

10. The Hallgren Collection, Combined Arms Research Library, 250 Gibbon Ave., Fort Leavenworth, KS 66027-2314.

11. Russell Barros, "Brief History of Lt. Col. Russell D. Barros' Extended Sojourn in the Philippine Islands," 14 July 1945. (http://www.west-point.org/family/japanese-pow//Barros%20files/barris-1), p. 2.
12. Murphy Papers, "Recommendation for Award of Medal of Valor," 26 July 1945.
13. FDR Chat 20, 23 February 1942 (24 February in the Philippines) (http://www.mhric.org/fdr/chat20.html).

Chapter 12 – Back to the North

1. Murphy Papers, diary entry, 24 February 1942.
2. Ibid., diary entry, 25 February 1942.
3. Francisco A. Delgado, (http://www.grandlodgephils.org.ph/2012/?page_id=141).
4. Murphy Papers, letter from Art to Lillian, 31 May 1945.
5. Ibid., diary entry, 26 February 1942.
6. Ibid., "Recommendation for Award of Medal of Valor," 26 July 1945.
7. Ibid., diary entry, 28 February 1942.
8. Ibid.
9. Ibid., diary entry, 1 March 1942.
10. Ibid., diary entry, 2 March 1942.
11. Ibid., diary entry, 4 March 1942.
12. Ibid., diary entry, 5 March 1942.
13. Stanley Falk, *Liberation of the Philippines* (NY: Ballantine Books, Inc., 1971), p. 15.
14. Murphy Papers, "Recommendation for Award of Medal of Valor."
15. Moule, *God's Arms Around Us*, p. 58.
16. Murphy Papers, diary entries, 18-21 March 1942.

Chapter 13 – A Homecoming, of Sorts

1. Moule, *God's Arms Around Us*, pp. 108-109.
2. Ray C. Hunt and Bernard Norling, *Behind Japanese Lines* (Lexington: The University Press of Kentucky, 1986), pp. 85-87. This account of Al Hendrickson's exploits differs markedly from that provided by William Moule, though both Moule and Hunt claim to have had considerable personal interaction with Hendrickson. Art Murphy's letters state only that upon arriving back at Lusod on March 22, 1942, an "American enlisted man" was in charge of some guerrillas there, but gives no further detail about Al Hendrickson.
3. Harley Hieb, *Heart of Iron* (Lodi, CA: Pacifica Publishing, 1987), p. 137. Colonel Hieb describes Major Warner as a member of the 26th Cavalry, which had been sent from Fort Stotsenburg to Baguio to

bolster the Philippine Army troops defending the beaches of Lingayen Gulf. Others place him as the provost marshal of Camp John Hay.

4. Norling, *The Intrepid Guerrillas of North Luzon*, pp. 94-95.

5. Moule, *God's Arms Around Us*, pp. 107-109.

6. Ibid., pp. 110-111.

7. Ibid., pp. 124-125.

8. Arnold, *A Rock and a Fortress*, pp. 6-9.

9. Ibid., pp. 16-39.

10. Donald Chaput, "Philippine Resistance in Candon, 1942," *Philippine Studies*, Volume 47, No. 1 (Quezon City, Philippines: Ateñeo de Manila University, 1999), pp. 102-105.

11. Louis Goldbrum, "Military Biography of Louis Goldbrum" (http://www.lindavdahl.com/bio%20pages/louis%20goldbrum/l.goldy_bio.html).

12. Volckmann, *We Remained*, p. 103.

13. Arnold, *A Rock and a Fortress*, pp. 46-47.

14. Ibid., p. 84.

15. Murphy Papers, letter from Art to Lillian, 4 October 1944, p. 3.

16. Harkins, *Blackburn's Headhunters*, p. 22.

17. Moule, *God's Arms Around Us*, p. 120.

18. Murphy Papers, letter from Art to Lillian, 4 October 1944, p. 3.

19. Ibid.

20. Moule, *God's Arms Around Us*, p. 113.

21. Murphy Papers, "Recommendation for Award of Medal of Valor," p. 2.

22. Murphy Papers, letter from Art to Lillian, 4 October 1944, p. 2.

23. Ibid.

24. Ibid., letter from Art to Lillian, 27 November 1944, p. 3.

Chapter 14 – The Dilemma of Surrender

1. Harkins, *Blackburn's Headhunters*, p. 101.

2. Morton, *The War in the Pacific: The Fall of the Philippines*, pp. 569-572.

3. Richard F. Miller, *In Words and Deeds: Battle Speeches in History* (Lebanon, NH: University Press of New England, 2008), p. 340.

4. Jonathan M. Wainwright, *General Wainwright's Story* (Garden City, NY: Doubleday & Company, Inc., 1946), p. 141.

5. Murphy Papers, letter from Art to Lillian, 4 October 1944, p. 2.

6. Morton, *The War in the Pacific: The Fall of the Philippines*, pp. 573-574.

7. Murphy Papers, letter from Art to Lillian, 28 June 1942.

8. Harkins, *Blackburn's Headhunters*, pp. 28, 32.

9. Ibid, pp. 38-39.

10. Volckmann, *We Remained*, pp. 40-43.

11. Murphy Papers, letter from Art to Lillian, 28 June 1942, pp. 1-4.

12. Ibid., document dated 26 November 1945, written and signed by Colonel Russell W. Volckmann, entitled, "Amendment of Date of Recognition of United States Army Forces in the Philippines, North Luzon (USAFIP, NL)."

13. Ibid., letter from Art to Lillian, 28 June 1942, p. 2.

14. Ibid., letter from Horan to Calvert, 3 July 1942, pp. 1-2.

15. Ibid., letter from Art to Lillian, 28 June 1942, p. 1.

Chapter 15 – Guerrilla Action Begins, Fizzles

1. Murphy Papers, letter from Art to Lillian, 22 July 1942.

2. Ibid., letter from Art to Lillian, 2 August 1942.

3. Ibid., letter from Art to Lillian, 3 August 1942.

4. Marines, *The 66th Infantry and the Igorot Diary*, p. 131.

5. USAFIP-NL, *Guerrilla Days in North Luzon,* p. 27.

6. Ibid., 26.

7. Marines, *The 66th Infantry and the Igorot Diary*, p. 142.

8. USAFIP-NL, *Guerrilla Days in North Luzon*, p. 26.

9. Volckmann, *We Remained*, p. 88.

10. Ibid.

11. John F. Ream, "An Interview with Lt. Col. Herbert Swick," "Military Magazine Online" (http://milmag.com/newsite/features/articles/swick), p. 1.

12. Volckmann, *We Remained*, pp. 57-58.

13. Harkins, *Blackburn's Headhunters*, pp. 58-93.

14. Ibid., p. 98.

15. Volckmann, *We Remained*, p. 84.

16. Murphy Papers, "Recommendation for Award of Medal of Valor," p. 2.

17. Ibid., "Citation for Award of Silver Star," 15 March 1951.

18. Moule, *God's Arms Around Us.*, pp. 327-337.

19. Murphy Papers, "Recommendation for Award of Medal of Valor," p. 2.

20. Ibid., letter from Art to Lillian, 27 November 1944, p. 2.

Chapter 16 – Buckling Down in the Bay Area

1. Captain James W. Hamilton and First Lieutenant William J. Bola Jr., *Gateway to Victory: The Wartime Story of the San Francisco Army Port of Embarkation* (Stanford, CA: Stanford University Press, 1946), p. 123.

2. Ibid., p. 37.

3. Murphy Papers, Lillian Murphy's Personnel File, NARA.

4. Hamilton and Bola, *Gateway to Victory*, p. 44.

5. Samuel Eliot Morrison, *The Two-Ocean War* (Boston: Atlantic-Little Brown Books, 1963), pp. 196-208.

6. Ibid., pp. 318-322.

Chapter 17 – Guerrilla Action Resumes

1. Marines, *The 66th Infantry and the Igorot Diary*, p. 217.

2. Maurice Melanes, "Unsung Hero Helps Tell Benguet History," "Philippine Daily Inquirer, North Luzon," 19 August 2008.

3. Moule, *God's Arms Around Us*, pp. 188, 297.

4. Ibid., p. 207.

5. Ream, "An Interview with Lt. Col. Herbert Swick," p. 2.

6. Murphy Papers.

Chapter 18 – MacArthur's "Lay Low" Order

1. Norling, *The Intrepid Guerrillas of North Luzon*, p. 30.

2. Arthur P. Murphy, "Corrections, Additions and Comments on Chapter VI of 'Guerrilla Resistance Movements in the Philippines'" (Military Intelligence Section, General Staff, GHQ, SWPA), p. 8.

3. Ibid.

4. Ibid.

5. Ibid.

6. Ibid., p. 9.

7. Douglas MacArthur, *Reminiscences* (NY: McGraw-Hill Book Company, 1964), p. 204.

8. Chris Schaefer, *Bataan Diary* (Houston, TX: Riverview Publishing, 2004), p. 123.

9. Norling, *The Intrepid Guerrillas of North Luzon*, p. 190.

10. Marines, *The 66th Infantry and the Igorot Diary*, p. 139.

11. Robert Lapham and Bernard Norling, *Lapham's Raiders: Guerrillas in the Philippines 1942-1945* (Lexington: The University Press of Kentucky, 1996), p. 141.

12. MacArthur, *Reminiscences*, p. 205.

Chapter 19 – Laying Low in Kapangan

1. Volckmann, *We Remained*, pp. 130-131.

2. Murphy Papers.

3. Ibid., "Recommendation for Award of Medal of Valor," p. 2.

4. Ibid., USAFIP-NL, *After Battle Report*, 10 November 1945, p. 15.

5. Ibid., letter from Art to Lillian, 29 May 1943.

6. Ibid., letter from Art to Lillian, 15 June 1943.

7. General John Henry "Gatling Gun" Parker (http://www.findagrave.com, Memorial #86445274).
8. Volckmann, *We Remained*, pp. 102, 111-112.

Chapter 20 – The Noose Tightens

1. Murphy Papers.
2. Moule, *God's Arms Around Us*, p. 266.
3. Volckmann, *We Remained*, p. 112.
4. Harkins, *Blackburn's Headhunters*, pp. 143-144.
5. Lapham and Norling, *Lapham's Raiders*, p. 55.
6. Murphy, "Corrections, Additions and Comments," pp. 10-11.
7. Ibid.
8. William B. Breuer, *MacArthur's Undercover War* (NY: John Wiley & Sons, Inc., 1995), pp. 46-47.
9. Murphy, "Corrections, Additions and Comments," pp. 10-11.
10. Ibid.
11. Ibid.
12. Ibid.
13. Harkins, *Blackburn's Headhunters*, p. 158.
14. Moule, *God's Arms Around Us*, p. 169.
15. Harkins, *Blackburn's Headhunters*, p. 175.
16. Murphy Papers, letter from Art to Lillian, 4 October 1944, p. 2.
17. Arthur P. Murphy, "Short History, USAFIP, North Luzon, and Guerrilla Activities in North Luzon," p. 3. It should be noted that on page 65 of *Lapham's Raiders*, the author has confused Enoch French and Jack Langley. It was Langley who died near Aritao, not French.
18. Marines, *The 66th Infantry and the Igorot Diary*, p. 131.
19. Schaefer, *Bataan Diary*, pp. 204-206.
20. Murphy Papers, letter from Art to Lillian, 12 July 1943.
21. Murphy Papers.
22. Ibid.
23. Ibid. The Red Cross nurse's name is unknown. Nona is a fictitious name derived by combining the words "no" and "name."
24. Ibid., letter from Art to Lillian, 22 August 1943.

Chapter 21 – Volckmann Takes Over

1. Murphy, "Corrections, Additions and Comments," p. 12.
2. Ibid., p. 14.
3. Ibid., pp. 14-15.
4. Volckmann, *We Remained*, p. 122.
5. Murphy, "Corrections, Additions and Comments," p. 15.

6. Murphy Papers, "Recommendation for Award of Medal of Valor," p. 3.

7. Ibid., *USAFIP-NL, After Battle Report*, p. 15.

8. Ibid., letter from Art to Lillian, 21 September 1943.

9. Volckmann, *We Remained*, p. 124.

10. Murphy, "Corrections, Additions and Comments," p. 16.

11. Volckmann, *We Remained*, p. 124.

12. Ibid.

13. Ibid., p. 125.

14. Murphy, "Corrections, Additions and Comments," p. 15.

15. Murphy, "Guerrilla Warfare in the Philippines," pp. 13-18, 28.

16. Murphy, "Corrections, Additions and Comments," pp. 15-16.

17. Murphy Papers, letter from Art to Lillian, 31 October 1943.

18. Volckmann, *We Remained*, p. 126.

19. Murphy Papers, letter from Art to Lillian, 27 November 1943.

Chapter 22 – The Grind Goes on at Home

1. Hamilton and Bola, *Gateway to Victory*, p. 136.

2. Ibid., pp. 63-68.

3. Murphy Papers, letter from Lillian to Art, 21 December 1944, p. 1.

4. Ibid.

5. Ibid.

6. Ibid., Lillian's official personnel file, NARA.

7. Ibid.

8. Ronald H. Spector, *Eagle Against the Sun* (NY: The Free Press, a Division of Macmillan, Inc., 1985), pp. 259-266.

9. Personal contact between the author and Lucille (Buffum) Fried, spring 2013.

10. Personal contact between the author and clerical personnel at St. Joseph the Worker Church, Berkeley, California, fall 2015.

Chapter 23 – Some Good News, Some Terrible

1. Murphy Papers, letter from Art to Lillian, 12 January 1944.

2. Murphy Papers.

3. John Costello, *The Pacific War: The Newly Revealed History of the Origins and Conduct of World War II in the Pacific, Based on Hitherto Secret Archives*, 1941–1945 (NY: Rawson, Wade Publishers, Inc., 1981), pp. 448-450.

4. Harkins, *Blackburn's Headhunters*, p. 188.

5. Ibid., p. 189.

6. Volckmann, *We Remained*, pp. 141-142.

7. Murphy papers, letter from Art to Lillian, 4 March 1944.

8. Volckmann, *We Remained*, pp. 126-127.

9. Ibid.

10. Murphy, "Guerrilla Warfare in the Philippines," p. 16.

11. Murphy Papers, assorted USAFIP-NL newsletters.

12. Ream, "An Interview with Lt. Col. Herbert Swick," p. 3.

13. Ibid., pp. 1-3.

14. Moule, *God's Arms Around Us*, pp. 325-327.

15. Ream, "An Interview with Lt. Col. Herbert Swick," p. 3.

16. Marines, *The 66th Infantry and the Igorot Diary*, p. 143.

17. Harkins, *Blackburn's Headhunters*, p. 194.

18. Murphy Papers, letter from Art to Lillian, 15 April 1944.

19. Volckmann, *We Remained*, p. 149.

20. Art Murphy, "Guerrilla Warfare in the Philippines," *The Rattle of Theta Chi* (Los Angeles, CA: *The Rattle of Theta Chi*, fall 1947), p. 16.

21. Murphy Papers, letter from Art to Lillian, 26 June 1944.

22. Ibid.

23. Murphy Papers, "Schematic Diagram Showing the Evolution and Growth of USAFIP North Luzon."

Chapter 24 – Nothing Comes Easy

1. Murphy, "Guerrilla Warfare in the Philippines," p. 16.

2. Lapham and Norling, *Lapham's Raiders*, p. 141. Although it is stated on page 141 that Major Parker Calvert had gotten a transmitter into working order, this is incorrect. Until April 1944, Calvert's war news came in via runner from agents in Baguio, who got it from loyal civilians who kept hidden short-wave radios. In April, Calvert's group got a receiver working, not a transmitter.

3. Volckmann, *We Remained*, pp. 156-157.

4. Marines, *The 66th Infantry and the Igorot Diary*, pp. 258-259.

5. Ibid.

6. Ibid.

7. *Staff Reports of General MacArthur: The Campaigns of MacArthur in the Pacific* (http://www.history.army.mil/books/wwii/macarthur&20reports/macarthur%20v1/ch10), pp. 298-300.

8. Department of the Navy, "Submarine Activities Connected with Guerrilla Organizations" (http://www.history.navy.mil/library/online/pi_subs_guerrillas.html), p. 4.

9. *Staff Reports of General MacArthur: The Campaigns of MacArthur in the Pacific*, p. 305.

10. Ibid.

11. Department of the Navy, "Submarine Activities Connected with Guerrilla Organizations," p. 5.
12. Lapham and Norling, *Lapham's Raiders*, pp. 144-148.
13. Ibid.
14. Murphy, "Corrections, Additions and Comments," p. 18.
15. Edward Dissette and Hans Christian Adamson, *Guerrilla Submarines* (Bantam Books, 1982), pp. 184-189; Department of the Navy, "Submarine Activities Connected with Guerrilla Organizations," p. 6; Celedonio A. Ancheta, *Exigencies of War* (Manila: Philippine Historical Association, 1966), pp. 77-78.
16. Ibid.
17. Ibid.
18. Murphy, "Corrections, Additions and Comments," p. 18. There are differing accounts of these events. Robert Lapham claims on page 148 of *Lapham's Raiders* (written in 1996) that he first requested permission from SWPA and then had an old friend, Esteban Lumyeb, deliver the radio to Volckmann's headquarters. Russell Volckmann on p. 157 of *We Remained* (written in 1954) gives a politically correct account involving intelligence reports to avoid criticizing Lapham. Murphy's version, written in July 1945 as part of the official U.S. government record, seems most believable. He says that Anderson notified SWPA, who in turn *ordered* Lapham to send Ancheta and Luz to USAFIP-NL headquarters. Murphy Papers, *USAFIP-NL, After Battle Report*, pp. 15-16.
19. Volckmann, *We Remained*, pp. 157-158.
20. Murphy, "Corrections, Additions and Comments," p. 18.
21. Murphy Papers, radiogram from Volckmann to HQ-SWPA, 29 August 1944.
22. Ibid., radiogram from HQ-SWPA received 13 September 1944.
23. Ibid., radiogram from HQ-SWPA, undated.
24. USAFIP-NL, *Guerrilla Days in North Luzon*, p. 57.
25. Marines, *The 66th Infantry and the Igorot Diary*, pp. 260-261.
26. Ibid., p. 261.
27. Murphy Papers, radiogram from HQ-SWPA received 21 September 1944.
28. Ibid., undated.
29. Volckmann, *We Remained*, pp. 159-160. Volckmann gives the estimated time of arrival as October 19, but official radiograms support the later date.
30. Murphy Papers, radiogram from HQ-SWPA received 30 October 1944.
31. Ibid., radiogram from HQ-SWPA received 31 October 1944.
32. Dissette and Adamson, *Guerrilla Submarines*, pp. 194-196.

Chapter 25 – A Damsel in Distress

1. Jose R. Rodriguez, *Philippine First Ladies Portraits* (Philippines: Tantoco-Rustica Foundation, 2003), pp. 30-35.
2. Ibid. pp. 39-47.
3. Ibid.
4. Ibid.
5. Ibid.
6. Ibid.
7. Marines, *The 66th Infantry and the Igorot Diary*, pp. 273-275.
8. Ibid., pp. 281-282.
9. Volckmann, *We Remained*, p. 161.
10. Murphy Papers.
11. Ibid., personal letter dated 20 September 2005 from Mrs. Rosie Osmeña Valencia to the author.
12. Suzanne Duque, ed., *Soldiers as Guerrillas, World War II in Northern Luzon* (Raleigh, NC: Lulu Publishing, 2015), pp. 102-103.
13. Murphy, "Corrections, Additions and Comments," p. 21.

Chapter 26 – MacArthur Keeps His Promise

1. Falk, *Liberation of the Philippines*, p. 18.
2. Ibid.
3. MacArthur, *Reminiscences*, pp. 210-211.
4. Falk, *Liberation of the Philippines*, p. 19.
5. Ibid., p. 21.
6. Ibid., pp. 26-27.
7. Ibid., p. 32.
8. MacArthur, *Reminiscences*, pp. 214-216.
9. Ibid., pp. 216-217.
10. Falk, *Liberation of* the Philippines, pp. 60-61.
11. William Manchester, *American Caesar: Douglas MacArthur 1880-1964* (Boston, MA: Little, Brown and Company, 1978).

Chapter 27 – A Comedy of Errors

1. Murphy Papers, letter from Art to Lillian, 12 November 1944.
2. Ibid., radiogram from HQ-SWPA received 1 November 1944.
3. Volckmann, *We Remained*, pp. 161-163. Although Volckmann gives the revised arrival date of the second submarine as November 21, actual radiograms received from HQ-SWPA in mid-November confirm the revised date as 22 November 1944. Murphy Papers, radiograms from HQ-SWPA received 14 and 15 November 1944.
4. Volckmann, *We Remained*, pp. 161-164.

5. Ibid., p. 163.

6. Ibid.

7. Ibid.; Murphy Papers, letter from Lillian to Jane (Buffum) Applegate, 6 March 2000, p. 2.

8. Ibid.

9. Ibid.

10. Ibid.

11. Volckmann, *We Remained*, p. 165.

8. Murphy Papers, radiogram from HQ-SWPA received 18 November 1944.

9. Ibid., radiogram sent by USAFIP-NL to HQ-SWPA on 18 November 1944.

10. USAFIP-NL, *Guerrilla Days in North Luzon*, p. 57.

11. Volckmann, *We Remained*, pp. 163-164.

12. Ibid.

13. Ibid.

14. Murphy Papers, radiogram from HQ-SWPA received 17 November 1944.

15. USAFIP-NL, *Guerrilla Days in North Luzon*, p. 57.

16. Murphy Papers, report sent to USAFIP-NL by George M. Barnett, 4 a.m. 23 November 1944.

17. Volckmann, *We Remained*, pp. 163-164.

18. Ibid.

19. Ibid.

20. Ibid., p. 165.

21 Murphy Papers., radiogram from HQ-SWPA received 17 November 1944.

22. Volckmann, *We Remained*, pp. 165-166.

23. Ibid., pp. 166.

24. Ibid., pp. 166-167.

25. Ibid., p.167.

26. Ibid., pp. 169-171; USAFIP-NL, *Guerrilla Days in North Luzon*, pp. 22-24.

27. Murphy Papers, "Corrections, Additions and Comments," p. 18; Volckmann, *We Remained*, pp. 170-172; USAFIP-NL, *Guerrilla Days in North Luzon*, pp. 22-24.

28. Ibid.

29. Ibid.

30. Ibid.

31. Volckmann, *We Remained*, p. 170.

32. Ibid., p. 172.

33. Murphy Papers, letter from Art to Lillian, 9 December 1944.

34. Ibid., radiogram from HQ-SWPA received 28 November 1944.

35. Ibid., radiogram from HQ-SWPA received 9 December 1944.

36. Volckmann, *We Remained*, pp. 171-172.

Chapter 28 – Taking Back North Luzon

1. Falk, *Liberation of the Philippines*, pp. 84-85.

2. Murphy Papers, *USAFIP-NL, After Battle Report*, pp. 18-25.

3. Duque, ed., *Soldiers as Guerillas,* pp. 117-123.

4. Volckmann, *We Remained*, pp. 180-181; Ancheta, *Exigencies of War*, pp. 126-128.

5. Murphy Papers, radiogram from HQ-SWPA received about 6 January 1945.

6. Falk, *Liberation of the Philippines*, pp. 88-89.

7. Ibid.

8. Wayne W. Parrish, "On the Beam," "Liberty Magazine," 23 June 1945, pp. 14-15.

9. The Rand Corporation Symposium on the Role of Airpower in Counterinsurgency and Unconventional Warfare: Allied Resistance to the Japanese on Luzon, World War II, Memorandum RM-3655-PR, July 1963, pp. 16-17.

10. Murphy Papers, radiogram from HQ-SWPA received 3 December 1944.

11. Marines, *The 66th Infantry and the Igorot Diary*, pp. 249-252.

12. Ibid.

13. Ibid.

14. Murphy Papers, letter from Art to Lillian, 23 January 1945.

15. Volckmann, *We Remained*, pp. 196-197.

16. Ibid., pp. 197-199.

17. Murphy Papers, *USAFIP-NL, After Battle Report*, pp. 18 and 27-36.

18. Ibid., pp. 58-81.

19. Arnold, *A Rock and a Fortress*, pp. 125-128.

20. Hieb, *Heart of Iron*, p. 395.

21. Arnold, *A Rock and a Fortress*, pp. 245-248.

22. Volckmann, *We Remained*, pp. 200-202.

23. Arnold, *A Rock and a Fortress*, pp. 259-268.

24. Murphy Papers, *USAFIP-NL, After Battle Report*, p. 103.

25. Harkins, *Blackburn's Headhunters*, pp. 295-304.

26. Volckmann, *We Remained*, pp. 202-205.

27. Murphy Papers, *USAFIP-NL, After Battle Report*, pp. 104-105.

28. Ibid., pp. 106-108.

29. Ibid., pp. 109-113.

Chapter 29 – Our Prayers are Answered

1. Murphy Papers, letter from Lillian to Art, 17 February 1945, p. 8.
2. Ibid., p. 5.
3. Murphy Papers, radio communiqué intercepted by General MacArthur's headquarters on 9 January 1945.
4. Murphy Papers, undated form document accompanying War Department letter dated 24 November 1944.
5. Murphy Papers, letters from Art to his uncle and brothers, 27 November 1944.

Chapter 30 – Stacking Arms

1. Murphy Papers, letter from Art to Lillian, 4 March 1945, p. 2.
2. Ibid., letter from Art to Lillian, 8 February 1945.
3. Ibid.
4. Ibid., letter from Art to Lillian, 7 April 1945, p. 2.
5. Ibid., letter from Art to Lillian, 28 May 1945, p. 1.
6. Ibid., letter from Art to Lillian, 31 May 1945, p. 1.
7. Ibid., 26 February 1945 letter from Connie Delgado to Mrs. John F. Spencer (grandmother of Grafton Spencer) enclosing 21 January 1942 letter written by Grafton Spencer while at Delgado's villa in Sibul Spring.
8. Ibid., letter from Art to Lillian, 6 June 1945.
9. Ibid., letter from Art to Lillian, 20 June 1945.
10. Ibid., USAFIP-NL Newsletter, 28 June 1945.
11. Ibid., letter from Art to Lillian, 16 August 1945.
12. Murphy, "Corrections, Additions and Comments."
13. Murphy Papers, letter from Art to Lillian, 6 September 1945.

BIBLIOGRAPHY

Primary Sources

Ancheta, Celedonio A., ed. *Exigencies of War.* Manila: Philippine Historical Association, 1966.

Arnold, Robert H. *A Rock and a Fortress.* Sarasota, FL: Blue Horizon Press, 1979.

Barros, Russell. "Brief History of Lt. Col. Russell D. Barros' Extended Sojourn in the Philippine Islands," 14 July 1945. http://www.west-point.org/family/japanese-pow//Barros%20 files/Barros-1.

Borneman, Walter R. *MacArthur at War.* New York: Little, Brown and Company, 2016.

Breuer, William B. *MacArthur's Undercover War.* New York: John Wiley & Sons, Inc., 1995.

Chaput, Donald. *Philippine Resistance in Candon, 1942.* Quezon City, Philippines: Ateneo de Manila University, 1999.

Costello, John. *The Pacific War: The Newly Revealed History of the Origins and Conduct of World War II in the Pacific, Based on Hitherto Secret Archives, 1941–1945.* New York: Rawson, Wade Publishers, 1981.

Delgado, Francisco A. http://www.grandlodgephils.org.ph/2012/?page_id=141.

Department of the Navy. "Submarine Activities Connected with Guerrilla Organizations." http://www.history.navy.mil/library/online/pi_subs-guerrillas.htm.

Dissette, Edward, and Hans Christian Adamson. *Guerrilla Submarines.* New York: Bantam Books, Inc., 1982.

Duque, Suzanne, ed. *Soldiers as Guerillas: World War II in Northern Luzon, Memoirs of Maj. Gen. Calixto Duque.* Raleigh, NC: Lulu Publishing, 2015.

Goldbrum, Louis. "Military Biography of Louis Goldbrum." http://www.lindavdahl.com/bio%20pages/louis%20goldbrum/l.goldy_bio.html.

Falk, Stanley. *Liberation of the Philippines.* New York: Ballantine Books, Inc., 1971.

FDR Chat 20, 23 February 1942. http://www.mhric.org/fdr/chat20.html.

Hallgren Collection. Combined Arms Research Library, 250 Gibbon Ave., Fort Leavenworth, KS 66027-2314.

Halsema, James J. "A Recollection of the Day after Pearl Harbor in Baguio." http://philippinecommentary.blogspot.com/2005/12/day-after-pearl-harbor.htm.

Hamilton, Captain James W., and First Lieutenant William J. Bola Jr. *Gateway to Victory: The Wartime Story of the San Francisco Army Port of Embarkation.* Stanford, CA: Stanford University Press, 1946.

Harkins, Philip. *Blackburn's Headhunters.* New York: W. W. Norton & Company, Inc., 1955.

Hieb, Harley. *Heart of Iron.* Lodi, CA: Pacifica Publishing, 1987.

Hunt, Frazier. *The Untold Story of Douglas MacArthur.* North Greenwich, CT: The Devlin-Adair Co., 1954.

Hunt, Ray C., and Bernard Norling. *Behind Japanese Lines.* Lexington: University Press of Kentucky, 1986.

Kaminsky, Theresa. *Angels of the Underground.* New York: Oxford University Press, 2016.

Lapham, Robert, and Bernard Norling. *Lapham's Raiders: Guerrillas in the Philippines 1942–1945.* Lexington: University Press of Kentucky, 1995.

Lee, Clark. *They Called It Pacific: An Eye-Witness Story of our War against Japan, from Bataan to the Solomons.* New York: The Viking Press, Inc., 1943.

MacArthur, Douglas. *Reminiscences.* New York: McGraw Hill Book Co., Inc., 1964.

Manchester, William. *American Caesar: Douglas MacArthur, 1880-1964.* Boston, MA: Little, Brown and Company, 1978.

Marines, Bonifacio Dulagan, and Caroline Marines Depaynos. *The 66th Infantry and the Igorot Diary.* West Conshohocken, PA: Infinity Publishing Co., 2010.

McMaster, Robert, ed. *'Lo Joe: Memoirs of Archie L. McMaster, Major, U.S. Army.* Unpublished. Archie McMaster's original typed manuscript, dated 29 October 1986, was donated to the Wahoo Public Library, Wahoo, NE.

Melanes, Maurice. "Unsung Hero Helps Tell Benguet Story." North Luzon, Philippines: "Philippine Daily Inquirer," 19 August 2008.

Miller, Richard F. *In Words and Deeds: Battle Speeches in History.* Lebanon, NH: University Press of New England, 2008.

Morrison, Samuel Eliot. *The Two-Ocean War.* Boston: Atlantic-Little, Brown Books, 1963.

Morton, Louis. *United States Army in World War II, The War in the Pacific, The Fall of the Philippines.* Washington, D.C.: Office of the Chief of Military History, Department of the Army, 1953.

Moule, William R. *God's Arms Around Us.* Grass Valley, CA: Blue Dolphin Publishing, Inc., 1990.

Murphy, Arthur P. "Corrections, Additions and Comments on Chapter VI of 'Guerrilla Resistance Movements in the Philippines,'" published by Military Intelligence Section, General Staff, GHQ, SWPA. Undated.

Murphy, Arthur P. "Guerrilla Warfare in the Philippines." Los Angeles, CA: *The Rattle of Theta Chi*, fall 1947.

Murphy, Arthur P. "Short History, USAFIP, North Luzon, and Guerrilla Activities in North Luzon." Undated.

Murphy Papers. "Citation for Award of Silver Star," 15 March 1951.

Murphy Papers. Diary December 1941–March 1942.

Murphy Papers. 26 November 1945 document, written and signed by Colonel Russell W. Volckmann, entitled, "Amendment of Date of Recognition of United States Armed Forces in the Philippines, North Luzon (USAFIP, NL)."

Murphy Papers. 26 February 1945 letter from Connie Delgado to Mrs. John F. Spencer, grandmother of Grafton Spencer, enclosing 21 January 1942 letter written by Grafton Spencer at Delgado villa in Sibul Spring.

Murphy Papers. Letter from John P. Horan to Parker Calvert, 3 July 1942.

Murphy Papers. Letter from Roberta Gallup to Lillian, 26 October 1941.

Murphy Papers. Letter from War Department to Lillian, 3 March 1941.

Murphy Papers. Letters from Art to Lillian 1937–1941.

Murphy Papers. Letters from Lillian to Art 1941–1945.

Murphy Papers. Letters from Art to his uncle and brothers, 27 November 1944.

Murphy, Lillian I. Personnel File 1942–1945, NARA.

Murphy Papers. Organizational Chart, "Schematic Diagram Showing the Evolution and Growth of USAFIP North Luzon." Undated.

Murphy Papers. Personal letter, 20 September 2005, Mrs. Rosie Osmeña Valencia to the author.

Murphy Papers. Radio communiqué intercepted by General MacArthur's headquarters on 9 January 1945, Pacific time.

Murphy Papers. Radiograms from HQ-SWPA 1943–1945.

Murphy Papers. "Recommendation for Award of Medal of Valor," 26 July 1945.

Murphy Papers. "Special Orders No. 229, Manila, P.I., 1 October 1941."

Murphy Papers. "Statement of Lt. Col. Arthur P. Murphy," 8 August 1958.

Murphy Papers. Undated form document accompanying War Department letter, 24 November 1944.

Murphy Papers. *USAFIP-NL, After Battle Report*. North Luzon, Philippines: 10 November 1945.

Murphy Papers. USAFIP-NL Newsletter, 28 June 1945.

Norling, Bernard. *The Intrepid Guerrillas of North Luzon*. Lexington: The University Press of Kentucky, 1999.

Norman, Elizabeth. *We Band of Angels: The Untold Story of American Nurses Trapped on Bataan by the Japanese*. New York: Random House, Inc., 1999.

Parker, John Henry. Memorial 86445274. http://www.findagrave.com.

Parrish, Wayne W. "On the Beam," *Liberty Magazine*, 23 June 1945.

Personal contact between the author and clerical personnel at St. Joseph the Worker Church, Berkeley, California, fall 2015.

Personal conversations between the author and Lucille (Buffum) Fried, spring 2013.

Rand Corporation Symposium on the Roll of Airpower in Counterinsurgency and Unconventional Warfare: Allied Resistance to the Japanese on Luzon, World War II, Memorandum RM-3655-PR, July 1963.

Ream, John F. "An Interview with Lt. Col. Herbert Swick." *Military Magazine Online.* http://milmag.com/newsite/features/articles/swick.

Rodriguez, Jose R. *Philippine First Ladies Portraits.* Manila, Philippines: Tantoco-Rustica Foundation, 2003.

Schaefer, Chris. *Bataan Diary.* Houston, TX: Riverview Publishing Co., 2004.

Spector, Ronald H. *Eagle Against the Sun.* NY: The Free Press, a Division of Macmillan, Inc., 1985.

Staff Reports of General MacArthur: The Campaigns of MacArthur in the Pacific. http://www.history.army.mil/books/wwii/macarthur&20reports/macarthur%20v1/ch10.

USAFIP-NL. *Guerrilla Days in North Luzon: A Brief Historical Narrative of a Brilliant Segment of the Resistance Movement during Enemy Occupation of the Philippines 1941–1945.* Camp Spencer, Luna, La Union, Philippines: United States Army Forces in the Philippines, North Luzon, July 1946.

Wainwright, Jonathan M. *General Wainwright's Story.* Garden City, NY: Doubleday & Company, Inc., 1946.

Volckmann, Russell W. *We Remained: Three Years Behind Enemy Lines in the Philippines.* New York: W. W. Norton & Company, Inc., 1954.

Secondary Works

Army Field Manual 31-20: *Operations Against Guerrilla Forces.* Fort Benning, GA: The Infantry School, 1950.

Army Field Manual 31-21: *Organization and Conduct of Guerrilla Forces.* Washington, D.C.: Government Printing Office, 1951.

Fitzgerald, John M. *Family in Crisis.* Bloomington, IN: John M. Fitzgerald, 2002.

General Staff. "Reports of General MacArthur: The Campaigns of MacArthur in the Pacific." http://www.history.army.mil/books/wwii/macarthur%20reports/macarthur%20v1/c10.

Guardia, Mike. *American Guerrilla: The Forgotten Heroics of Russell W. Volckmann.* Philadelphia: Casemate Publishing, 2010.

Gugliotta, Bobette, *Pigboat 39: An American Sub Goes to War.* Lexington: University Press of Kentucky, 1984.

Haggerty, Edward. *Guerrilla Padre in Mindanao*. New York: Longmans, Green & Company, Inc., 1946.

Hilsman, Roger. *American Guerrilla: My War Behind Japanese Lines*. New York: Brassey's (U.S.), Inc., 1990.

Hoyt, Edwin P. *The Battle of Leyte Gulf: The Death Knell of the Japanese Fleet*. New York: Weybright and Talley, 1972.

Ingham, Travis. *Rendezvous by Submarine: The Story of Charles Parsons and the Guerrilla-Soldiers in the Philippines*. Garden City, NY: Doubleday, Doran & Company, Inc., 1945.

Keith, Agnes. *Three Came Home*. Boston: Little Brown, 1947.

Kerr, E. Bartlett. *Surrender & Survival: The Experience of American POWs in the Pacific 1941–1945*. New York: William Morrow & Company, Inc., 1985.

Lawton, Manny. *Some Survived: An Eyewitness Account of the Bataan Death March and the Men Who Lived Through It*. Chapel Hill, NC: Algonquin Books, 2004.

Miller, Col. E. B. *Bataan Uncensored*. Long Prairie, MN: The Hart Publications, Inc., 1949.

Mills, Scott A. *Stranded in the Philippines*. Annapolis, MD: Naval Institute Press, 2009.

Murphy, Arthur P. "Principles of Anti-Guerrilla Warfare." Fort Benning, GA: *United States Army Infantry School Quarterly*, vol. 38, no. 1, July 1951.

Murphy Papers. USAFIP-NL Newsletters.

Nova, Lily, and Iven Lourie, eds. *Interrupted Lives: Four Women's Stories of Internment during World War II in the Philippines*. Grass Valley, CA: Artemis Books, 1995.

Ramsey, Edwin, and Stephen J. Rivele. *Lieutenant Ramsey's War*. New York: Knightsbridge, 1990.

Rand Corporation. "Symposium on the Role of Airpower in Counterinsurgency and Unconventional Warfare: Allied Resistance to the Japanese on Luzon, World War II," Memorandum RM-3655-PR, July 1963.

Sanderson, James Dean. *Behind Enemy Lines*. Princeton, NJ: Van Nostrand Company, Inc., 1959.

Sinclair, Peter T. II. *Men of Destiny: The American and Filipino Guerillas during the Japanese Occupation of the Philippines*. Fort Leavenworth, KS: School of Advanced Military Studies, United States Army Command and General Staff College, 2011.

Stewart, Adrian. *The Battle of Leyte Gulf*. New York: Charles Scribner's Sons, 1979.

Welch, Bob. *Resolve: From the Jungles of WWII Bataan, the Epic Story of a Soldier, a Flag, and a Promise Kept*. New York: Berkeley Books, a Division of The Penguin Group, 2012.

Willoughby, Charles A. *The Guerrilla Resistance Movement in the Philippines,*

1941–1945. New York: Vantage Press, 1972.

Willoughby, Charles A., and John Chamberlain. *MacArthur, 1941–1951*. New York: McGraw-Hill, 1954.

White, W. L. *They Were Expendable*. New York: Harcourt, Brace & Company, 1942.

Wolfert, Ira. *American Guerrilla in the Philippines*. New York: Simon & Schuster, 1945.

Zuckoff, Mitchell. *Lost in Shangri-La*. New York: Harper Collins Publishers, 2011.

INDEX

CPSIA information can be obtained
at www.ICGtesting.com
Printed in the USA
LVHW082305231118
597870LV00004B/9/P